D1097951

AMERICAN FAITH

AMERICAN FAITH.

Its Religious, Political, and Economic Foundations

Ernest Sutherland Bates

New York · W·W· NORTON & COMPANY · INC · *Publishers*

Contents

Introduction 9

BOOK 1. THE EUROPEAN HERITAGE

CHAPTER 1. The Reformation as a Social Revolution 17
CHAPTER 2. The Left Wing of the Reformation 34
CHAPTER 3. The Right Wing of the Reformation 59

BOOK 2. THE REFORMATION COMPLETED IN AMERICA

CHAPTER 4. The Significance of America 83
CHAPTER 5. "Earth's Only Paradise—Virginia" 87
CHAPTER 6. The First New England Colony—Maine 99
CHAPTER 7. The Pilgrim Experiment in Separatism 104
CHAPTER 8. The Beginning of the Puritan Experiment in Theocracy 120
CHAPTER 9. The Rebellion that Became Rhode Island 127
CHAPTER 10. Liberalism and Reaction in Connecticut 151
CHAPTER 11. The Decline and Fall of the Puritan Theocracy 155
CHAPTER 12. Tolerance and Intolerance in Maryland 171
CHAPTER 13. The Rise and Rule of the Quakers 176

v

BOOK 3.   FROM RELIGION TO POLITICS

CHAPTER 14.   *Jonathan Edwards and the Great Awakening*   207
CHAPTER 15.   *The Rise of Deism*   218
CHAPTER 16.   *European Political Theory and American Political Fact*   234
CHAPTER 17.   *The American Revolution as a Popular Movement*   257
CHAPTER 18.   *The Democratic Compromise*   286
CHAPTER 19.   *The Federalist Elite*   298
CHAPTER 20.   *The Secondary Jeffersonian Revolution*   304
CHAPTER 21.   *The Tertiary Jacksonian Revolution*   312

BOOK 4.   THE FAITH ROMANTICIZED

CHAPTER 22.   *The Creedless Frontier*   329
CHAPTER 23.   *The Rowdy Church of the Latter-Day Saints*   341
CHAPTER 24.   *God's Peculiar People—the Shakers*   359
CHAPTER 25.   *Philanthropic Communism: the Owenists* 367
CHAPTER 26.   *The Fourierist Folly*   374
CHAPTER 27.   *Perfectionism and Sex: the Oneida Community*   390
CHAPTER 28.   *The Complex Faith of New England*   400
CHAPTER 29.   *Southern Romanticizing of Slavery*   434
CHAPTER 30.   *The Northern Faith Militant*   453

              Index   471

AMERICAN FAITH

Introduction

IT MAY seem strange that an account of American faith should begin with a brief survey of the Reformation in Europe. But the complex American faith which is summarized today in the term "democracy" has world derivations as well as world implications. In the form in which we hold it, it is the fruit of centuries of struggle watered by the blood of thousands who had never even heard of democracy but who none the less bled and died for what Charles Beard has called those "inner powers," "unexplored capacities," and "hints of emancipation" that are of its essence.

Democracy did not arise out of eighteenth century political and industrial conflicts, as a momentarily popular view misconceives. Its roots are to be found in the attempted revival of primitive Christianity by the radical lower-class sects of the Protestant Reformation, those peasants and yeomen who were our own ancestors, and who initiated the Reformation and eventually carried out its basic principles—especially in America—to conclusions undreamt of in the beginning. The ideal of local self-government was brought to America by the Pilgrims; the separation of church and state was derived from the Baptists; the right to free speech was a development of the right to freedom of conscience established by Roger Williams and William Penn; the equality spoken of in the Declaration of Independence was an outgrowth of the equality practiced by the Quakers. Democracy was envisaged in religious terms long before it assumed a political terminology.

Unfortunately, the knowledge of religious history has almost vanished from our modern world. How many contemporary American Presbyterians, Baptists, Methodists, or Disciples could tell you much about the origin of their respective sects, the meaning of what they stood for, or the smallest part of their often heroic achievements? The average college student of whatever sect could pass a better examination on Greek mythology than he could on the history of modern Protestantism. The last encyclopedic attempt to deal with it was the American Church History Series brought out in the nineties, and it was produced by clergymen for clergymen only.

Granted that it is better to stand for something today than merely to know what one's ancestors stood for; granted, too, that the decline of religious knowledge has resulted from the decay of narrow sectarianism; the result is still a misfortune, just as it is a misfortune for one not to be able to recall his own parents. And it is doubly so when it is connected with anything so vital as the origin of the American faith in democracy.

To recover the human meaning of that forgotten religious period is a task of particular difficulty because the early formulations of the religious democratic faith of which we are speaking were cast in a theological language and dealt with ecclesiastical dogmas which no longer have any significance for us. When we read that thousands of men were slaughtered simply for persisting in the heretical rite of adult baptism it is likely to seem to us an unaccountable instance of sadism on the part of the persecutors, and sheer senseless stubbornness on the part of the victims. Or when we hear of other thousands leaving England rather than attend churches where priests wore surplices and carried the Cross, we are likely to be ashamed of the narrow bigotry of our ancestors. If we would understand such situations, it is necessary to see them in terms of their modern equivalents, to reduce attitudes and concepts to what William James called their "cash value," when indeed we will perceive them to have been expressions of the same class struggles and clashing interests with which we are familiar today.

We may smile at the title of Roger Williams' work, "The Bloody Tenent of Persecution for Cause of Conscience," or at that of John Cotton's reply, "The Bloody Tenent Washed and Made White in the Blood of the Lamb," or at that of Williams' answer to Cotton, "The Bloody Tenent Yet More Bloody through Mr. Cotton's Endeavor to Wash it White in the Blood of the Lamb." But beneath the strange language the arguments of John Cotton were the arguments of fascism today and the issues debated by him and his liberal opponent were the identical issues that arise in every civil liberties case of the hour.

It is hoped that the reader will be led through interpreting the Reformation as a social, rather than merely religious, revolution, to find the dust of forgotten dogmas taking on new life and a contemporary significance penetrating the tangled thickets of ecclesiastical strife. Thereafter, the track will gradually emerge from the brush and lie in the open as it follows the course of the middle-class autocracy in Calvinistic New England at war with Baptist individualism and Quaker equalitarianism, through the rise of rationalistic Deism into the popular revolutionary movement, and out of it into the counterrevolution of Federalism, and so on to the familiar Jeffersonian and Jacksonian revolutions, the defeated endeavors of the Utopian socialists to carry democracy into economics, the mystical flight of the Transcendentalists, the return of New England to solid earth in the reform movements ending with the abolition of slavery, and the reassertion of freedom in the Civil War. If told as it should be, the story will reveal less of the simple pattern of direct narrative than the intricate movement of a symphony, with its major themes, rising, falling, and re-emerging more powerfully, accompanied intermittently by such minor but integrally related motifs as the liberation of women, the education of children, the dream of world peace.

However told, if told truthfully, it cannot be an unmixed "Heroica." It begins with the picture of a formally unified Europe, but it is impossible for it to end, at the Civil War or even if continued down to the present, with any picture of a really unified America. The old class struggles and political struggles are still with us, and with us in an exacerbated form, in the twentieth century. Every gain has been provisional only, eternally subject to the chance of relapse, and every further gain remains problematic.

Under such circumstances, it is not surprising that many idealists, looking wistfully back to the Middle Ages when such conflicts, though no less existent, were less apparent, should be tempted to return to an authoritarian philosophy and ways of thinking that are unconscious preparations for the acceptance of an authoritarian politics, such as that which has at the moment conquered more than half of Europe. Henry Adams long ago charted the movement from tenth century unity to twentieth century diversity, and there will always be many minds who prefer apparent unity and apparent security to overt diversity and overt hazard.

Yet the medieval unity was only formal and in the interest of a small class; and its fancied security turned out in the end to be insecurity. The different path followed by American democracy, if followed resolutely to the completion of the unfinished program, promises a far more real unity, a far more actual security—the unity of a whole people without class divisions; the physical security that can come only with the control of the means of production, now for the first time really possible; and the mental security that arises from a confirmed habit of recognizing truths wherever found.

Owing to the emphasis laid upon economic conditions and class divisions throughout this work, its pluralistic "multiple-causation" philosophy may possibly be misconstrued as an example of the exactly opposite single-cause philosophy of economic determinism. The latter has undoubtedly done great service in calling attention to formerly neglected truths of the utmost importance; it has done great disservice by distorting these truths into equally important falsehoods. That social classes, based upon economic conditions, do exist is an obvious truth, however deplorable, and that the majority of men tend usually, though by no means always, to defend their economic interests, their group and class interests, is also fairly obvious once attention is called to it. But the theory of economic determinism, as generally advanced, is not simply that economic interests affect other interests but that they exclude other interests, and that the manifold class struggles inevitably polarize in a single great conflict between the bourgeoisie and the industrial proletariat. This is to magnify the economic factor out of all due proportion. The point is well exemplified by a striking passage, which happens to concern the American faith in freedom, in John Strachey's book, *The Coming Struggle for Power:* [1] "The freedom for which Henry Tudor broke with Rome, for which Hampden and Cromwell fought, . . . for the sake of which Washington and Jefferson

[1] By permission of Random House, Inc. (New York: 1933).

defeated George III . . . was the freedom to buy and to sell. The whole long struggle for Liberty, about which the historians tell us everything except what it accomplished, was a struggle for that freedom of contract, which is the legal expression of the free market." And again, "All men, they were now assured, were at last 'free and equal'; they were to approximate as nearly as possible to perfect social atoms, without ties or impediments, whether human or divine, bent only on one activity, namely to produce in order to buy and to sell." The passage is striking, but it turns a truism into an absurdity. The long struggle for liberty did include a struggle for freedom of contract (in its day an advance), but it also included a struggle for free land, a free church, free schools, and politically free individuals; and what it accomplished was, among other things, to bring these into being.

The democratic faith demands whole men, not half-men. The compartmentalized philosophy which separates economics from life, which degrades scholars into specialists and is content to regard laborers as cogs in the machines which they serve, instead of the machines' serving them, is fundamentally inconsistent with the democratic spirit. And the whole man is the moral man, concerned everywhere with values, a field too often pre-empted by religion: for politics, also, is a realm of values, governed in theory, though rarely in practice, by an ideal of "the best government"; so, too, is economics—for few would deny that a "better" economic organization than that which we have surely can and surely must be found. All this has been glimpsed many times in American history.

With this viewpoint in mind, we are ready to take up the study of our own beginnings in the distant Europe of ten centuries ago.

BOOK I. *The European Heritage*

CHAPTER I. *The Reformation as a Social Revolution*

THE GREATNESS OF MEDIEVAL CATHOLICISM

THE older Protestant historians were fond of pointing out that in the providence of God the settlement of America was delayed until after the Reformation in order that the new country might be free from the atrocious superstitions engendered by Roman Catholicism. As late as 1897 the prominent ecclesiastical historian, Leonard Woolsey Bacon, could write in the concluding volume of the American Church History Series: "The grandeur of human enterprise and achievement in the discovery of the western hemisphere has a less claim on our admiration than that divine wisdom and controlling providence which, for reasons now manifested, kept the secret hidden through so many millenniums, in spite of continual chances of disclosure, until the fullness of time. . . . If the discovery of America had been achieved four centuries or even a century earlier, the Christianity to be transplanted to the western world would have been that of the Church of Europe at its lowest stage of decline." [1]

No enlightened Protestant today would be inclined to regard Roman Catholicism quite so simply. The medieval centuries cited by Bacon—the eleventh to the thirteenth—as a period of decline, were in reality one of the great periods of human culture. During

[1] L. W. Bacon, *A History of American Christianity* (New York: The Christian Literature Co., 1897), pp. 1-2.

17

those very centuries the Roman Catholic Church reached the culmination of its power. It had behind it a history of a thousand years, and for half that time had ruled unchallenged over the mind and conscience of western Europe. To all outward appearance it seemed assured of an equally long continuance of power in the future. Its organization was more strongly centralized than that of the Roman Empire had ever been, yet the authority of its multitudinous officials was recognized on the fringes of Europe in far distant England, Ireland, and Spain. It could point to a mighty line of theologians in the Church Fathers from Justin Martyr to Augustine; to an equally notable group of statesmen in Leo the Great, Gregory the Great, Hildebrand, Innocent the Third; and, most recently developed, to schools of philosophy headed by such thinkers as Albertus Magnus and Thomas Aquinas, which rivaled in glory the ancient Academy and Lyceum. Art had never flourished so widely as under the patronage of the church: Romanesque and Gothic cathedrals, with their interior paintings and stained glass windows, their wood carving and sculpture; Gregorian music; folk arts of weaving and furniture; a folk literature of balladry; the romances in verse and prose, centering in the legend of the Holy Grail and the celebration of the Eucharist; the lyrics of the troubadours, and the world epic of Dante.

In the many-chambered temple of the church there seemed to be room for almost every variety of culture. Just as it had been able to absorb both the dying paganism of the ancient world and the youthful paganism of the North, so the church took over the best of Arabic philosophy and, after the fall of Constantinople, made its peace with the revival of Greek learning and with the worldly art of the Renaissance. If clerical morality tended, as it undoubtedly did, to become corrupted by excess of power, the church nevertheless seemed able to revitalize itself periodically from within through such movements as the Cluny Reform, the rise of the Franciscans, and, after the Reformation, the organization of the Jesuits. Warriors, saints, philosophers, poets, and artists were all made welcome within the church.

In the realm of conduct, every important event in life had been brought under the church's idealizing control. Birth, marriage, and death were given a sacred meaning by the ecclesiastical sacraments and ceremonies. Throughout the year, the calendar of the Saints' Days made every twenty-four hours as they passed a reminder and celebration of the church. The institution stood prepared to meet every need. For the sinful, penance and pilgrimage; for the sick, healing images and relics; for the ordinarily good man, the promise of salvation symbolized by the miracle of the mass, daily repeated on his behalf; and for the specially righteous, entrance into the monastic orders with their vowed devotion to wholly religious ends.

In the realm of thought, men enjoyed what is considered by many an inestimable blessing, that of mental security in the inerrant dogmas of the church. As Lewis Mumford points out in *The Culture of Cities*, the church's dogmas corresponded to the city walls, the former protecting the mind, as the latter protected the body. For the church claimed to know once and for all the very innermost scheme of the cosmos. The Scholastic philosophers, though they were profoundly ignorant of their own bodies, uncertain whether the earth was round or flat, and unable to construct a reliable map of more than their own little Europe, nevertheless conceived themselves able to chart the outlines of the whole physical and spiritual universe. For the two were essentially one, the physical world existing as a means to the realization of spiritual values. The earth, around which sun, planets, and stars were supposed to revolve in a divinely symbolic order, was believed to have been created, with all its plants and animals, for the sake of its chief inhabitant, man, as the temporal scene on which the drama of his eternal destiny could be worked out. The universe, man, and destiny alike revealed the purposes of God, which, however difficult to understand in detail, were known in principle. This, the unchanging philosophy of the Catholic Church, was eloquently summarized by the present Pope, then Cardinal Pacelli, on May 31, 1937, at the opening of the Pontifical Academy of Sciences in Rome: "All of nature is directed towards man, and the end of the motion of the skies, as says Saint Thomas Aquinas, points to man as the last end in the circle of things that can be generated and moved. But man in his turn is directed and formed in that image and similitude which marks him in the face of God, to that glory that the skies sing forever."

In the medieval period, life was, in theory, unified as never before or since. Nominally, at least, every human activity was brought under the moral guidance of the church. Trade was supposed to be governed, and in large part actually was governed, by the ethical principles of the church operating through the rules of the guilds to secure fair practice and the production of goods at once durable, useful, and beautiful. Princes were supposed to acknowledge the same moral law as the peasant. Political conduct was often brutal and shameful, but prior to Machiavelli no one dared to suggest that this was as it should be, or ventured to set up a separate code for either political or economic activity.

No other human institution ever began to exercise the influence wielded by the Roman Catholic Church in its prime. It is not surprising that by millions of men, then and now, it should have been regarded, and should still be regarded, as not fundamentally a human institution at all but one divinely instituted, divinely guided, even as the church itself claimed.[2] What, then, were the reasons which led other millions of men to conclude that the blessings of the church were purchased at too high a price, and so to deny its claims and ultimately its whole philosophy? The answer must be found in the consideration of the church in relation to the social system of feudalism—that system of which the church was the crown and glory, the ultimate sanction, and the sustaining principle.

In all three of the Synoptic Gospels, Peter appears as the foremost of the disciples; he was the first to acknowledge Jesus as the expected Messiah, and in Matthew 16:18–19 that acknowledgment is immediately followed by the extraordinary statement of Jesus, wherein, punning on the meaning of the name of Peter, he says: "Thou art Peter (the rock), and upon this rock I will build my church; and the gates of hell shall not prevail against it. And I will give unto thee the keys of the kingdom: and whatsoever thou shalt bind on earth shall be bound in heaven: and whatsoever thou shalt loose on earth shall be loosed in heaven."

The authenticity of this passage has been much questioned by

[2] The claim of the church rests upon the authority conferred upon the Apostle Peter in the New Testament, and upon the tradition that he was martyred in Rome after founding the church there.

modern critics. It does not appear elsewhere in the Gospels. Mark, the companion of Peter on his missionary journeys, might certainly have been expected to mention those words of Jesus if they were genuine, yet he makes no faintest reference to them. There is no further recognition anywhere of the tremendous authority supposed to have been conferred upon Peter; it was not acknowledged by Paul, who in his own words "withstood him to the face" in Antioch; [3] James, not Peter, was head of the Apostolic church in Jerusalem; no mention is made in the Book of Acts of Peter's missionary journey to Rome or his martyrdom there, which, if they occurred at all, must have been subsequent to the journey and death of Paul, at which time the church was already well established in Rome.[4] These arguments are convincing but quite irrelevant to the thoughts of men at a time before higher criticism of the Bible existed or any historical examination of the chronology of the early Christian missions.

SOCIAL CAUSES OF THE REFORMATION

THE characteristic of feudalism that contrasts it most strikingly with the modern world is that it was a static *class society* of a rigidly hierarchic character. From the lowest serf bound for life to the soil up through the "free" yeomanry and the rising grades of nobility to the monarch, social status and function were determined by birth. Looked at from a distance, this fixed social order, unchanging from generation to generation, had many of the characteristics of those admirable communities of the bee and the ant to which philosophers have often sent us for instruction. "The idea of individual autonomy, of individual action independent altogether of the community," wrote Belfort Bax, "is a modern idea which never entered the medieval mind." [5] So again Lewis Mumford: "The unattached person during the Middle Ages was one either condemned to exile or doomed to death: if alive, he immediately sought to attach himself, at least to a band

[3] Galatians 2:11.
[4] See the excellent discussion of these points in Hall Caine, *Life of Christ* (New York: Doubleday, Doran and Company, Inc., 1938), pp. 1137–1141.
[5] E. Belfort Bax, *German Society at the Close of the Middle Ages* (London: S. Sonnenschein and Co., 1894), p. 19.

of robbers. To exist, one had to belong to an association: a household, a manor, a monastery, a guild; there was no security except in association, and no freedom that did not recognize the obligations of corporate life. One lived and died in the style of one's class and corporation." [6]

In this society, the church held a unique and privileged position. In it alone status was determined, not by birth, but by ability. And this ability was supposed to be devoted not simply to the advancement of the church—though the institution of a celibate priesthood [7] in the fourth century prevented any conflict of family affection with the larger loyalty to the church—but to the spiritual welfare of the whole society. Like modern governments, in theory the church stood apart from all the various classes in the community, an arbiter among them and a friend to all. Actually, however, the church stood apart only in the sense that it was a class in itself, enjoying the privileges of the nobility and monarchy and much more besides. It was a temporal sovereign, holding, in addition to the Papal States in Italy, vast areas in Sicily, Sardinia, Dalmatia, and North Africa, besides its indirect ownership of great stretches of monastic land in every country of western Europe. It had its own serfs, like the nobility; it had its own courts in every nation; it could declare war, when this was called "a crusade," and raise armies and navies; it could exact tribute; it could excommunicate monarchs; it was a state within the state and above the state. Of all classes, the church had the largest vested interest in the maintenance of the feudal system. Hence, if any class felt unjustly used under that system, its attack was first and foremost against the church.

Those with most cause for discontent were naturally the great masses of the people at the bottom of the social scale. These included the serfs bound to the soil and often obliged to contribute as much as half their labor for the landlord's maintenance, the tenant farmer yeomanry, and an increasing class, recruited from the yeomen, engaged in city handicrafts. All of these had reason to complain of the exactions of the church. The peasants asserted

[6] Lewis Mumford, *The Culture of Cities* (New York: Harcourt, Brace and Company, 1938), p. 29.

[7] Ironically, the supposed founder of the church, St. Peter, was a married man. "But Simon's wife's mother lay sick of a fever. . . ." Mark, 1:30.

that in the capacity of landlords the clergy were more onerous taskmasters than the nobility. What with plowing, sowing, and harvesting my Lord Bishop's crops, draining my Lord Bishop's estates, cleaning my Lord Bishop's stables, cutting wood and carting it to my Lord Bishop's palace, and providing for my Lord Bishop on his frequent journeys to Rome, the poor laborer had little time or energy left to cultivate his own mean plot of ground.

Then there was the death-tax whereunder at the decease of any peasant householder, the landlord had the right to take from the widow the best article in her possession, depriving her of this at the time she most needed it—a privilege of which the monasteries were said to avail themselves with especial ruthlessness.

And there was the *pallium*, which bore alike on peasants, tradesmen, and the nobility—a special investiture tax which had to be raised by the inhabitants of the diocese on every change of archbishop, bishop, or abbot.

And there were the indulgences in connection with the confessional. The practice of private auricular confession, made obligatory in the eighth century, took on a somewhat different cast when in the thirteenth century the formula of absolution was changed from the conditional *Dominus absolvat*—"May the Lord absolve thee"—to the absolute *Ego te absolvo*—"I absolve thee," whereby the most disreputable priest was given the power to open or close the gates of Heaven, and as the direct dispenser of eternal salvation was encouraged to inflict much heavier penances. But this was of less moment than the growing custom of remitting the penalty through an indulgence granted on the payment of a specified sum, a practice upheld by the casuistry of Thomas Aquinas on the ground that the church, as the custodian of all the supernumerary "good works" performed by the faithful down through the ages, had full right to extend credit from this general sum to any weak brother whom it might select—a kindly operation of spiritual banking which, in the satirical words of Shelley, both "enriched the Church and respited from Hell an erring soul which might repent and live." This form of special privilege was bitterly resented by the poor who saw themselves condemned to penances for sins in which the wealthy could indulge at the cost of what amounted merely to a small fine.

Other practices of the church bore still more hardly upon the masses of the dispossessed. They were taught to believe that, if sick, they could be cured by the possession of relics; but the sale of relics was another ecclesiastical perquisite. They were taught to believe that their dead parents, relatives, or friends were suffering the torments of purgatory; a few masses and candles would shorten that time of agony; but masses and candles cost money. It was not enough that the rich should enjoy most of the goods of earthly life; their special privileges were extended to the future life as well. The church that had started out to save the common man had become the chief agent in grinding him into the dust.

From the haughty point of view of the First and Second Estates, "the lords spiritual and the lords temporal," the Third Estate was all one. In that great class were thrown, without distinction, ordinary laborers, the professional classes, merchants, and incipient bankers or "money-changers." In the famous allegorical interpretation of chess by Jacobus de Cassolis in his *Liber de Moribus Hominum* (known in England as "The Chess Book" through Caxton's translation from the French), the eight pawns were said to signify: (1) field laborers; (2) smiths; (3) clerks, meaning notaries, advocates, or scriveners; (4) merchants or moneylenders; (5) physicians; (6) tavernkeepers; (7) customs officers; (8) ribalds or dice players. Of these pawns, to carry out the chess symbolism, the merchant, supported by the others, was now about to start on his long journey across the board to the crowned king. But he had against him the whole weight of the feudal agrarian tradition.

The notion that money should breed money, thus aping the prerogative of life, seemed monstrous to the medieval mind. The church in theory consistently condemned, under the name of usury, all taking of interest on loans, although it is true that a tacit exception was made in the case of those bankers who supplied the needs of throne and papacy. The condemnation of interest was a part of the *mores* of the period. William Dunbar in his *Dance of the Deadly Sins* placed "caitiffs, wretches, and usurers" in a common group, and Dante assigned to usurers a lower station in Hell than that allotted to those guilty of manslaughter. It was one of the charges against the Jews that they failed to conform to Christian ethics in this matter, the Deuteronomic law condemning only the taking of interest among Jews themselves; hence, it was quite justifiable to cheat a Jewish moneylender as did the knightly hero of *The Cid* who deposited with two Jews a bag of sand, affirming it to be a bag of gold, as security for a heavy loan spent virtuously in private warfare.

Medieval thought, both lay and clerical, looked askance at economic activity unless it was incidental to war or religion. There grew up, to be sure, great commercial cities in Italy and Flanders. Florentine and Lombard bankers had little to learn from Wall Street, and Dante's thirteenth century picture of the business corruption of his day seems singularly modern. Nevertheless, the commercial districts were exceptions in a European society which as a whole was still distinctly agrarian. In general, commerce was condoned but not approved. Trade was recognized as a necessity, but the tradesman was usually regarded as a low fellow. In the words of Gratian, founder of the canon law, "Whoever buys a thing . . . in order that he may gain by selling it again unchanged and as he bought it, that man is of the buyers and sellers who are cast forth from God's temple."

The greatest potential foe of feudalism and the Catholic Church was commerce. Livelihoods dependent upon the individual's own efforts for self-advancement instead of upon his satisfactory fulfillment of a given role in society would demand individual initiative and self-confidence. Obedience would cease to be a virtue. Whenever commerce should become a major interest of man, feudalism would be doomed.

This was already beginning to happen in the period under discussion. In Bohemia, Austria, and Germany the discovery and successful working of silver, copper, and iron mines drew men by thousands from agriculture into industry. These new mineral resources led in turn to new commercial developments. Martin Butzer, writing not in the nineteenth but in the fifteenth century, lamented, "All the world is running after those trades and occupations that will bring the most gain. . . . All the clever heads, which have been endowed by God with capacity for the nobler studies are engrossed by commerce, which nowadays is so saturated with dishonesty that it is the last sort of business an honorable man ought to engage in."

The opening of the sixteenth century saw the rise of the first great family of modern bankers, the Fuggers of Augsburg. With their vast mining interests, their mortgages on the lands of impoverished noblemen, and their extortionate banking loans, they increased their already large wealth almost twentyfold in the sixteen years from 1511 to 1527. They were also, incidentally, philanthropists of the modern type, creating in the Fuggerei a model community in the midst of the turbulent city of Augsburg. Meanwhile, a few miles away in Nuremberg, worked Albrecht Dürer, who, with his mysticism, deep spirituality, and subtle allegories, is likely to be regarded by us as the very incarnation of the spirit of medievalism—although in actual fact he was using medieval methods to destroy medievalism. As always, the past and the future lived together side by side and often within the same man.

Thus, in the Middle Ages there were two mighty social classes with a common grievance against the church: the lower class, earlier in the field, struggling for existence, and the middle class, struggling for power. Their ultimate aims were divergent and conflict between them was certain, but for the time being the two classes could be counted upon to make common cause against the authority of the church. Since the spiritual and the temporal were inextricably intertwined in the church, the field of conflict covered the whole terrain of dogma, ritual, and ecclesiastical organization. For centuries the supreme standard of reference in the world had been Christianity, and it would take centuries to displace Christianity from this position. No one as yet desired to do so. But the Roman Catholic Church could be displaced as the custodian of Christianity if the majority of men should become convinced that it had irretrievably violated its sacred trust. In the course of arriving at this settled belief, the two insurgent classes developed new types of religion suitable to their needs. These new types became the manifold forms of Protestantism.

RELIGIOUS ISSUES IN THE REFORMATION

THE inner strength of Catholicism resided in its control of the means of salvation through its alleged efficacy in preventing sin or at least the consequences of sin. Sin falls into a different category from crime or immorality. Immorality consists in disobeying an accepted moral code, crime is disobedience to the laws of the state, but sin is disobedience to God. The higher the idea of God, the greater the enormity of sin, until, if God is regarded as infinite, sin also acquires an infinite character. Immorality and crime may be expiated by finite punishments: an eye for an eye and a tooth for a tooth; but sin demands an infinite punishment. The conception of Hell was a logical consequence of this conception of sin.

To one really believing in Hell, not merely verbally but with full organic conviction, the question of how to substitute eternal salvation for eternal damnation is manifestly a matter of the utmost concern. The prevalence of magical beliefs and practices in the later Roman Empire made it inevitable that these should creep into Christianity and transform the few simple ceremonies bequeathed by the New Testament into an elaborate salvation ritual.

The magical character of baptism became widely accepted during the second century. Heretics and orthodox agreed that the mere ceremony carried with it remission of sins and assurance of salvation. The custom of infant baptism arose naturally because men holding such beliefs sought to secure the salvation of their children as early as possible. But a difficulty soon presented itself. Common sense and ordinary morality forced the concession that if one of the redeemed later fell into mortal sin his redemption became void. Under these circumstances, was it not safer to postpone baptism until late in life when temptations to sin would be less numerous? Tertullian in the third century argued strongly for this view, and his prudent advice was generally followed until, in the fifth century, the Ambrose-Augustine emphasis upon original sin complicated the whole question. Since the dogma of original sin became so important during the Reformation and played such a large part in the history of American faith it is necessary to go into its origin in some detail.

The theological dogma was technically based upon the story of Adam's Fall related in the second chapter of Genesis. That story was simply a bit of primitive mythology, linked up with the similar tales of Prometheus, Orion, Nimrod, and many others which warned against human attempts to rival the gods in the attainment of power or pleasure. Its original meaning had nothing to do with the implications read into it by theologians many centuries later. The story merely took its place in Jewish literature along with other early myths and legends, and it exercised no great influence on the development of Jewish thought, which took as the point of departure for its philosophy of history the tale of Abraham, the father of the Chosen People. It may have been partly responsible for the Jewish conception of inheritable sin, but none of the Old Testament writers saw in the account of the Fall any hint that the sin of Adam involved the condemnation of the whole human race. The notion of original sin was not a Jewish but a Christian conception and essentially a Catholic conception, however much the church strove to minimize it after John Calvin took it over.

The germ of the idea, to be sure, is to be found in St. Paul as a part of his emphasis on the redemptive power of Christ. In the fifth chapter of the Epistle to the Romans we read: "Wherefore, as by one man sin entered into the world, and death by sin; and so death passed upon all men, for that all have sinned: therefore, as by the offense of one, judgment came upon all men to condemnation; even so, by the righteousness of one, the free gift came upon all men unto justification of life." It is to be noted that although St. Paul here connected the idea of inheritable sin with Adam, he limited its baleful activity to the period before Christ; after Christ, the free gift of justification was available to "all men." In the Epistle to the Ephesians, more likely the work of a Paulist disciple than of St. Paul himself, there is a longer exposition of essentially the same doctrine.

St. Paul did not offer any explanation of the *modus operandi* whereby Adam's sin was inherited, but the scientific-minded Tertullian brought to the support of the theory his celebrated "traducian" interpretation which was destined to an important place in the development of Lutheran theology. According to Tertullian, all human souls were contained in that of the first man, subsequent generations arising by a kind of spiritual cell division. Adam's sin was, as it were, inherited spirituo-biologically. But Tertullian, like St. Paul, held that the new dispensation freed men from this ancestral curse.

The other early Church Fathers—Justin Martyr, Tatian, Athenagoras, Theophilus of Antioch, Irenaeus, Clement of Alexandria,

Origen, Athanasius, Gregory of Nazianzus, Gregory of Nyssa, Chrysostom, Cyril of Jerusalem, Methodius—one and all believed in the freedom of the will and in man's ability through faith and virtuous living to overcome whatever disposition toward sin he might have. Origen, the most philosophical among them, thought that man in this life suffered a reformatory punishment for sins committed in some previous existence, and he even went so far as to advance the theory held by modern Universalists that all men would eventually attain salvation.

These generous views suffered a rude setback in the fourth and fifth centuries. The Roman Empire was obviously becoming less and less capable of resisting the incursions of the barbarians; it had long since passed from the aggressive to the defensive and was engaged in fighting a series of rear-guard actions that brought the enemy ever nearer to Rome. Confidence in the ability of human nature to manage its affairs even tolerably well steadily declined. On the other hand, while the Empire was going to pieces the church was prospering; it seemed to afford the only haven of refuge in an otherwise evil world; whatever increased the power of the church was therefore looked upon with added favor. Furthermore, within the church an economic hierarchy was forming. Recruited originally from artisans and slaves, the church had gradually risen in the social scale until it now represented the upper bourgeoisie and the nobility. These were less eager for a doctrine of universal salvation than for one that duly recognized a distinction between what might be called superlative Christians and merely ordinary Christians.

Various influences thus brought about a renewed emphasis upon the doctrine of original sin, a more stringent interpretation of baptism, and the limiting of God's grace to a favored few. Even Ambrosiaster, in many respects a follower of Origen, came forward with a theory to justify the damnation of unbaptized infants: God in His righteous government of the world suffered only those infants to die unbaptized who, had they lived, would have proved unrepentant sinners; there was therefore no injustice in damning at birth souls that would have merited damnation in any case. Ambrosiaster's contribution to Catholic theology was a little too tenuous to win acceptance, but St. Ambrose, bishop of Milan and the most influential churchman of the period, brought the prestige of his personality and position to the support of a "creationist" explanation of original sin which made use of that distrust of the physical which was common to both later paganism and Christianity. St. Ambrose maintained that each individual soul was freshly created by the deity and was infused into the body after conception, but that this body was already corrupted by its contact with the lust-defiled womb of the mother and hence in turn corrupted the newly arrived soul. In this subtle theory, St. Ambrose sought to harmonize two apparently contradictory ideas: that the soul was created perfect and was yet at birth already tainted with sin. So tainted, indeed, was it in the view of St. Ambrose that the human being could achieve no virtue whatever prior to baptism. With the acceptance of this theory, the door of Heaven was irrevocably closed upon unbaptized infants.

A greater one than Ambrose, St. Augustine, became the chief proponent, elaborator, and defender of a doctrine which he had not originated and which was repugnant to his gentle nature; but he saw no other logical way of reconciling the existence of evil with God's omnipotence than by the assumption of predestined sin. St. Augustine deplored the hapless lot of the unbaptized infants, and in a passage which was versified and elaborated centuries later in the most popular of early New England poems, *The Day of Doom* by Michael Wigglesworth, he ventured to express the belief that God would mitigate the full rigor of His justice toward these victims of inherited sin, just as He might be expected to show some little mercy toward the ignorant heathen. In St. Augustine's words: "It may . . . be correctly affirmed that such infants as quit the body without being baptized will be involved in the mildest condemnation of all. . . . But even the ignorance which is not theirs who refuse to learn knowledge, but is theirs who are, as it were, simply ignorant, does not so far excuse a man as to exempt him from the punishments of eternal fire, even if his failure to believe in Christ has been the result of his not having at all heard what it is that he should believe; though probably his punishment will be a milder one."

Owing to St. Augustine's divergence from the earlier Church Fathers, the church never gave official sanction to his theories of predestination and original sin, but it adopted them by implication in making obligatory the practice of infant baptism. Those Protestant sects which opposed the practice did so because they were opposed to the theory of human nature that lay at its root.

The Christian ceremony of the Lord's Supper underwent a development not unsimilar to that of baptism. The magical rite of eating the flesh and drinking the blood of a sacrificed animal god was a very old one, the idea underlying it being that the participant was thus enabled to share in the strength of the sacrificed god, who, of course, being immortal, in some way survived the sacrifice. Under the influence of Mithraic example, the Lord's Supper, originally a simple symbolic ceremony in memory of the last meal eaten by Jesus with his disciples, was given a magical interpretation as early as the second century by Justin Martyr, who announced the presence of the literal body and blood of Christ in the sacrament. This view was frequently, though by no means universally, affirmed by Catholic theologians until its denial by Berengar of Tours in the eleventh century provoked a furious theological controversy which was finally quieted when the doctrine of literal transubstantiation was declared an article of faith by Pope Innocent the Third in 1215.

It should now be obvious why the first attacks on the church that were made by the Reformers were usually centered upon its rites and ceremonies. The greater the place of ritual in life, the greater the authority of the church administering the ritual. By making participation in the sacraments necessary for salvation the church had obtained a strangle hold on its members. No amount of corruption in its administration could affect this in the least since the church, following St. Augustine, taught that the efficacy of a sacrament was not weakened by any unworthiness on the part of the officiating priest—for the keys of Heaven had been confided to the church irrespective of the personal worthiness or unworthiness of its priests.

Medieval Christianity with its celibate clergy, its confessional and indulgences, its fourth century dogmas, and its magical sacraments, differed utterly from the Christianity of the New Testament. In fact, the church's tremendous affirmation of the Trinity in its sixth century Athanasian Creed did not even pretend to be drawn from the Scriptures. The Creed never referred to the Christian faith or religion; it was avowedly, in its own words, the creed of "the Catholic faith," "the Catholic religion." The relation between the Bible and the church had become inverted so that instead of the church's resting upon the authority of the Bible, the Bible rested upon the authority of the church. St. Augustine frankly declared, "I should not believe the Gospel, did not the authority of the Catholic Church move me thereto." The efforts of Charlemagne and Alfred the Great to foster vernacular translations of the Bible in the ninth and tenth centuries were permitted, but when the medieval church became fully self-conscious and realized its true relation to the Bible, all such efforts were strictly forbidden. So, too, the church declined to furnish its members with translations of its Latin services, because it was necessary to the maintenance of its power that the faithful should not understand what they heard. Even the Latin Bible gradually disappeared from the schools. Amazing as it may seem, Martin Luther studied in the Franciscan school at Eisenach and obtained his bachelor's degree at the University of Erfurt without ever having had a copy of the Scriptures in his hands.

Nevertheless, as a result of the growing dissatisfaction with the church, vernacular translations continued to be made in defiance of its commands. When members of the two great discontented classes were able to read the Bible, what did they find there? They found the record of a lowly people, exiled in Egypt, exiled in Babylon, exiled in Persia—a story of trial and tribulation and persecution nobly borne because of belief in a God who cared directly for men, a God with whom they could come into communication without intermediaries. They found the magnificent denunciatory poetry of the Prophets thundering against formal rites and ceremonies and the exactions of the rich and powerful. They found the teachings of the brotherhood of man enunciated by Jesus, they found him associating with the poor and the outcasts, speaking to them and for them and preaching a religion of joy and freedom that regarded the humblest of men as equal to the highest and gave them a sense of transcendent individual dignity and importance. They learned that the persecuted congregations which cherished these exalted beliefs lived as nearly as possible like loving families, having all their possessions in common.[8] And they learned that a classless society was to be instituted when Christ should return in his glory and establish the Kingdom of Heaven on earth.

"Ideas are weapons," writes Max Lerner. No better weapon than the Bible could have been forged for the overthrow of medieval Catholicism.

[8] The church itself admitted that communal ownership represented the ideal condition of man. In the words of Gratian, "By the law of nature all things are the common property of all men—a principle followed by the primitive church in Jerusalem and taught by Plato." But though the church held that private property, like cohabitation, was a result of sin, it also held that this sin was so ineradicable in fallen human nature that to attempt to remove its results, when it was impossible to remove the cause, was blasphemous; the best that could be done was to sanctify cohabitation through the institution of marriage, and to sanctify property by subjecting it to the uses and rules of the church.

CHAPTER 2 . *The Left Wing of the Reformation*

THE EARLY RADICAL SECTS

THE popular conception that the Reformation began with Martin Luther, and was carried to success by Luther and Calvin, misrepresents the facts and the significance of the entire movement. Luther and Calvin came late in its development, riding to triumph on the crest of a tide that had been rising for centuries. In many ways they represented a betrayal of the Reformation, a counterrevolution which embodied an unstable compromise with the principles of Catholicism—a compromise eventually left behind in a further resurgence of the original anti-Catholic forces. Put in modern political and economic language, the Reformation began as a radical lower-class movement which was largely taken over by the rising bourgeoisie under Luther and Calvin, to be followed by a renewed struggle between these two classes within Protestantism itself. This interpretation gives meaning to the otherwise senseless conflicts that developed within Protestantism even before the victory over Catholicism was surely won.

There were no less than four essentially Protestant sects of great historical importance—the Cathars, Waldenses, Lollards, and Hussites—which arose during the period from the eleventh to the fifteenth century when Roman Catholicism was at the very height of its power. All of them expressed a revolt of the submerged classes in medieval society.

The first and most interesting of these movements was that of the

Cathars. This amazing sect had its origin in survivals of primitive Christianity, with Gnostic and Manichean additions, among the Paulicians and Bogomils of Thrace and Bulgaria whose doctrines were brought into western Europe by soldiers returning from the Crusades. Those vast enterprises of useless slaughter provoked a widespread pacifist reaction—but only among the common people who then, as now, bore the brunt of all wars. No faintest echo of this was heard in the knightly or churchly literature of this or subsequent periods. Speaking of the attitude of orthodox Christianity toward the Christian principle of nonresistance, that admirable humanist, Edith Hamilton, is quite correct in writing: "Except for Christ . . . we do not know of anyone else who disbelieved in violence as a means of doing good. None of Christ's followers seems to have followed Him there until comparatively modern times. Not one medieval saint stands out to oppose the thousands of saintly believers in the holiness of this war or that." [1] Not one official saint, truly; but as we shall see there were thousands of forgotten medieval Christians who followed the lead of the Cathars in denouncing violence.

Their popular origin also explains the second point in which the Cathars resembled the modern Quakers: their opposition to the giving of oaths in law courts; for they had learned the harsh truth that that supposed agent of justice, the law, is in practice accustomed to support the rich and the powerful.

The Cathars possessed an intricate Gnostic theology which does not concern us here. They also had a definite ecclesiastical organization without corporate wealth—the Perfecti, who were the spiritual heads of the Cathar communities, being forbidden to marry or to own property. As a matter of principle, and also perhaps because of their lack of financial means, as well as from a desire to avoid Catholic investigation, they built no churches but contented themselves with simple oratories unadorned with images. The Mosaic books of the Old Testament were rejected by them, and although they retained the Prophets, Psalms, and Wisdom literature, they looked for religious guidance to the New Testament, of which they had their own translations based on Greek texts instead of the Catholic

[1] Edith Hamilton, *Three Greek Plays* (New York: W. W. Norton and Co., Inc., 1937), p. 20.

Vulgate. Their Christology was semi-Unitarian rather than Trinitarian, insisting upon the subordination of the Son to the Father. They interpreted the miracles in the Bible symbolically, and they denounced the worship of saints and relics. For the Catholic ceremonies of water baptism and the bread and wine of the Eucharist, they substituted an adult spiritual baptism by the laying on of hands as an initiation to the order of the Perfecti, and a symbolic Eucharist of bread alone, wherein all went up to a common table and the leader divided the bread among them after saying: "Thanks be to the God of our Jesus Christ. May the Spirit be with us all." Finally, they denied the right of the secular power to intrude in matters of religion or to punish heresy.

Such was this almost incredibly modern sect which flourished in the south of France in the very heart of the Middle Ages. Among the Cathar tenets one finds nearly all of the most radical doctrines of later Protestantism: the separation of church and state (Baptists, Quakers, ultimately all American Protestants); restriction of the power of the clergy (Baptists, Quakers, Methodists, and Disciples); restriction of rites and ceremonies (all Protestant sects, except the half-Protestant Anglo-Catholics); the institution of adult baptism (Baptists and Disciples); the institution of the purely symbolic Eucharist (all Protestants except the Lutherans); opposition to war and oaths (Quakers, Shakers, and German Baptists). The forgotten leaders who built up the Cathar system were true prophets. Four centuries before Luther, they also leaped four centuries beyond Luther in their democratic and humanitarian outlook.

Fortunate in obtaining the favor of William, Duke of Aquitaine, patron of the troubadours, and that of the powerful Counts of Toulouse, the Cathars came out into the open during the eleventh century, and under the name Albigensian, derived from their congregation at Albi, they practically dominated the religious field in the fairest and most cultured region of France. The motives which actuated the Languedoc nobility in patronizing this poor man's religion may readily be conjectured. The "bons hommes" or "bons Chrétiens," as the Albigensian preachers were called, enjoyed great popularity with the masses of the people, and since the nobility had nothing to fear from an "invisible church" without corporate wealth, its fostering offered an easy way by which to retain their subjects' fealty.

The church hesitated long before attacking so powerful a group, but eventually the Cathars were made to feel its wrath. With the support of the King of France, always jealous of the Counts of Toulouse, Pope Innocent III declared a religious crusade in 1208, promising to all who took part in it that the rich domains of Toulouse should be divided among them. With such an incentive, warriors for God were not difficult to obtain, and a large army led by Simon de Montfort and Arnold, the abbot of Citeaux, carried fire and sword into Languedoc. The war endured for twenty years, and at the end of that time the once smiling region had become a wilderness. The organized resistance of the Counts of Toulouse was broken, but separate Cathar groups held out much longer. As late as 1245, when the heretical citadel of Montségur was captured, two hundred Cathars were burned at the stake in a single day. In fact, the Inquisition found abundant work to do in the south of France during the whole of the thirteenth century, and a large part of the fourteenth.

How many Cathars fled to other countries in the course of the persecution there is no means of estimating, but we know that the number was considerable. There were later Cathar groups in Germany, Holland, and Flanders, and as early as the year 1210 a Cathar congregation was discovered in London. Scattered too widely to preserve any organization of their own, they gradually merged with other heretical groups until even their name disappeared. But not their doctrines, which continued to work as a leaven beneath the surface. Even from the Catholic viewpoint, the Cathar persecution merely succeeded in extirpating a local disease at the cost of spreading its germs over Europe. Heretics may be slain by the sword, heresies never.

Unlike the Cathars, whose origins are shrouded in obscurity, the Waldenses came into being at a definite time and place. In the year 1176, Peter Waldo, a rich banker of Lyons, was moved to take literally the injunction of Jesus, "Sell all that thou hast and distribute unto the poor." [2] When he had done so, he gathered around

[2] Luke xviii:22; Matthew xix:21.

him a group known as the "Poor Men of Lyons," who went out, like Christ's disciples, as preachers among the people. This revival of the practice of the early church being condemned by the archbishop of Lyons, Waldo appealed—but appealed in vain—to the Third Lateran Council in 1179. Answering the hostile decision of the Council with the words of Peter, "We ought to obey God rather than men," [3] Waldo was excommunicated. He and his followers fled to the mountainous regions of Vaudois and Piedmont, where, under the stress of persecution, they became definitely heretical and adopted many Cathar doctrines, entirely repudiating the Roman Catholic Church, water baptism, indulgences, purgatory, and the saying of masses for the dead. Their economic organization was definitely communistic. In politics they were opposed to capital punishment and to the taking of oaths. They had their own vernacular translations of some of the Scriptures. Waldo, who remained at the head of the community until his death, set up a system of bishops and priests, but lay preachers were allowed to administer the Lord's Supper, the only Catholic sacrament which was retained.

For the next two centuries a constant stream of missionaries went out from the Vaudois and the Piedmont to found Waldensian communities in Germany and Moravia, where they joined with other groups to play an important part in the further development of the Reformation. It is estimated that by the end of the fifteenth century the Waldenses had a hundred thousand members in France and Italy, and an equal number in Switzerland, Germany, and Moravia. The Catholic Church at last became so incensed that, in 1487, Pope Innocent the Eighth preached a crusade against the Waldenses, but the experience of the Albigensians was not to be repeated. The hardy mountaineers inflicted a crushing defeat on the army of Alberto dè Capitanei, archdeacon of Cremona, and thenceforth sustained themselves against intermittent Catholic persecutions, one of which inspired Milton's noble sonnet, "Defend, O Lord, thy slaughtered saints," until at last the eighteenth century brought peace to the religious world. After seven hundred years, the Waldenses still are to be found on the same mountain slopes to which Peter Waldo led them in 1179.

[3] Acts v:29.

The Lollards of England had a more direct connection with the later Reformation than had either of the sects which we have just considered. They were able to go far because of local conditions. In England, the local church, secure in its distance from the papal seat at Rome, had always managed to preserve an unusual degree of independence. The Anglo-Saxon clergy had maintained its footing in the lower orders of the church and had even perpetuated the original noncelibate organization which permitted its members to marry and have children. Reformation of the church from within seemed more possible in England than elsewhere, and there were leaders ready for the task. Oxford University supplied the Scholastic movement with its most original and daring philosophers, those who stressed an empirical approach: Duns Scotus, William of Ockham, Roger Bacon, and, boldest of them all, John Wiclif, the "Morning Star of the Reformation."

Elected master of Balliol in 1360, Wiclif was not only a philosopher and theologian but also a statesman, being largely responsible for the refusal by King Edward the Third and his Parliament to continue the feudatory tribute to the Papacy that had been wrung from King John many years before. In upholding the state against the church, Wiclif was treading in the steps of William of Ockham, but in his general ecclesiastical theory he was even more radical, insisting that the church should be supported, without tithes, by voluntary contributions; that its emphasis should be laid upon preaching rather than upon the sacraments; and that the merit of the latter was lost when administered by unworthy priests. He held that lay preachers should be installed, and that pilgrimages to shrines and the worship of relics should be abolished.

Boldly carrying his theories into practice, Wiclif sent out his Oxford students as itinerant preachers and diligently labored to supply them with vernacular translations of the Bible. Using the Vulgate text, he himself translated the Gospels and possibly the whole of the New Testament; his disciple, Nicholas of Hereford, translated the Old Testament as far as the middle of the Book of Baruch; the work was completed in 1382, either by Wiclif himself or by some disciple. Thus, England became the first nation to possess a complete translation of the Bible in the native tongue.

Meanwhile, the Papacy was active in endeavoring to thwart

Wiclif's dangerous influence. Five papal bulls were launched against him in vain. Secure in the powerful support of John of Gaunt, Wiclif was able to ride out the storm until Wat Tyler's rebellion in 1381. Although Wiclif disapproved of the peasant rebellion, declaring that all unloving violence was evil and of Hell, there can be little doubt that it was partly inspired by a misinterpretation of Wiclif's economic teachings which verbally had a strongly communistic cast. "Every one in a state of grace has real lordship," he said, and went on to deduce a rightful community of property—but only among those in a state of grace. The limitation was easily overlooked, and Wiclif was further connected with the insurrection through the fact that John Ball of Kent, an unfrocked Wiclifite priest, was one of those who marched at the head of the rebel columns as they moved on London, singing the popular incendiary lines that insulted the whole medieval order of society:

> "Whaune Adam dalf and Eve span
> Who was thane a gentilman?"[4]

Although the rebellion was broken when Wat Tyler was treacherously killed by the Lord Mayor of London during a parley (the code of chivalry not applying to peasants!), nevertheless it had developed enough strength to strike terror into the hearts of the nobility; and Wiclif, like Socrates long before him, was held responsible for the deeds of his followers. On the ostensible ground of his denial of transubstantiation, he was dismissed from Oxford, although permitted to retire to the living of Lutterworth, where he died in 1384.

The movement which he had started continued to grow without him. Ten years after Wiclif's death, the Lollards, as his followers had come to be called (the word having been used originally as a term of contempt meaning "prayer-mumbler"), were strong enough to present to Parliament a long petition in twelve articles, calling for a reformation of the church through the abolition of the celibate clergy, pilgrimages, relics, auricular confession, and prayers for the dead. The Lollards also attacked the doctrine of transubstan-

---

[4] These lines were much older than Wat Tyler's rebellion, as they were known to Richard Rolle half a century earlier.

tiation, and denounced capital punishment and war. Distant influences from both Cathars and Waldenses, as well as the immediate influence of Wiclif, seem to have mingled in their doctrines.

A few years later, Henry Knighton of Leicestershire wrote in his "Chronicle" that the Lollard sect "is held in such great honor in these days and has so multiplied, that you can hardly see two men passing in the road, but one of them shall be a disciple of Wiclif." Even allowing for exaggeration in this passage, it indicates that the movement had acquired an extraordinarily large following. The rise of the Lollards was in fact the most important cultural event in fourteenth century England.

Both Chaucer and Langland were profoundly influenced by it. In choosing the Canterbury Pilgrimage as the theme of his major work, Chaucer deliberately selected the most controversial subject of his day. In his treatment, the great pilgrimage becomes as secular as a fair, and the individual characters, though regarded with a kindly tolerance for human frailty, are shown to be animated by the most mundane motives. Of the many representatives of the clergy, the only one not handled satirically is the poor parson, the single cleric in the group of whom Wiclif also would have approved. Beneath its infinite discretion, the work is essentially a satire.

The other important poem of the period, William Langland's *The Vision of William concerning Piers Plowman*, with its contrasted figures of "Do-well" (outward morality), "Do-bet" (outward morality inspired by love), and "Do-best" (complete reformation of character through union with the spirit of Christ), is almost a preliminary sketch of Quakerism. Its Lollard sympathies are evident throughout but especially in the conclusion where the figure of Piers Plowman merges mystically into that of Christ himself.

The fifteenth century, however, saw the fall of Lollardry. Henry the Fourth, who obtained the throne by usurpation in 1399, was eager to strengthen his position by the closest possible alliance with the church and therefore secured from Parliament the passage of an act in 1401 which introduced into England the death penalty for heresy. For over a century the drastic persecution continued. All copies of the Wiclif Bible that could be discovered were destroyed. Year after year, the Lollards paid for their beliefs with their lives.

Yet Lollardry, though suppressed, was never exterminated. After more than a hundred years of persecution, Bishop Tunstal asserted in 1525 that Luther's teachings "simply put new weapons in the hands of already existing bands of Wyclif heretics." And in 1528 the Convocation lamented that Lollard heresy was spread abroad in Canterbury itself. Lollardry survived, only awaiting some external stimulus to be roused into new life. And the stimulus, by a strange chance, was to come in the form of a return of its own teachings after they had traveled across the continent of Europe and back again.

It was a historical accident that sent Wiclif's influence pulsing through far-off Bohemia. Richard the Second's queen was a Bohemian princess, and in her train came Bohemian scholars to study at Oxford. One of them, Jerome of Prague, obtained a number of Wiclif's manuscripts, which he carried back to Prague in 1397. His brilliant young friend, John Hus, already a professor of philosophy, copied five of the manuscripts, and both he and Jerome began to expound Wiclif's doctrines. In 1403 Hus became rector of the University of Prague, where his daring eloquence aroused the enthusiasm of the students. A less original thinker than Wiclif, he avoided the awkward subject of transubstantiation, but waged relentless war on the sale of indulgences and the worship of relics. He also followed the example of his English master in inaugurating a vernacular translation of the Bible. For these "crimes" he was condemned by the Council of Constance in 1415, and in spite of a safe-conduct from the Emperor Sigismund, who betrayed him at the critical moment, he was burned at the stake. Two hundred and sixty-seven heretical theses, discovered in Wiclif's writings by the assiduity of his subservient successors at Oxford, were also condemned by the Council. Jerome of Prague, who went to Prague to assist Hus, was tried, recanted, recanted his recantation, and was burned in 1416.

During this wintry season for the reformers, a large number of Lollards under Peter Payne, fleeing from persecution in England, arrived in Bohemia to meet persecution there. But history did not repeat itself. In Bohemia hundreds of the nobility actuated by nationalistic sentiments made common cause with the reformers. By an unwise alliance with Germany against the Czechs, the church converted a religious struggle into a war for national independence in which the Czechs were wholly successful. For the first time in its history, the church was obliged to compromise and permit the establishment of a national church under little more than nominal Catholic supervision.

After about 1440, Bohemia and Moravia enjoyed a century of relative peace during which Catholics and Protestants lived side by side. The Reformation was thus virtually established among the Czechs almost a hundred years in advance of other European countries. Although these gains were later largely nullified when national independence was lost, something of the democratic spirit which characterized modern Czechoslovakia until its recent betrayal to Hitler was a direct inheritance from the Hussites.

Of special interest to Americans is the fact that the strongest of the Hussite sects, surviving all the devastation and destruction of the religious wars, found shelter at last, after two hundred years, in Quaker Pennsylvania, where it helped in building our own democracy. This was the sect of pacifist communists known as the Unitras Fratrum or Moravian Brethren, important in themselves and also, as we shall see later, because of their creative influence on the beginnings of the largest American church, that of the Methodists.

THE LUTHERAN COMPROMISE

In Germany, as in England and Bohemia, the Reformation began as a protest against the economic exactions of the Roman Catholic Church. It was supported at the outset by the lower classes, by those members of the nobility who were jealous of the foreign influence of the Papacy, and by the intellectuals. As in the cases of Wiclif and Hus, its leader was a professor of philosophy. But never was there a professor of philosophy of such unphilosophic temperament as Dr. Martin Luther of Wittenberg.

The son of a peasant, Luther always claimed to be proud of his lowly origin. Its traces were evident in his healthy animality—he could quote with approval the popular folk distich—

"Wer liebt nicht Wein, Weiber, und Sang,
Der ist ein Kerrl sein Leben lang—" [5]

and in his coarse manners, his fondness for ribaldry, his tempestuous fits of anger, his impassioned language, often vulgar and violent, but at its best rich with the tang of earth and all growing things. He was a creature of imagination and emotion rather than reason, a mystic without the ascetic tendency that usually accompanies mysticism.

But he was born under medieval skies. After taking degrees at the University of Erfurt, intending to study law, he was shocked into recognition of the nullity of such pursuits by two terrifying personal experiences. The death of a friend cut off in the flower of youth; his own narrow escape from a stroke of lightning while traveling through a forest: these brought home to him with irresistible force the precariousness of human life. He accordingly became an Augustinian monk and did weary battle in prayer and fasting with the natural inclinations which he was forced to regard as sin. Not being an original thinker, he fully accepted the Augustinian doctrine of natural depravity; the human soul, conceived in sin and born in corruption, had no escape from merited perdition except through the gift of the grace of God. Why did not God extend this gift to all instead of only to a chosen few? God's will is not to be judged by human standards of good and evil, justice or injustice. Had not Duns Scotus and William of Ockham proved that the reason cannot search out God? As the creator of all good, He cannot be subject to His own creation; whatever He wills must be right simply because He wills it. Then how could Luther ever be sure that he would not die in his sins, struck down next time by the merited lightning that had narrowly missed him? In the Bible he found the solace that his ailing spirit demanded. Those who are able to give themselves wholly to Christ will attain through the sense of union with him an assurance of their redemption. This was the mystical meaning of that justification by faith taught by St. Paul and recently stressed by Bishop Lukas of Prague. In it Luther found comfort and peace. But he was nevertheless all unwittingly treading on dangerous ground.

[5] Often attributed to Luther himself. A contemporary Lutheran once told me that in his boyhood he supposed it to be part of the catechism.

Since the phrase, "Justification by Faith," became the great Protestant war cry as against the Catholic slogan of "Justification by Works," it is well to be clear as to just what the terms meant. By "faith" the Protestants implied, as did St. Paul, much more than mere belief: the word conveyed to them the idea of an inner union with Christ and immediate direction by his spirit. And, on the other hand, the Catholics meant by "works" much less than the whole range of moral activities, the performance of "good works" referring to the fulfillment of tasks specially enjoined by the church, such as pilgrimages and crusades, regular attendance at church ceremonies, fasting, confession, masses for the dead, and, occasionally, the giving of alms to the living. The Protestant ideal was that of inward inspiration, the Catholic ideal was that of outward authority. Compromise between the two was, of course, possible, but fundamentally they were irreconcilable.

In 1517 the sale of indulgences in the vicinity of Wittenberg by Dr. John Tetzel, acting under a commission from the Archbishop of Mainz, offered a sudden test as to how far Luther would dare to carry his principles. The famous ninety-five theses, to the writing of which he was spurred on by Andreas Carlstadt, professor of theology, were Luther's reply. They took up with Scholastic thoroughness every aspect of the question and boldly denied that a papal indulgence could remove the guilt of even the smallest transgression.

To Luther's own surprise the theses were caught up everywhere, and the thirty-four year old professor of philosophy found himself suddenly famous. Such Humanists as Erasmus, Melancthon, Reuchlin, and Oecolampadius rallied to his support; Franz von Sickingen and Silvester von Schauenberg offered him the refuge of their castles for a time of need; students from all parts of Germany hurried to Wittenberg. There ensued a three years' war of pamphleteering in which Luther as a fighting polemicist proved himself more than a match for the various papal emissaries who sought to refute him. Under the stress of argument, his heresies grew. The high point of his radicalism was reached in a long debate with John Eck from June 27 to July 16, 1519, in the course of which he declared:

"I believe that there is on earth, wide as the world is, not more than one holy, universal church, which is nothing else than the community of the saints. . . . I believe that in this community or Christendom, all things are common and each one shares the goods of others and none calls anything his own."

Such utterances made Luther the hero of the common man as well as of the intellectuals. In his tract, *The Babylonish Captivity of the Church of God* (1520), he denied the literal presence of the body and blood of Christ in the mass, and rejected the doctrine that baptism carried with it regeneration. He seemed definitely to be following in the footsteps of the Cathars, Waldenses, and Lollards. But with a shrewd sense of actual forces, he declined to entrust his cause either to the populace or to the intellectuals. Instead, in *An Address to the Christian Noblemen of Germany*, he called upon the aristocracy to take the lead in ecclesiastic reformation by refusing to recognize the temporal authority of the church. He had learned from his study of the Hussites the value of having a nationalistic movement behind him.

Summoned before the princes of the Empire at Worms to answer a papal bull of excommunication and required to recant his opinions, Luther replied in the oft-quoted words: "I shall not be convinced, except by the testimony of the Scriptures or by plain reason; for I believe neither the pope nor councils alone, as it is manifest that they have often erred and contradicted themselves . . . I am not able to recall, nor do I wish to recall, anything; for it is neither safe nor honest to do anything against conscience. Here I stand, I cannot do otherwise. God help me. Amen." Memorable words, which marked the point that the world had reached. Luther was substituting for the authority of the church the double authority of the Bible and private conscience. And since interpretations of the Bible might differ, this would inevitably mean in the long run the single authority of the private conscience. Such a development, however, was something that Luther did not foresee.

On his departure from the Diet of Worms, Luther was abducted, with his own consent, by the Elector of Saxony, and for nearly a year was kept in voluntary imprisonment in the safe castle of Wartburg where he devoted himself to the translation of the Scriptures. Only an inspired poet, a great lover, and a great hater could have succeeded in the task; and Luther was all of these. He had the tenderness of a St. Francis for birds and flowers and children, and he had the sternness of a Dante toward those whom he regarded as sinners. He was the greatest of the world's translators, his only rival being William Tyndale, who had the benefit of Luther's example. Avoiding both the pedantry of literalness and the license of easy paraphrase, he produced a version which was as accurate as his texts permitted, and in style he captured to perfection the marvelous union of dignity and familiarity found in the Hebrew and Greek originals. It established the High German dialect in which it was written as the language of Germany, even though of itself it could not create a united Protestant Germany.

During Luther's retirement at the Wartburg, another leader of the Reformation arose at Zurich in the person of Huldreich Zwingli, a much more logical and radical thinker than the German reformer. Influenced like Luther by John Hus, he too began by denouncing the sale of indulgences but swiftly moved on to a wide-ranging attack on the whole Catholic system, including the ceremony of the mass, auricular confession, the institution of monasticism, and the celibacy of the priesthood. The last-mentioned issue was effectively dramatized by Luther through his marriage with Katherine Bora, the spectacle of the ex-monk and ex-nun both renouncing their vows furnishing a suitable symbol of Protestant freedom and the Protestant ideal that the clergy should be representative of the people. It was Zwingli, rather than Luther, however, who first gave prominence to the ideal. And it was Zwingli who developed what was later to become one of the most distinctive features of radical Protestantism: the conception that the seat of religious authority lay in the individual congregation, as in the practice of the early church, rather than in the priestly hierarchy, as developed by Catholicism and later by the Church of England. Victorious over his Catholic opponents in a public discussion of sixty-five theses in January, 1523, Zwingli persuaded the magistrates of Zurich to adopt his principles and to set up a virtual theocracy under his direction.

Now the Achilles' heel in Luther showed itself. It was of the utmost importance for the progress of the Reformation that the Swiss and German Protestants should maintain the most close of alliances. But Luther could not brook a rival leader in the movement. Violently rejecting Zwingli's rationalistic interpretation of the Eucharist which allowed a merely symbolic significance to the bread and wine, he upheld William of Ockham's theory of "consubstantiation," according to which the bread was not literally changed into the body of Christ yet the body of Christ was still present in it *substantialite* though not *locasliter*—a heavenly body not in space but none the less received through the mouth of the participant. When Zwingli professed to be unable to understand this effort of Scholastic subtlety, Luther flew into a rage, and an unedifying exchange of pamphlets followed. Through the mediation of the irenic Philip of Hesse, the contestants were brought into personal conference, but Luther refused to budge from the words, *Hoc est meum corpus*.[6] *Est*, he insisted, meant "is," not "symbolizes"; the bread must be the body, even though it could not be. The conference broke up, and Luther in parting wrathfully refused to take Zwingli's hand. Hotly he wrote, "Zwingli, Carlstadt, and Oecolampadius would never have known Christ's gospel rightly had not Luther written of it first." He compared their refusal to accept his dictation to the undutiful rebellion of Absalom against David and even to the betrayal of Christ by Judas.[7]

Disgusted by Luther's growing dogmatism, Erasmus, and most of the other Humanists who had given him their qualified support, now broke with him entirely. They could see little point in forsaking the Catholic Church for another which promised to be equally intolerant. In 1524 Erasmus published his *Diatribe on Free Will*, maintaining that the doctrine of predestination, as understood and asserted by Luther, was tantamount to a denial of God's sense of justice. Luther in his reply, *The Bondage of the Will* (1525), reiterated his position that it was perfectly just for God to save or damn men regardless of their efforts or temptations. God, he asserted, had "an eternal hatred of mankind, a hatred not only on account of demerits and the works of free will, but a hatred that existed even before the world was created." Such, he maintained, was the teaching of the infallible St. Paul.

Meanwhile, other interpretations of the Bible (and also of Luther) were being made, some of which were less to the reformer's taste. Nicholas Storch, a master weaver, developed an astonishing pro-

---

[6] The word "hocus-pocus" is significantly derived from the phrase *Hoc est corpus*.

[7] When Zwingli was later killed in battle against the Roman Catholics, Luther announced that his death was a judgment of God.

ficiency in applying Scriptural apocalyptic prophecies to his own time. Thomas Münzer, a Lutheran priest, took seriously Luther's words that in a Christian community all things should be in common. When Storch and Münzer came together, and the prophetic visions of the one were united with the communistic aspirations of the other, a dangerous revolutionary force was engendered, which was further strengthened by the adherence of the influential Andreas Carlstadt.

The great Peasants' Revolt of 1525 was not, however, the work of Münzer, Storch, Carlstadt, or any other individual, but came as a spontaneous outbreak in many separate localities. The peasants were driven to desperation by the enormous rise in the cost of living at the close of the fifteenth century, occurring at a time when they were being subjected to increased tithes and taxes and were also steadily losing their former communal rights. There had been similar local revolts in 1476, 1491, 1493, 1502, 1512, 1517, but that of 1525 was by far the most serious. The justice of the peasants' demands even drew into the movement such generous apostates from the aristocracy as the knightly Florian Guyer, and that stormy Goetz von Berlichingen celebrated by Goethe in his early radical period. The famous Twelve Articles of the Peasants, drawn up by the Swiss pastor Schappeler, show how completely the religious and economic motives had become intertwined. The first article asserted the right of the peasants to choose and depose their own pastors. The second asserted their right to determine the amount of the tithes. The third demanded the abolition of serfdom. Appealing to the Bible, the peasants declared, "We find in the Scriptures that we are free, and we will be free." The other articles concerned the restoration of former rights, such as those to fish in the streams and to cut wood on unoccupied land.[8]

By all the laws of consistency, Martin Luther, rather than Münzer, Storch, or Carlstadt, should have been the religious leader of the peasants. He had come from their class, and he understood their plight. In words as incendiary as those later used by Münzer he had

---

[8] Even these rebellious medieval peasants showed more sense of the need for conserving natural resources than was possessed by nineteenth century Americans and Australians. The demand for a renewal of the right to cut wood was accompanied by the qualification: "with the knowledge of them who are chosen to this end, whereby the destruction of the wood may be hindered."

warned the nobility: "The people neither can nor will endure your tyranny any longer. God will not endure it; the world is not what it once was when you drove and hunted men like wild beasts." Luther had no love for the aristocracy, and still less did he have any love for the merchant class. Holding to the medieval condemnation of interest, he had often enough denounced the wiles and trickery of commerce and trade. When the workmen of the cities began to join the peasants, as they did, that should have been an added reason for his supporting the revolt.

But Luther knew that his own safety had depended upon his aristocratic following, and now that his religion had been taken up by so many of the princes was he to see these gains imperiled by the impracticable demands of an illiterate populace? For a time he strove to steer a middle course, but when the crisis became acute he definitely joined the party of wealth and authority. His attitude may well have been conditioned in part by personal envy of Münzer's popularity among the peasants; yet the peasants really only turned from Luther to Münzer after the former clearly indicated that he was preparing to abandon their cause. By successive steps he had declined from the once idolized Dr. Luther to the execrated "Dr. Lugner" (Dr. Liar).[9]

In *An Admonition to Peace* (1525), Luther appealed to the peasants to return to their "duty." Emphasizing the distinction between the "spiritual" and the "temporal," he who had himself defied both the ecclesiastical law of Rome and the political law of the Empire, now preached the duty of submission to all political laws, no matter how unjust. "Render unto Caesar," he cried, "the things that are Caesar's." One's divine *Beruf* or calling, he argued, consists in doing one's duty in that state of life in which he finds himself. Concerning the abolition of serfdom, he wrote that it would make Christian liberty "an utterly carnal thing." "Did not Abraham and other patriarchs have slaves?" he asked, with the same line of reasoning that was to be followed by the southern clergy in America three centuries later.

When the initial successes of the peasants were accompanied by the looting of monasteries and a few instances of terrible cruelty, the conflict became simplified in Luther's eyes to one between God

[9] Münzer's term for him.

and the Devil. In the relatively mild *Admonition* he had addressed the peasants as "Dear Christians" and "Dear Brethren," but now two months later they had become "the Murderous and Thieving Peasant Bands," to whom no quarter should be given. "Let everyone who can," he wrote, "smite, strangle, stab—secretly or openly." "It does not help the peasants," he continued, "that they claim that in Genesis I & II all things were created free and common and that we have all been equally baptized. For in the new testament Moses counts for nothing, but there stands our Master Christ and casts us with body and possessions under the Kaiser's and worldly law." [10]

If it suited Luther's purposes, the example of Abraham in the Old Testament was absolutely binding, but if the Old Testament could be used against him it counted "for nothing." This playing fast and loose with the Scriptures was later still more characteristic of the Calvinists. Protestant insistence upon the literal interpretation of the Bible usually meant that it should be interpreted literally whenever it was to the Protestant interest to make that interpretation.

When Luther's ferocity aroused unfavorable comment among many of his own followers, he turned savagely upon his critics, supplementing *Against the Murderous and Thieving Peasant Bands* (1525) with another tract, *Concerning the Hard Book Against the Peasants* (1525), in which he said: "I must warn those who criticize my book that they ought to hold their tongues and have a care lest they make a mistake and lose their own heads; for they are certainly rebels at heart. . . . The rulers, therefore, ought to seize these people by the cap and make them hold their tongues. . . . If they think this answer too hard, and that this is talking violence and only shutting men's mouths, I reply that this is right. A rebel is not worth answering with arguments, for he does not accept them. The answer for such mouths is a fist that brings blood from the nose." All this when the revolt of the peasants had already failed and they were being subjected to mass reprisals in a bloody reaction which Luther, although he mildly deplored its severity, did much to encourage by his general attitude.

Luther's capitulation to the German princes was to have dire con-

[10] Quotation taken from V. F. Calverton, *The Passing of the Gods* (New York: C. Scribner's Sons, 1934), p. 151. Chapter IV of this work is the best brief account of the Reformation that we have.

sequences for his church centuries later. He had purchased safety at the cost of liberty, which is never a secure thing to do. Lutheranism became the established church of the North German states, but this meant that the supreme ecclesiastical power was turned over to the government with the authority to appoint and remove the clergy. The Lutheran ministry was subjected to a system of church visitation by government officials empowered to pass upon clerical competence. The church became simply a department of the state which remained, beneath all the later industrial development, essentially feudal in spirit. Thus, the end of the Lutheran compromise was that the Lutheran rebellion had merely exchanged the ecclesiastical domination of the Roman Catholic Church for various forms of political domination: first that of the principalities, then that of the German Empire, and finally that of the Nazi dictatorship. So when in these sad latter years the Hitlerian oligarchy began their attempt to replace Christianity by a return to primitive paganism, the Lutheran clergy were rendered almost powerless by the concessions of Martin Luther four centuries earlier.

THE GREAT ANABAPTIST MOVEMENT

THE Anabaptists were the direct descendants of the Waldenses and the direct ancestors of our own Congregationalists, Baptists, Quakers, and Unitarians. They first became prominent in Zurich, where the Waldensian influence was strongly felt, during the early years of the liberal, antiritualistic phase of Zwingli's reformation. They were at first merely left-wing followers of Zwingli, who himself had decided objections to the doctrines of original sin and infant baptism. These objections they carried to the logical conclusion that infant baptism, a thing involuntary and of no value, must be replaced by adult baptism—whence their name of Anabaptist or "rebaptizers." This radical reform Zwingli might perhaps have permitted save that its advocates were members of the lower classes who went on to object to the payment of tithes and to agitate for agrarian reforms. Zwingli, like Luther, made his choice, and it was the same choice. In 1526 the magistrates of Zurich under his direction decreed the penalty of drowning for any who underwent the Anabaptist ceremony of adult rebaptism.

Expelled from Zurich, the Swiss Anabaptists found a temporary refuge under the tolerant rule of Philip of Hesse. To the importunate demands of Luther that he adopt measures of persecution, Philip replied: "We are still unable at the present time to find it in our conscience to have any one executed with the sword on account of his faith," and again, "To punish capitally . . . those who have done nothing more than err in the faith cannot be justified on gospel grounds."

But Philip of Hesse stood alone. The Diet of Spires in 1529 passed an edict that reached a new high level of intolerance: "By the plenitude of our imperial power and wisdom we ordain, decree, oblige, declare and will that all Anabaptists, men and women who have come to the age of understanding, shall be executed and deprived of their natural life by fire, sword, and the like, according to opportunity and without previous inquisition of the spiritual judges." In passing this decree of execution without even the shadow of legal trial, Lutherans joined with Catholics, and both were equally zealous in enforcing it, actuated ultimately by the same economic fear that the lower classes would once more get out of hand.

The lower classes were, however, already again out of hand. In spite of the execution of two thousand Anabaptists prior to 1530, their movement continued to grow, especially in the cities, where the artisans were now ready to lead a new rebellion against the rule of the princes. The fiery Thomas Münzer was dead, executed after the failure of the Peasants' Revolt, but a successor appeared in the person of Melchior Hofmann, who claimed to be a reincarnation of Elias and promulgated an order for the suspension of baptism for two years, after which another prophet, Enoch, would set up the kingdom of the Lord in Strassburg. The second year saw Melchior imprisoned for life, but the promised Enoch arrived in Johann Matthiesen, a baker of Haarlem, who had the wisdom to change the seat of the New Jerusalem from Strassburg to Münster where a radical Lutheran preacher, Bernard Rothmann, had already organized the workingmen in a successful drive to close the monasteries and expel all priests from the city. Matthiesen obtained control of the municipal government, and thousands of Anabaptists thronged into Münster, which was soon closely besieged by the forces of the nobility. Matthiesen was killed in a sally, to be succeeded by Johann

Bockholdt, a Leyden tailor usually known in history as John of Leyden. The latter instituted polygamy, married four wives himself, and, when one of them was discovered to be in communication with the enemy, publicly beheaded her with his own hands. E. Belfort Bax in *The Rise and Fall of the Anabaptists* (1903) makes out a good case for the thesis that polygamy was adopted as a political expedient since there were twice as many women as men in Münster; he is less successful in arguing that John's assumption of the executioner's role was due to a democratic desire to remove the obloquy unjustly attached to that office—a hypothesis inconsistent with the dictator's very undemocratic assumption of kingly powers and pomp. His part in the execution was more likely taken to assure his followers of his own loyalty to their cause. According to his finally triumphant opponents, Münster under John of Leyden's rule was a scene of riot and anarchy, but these stories are difficult to reconcile with the fact that the city heroically withstood its besiegers for an entire year and was only conquered at last through treachery. When it fell, John and his leading followers were, of course, cruelly tortured and then put to death.

As always, the winners vilified the memory of the losers and transmitted their own distorted account of events to posterity. But, contrary to the accepted tradition, it was not the excesses of the Anabaptists in their brief moment of power that discredited them with sober-thinking people, for these excesses were mild indeed compared to those of the reign of terror that followed their defeat. The Anabaptists were discredited in advance with both nobility and bourgeoisie by the nature of their demands and the class they represented. "Anabaptism," like "communism" in the twentieth century, became the stalking-horse of reaction. Francis the First, hoping for the assistance, or at least the neutrality, of the German princes in his war with Charles the Fifth deemed that he offered a sufficient excuse to them for his persecution of the French Protestants by accusing the latter of being "Anabaptists." It was initially to refute this sufficiently absurd accusation that John Calvin sat down to write his *Institutes*, the work which was, when fully elaborated, to establish a new code of bourgeois morals.

In Germany and Holland the Anabaptists were too thoroughly crushed to leave any enthusiasm for armed rebellion in their descendants. But meanwhile the movement was carried into Austria and Moravia by Balthasar Hubmaier, who set up an influential printing press at Nikolsburg. After Hubmaier was burned at the stake in 1528 new leaders arose in Jacob Huther and Jacob Wiedemann, who found support for their communistic teachings among the surviving groups of Waldenses and Taborites. "Notwithstanding frequent bitter persecution," writes a conservative Baptist historian, "the Moravian Anabaptists by their skill and industry made themselves indispensable to the Moravian nobles, and their strong communistic organization enabled them to husband their resources and even in times of severe persecution to hold together." They continued to prosper until the Thirty Years' War involved them in the general devastation brought to their country by that ruinous struggle.

The significance of all these militant lower-class movements—Lollard, Utraquist, the Peasants' Revolt, Moravian communism—lay in their combination of religious reform and social amelioration. They were bold drives for power which were pathetically premature, bound to be crushed in the long run by the united opposition of the nobility and bourgeoisie, the former slowly declining, the latter representing the economic forces of the immediate future.

Destined to move forward, not in opposition to the bourgeoisie but in conjunction with it, the lower classes in the sixteenth and seventeenth centuries were in no position to struggle for power; the most they could hope for was tolerance and the opportunity to rise as individuals. Hence, outside of Bohemia and Moravia, the later Anabaptists tended to abandon the direct economic issue and to devote themselves entirely to the attack on religious and political authoritarianism.

TRANSFORMATION OF THE ANABAPTISTS INTO THE BAPTISTS

WITH the intellectual climate what it was, the most promising approach to heresy was through mysticism. This was the form ultimately assumed by religious radicalism among the Lutheran Anabaptists. Hans Denck, director of St. Sebald's school in Nuremberg, and one of the many early Lutherans who had turned to Münzer, when called to make a profession of faith before the City

Council declared that although he had not yet "a full experience of the inward powerful Word of God," he distinctly felt its life as an inner witness which God had planted within him, and in the strength of this direct experience he denied the value of external ceremonies and asserted that "even the Bible itself cannot bring men to God without the assistance of this inner Light and Spirit." Here at last a new note was struck in Protestantism, and one destined to vibrate ever more loudly in the coming years, as the inner logic of Protestantism would slowly force an acceptance of this appeal to direct experience as the central core of philosophic meaning in the new religion—an appeal that would in time be carried far beyond the bounds of religion into art, science, politics, and every walk of life.

Denck's mysticism was shared by Menno Simons and Caspar Schwenkfeld, who established sects which in due time were to be carried to Pennsylvania on the heels of the Quakers, helping to give its religious character to that distant part of the world. Menno, a former follower of Münzer, was scornfully described by Luther as "a hedge-preacher, one of those sneaking fellows who associate themselves with laborers in the harvest fields, or charcoal burners in the woods." A price was put on his head, and a description of his appearance was posted on the doors of all churches. Preaching to the peasantry, he, like Schwenkfeld, emphasized the old familiar themes of the Left Reformation—the separation of church and state, and the opposition to oaths and war and capital punishment, to infant baptism and to ecclesiastical ceremonies. But warned by the fate of Münzer and Johann Matthiesen, they had nothing to say in regard to economic reform. Both the Mennonites and Schwenkfeldians preferred to be called Baptists rather than Anabaptists, in order to avoid the opprobrium attached to the older term. Laboring chiefly in the scattered communities of the Waldenses, Menno gained a wide following in Switzerland and the Netherlands. Unfortunately, as Menno's church increased, his own liberalism diminished. After he became bishop of the Brethren in Groningen, he fulminated excommunications like any pope, forbade marriage outside of the sect, and declaimed against any attempts to raise women from their Pauline position of inferiority. As a result, the Waterland Mennonites in Amsterdam seceded and formed a separate church of great importance for American history—for from it sprang the English Baptists, led by John Smyth, a man who should not be forgotten.

John Smyth was a onetime Cambridge graduate and minister of the Church of England. It was his good or ill fortune to be so open-minded and logical that if anyone thoroughly confuted his position he at once abandoned it and assumed that of the victor. Setting out to convert a group of Separatists at Gainsborough, he found himself converted by them, with the result that he remained in Gainsborough as their pastor. When the danger of persecution became too great in 1606, he succeeded in getting his flock safely across to Amsterdam. But there he entered into debate with the Mennonites regarding their doctrines of adult baptism and the separation of church and state, and his earlier experience was repeated. In order to signalize his conversion, Smyth publicly baptized himself (whence his sobriquet of "the Se-Baptist") and then baptized Thomas Helwys as his first disciple. The two together then baptized those other members of Smyth's congregation who had followed him in this his second and greater heresy.

Smyth's congregation published a Declaration of Faith in 1611, notable as containing the first English demand for the complete separation of church and state: "The magistrate is not to meddle with religion, or matters of conscience, nor compel men to this or that form of religion." It also set forth the principle of local autonomy—"No church ought to challenge any prerogative over any other"—and repudiated infant baptism. The Baptists began as the most democratic and rational of all English sects.

Smyth fully deserved the praise accorded by Mandell Creighton: "None of the English Separatists had a finer mind or a more beautiful soul than John Smyth. None of them succeeded in expressing with so much reasonableness and consistency their aspirations after a spiritual system of religious beliefs and practice. None of them founded their opinions on so large and liberal a basis." Smyth, like his later follower Roger Williams, understood that true consistency resides in a unified pattern of personality animated by a coherent dynamic purpose rather than in a static clinging to one set of ideas.

"To change a false religion," he wrote, "is commendable and to retain a false religion is damnable. For a man of a Turk to become a Jew, of a Jew to become a Papist, of a Papist to become a Protestant, are all commendable changes though they all of them befall one and the same person in one year; nay, if it were in one month: . . . and therefore, that we should fall from the profession of Puritanism to Brownism, and from Brownism to true Christian baptism, is not simply evil or reprovable in itself, except it be proved that we have fallen from the true religion."

Smyth was a bold and able thinker, and so good a scholar that he insisted upon preachers always verifying their quotations from the Bible by going directly to the Hebrew and Greek originals. Nevertheless, he had his crotchets. He carried his idea of the separation of church and state to the extent of excluding magistrates from the congregation, and, on the other hand, fearing a lapse into religious anarchy, he stressed the notion of apostolic succession and required that elders be ordained by ministers or elders who had themselves been ordained. These opinions, unfortunately, broke the bond of brotherhood in his congregation, and Smyth had the mortification, shortly before his death in 1612, to be expelled from the church that he had founded. To make his defeat more bitter, the anti-Smyth group was led by his first convert, Thomas Helwys.

Helwys was one of those ardent liberals who become illiberal in their support of liberalism. He detested the idea of infant damnation so heartily that he declared that all those who held it were certain to go to Hell themselves. Conceiving that it was the duty of all Separatists and Baptists to return to England and endure whatever persecution might befall them there, he led his congregation to London, where, however, heterodoxy had become so rife that they escaped attention in the general confusion. Slowly, though very steadily, the Baptists increased in numbers until by 1624 they had five churches in the south of England; but they were not to become a major sect until the time of the Cromwellian Revolution.

CHAPTER 3. *The Right Wing of the Reformation*

THE CHURCH OF ENGLAND

IN ENGLAND, the character of the Reformation was determined by the fact that the decline of the nobility had proceeded much further than in Germany. The prolonged War of the Roses (1455–85) had wrought such frightful carnage that on the accession of Henry the Seventh only twenty-nine lay peers were left in the whole realm to take their seats in the House of Lords. Feudalism may fairly be said to have committed suicide in England. The surviving noblemen found it necessary to recuperate their fortunes by devotion to sheep raising in order to participate in the growing woolen trade with the Continent. In order to remain noblemen they were obliged to become merchants. The Tudors, of course, were too shrewd to allow aristocracy to perish, and constantly recruited the members of the class by new patents of nobility to court favorites and men of wealth who could be depended upon to support the authority of the Crown. But they had the wit to see that the future of the nation would lie in commerce. They were willing to protect the rising bourgeoisie as long as the latter respected the sovereign rights of the Crown; and the bourgeoisie were quite willing to respect those rights as long as they did not interfere with their own prosperity.

Beneath the surface smoldered the old Lollard discontent among the lower classes, increased by the recent practice of enclosing the commons for sheep pasture. As on the Continent, the first interest

59

in the Reformation was shown by representatives of the commonalty. William Tyndale, whose translation of the New Testament was the initial step in restoring the Bible to the English people, had the common man in mind in all his efforts. His attitude was shown as a young priest when to the pompous assertion of a high ecclesiastic—"We were better without God's laws than without the Pope's"—he replied prophetically, "If God spare my life, ere many years I will cause a boy that driveth the plough to know more of the Scriptures than thou dost." But Tyndale was obliged to flee from England in order to make his translation in even relative safety, and when published it was suppressed in England as rigorously as Wiclif's had ever been. The English yeomanry might be in sympathy with the Reformation, but they were almost powerless to further its cause as long as the church, the throne, the nobility, and the bourgeoisie were united in their opposition to it.

The dissolution of this powerful alliance was in the first instance a historical accident. Henry the Eighth, lustful, proud, and tyrannical, was the last man to be interested in religious reform. Being himself something of a scholar in a minor way, he produced a work against Luther which earned him the title "Defender of the Faith," still claimed by British monarchs regardless of history. But Henry grew weary of his virtuous but somewhat tiresome Catholic queen, the Spanish Catherine of Aragon, and became infatuated with her vivacious maid of honor, the English Anne Boleyn. The fact that he had no heir by Catherine, which endangered the stability of the throne, furnished a convenient rationalization of his desires. When the Pope, confronted with the dilemma of offending England or Spain, chose the former and stubbornly refused to countenance Henry's divorce and remarriage, the King had little difficulty in obtaining from a complaisant Parliament the Act of Supremacy of 1534 by which he became "the only supreme head in earth of the Church of England, called the 'Anglicana Ecclesia.'" No other Protestant church ever had so simple or so discreditable an origin.[1]

[1] Under the circumstances it is not surprising that numerous Anglican writers have sought to show that the Church of England was an independent organization dating from Apostolic times, thereby justifying the notion of "Apostolic succession," dear to high churchmen. But there is no evidence that any Apostle ever visited the British Isles, the history of the early Briton church is confused and legendary, and the actual Christianizing of the country was accomplished by the

Neither in name nor in fact was the Church of England at the time of its establishment a truly Protestant body. The only change made by the Act of Supremacy was the transfer of final authority from the Pope to the King. Being in need of money, Henry soon made use of his new power to abolish the monasteries, on the specious plea of their immorality, and to confiscate their wealth amounting to several hundred million dollars. But at that point reform, if it could be called such, was halted. The celibacy of the clergy, auricular confession, the dogmas of purgatory and transubstantiation, the worship of the saints, the use of images, the Latin service—all were retained. On the Continent, Tyndale paid with his life for his translation of the New Testament and denial of transubstantiation, and Henry the Eighth made no effective protest against the execution which he might easily have prevented. His church was merely an English edition of Roman Catholicism.

But the forces unloosed by Henry for purely personal considerations could not be restrained for long within such narrow limits. Too many of the clergy and prominent laity were in direct communication with the Continent. The influence of Luther and Zwingli steadily increased.[2] By clever political tact Miles Coverdale secured the royal permission to introduce his vernacular translation of the Bible, and by 1540 four such versions were in circulation. During the reign of Edward the Sixth an English Prayer Book was drawn up, and in 1552 the Forty-two Articles (afterwards reduced to thirty-nine) were adopted as a formulation of faith. The celibacy of the clergy and auricular confession were discontinued, English was substituted for Latin in the services, and the Zwinglian symbolic interpretation of the Eucharist was accepted.

The reign of the Catholic Mary Tudor with its revival of persecution tested the courage and sincerity of the Anglican clergy. The majority hoisted the white flag at once. Out of the ten thousand parishes in England only three hundred were vacated. Just as most of the clergy had submissively abandoned Catholicism under Henry the Eighth, they submissively returned to it under Mary, to abandon

---

monk Augustine, an emissary of Pope Gregory I. Furthermore, it is unquestionable that after the time of King John the English church fully accepted the ultimate authority of the Papacy.

[2] See H. E. Jacobs, *The Lutheran Movement in England* (Philadelphia: G. W. Frederick, 1890).

it once more under Elizabeth. With this should be contrasted the situation in Holland, where in 1772, when the Protestant cause seemed hopelessly lost, Requesens offered a general amnesty to all who would return to the Catholic faith—and only two persons in the whole country responded. In England, on the other hand, the celebrated case of Owen Oglethorpe was, in all but its ending, quite typical. That distinguished member of the House of Oglethorpe held, in the reign of Henry the Eighth, the offices of Fellow and President of Magdalen College, Vice-Chancellor of Oxford University, and Canon of Windsor; under "Bloody Mary" he rose to be Bishop, first of Carlisle, later of Lincoln, Dean of Windsor, and Scribe of the Order of the Garter; on the accession of Elizabeth he officiated at the coronation ceremonies; and then his career of tergiversation plunged downward, when the new queen, having no further need of his services, sent him to the prison in which he died.

During the Marian persecution, a few of the Protestant leaders did indeed show more character. "At the ditch over against Balliol College" in Oxford where Wiclif had first dared deny the myth of transubstantiation, Nicholas Ridley, Bishop of London, and Hugh Latimer, Bishop of Worcester, went unyieldingly to the stake rather than disavow their acceptance of Wiclif's position. The more pliant head of the church, Thomas Cranmer, Archbishop of Canterbury, who had purchased his high place by subservience to Henry, seven times vainly recanted, but, too deeply involved politically to be pardoned, he atoned in some degree for his past by the courage with which he finally faced the flames. Many of the lesser clergy, the impoverished heirs of Chaucer's "poor parson," fled to Geneva where they came under the influence of the hardening doctrines of Calvin which they brought back with them on their return. The Marian persecution, like all persecution, ended in self-defeat, for its one permanent effect was to introduce Calvinism into England and substitute a militant Protestantism for a compliant Anglo-Catholicism.

With the accession of Elizabeth, the terms of the religious conflict shifted to those of a struggle within the Church of England itself between the conservative Anglo-Catholic party supported by the throne and an increasingly assertive minority of Calvinistic Puritans. To understand the ideals of the latter, it is necessary to turn to the most important of all Protestants after Luther, the French legalist, Jean Cauvin or John Calvin.

THE PHILOSOPHY OF CALVINISM

ONE would have said that Calvin came into the world bound hand and foot to the established order. His mother was a particularly strict and devout Roman Catholic; his father was notary to the ecclesiastical court at Noyon, secretary to the Bishop of Noyon, and fiscal attorney of the county. Their son was taken under the patronage of the noble family of Mommor and was educated with the children of the family. At the age of twelve he was made recipient of the income of a chaplaincy, and was destined for the priesthood. These early experiences sufficed to alienate him completely from the common people for whom he always had the utmost contempt. He was of far too strenuous a temper, however, to be satisfied with the religious sinecures that lay ready at hand, and instead devoted himself to the study of law at the universities of Orléans and Bourges. There he became acquainted with the aspirations of the rising middle class, largely represented in France as in England by the legal profession. Such was the intensity of his application to his legal studies that he permanently ruined his health, thereby aggravating an inherently censorious and irascible disposition that caused him to be nicknamed by fellow-students "The Accusative Case." His ill health also probably had a part in the growing sense of sin which led him to a serious study of the Bible resulting in a Lutherlike conviction of unmerited redemption through God's grace. But the conversion to Protestantism that followed was really a conversion to Calvin's own type of Protestantism, very different from that of the by nature kindly, poetic, and mystical Luther.

Kindliness, poetry, and mysticism were foreign to Calvin's make-up. Their place was taken by a legalistic conception of duty. He looked upon the Bible through the eyes of a lawyer, seeing in it an absolutely fixed and sacred system of laws and punishments decreed by God and upheld by His ministers. Since the Catholic Church had proved unable to maintain discipline, some stronger organization was needed, which should exercise a more pervasive influence over conduct. A theocracy was required, an organization of churchmen and strenuous laymen who should have direct control of both private and public morals and should dominate the civil authority to the extent of guiding its fundamental policies. Calvin's ideal was thus a kind of revised Catholicism, equally authoritarian, equally intolerant, but more broadly based and strengthened by the inclusion of an upper middle-class laity in its counsels.

In 1534, the year after Calvin's conversion, Francis the First decided to initiate a drastic persecution of the Protestants, and in January of the ensuing year six heretics were burned to death in an auto-da-fé graced by the monarch's presence. With Paris unsafe, Calvin became a wanderer through the south of France and into Switzerland, brooding incessantly over the theology and ecclesiastical organization needed by his ideal theocracy. At last he took up his residence in Basle, where at the age of twenty-seven he wrote the first version of his *Institutes*, later much enlarged but never altered in any of its main conceptions. The work embodied his religio-legalistic convictions of the nature of God, man, society, and the church.

Calvin believed that he derived his theology from the Bible, but in reality it was derived from the kind of church government he had in mind for the control of the community by a select minority fitted for such control. In the Augustinian-Lutheran doctrine of pre-destination, if taken in the most stringent supralapsarian form and made the very foundation of a creed instead of a mere adjunct to it, Calvin perceived a suitable theological basis for his theocracy. The dogma of the innate depravity of man, combined with the conception of an elect few divinely chosen to be saved for no reason except that of God's inscrutable will, symbolized on a cosmic scale the actual world in which the French Protestant found himself—a member of an oppressed minority surrounded by the masses of the wicked, whose mundane advantages of inherited authority and power could not be supposed to weigh with the deity. At the same time, the doctrine looked forward to the ultimate victory of those who held it. The elect of God, if one could but determine who they were, should obviously be the ones to exercise political and social power. Nor did this problem of determining who were the elect cause any difficulty to the Calvinists, either in Switzerland or later in Scotland, England, or New England. The elect were, self-evidently, the Calvinists.

Just as the awakening mind of youth may entertain its first religious doubt when it asks vainly why the Israelites rather than the more talented Greeks should have been the Chosen People, so the question is often asked: How could the Calvinists be so sure that they were the elect? But to ask the question in this form is to disregard the emotional origin of the teachings. The mythical history and the dogma were the expression of vital desires so coercive that they needed no evidence beyond themselves. The Calvinists knew instinctively that God would elect the kind of people who were deciding whom He would elect. The absolute duty to regard one's self as of the chosen, once the novitiate of conversion was passed, was explicitly taught and was defended by the argument that lack of faith was a sign of lack of grace: the surest token of probable salvation was the firm belief that one was to be saved.

Nor were outward tokens lacking. Theoretically, to be sure, God might extend His grace to the sinner equally with the saint since both alike through their innate depravity deserved damnation; but, practically, could one doubt that He would as a rule prefer saints for His celestial company? And the saints were clearly the "unspottyd lambs of God," the frugal, serious-minded folk who eschewed prodigality and wantonness, light speech or frivolous dress, the pleasures and vanities of the worldling and eschewed equally the blasphemous discontent with God's world shown by those at the bottom of the social scale. Who could believe that God would elect any luxury-loving Papist or ranting Anabaptist to His Heaven? It was perfectly obvious that the elect would be chosen from the members of the sober middle class to whom Calvin directed his teachings.

An opportunity came to Calvin to apply in practice the principles of his *Institutes* when William Farel, leader of the Protestants in Geneva, asked him to join in an attempt to enforce ecclesiastical discipline. Farel was a vulgarized edition of Calvin himself. He was described by Erasmus as the most arrogant, abusive, and shameless man he ever met, whose only method of meeting argument was to shout down his opponents with a stentorian voice. The two Geneva reformers found each other congenial, but Calvin, as the abler and more intellectual, soon took the lead. Together they insisted ever more rigorously upon a censorship of private morals until, after two years, a popular reaction drove them from the city. During their absence, the Catholics made a vigorous attempt to recover their power, and in 1541 the municipality, in order to preserve Protestantism, begged Calvin to return with virtually autocratic authority. He immediately established a consistory of six clergymen and twelve elders which met every Thursday as an ecclesiastical court to suppress heresy, enforce attendance at church, and punish every form of personal immorality and laxity. The death penalty would seem to have been almost its favorite decree. In 1555, Calvin succeeded in reducing the civil legislative body to a purely nominal position, thus placing the church definitively over the state. Twenty years after the first publication of the *Institutes*, Calvin's ideal theocracy had become a fact.

The greater Calvin's power the more tyrannical he became. A woman was excommunicated for having her hair dressed in what he considered an immodest manner. A child was beheaded for striking his father and mother. The learned Unitarian physician, Michael Servetus (who had very nearly anticipated Harvey's theory of the circulation of the blood), when he sent to Calvin a copy of his privately circulated work on *The Errors of the Trinity*, was betrayed by the reformer to the Catholics, and when he escaped to Geneva he was seized, contrary to Swiss law, condemned for heresy, and burned at the stake. Although in the case of Servetus Calvin did make a halfhearted plea for a milder death than burning, in other instances he thanked God when the agonies of his victims happened to be prolonged by the bungling of the executioner. Later Protestants have usually apologized for Calvin's conduct on the ground that he was merely conforming to the custom of the period. But this is an utterly unhistorical view. The age was a cruel one, true enough, and Catholics and Lutherans were equally ready to persecute organized heretical movements, such as that of the Anabaptists; but Calvin was unique in invading the realm of trivial private conduct and in outlawing expressions of purely personal opinion like that of Servetus. He was also unusual in gloating over the sufferings of his victims. When all is said on his behalf that can be said, he remains the outstanding example among Protestants of the way in which religious fanaticism can change men into monsters.

The harshness of Calvinism did not mean, however, that it was devoid of survival value. That was exactly the value which it did possess. The narrowness and fanaticism of the Calvinists enabled them to be more completely themselves, unconfused by alien viewpoints. The character of their war on Catholic feudalism appealed to motives of envy in both the bourgeoisie and the lower classes. Whatever was connected with the aristocracy was denounced: not only the aristocratic vices of prodigality and licentiousness, but polite manners, expensive costumes, beautiful architecture, stained glass, instrumental music, the theater, painting, and sculpture. In its discipline, standardization of doctrine, and elite membership, Calvinism irresistibly reminds one of twentieth century Bolshevism, just as, in its attack on culture, it reminds one of Nazi fascism. But there was one limitation of its anticultural attitude. It did foster learning among its leaders as a defense of its dogmas; and in the long run the learning would outlast the dogmas.

The ethical attitude of Calvinism has been generally known as "Puritanism." Strictly speaking, as will be pointed out, the term Puritanism had a somewhat different historical meaning, but it has been so generally accepted as expressing a certain conception of life for which there is no other word that it seems pedantic to decline to use it. In this larger sense, Calvinism was only one example of an ethical attitude which is perennially possible. And since it was an attitude more permanently emphasized in America than elsewhere it may be well to discuss it briefly at this point.

Puritanism is the natural way of survival in periods when the struggle for existence is sufficiently intense. Wherever men are beset by an adverse environment, physical or human, that must be subjugated if they are to continue to exist, every pulse of energy is needed for the direct offense against the enemy. Activities merely pleasant in themselves have no place in such a hurried scheme of things. The utilitarian end of every act must be apparent in the act itself. Puritanism battens upon necessity. What the law of survival has said must be the Puritan calls good.

The spectacle of men, not all men or most men but some men in every age, voluntarily depriving themselves and their neighbors of natural, spontaneous, human pleasures is sufficiently striking to account for its having often been cited to prove the supernatural origin of man and his supernatural destiny. Man denying himself the comfort and warmth of his own humanness suggests that he is striving toward something higher than himself. Unfortunately for the argument, the puritan, the archdenier, always turns out, upon examination, to be not superhuman but infrahuman. He has denied his natural impulses, it is true, but not for any more godlike end; he has taken on the burden of asceticism only because that is necessary in order to gain another human, all-too-human goal. He has curbed his expansive nature in order to strengthen his acquisitive will.

The acquisitive will leads directly to property. Throughout history the acquisition of property, either private or collective, has been the surest means of gratifying the bodily craving for food, shelter, and security. Puritanism, the philosophy of hunger and acquisition, is, *ipso facto*, the philosophy of the struggle for property. It is as firmly rooted in the body, its original source, as is the sensuality it affects to despise. Vehement as are its denials of its lowly birth, it springs, like all things human, out of the dust of the earth.

CALVINISM AND CAPITALISM

CALVIN set out deliberately to justify the acquisition of capitalistic profits. In harmony with this position he drew the wholly arbitrary modern distinction between interest and usury, the latter being redefined by Calvin as "excessive interest" tentatively fixed as anything over five per cent. In this way he gave a religious sanction to the general principle of interest, which is, of course, basic to capitalism.

Still more significant was Calvin's revolutionary reinterpretation of the Lutheran *Beruf* or "calling," which was transformed by him from the duty of remaining in that state of life into which it had pleased God to call one, into a new duty to utilize one's talents to the full and thereby rise in the world and improve one's status and opportunities. Calvin explicitly taught that the amassing of property is an important part of one's "divine call," an obligation laid upon the individual by God Himself. What was to be one of the most fundamental convictions of the American mind, often treated as due to its own obliquity, was thus really forged long before at Geneva. Calvin, however, always mindful of the Anabaptists, was careful to add that the duty of gaining wealth must not be taught to the masses, who, as he pointed out, obey God only as long as they are poor.

Among later Calvinists the union of commerce and godliness was especially preached by the Reverend Richard Baxter, whose *Saint's Everlasting Rest* (1650) was a popular textbook of piety in England and the colonies. "If God show you a way," he wrote, "in which you may lawfully get more than in another way (without wrong to your soul or to any other), if you refuse this, and choose the less gainful way, you cross one of the ends of your calling, and you refuse to be God's servant." Earnestly he exhorted: "Be wholly taken up in diligent business of your lawful callings when you are not exercised in the more immediate service of God," and again, "See that you have a calling which will find you employment for all the time which God's immediate service spareth."

It would, of course, be unfair to both Calvin and Baxter to imply that they countenanced any exploitation of the public. Both of them, and especially Baxter, emphasized honesty and fair dealing. In fact, Baxter's rules for the conduct of business in his *Christian Directory* would have made the conduct of business very difficult. The seller must never take advantage of the buyer's ignorance or necessity; if he foresees that prices are going to rise, he must warn the purchaser of this fact; he must not conceal any defects in the articles he sells but must call attention to them; if the seller himself has been so unfortunate as to purchase an inferior article he may not pass it on to another any more than one who has been robbed may recoup his losses by robbing another. And, on the other hand, the buyer must always pay the full price that the goods are worth to himself even though the seller, pressed by competition, should offer them for less. It is probably unnecessary to observe that Baxter's rules for the Christian government of trade never seem to have been widely adopted by the business world.

The Calvinists, in fostering the alliance of religion and commerce, undoubtedly intended to idealize commerce, not to materialize religion. But they welcomed the camel into the tent, and the natural result followed. Calvin's legalization of interest "took with the brethren," we are told, "like polygamy with the Turks," and the injunction to exact interest for the sake of widows and orphans appealed to "divers zealous ministers who themselves desired to pass for orphans of the first rank." Baxter's example led to numerous other works on religious economics, such as *The Religious Weaver, Husbandry Spiritualized, Navigation Spiritualized, The Tradesman's Calling*, and, finally, *The Complete English Tradesman* by Daniel Defoe, in all of which the union of religion and business was celebrated with devout and canny enthusiasm. Indeed, in *The Tradesman's Calling*, by the Reverend Richard Steele, business already began to be looked upon as more sacred than religion itself, the author denouncing those who neglected "a man's necessary affairs upon pretense of religious worship," and asserting that "the presence of God" is to be found most frequently in the tradesman's shop.

In the first covenant of the church at Salem, Massachusetts, were the words, "We resolve to approve ourselves to the Lord in our particular callings; shunning idleness as the bane of any state." The Cambridge Platform of 1648 assigned to the elders the special duty "to see that none in the church live inordinately out of rank and place without a calling, or idly in their calling." One sees that the Lutheran "rank and place" had crept back into Calvinism as soon as Calvinism became successful. Yet the notion that leisure and idleness were definitely irreligious persisted. One must have a trade or a business and be about it.

A century after Baxter, John Wesley, contemplating the result of such teachings, was sadly perplexed. The teachings, he felt, were sound, yet the effect had been a great increase of worldliness. "Is there no way," he asked despondently, "to check this continual decay of pure religion?" Certainly there must be no lessening of emphasis upon one's economic calling. "We ought not to prevent people from being diligent and frugal; we must exhort all Christians to gain all they can and to save all they can; that is, in effect, to grow rich." Yet Wesley perceived that rich Christians, like Calvin's poor, had a habit of ceasing to obey God. The dilemma was embarrassing. Wesley eventually found the solution of his problem where most later Christian churches have found it. People, he said, should gain all they can, but they should also give all they can. The greater the wealth, the greater the opportunity to exercise the virtue of charity. Hence, instead of its being hard for a rich man to enter the Kingdom of Heaven, the path was made easy for him if he would but follow it.

Other Protestant ministers, less adept than Wesley, would sometimes embog themselves hopelessly in the same problem. Thus the Reverend Joseph Morgan, an early New England ancestor of J. Pierpont Morgan, managed to make a veritable quagmire out of a sermon on covetousness:

"Covetousness (which is idolatry), must be the Support of the World and the misery of it both. Each man coveting to make himself rich, carries on the Publick Good: Thus God in His Wisdom and Mercy turns out Wickedness to Publick Benefit. It were better for the most of people to be poor than to be born rich. For such have in general, really a more comfortable Life here and far less dangerous as to the next Life. . . . A Rich Man has a *miserable* life: for he is always full of Fear and Care. . . . Whereas a Man that has but Food and Raiment with honest labor, is free from these Fears and Cares. . . . We need to *pity* and *love* Rich Men. But what am I doing? If this discourage People from seeking after Riches, it would be a great detriment to the Publick, if not the undoing of the World. . . . A Rich Man is a great friend to the Publick, while he aims at nothing but serving himself. God will have us live by helping one another; and since Love will not do it, Covetousness shall."

This emendation of the Sermon on the Mount, while hardly worthy of Calvinistic logic, was apparently accepted in good part by the wealthier members of the Reverend Joseph Morgan's congregation, since some time later they secured his reinstatement after a suspension for drunkenness. It was, after all, only a particularly awkward assertion of what had been the underlying spirit of Calvinism from the beginning.

THE RISE OF PRESBYTERIANISM

THE spearpoint of the Calvinistic attack upon the feudal order was its program of ecclesiastical reorganization known as Presbyterianism. The distinction between Presbyterianism and Episcopacy was not doctrinal; it turned primarily on the question of the elimination or retention of the bishopric. Under Presbyterianism in its fully developed form immediate authority was vested in presbyters, consisting of both ministers concerned with doctrine, and lay elders concerned with discipline, but with the individual congregations united in the equivalent of church councils in a rising series of *presbyteries* (composed of all the ministers and selected ruling elders within a prescribed area), *synods* (composed of a similar group from a prescribed number of presbyteries), and a *general assembly* meeting annually as a court of last appeal. Distinctive features of the system were: first, the prominence given to the lay elders, who were regarded as of equal rank with the clergy; and second, the attempt to combine the independence of separate congregations with the principle of strong centralized government, through giving each congregation the right to elect its clergymen but requiring confirmation by the presbytery. This form of organization was a strong fighting force against the feudalism of the Anglican Church, with its royal head and appointive bishops. Presbyterianism contained the germ of democracy in the limited right of election permitted to the separate congregations, but beyond that it was strongly authoritarian and theocratic with the real power vested in the presbyters, presbyteries, and synods.

English Presbyterianism arose as a reform movement within the Anglican Church. Not venturing as yet to attack the bishops, it directed its efforts toward simplifying the ritual and securing greater freedom of clerical appointment. In neither direction were its efforts successful.

The church met the attempted reforms by more repressive measures. In 1583 private prayers were forbidden if more than the immediate family were present, clergymen were compelled to wear their ecclesiastical habits at all times, none but ordained ministers were permitted to preach, and only those could be ordained who agreed to use no other than the Book of Common Prayer in conducting the services. To enforce these and other laws an Ecclesiastical Commission was established, similar to the Catholic Inquisition, with autocratic power to suspend trial by jury, to use torture in order to obtain confessions, and to fine or imprison at will. In 1592 an act "for the Punishment of Persons obstinately refusing to come to church" prescribed the death penalty. In its war on Calvinism the church had itself become Calvinistic. The Ecclesiastical Commission was given authority to inquire into private morals and to punish incest and "exaggerated adultery." England, even under Elizabeth, had started on the path to Geneva.

Thus far the mass of the people had not been seriously affected. The Puritans, as the Calvinistic party within the Anglican Church began to be called because of their claims to special purity of life and doctrine, were still a small minority group. Outwardly, England was the unified nation that responded as one man to defeat the Spanish Armada, that thrilled to every new tale of romantic exploration and adventure, that rejoiced in the spirit of the Renaissance and carried English literature to a new world height in Elizabethan poetry and drama. But the dramatists themselves sensed the chill winds of the future blowing upon them. Every year more trouble was made for them by the Puritans. At each outbreak of the plague the theaters were closed, not as a sanitary measure, but because the plague was considered a visitation of God because of the sins of the drama. The audiences more and more consisted of the nobility and the groundlings, with the middle class refusing to attend. Had it not been for the steady patronage of the court and the nobility, with some aid from the legal profession and the university wits, the theater could not have survived. The grateful dramatists in return drew their pictures of heroism from the aristocratic world, talked of "the divinity that doth hedge a crown," deplored the rise of trade, and satirized the Puritans. Shakespeare in *Twelfth Night* ridiculed the Puritan hostility to "cakes and ale" and all forms of jovial amusement, and Ben Jonson in *Bartholomew Fair* denounced their hypocrisy and their addiction to money getting.

The English middle class, however, was not reading Shakespeare or Jonson but the Bible—and not the expensive King James Bible of 1611 but the earlier, cheaper, and more portable Geneva Bible bristling with Calvinistic annotations. And it was devoting itself to money getting with such increasing success that it was becoming impatient of dictation or criticism. Engaged in an absorbing struggle to better its position, it had no time to spend on lighthearted gaiety, romantic poetry, or theories of the divine right of kings.

Meanwhile, Presbyterianism had won a great victory in Scotland. The Reformation, when first introduced there in 1560, had been as purely economic and nonreligious as it was in England under Henry the Eighth. Two thirds of the confiscated wealth of the Catholic Church was seized by the nobility, who reluctantly left the rest to the new Church of Scotland as long as it behaved itself as a docile church should. Of the period that followed, James Melville, writing in 1584, said, "By the insatiable avarice of the earls, lords, and gentlemen of Scotland, the ministers, schools, and poor were spoiled of that which should sustain them . . . whereof came fearful darkness of ignorance, superstition, and idolatry." Eager to perpetuate their puppet Scotch-Catholic church, the nobility resisted any change; but the crimes of the Roman Catholic Mary Stuart made anything connected with Catholicism so unpopular in Scotland that the more earnest reformers, headed by Alexander Melville and John Knox, each of whom had spent five years in Geneva under the direct influence of Calvin, succeeded in 1592 in establishing Presbyterianism as the form of ecclesiastical government.

When James the Sixth of Scotland became James the First of England, the Presbyterians at first hoped that he might be persuaded to introduce the Scottish system in the southern kingdom. But the new monarch, happy in having escaped at last from ecclesiastical domination, had no disposition to put his head back in the noose. "A Scottish presbytery," he passionately asserted, "agreeth as well with a monarchy as God and the Devil. Then Jack and Tom and Will and Dick shall meet, and at their pleasures censure me and my council, and all our proceedings. . . . Stay, I pray you, for one seven years, before you demand that from me, and if then you find me pursy and fat, and my windpipes stuffed, I will perhaps hearken to you." This speech, which an Anglican bishop declared "inspired," put an end to Presbyterian hopes of help from the Crown.

Nevertheless, Presbyterianism continued to grow, half underground, half in the open. The most radical English Presbyterian of the day, Thomas Cartwright, exiled in Holland, sent over the manuscript copy of a book of discipline called *A Directory of Church Government* which was passed secretly from hand to hand until as many as five hundred ministers had subscribed to its rules. And meanwhile a dangerous and heretical offshoot from Presbyterianism had appeared in the sect known variously as "Brownists," "Separatists," "Independents," or "Congregationalists," which was destined to be one of the three most important influences in the religious history of America.

THE BEGINNINGS OF CONGREGATIONALISM

ROBERT BROWNE, the founder of Congregationalism, and so one of the direct spiritual ancestors of New England, began his career like a hero but long ere his death was considered a craven. Being a kinsman of Lord Burleigh and grandson of a baronet, he could have found advancement easy in the Anglican Church. By the time of his graduation from Cambridge, however, he had developed heretical views which prevented his ordination. He was the first Englishman who dared openly to support the Anabaptist position that the church should return to the pattern of Primitive Christianity with autonomous congregations organized by voluntary agreement or covenant;[3] he was also the first Englishman to countenance even partially the Anabaptist notion of the separation of church and state. As a Calvinist, he was willing that the magistrates should punish idolatry, blasphemy, or Sabbathbreaking, but, unlike other Calvinists, he did not wish them to meddle with heresy. The individual congregation, he held, should not be responsible to any presbytery, synod, convention, or ecclesiastical authority outside itself. In Browne's religio-political philosophy, worked out fully in several able works later published by him in Holland,[4] there were already present the germinal ideas of democracy: government by consent, local autonomy, the separation of church and state, and at least the beginnings of religious tolerance. In accordance with these independent principles, a congregation was formed under his leadership at Norwich of which we fortunately have a fairly detailed account from his own pen.

"A covenant was made," he writes, "and their mutual consent was given to hold together. . . . Further they agreed of those which should teach them, and watch for the salvation of their souls, whom they allowed and did choose as able and meet for that charge.

[3] How far Browne was directly influenced by the Anabaptists is problematical. There was a Mennonite group at Norwich, but Browne's views seem to have been matured before he came there. He never accepted the basic Anabaptist principles of Arminianism and adult baptism.

[4] *A Treatise of Reformation without Tarrying for Anie, A True and Short Declaration,* etc.

. . . Likewise an order was agreed on for their meetings together, for their exercises therein, as for prayer, thanksgiving, reading of the scriptures, for exhortation and edifying, either by all men which had the gift, or by those which had a special charge before others. And for the lawfullness of putting forth questions, to learn the truth, as if anything seemed doubtful and hard, to require some to show it more plainly, or for any to show it himself and to cause the rest to understand it. . . . Again it was agreed that any might protest, appeal, complain, exhort, dispute, reprove, etc., as he had occasion, but yet in due order, which was then also declared."

Browne's extraordinarily democratic procedure in organizing a church in which any who had the gift could preach and all were free to question or criticize was clearly a much more heretical action than any of which the English Presbyterians had been guilty. Threatened with drastic persecution by the Bishop of Norwich, Browne and his congregation sought refuge in Holland, where they reorganized their church at Middelburg. This was the first example of what was to become one of the most astonishing phenomena of the period—the emigration of whole parishes led by their pastors in search of the religious freedom denied them in England but possible in Holland, and later in parts of America.

Those religious and political conservatives who regarded "Brownism" as the equivalent of moral anarchy felt that the truth of their position was demonstrated by the disasters that soon befell the heretic. After two years, his group at Middelburg broke up through internal dissensions. Utterly discouraged, Browne returned to England, where he was subjected to a year's imprisonment, at a time when prison conditions amounted to daily torture. Broken in health and spirit, he retracted all his views, supplementing his recantation with a new volume entitled *A Reproofe of Certaine Schismatical Persons and their doctrine touching the hearing and preaching of the word of God.* He was rewarded, through Lord Burleigh's influence, with the rectorship of Achurch-cum-Thorpe Waterville, a small village in Northamptonshire, where he lingered out an inglorious career for forty-two years. Enough of the old fire remained at the age of eighty to involve him in a fight with the parish constable over a tax rate, for which he was consigned to Northampton jail, where he died.

While Browne himself was sinking into ignominy and obscurity, his original heresies were propagated ever more boldly by others. Between November, 1588, and July, 1589, a series of seven Brownist tracts published secretly over the pseudonym "Martin Marprelate" assailed the bishops with such combined wit and fury as to throw London into an uproar. Four years later, Congregationalism had its first martyrs in John Penry (suspected of being the author of the Marprelate tracts), Henry Barrowe, John Greenwood, and three others, all of whom were executed after trials that were the merest parodies of justice. Continued persecution drove numerous Separatists to Holland, where they organized a strong church in Amsterdam under Francis Johnson as pastor and Henry Ainsworth as teacher. Other groups followed later, among them the original nucleus of the New England Pilgrims. In spite of all the efforts of the authorities, the principles of independency continued to spread. By the time of the first emigrations to America, Separatism or Congregationalism—two names for the same thing [5]—had many followers in England, especially among the lower classes.

The religious independency of the "Independents" had nothing to do with individual freedom of conduct. The Separatists in Holland and England, like their first representatives in America, the Pilgrims, exercised the most rigid inquisitorial control over manners and morals—which, being Puritans, they always confused. The amusing difficulties which Francis Johnson met with from his congregation in London (to which he returned after breaking with Ainsworth in Amsterdam) on account of his wife's behavior perfectly illustrate the censorial spirit of all these communities. Francis Johnson, we are told, was a man of most solemn and seemly deportment who never laughed and rarely smiled; perhaps this may partly explain the frivolous behavior of his worser half. At any rate, the congregation brought terrible charges against Mrs. Johnson: she wore "a copple crowned hat, immodest and toyish in a Pastor's wife," great sleeves set out with whalebones and an "excess of lace," "laune coives," and a "long busk"; she displayed "the painted Hypocritical brest" with dresses too low in the bosom; she carried "four

---

[5] Champlin Burrage, in *The Early English Dissenters* (Cambridge: University Press, 1912), endeavors to prove that there was a substantial difference between the beliefs of the early Separatists and the later Congregationalists, but the minute divergencies which he is able to cite are insufficient to establish his conclusion.

or five rings" on her fingers; she "stood gazing, bracing or vaunting in shop doores"; she "laid in bedd on the Lordes day till nine o'clock." It is indeed abundantly clear that Mrs. Johnson was out of place as the wife of a Puritan pastor.

This completes the account of the British Reformation up to the time of the American settlement. In comparison with the continental movements, those in Great Britain were imitative, hesitant, and conservative.

At the extreme right stood the Church of England, representing the same class which had formerly supported Catholicism, still feudal in outlook but more ready to compromise with the rising commercial forces. For "the divine right of the pope," it had merely, like Lutheranism, substituted the even less defensible doctrine of "the divine right of the prince." In the long run, the nationalism of the English Church would mean the priority of politics to religion, but at the moment Anglicanism was too much infected with Calvinism for this to be entirely true.

Equally authoritarian but representing the upper middle-class commercial interest was the party of Presbyterianism, in which the driving force was the Calvinistic ideal of a trade-based theocracy. Slightly to the left of the Presbyterians were the Separatists, still weak but growing rapidly, who tended to draw their strength rather from the lower middle class. Further down in the social scale were the real left-wing Baptists, mainly confined to the small city tradesmen and artisans, religiously the most liberal of any of the English sects and the one most closely touched by the radical movements on the Continent.

At the same time, the decline of feudalism had already blurred the old immutable distinctions of social status. Class interests had become less definite as soon as it became possible for men to change their class. The medieval communist dream of a classless society had not been realized; what had come to pass, however, was a fluctuating condition in which men were sufficiently dislocated from ancestral ties to permit a wider development of individual self-consciousness.

None of the great ideals implicit in the Reformation had come to full fruition at the time the American colonies were settled. Freedom of conscience was recognized even formally only in Holland;

separation of church and state nowhere existed; government by consent and co-operation, in either religion or politics, was still in its infancy; personal liberty and social equality were only dreams. These, the radical master ideas of the Reformation, born in and of it, existed in theory but without practical application when they were brought to America. It was America's function to give them that application, to develop them much further than was done elsewhere, and to make them eventually the basis of a national faith.

BOOK 2. *The Reformation Completed in America*

CHAPTER 4 . *The Significance of America*

THE great American myth that the colonies were founded for the sake of religious liberty—a myth that came into existence at about the time of the Revolution when men had forgotten the facts—has been thoroughly discredited by modern historians. In only one colony, Rhode Island, did the myth completely fit the facts, and the founders of "Little Rhody" fled thither not to escape from religious tyranny in England but to escape from persecution by their fellow-colonists in Massachusetts. In New Hampshire, Connecticut, New Jersey, Pennsylvania, and Georgia, religious liberty was only one among other factors. In the colonies of Massachusetts Bay, New York, Virginia, and the Carolinas it had originally no place at all. Religion there was aplenty everywhere, but this religion was usually the very opposite of religious liberty.

The long-continued acceptance of this myth of religious liberty created in the minds of most Americans in the nineteenth century an utterly distorted picture of their own beginnings. By presenting the ideals of religious and democratic freedom as already fully present in the minds of the first New England settlers, alike at Plymouth and Boston, and by regarding the Quaker and witch hangings as temporary aberrations instead of as part of a settled policy, the myth stood facts on their head. It not only gave undue importance to New England, great though that importance really was, but it also misread the meaning of events in New England itself as well as in the other colonies. Religious liberty was not simply something brought ready-made to the colonies from Europe; it was in part a natural

growth *within* the colonies, paralleling similar European developments. And it was never isolated, as the myth would have it, from an
economic or political background. The struggle for liberty, whether
political or religious, was essentially part of a larger struggle between
social classes which eventually developed, not in this place or that
place alone, but everywhere from Maine to Georgia, though it took
on manifold and divergent forms according to the prevailing local
conditions.

In reaction against this mythological interpretation, recent realistic historians have greatly emphasized the economic motive as a
driving force in the settlement of America. "With very few exceptions," writes Charles M. Andrews, "the British colonies in America
were founded for commercial purposes, and even those the original
motive for which was religious or philanthropic, had in most cases a
commercial aspect." Still more emphatically, Thomas J. Wertenbaker states that "The settlements of Virginia and New England
were mere incidents in the story of English expansion, an expansion
impelled chiefly by economic necessity." There can be no quarrel
with such utterances except for the implication that the economic
motive was not at the same time a religious motive. The two were
absolutely blended in the minds of the first settlers. The one common
article of faith in all the colonies was the abiding Protestant conviction that spiritual and material prosperity went hand in hand, each
aiding the other. Radical and conservative, left, right, and center,
held the same ideal of establishing the Kingdom of God *on this
earth*. They were separated, not by any difference of ultimate values,
but by questions of power and distribution, as to who should wield
authority in God's kingdom and as to how far its combined material
and spiritual goods could be shared by everyone—the chief questions
which have continued to occupy the American mind ever since.

The most important fact about North America in the seventeenth
century, and even in the eighteenth and nineteenth centuries, was
its size. That and its emptiness—for to the general European mind
of the seventeenth century the scattered Indian tribes had little more
right to the land they occupied than had the bears and the wolves.
The discovery of an enormous, empty continent open to colonization revolutionized European history. America was to Europe as
later the West was to the East in America. To the ruling classes it

meant the opportunity for exploitation and so favored the growth of capitalism. But to the oppressed classes it also meant opportunity —the opportunity to escape and to live under freer conditions. Democracy, like capitalism, was implicit in the situation.

The second most important fact about the new continent was its distance from Europe. A perilous voyage of from six to eight weeks effectually prevented any large emigration of those who did not have strong reasons for coming. Usually only the poor would be eager to come and of these only the hardiest would survive. The attempt to govern the colonies from England, when it took between three and six months for communications to go back and forth between the two continents, was from the outset foredoomed to ultimate failure. In all these ways the element of distance made for the development of a radically different type of culture in America from that in Europe.

The factors of space and distance both worked to make America a fertile field for experiment. All kinds of commercial undertakings, all sorts of governmental control, were attempted: joint stock companies in Virginia, Massachusetts Bay, New York, and Georgia; proprietaries in Maryland, Maine, the Jersies, Pennsylvania, and the Carolinas; virtually independent communities in Plymouth, Connecticut, and Rhode Island. Cutting across these divisions were various types of religious and social experiments which gave many forms of organization a trial, ranging through theocracy, paternalism, local self-government, equalitarian communities, philanthropic enterprises. The American Revolution was a political and social experiment on the grand scale, and the creation of the Federal Constitution was another experiment. During the first half of the nineteenth century America saw more further-going attempts at social change, always inspired by one or another religious or moral ideal, than were seen anywhere in Europe. The system of private property was attacked in scores of co-operative, semicommunistic, or communistic enterprises. The monogamous basis of the family was successfully defied in the long-lived ascetic communities of the Shakers, in Mormon polygamy, in the plural marriages at Oneida. The principle of racial unity went down before that of racial amalgamation through the assimilation of millions of foreign immigrants. During all these years America was not only a melting pot of nationalities, it was equally a melting pot of political, social, and religious ideas. The intense conservatism that came with the development of capitalism after the Civil War was unknown in the earlier centuries. For two hundred years America was pre-eminently the land of hope, opportunity, and experimentation.

The American faith that came out of it all was a complex, an amalgamation, of hundreds of warring faiths. It could not possibly be closely knit or approach a logical unity such as we find in medieval Catholicism or in modern fascism or communism. Tolerance of diversity was one of its essential characteristics. At its basis was a kind of residuum of common qualities found in nearly all of its constituent movements. Above that were elements, adopted now from one group, now from another, because they proved to possess, for one or another reason, survival value. It was bound to be shot through and through with logical contradictions. Such unity as it possessed, over and above a certain basic identity of spirit, was largely a union of opposites. Its method was compromise, its result assimilation. It was not "thinly dieted on dew," but lived like an organism through the neutralization of poisons. Such was the movement which began with the first settlers at Jamestown.

CHAPTER 5 . *"Earth's Only Paradise-Virginia"*

ROMANCE AND REALISM IN EARLY VIRGINIA

IT IS pleasant to remember that the first English settlement on American soil was attempted by that prince of adventurers, Sir Walter Raleigh. Soldier, sailor, courtier, and scholar, he had ideas of colonization far in advance of any other man of his time. He saw, what the Spanish and French never saw, and the English but tardily, that it was necessary to send out families instead of individuals if one wished to have not a mere trading post but a colony. Whereas it later took the Virginia Company thirteen years to learn this cardinal point of policy before the first famous "shipload of maidens" was sent over in 1619 "for the making of the men feel at home," Raleigh thirty-two years earlier was taking pains to send husbands and wives and young boys and girls to his proprietary colony at Roanoke Island, North Carolina. Virginia Dare, the first English child born on American soil, was a symbol of the future. Raleigh also carefully planned a political government for the colony. His undertaking deserved to succeed, and failed through no fault of his. Had the settlement of one hundred and fifty persons left on Roanoke Island by John White in 1587 received the supplies that were planned to be sent, it would probably have become established as the earliest successful American colony. But war with Spain intervened, Raleigh was kept busy helping Drake and Hawkins fight the Spanish Armada, and when after four years White returned to Roanoke, the settlement, including his daughter Eleanor Dare and his granddaughter Virginia, had vanished with nothing to indicate its fate save the word "Croatoan" carved on a tree—meaning perhaps that the survivors had gone with the Croatoan Indians to their distant hunting grounds south of Cape Hatteras. That one word was all that remained of Raleigh's great undertaking.

It is hardly surprising that after this experience Raleigh should have turned to quicker gains in imitation of the Spaniards. On his expedition to Guiana in 1595 he heard tales of the mythical land of Manoa with its fabulous monarch. "All the vessels of his home, table and kitchen were of golde and silver and the meanest of silver and copper. . . . He had in his wardrobe hollow statues of golde. . . . He had also ropes, budgets, chests and troughs of golde and silver, heaps and billets of golde." Raleigh preferred the bright myth of Manoa to the sad reality of Roanoke. It haunted him thereafter until at the end of his life, and in the shadow of the scaffold, he worked on the cupidity of King James to release him from prison through the promise of Manoan gold, went on one last desperate search for the mines, found them not, and returned to die like a philosopher at the hands of his unjust executioner.

Manoa, Quivira, the Seven Cities of Cibola, El Dorado, the Fountain of Youth in the Land of Bimini—these imaginary projections of Mexico and Peru—these and the notion of the Northwest Passage, a persistent survival of the original idea of Columbus to find a short route to Cathay, all had to be dissipated from the minds of Spaniards and Englishmen through a long series of tragic expeditions before the sober merchant companies would again take up the task of colonization begun by Raleigh at Roanoke.

Regularly incorporated trading companies had long existed in England, the oldest going back as far as Edward the Third. At first, the trade had been almost entirely with Holland, but with the gradual development of the commercial classes they expanded their operations until by the time of James the First they reached every accessible part of the world. There were among others the Muscovy, Levant, East India, Morocco, and Guinea companies, with their stock widely diffused among lords and commoners but with almost an interlocking directorate of the largest owners holding stock in several companies. The method was everywhere the same:

to secure from the Crown monopoly rights for the trade of some special region. Thus, one of the leading characteristics of latter-day capitalism—the existence of great monopolistic corporations—is in essence a reversion to the methods of early capitalism. So also the latter-day regulation or control by the state is paralleled by the power over industry which the state exercised in the beginning. In these respects, as in others to be mentioned during the course of this study, contemporary society is clearly turning back toward the seventeenth century.

The commercial companies, representing aggregations of capital far in excess of the private resources of even a Raleigh, were evidently the most suitable bodies to undertake colonization on a large scale. Trade meant the establishment of permanent trading posts, and from this to the establishment of self-supporting colonies seems so slight a transition that one may wonder that it was not accomplished earlier. Yet the difference between a trading post and a colony, though slight in theory, was enormous in practice, since the colony involved an outlay of capital and labor many times that of the trading post. A defeated colony, as we shall see in Maine, could lapse into the state of a trading post more easily than the latter could develop of its own initiative into a colony.

The London and Plymouth companies, so named from the residence of their leading promoters, were organized under a single charter in 1606 for both trade and colonization in North America. All of that part of the continent north of the Spanish possessions then went by the name of Virginia and was claimed by England, but following current custom the two companies carefully divided the region between them, the London Company having rights between the thirty-fourth and thirty-eighth parallels, the Plymouth Company between the forty-first and forty-fifth parallels, the intervening territory being left as a kind of no man's land which either might settle provided it did not come within one hundred miles of the other. Actually, this no man's land was settled by neither, but by the Swedes and the Dutch. The London Company, finding it enough of a task to support the single settlement at Jamestown, was reorganized under a new charter in 1609 as the Virginia Company, while the Plymouth firm after a number of vicissitudes eventually became the Council for New England when the latter name first given that region by Captain John Smith had come into general usage.

The second great American myth, almost as popular as that one concerning religious freedom which has already been discussed, is the notion that Virginia, the oldest colony, was settled by Cavaliers. This myth, sedulously cultivated in the South between the Revolution and the Civil War, is even more discredited than the first myth by historical research.[1] Only three important Virginia families of direct connection with the nobility have been discovered. It is true that on the first four voyages there was a great preponderance of "gentlemen" who occasioned difficulty by their refusal to engage in manual labor, but most of these either died in the terrific mortality of the early years or took the first opportunity to escape from that land of death back to England. It is also true that, after the overthrow of Charles the First, eight hundred to one thousand Cavaliers fled to Virginia, but nearly all of them returned to their British estates at the time of the Restoration. The permanent inhabitants of Virginia, as of the other colonies, were a mixture of gentry and yeomen with the latter greatly preponderant. For every gentleman that came, there were three or four indentured servants, bound out for a term of labor of from three to seven years. In so far as there was any difference between the population of Virginia and that of the northern colonies, it lay in the much larger representation of the very lowest classes, since until nearly the end of the seventeenth century the British government made a special practice of sending "sturdy beggars" and transported criminals thither. For the first ten years, in fact, Virginia resembled a penal colony. All of the early governors complained of the quality of the settlers. In its beginnings, at least, Virginia was much less "aristocratic" than Massachusetts.

The London Company made the typical capitalists' mistake of failing to consider the human elements of its problem. Once the initial capital for the enterprise had been raised and the legal rights

[1] See Thomas J. Wertenbaker, *Patrician and Plebeian in Virginia* (Charlottesville, Va.: the author, 1910), and Arthur W. Calhoun, *Social History of the American Family* (Cleveland: The Arthur H. Clark Company, 1917–19).

of the Company guaranteed, the one thought of the directors was to get their colony started as quickly as possible regardless of the suitability of the settlers sent over. In the first expedition, out of one hundred and five immigrants there were only twelve laborers, four carpenters, and a few mechanics. The rest were gentlemen of leisure and fortune hunters who came in the dream of discovering gold, which indeed was one of the Company's aims and the one that it found hardest to dismiss as groundless. Three later ships brought more colonists of the same color, until Captain Smith wrote to the Company in exasperation, "When you send again, I entreat you rather send but thirty carpenters, husbandmen, gardeners, fishermen, blacksmiths, masons, and diggers up of trees' roots, well provided, than a thousand such as we have." But the only result of Smith's expostulation was that the Company, after finding an exclusive colony of gentry impracticable, went to the other extreme of bringing over too many of the indigent and even some of the transported criminals mentioned above.

The other arrangements of the Company were equally inefficient. The first expedition, provided with adequate food for a voyage of only two months, took the long route through the West Indies and was four months at sea so that it arrived already short of provisions. The location of the settlement at Jamestown was on low-lying land which became a perfect breeding place for malaria and dysentery. At the end of the first year but thirty-eight of the original one hundred and five settlers survived.

In order to procure the needed number of colonists the Company had offered to feed them all from the common supplies. As later at Plymouth, this proved a sufficient deterrent to private initiative so that even in the face of approaching starvation most of the settlers worked in only a halfhearted manner. It was probably the energetic action of Captain John Smith who took the law into his own hands by declaring that he would expel all of the drones from the fort (under the good socialistic motto—"He that will not work shall not eat") which saved the colony from extinction. Writing of this period, Smith declared, "When our people were fed out of the common store and laboured jointly together, glad was he who could slip from his labour, or slumber over his taske, he cared not how, nay the most honest among them would hardly take so much true paines in a weeke, as now for themselves they will doe in a day; neither cared they for the increase, presuming that howsoever the harvest prospered, the general store must maintaine them, so that wee reaped not so much corne from the labours of thirtie, as now three or four doe provide for themselves."

Captain John Smith was never one to minimize his own accomplishments. Certainly the communal rationing of food was not likely to succeed in so ill integrated a group as that at Jamestown, but one may doubt whether it was so important as Smith assumes. The colony, after its abandonment, still did not succeed. Continued efforts were made by the Company, and in 1609 six ships were sent over with eight hundred immigrants, but by 1611 the population had fallen to one hundred and fifty. The colony continued undernourished, and disease continued to take its terrific annual toll.

From the beginning the colony was governed in the most autocratic manner, at first by a local council of company representatives and after 1609 by the governor, who combined in himself executive, legislative, and judicial powers. To quell the discontent and insubordination of the settlers the common law was suspended and a drastic code adopted which has been somewhat unfairly identified with Sir Thomas Dale, the governor chosen to bring order out of chaos. Dale, though tyrannical, was at least efficient, but his successor, Sir Samuel Argall, chiefly known for his exploits in treacherously kidnaping Pocahontas and in destroying a peaceful Jesuit settlement at Mount Desert, Maine, appropriated to his own use all the public cattle and the grain from the public lands, whereby he succeeded in reducing the colony to its customary condition of penury.

The reputation of Virginia, "Earth's Only Paradise," as it had been entitled by the poet, Michael Drayton, had now sunk so low that Gondibert, the Spanish ambassador, was able to send home an amusing tale of two murderers who, given their choice between hanging and transportation to Virginia, immediately chose the former. Naturally, no one was any longer willing to go to a colony where the settlers had no political privileges and only one in five survived.

THE GREAT REFORMS OF SIR EDWIN SANDYS

THE Company was millions of dollars in debt, and it was realized that a drastic change in methods was necessary. Under the leadership of the widely traveled and liberal-minded Sir Edwin Sandys (pronounced Sands), a most remarkable alteration of policy ensued in 1618. The Company adopted a charter of grants and liberties by which, in the words of the new governor, Sir George Yeardley, "those cruell lawes by which we had soe longe been governed were abrogated," forced labor was abolished, and provision was made for an annual assembly "to have power to make and ordaine whatsoever lawes and orders should by them be thought good and proffittable." More remarkable still, for the election of this, the first representative body in America, the suffrage was granted to all inhabitants over seventeen, including even indentured servants. This extraordinarily democratic venture, undertaken on Sandys' initiative, extended the right of voting beyond anything known in England, or indeed elsewhere in America prior to the Revolution.

The new policy further envisioned the creation of inns, hospitals, churches, schools, and a college. Funds were raised to establish a free school at Charles City and a college at Henrico. Fifteen thousand acres were set aside for the support of the latter and the governor was instructed by the Company to see "that each town, borough, and hundred procured, by just means, a certain number of their children to be brought up in the first elements of literature, that the most towardly of them should be fitted for college."

Considered in the light of its time, this conception of a service or welfare state was truly revolutionary. There was, it is true, no open profession of religious liberty, which King James would hardly have tolerated, but the Company opened its lands for "particular plantations" with local self-government under the general laws of the colony and was willing to grant a charter and an educational fund of five hundred pounds to the Pilgrims, indicating that a considerable degree of religious freedom was actually contemplated. Had the program of Sandys been actually carried out there is every reason to believe that Virginia, the first of the colonies, would also have been the most enlightened.

But the colony was still followed by the ill fortune that had overshadowed it from the beginning. The Indian massacre of 1622 wiped out nearly half of the settlers. The newly erected college buildings at Henrico were burned, and among the killed was George Thorpe, the college superintendent. With their fields ravaged and crops destroyed, the surviving settlers, huddled together within their forts for safety, were once more confronted with the problem of bare subsistence.

To make matters worse, a feud broke out among the stockholders as to the treatment to be accorded the infamous Argall, who was attacked on various counts by Sandys but was stoutly defended by Robert Rich, Earl of Warwick. This specific point of conflict was soon extended into a general line of battle between the aristocratic and merchant groups in the Company, the aristocrats having little sympathy with the reform policy of 1618. The acrimonious quarrels at the stockholders' meetings became so notorious as to be a public scandal. The result was that both parties were undone. The King and Privy Council stepped in, and after prolonged investigation and discussion the charter of the Company was abrogated in 1624, and Virginia became a crown colony.

RELIGION IN OLD VIRGINIA

THE Anglican Church had, of course, always been officially recognized, but after this time its authority was asserted much more conspicuously. In 1631 an Act of Uniformity was passed, and in 1642 three Congregationalist ministers who attempted to preach in the colony were promptly expelled. The Puritans were as unwelcome in Virginia as the Anglicans were in Massachusetts. This makes all the more interesting the fact that the blue laws of Virginia were fully as "puritanic" as those of Massachusetts itself, revealing the extent to which the Calvinistic ethics had penetrated the Anglican body. Regular attendance at church was rigidly prescribed; all traveling on Sunday, except to church, was prohibited; indulgence in profanity was subject to a heavy fine; and no one was allowed to "disparage a minister . . . upon pain of severe censure of the governor and council." As late as 1662 an act was passed, reading:

"Every person who refuses to have his child baptized by a lawful minister shall be amerced 2,000 pounds of tobacco; half to the parish, half to the informer." It would have been difficult to think of a law more certain to encourage the habit of spying upon the private conduct of neighbors.

All of these regulations, however, had one saving grace: they could not be enforced. It was no lack of will on the part of the Anglican clergy that prevented their endeavoring to turn Virginia into as rigid a theocracy as Massachusetts. But a system which depended so largely on personal espionage was only adapted to the life of the small community in village or town; it could not flourish under a plantation economy. As Virginia increasingly devoted itself to tobacco planting, the actual power of the clergy, in contrast to its nominal authority, automatically declined. On one's plantation miles from Jamestown or Williamsburg, one could criticize the church or indulge in profanity to his heart's content and no one be the wiser. To demand attendance at church services became impracticable when it might take a day to get there. So the blue laws became mere adornments of the statute books rather than living codes of conduct.

Meanwhile, after 1640, the Church of England was kept too busy fighting for its existence at home to be able to take much interest in Virginia. In spite of repeated requests, no bishop was sent over; the Anglican churches remained small, mean structures with none of the architectural beauty of those in England; the clergy, dependent upon the landlord class for their subsistence, adopted the plantation ideals and became landowners and slaveholders themselves to the extent of their means. "It gives me much uneasiness," wrote the Reverend Anthony Gavin in 1738, "to see the greatest part of our brethren taken up in farming and buying slaves, which in my humble opinion is unlawful for any Christian and particularly for clergymen." [2] The ministry gradually abandoned all pretense of moral leadership. The hard-drinking fox-hunting Virginia clergy became so notorious that it was necessary to adopt special laws to restrain clerical drunkenness. Meanwhile, as the population grew and boundaries expanded, the Dissenters—Congregationalists and

[2] Quoted in Henry Beston, *American Memory* (1837), p. 96.

Baptists—crept into the colony in increasing numbers until by the beginning of the eighteenth century they constituted considerably more than half of the inhabitants.

Thus, the plans of the two major groups originally interested in the settlement of Virginia came to naught. The great commercial company which had labored for eighteen years to extract profit from the colony had ended in bankruptcy. And the Church of England, though nominally established, had little hold on the affections of the people, little influence on their conduct. What then of the people themselves, the third estate completely disregarded at first, tardily recognized in the reforms of 1618, and afterwards once more largely forgotten? What of this mass of Virginia men and women?

THE YEOMANRY AND THE PLANTERS

THERE can be no doubt that the prosperity ultimately attained by Virginia was due to the people themselves, the descendants of those despised indentured servants, paupers, and transported criminals who made up the bulk of the early inhabitants. The Virginia Company and King James both did their best to persuade them to plant diversified crops and to develop such industries as saltmaking, brickmaking, shipbuilding, iron and glass works, but their efforts were vain. Beginning with John Rolfe's modest experiment in tobacco-raising in 1612, the settlers obstinately devoted themselves to this one staple, easy to cultivate and bringing huge profits. They planted it in the very streets of Jamestown. King James could write his moralistic declamations against the filthy habit of smoking, Sir Edwin Sandys could declare that tobacco was a "deceavable weed which served neither for necessity nor for ornament to the life of man," the Company might even prohibit its planting, but the settlers went on planting it none the less. In spite of the admonitions of the moralists against their "laziness," they could see no sufficient reason why they should work harder for less profit at something else, particularly when the Company was always willing to transport it and sell it and when the King's denunciations became notably milder after he made an arrangement whereby he should receive one third of the profits from the augmenting trade. The laziness of the settlers was wiser than the diligence of the merchants;

tobacco saved the colony and became the basis of Virginia's prosperity.

Politically, as well as economically, the people took their future into their own hands. After the creation of the crown colony in 1624, the Stuart monarchs for fifteen years declined to answer any of the numerous petitions for a continuance of the popular assembly established by the Sandys regime, but meanwhile the House of Burgesses met year after year exactly as if it had a legal right to do so, until in 1639 Charles the First officially recognized the *fait accompli*.

Up to about 1640 there was little distinction of social classes, but then slave labor, introduced in the twenties, began to tell. At first, the imported Negroes were treated like indentured servants and given their freedom after a few years of labor. In the absence of laws to protect them, however, they were gradually forced into permanent slavery. Two results followed. The number of indentured servants began to decline as slavery was discovered to be more profitable; and a wealthy class of large plantation-owners employing many slaves began to develop. In a single lifetime the second William Byrd enlarged his estates from twenty-six thousand acres to over a hundred and fifty thousand acres. The British officials were generous in their gifts of public lands to themselves and their favorites. Alexander Spottswood, not the worst of the governors, calmly deeded himself sixty thousand acres. Through bribery and fraud, as well as legal investment, the Virginia planting aristocracy came into being. Their economic power soon brought in its train political power. By 1653 they were able to deprive indentured servants of their right to vote, and in 1671 leaseholders also were disfranchised. The popular discontent aroused by these measures took form in the gallant rebellion of Nathaniel Bacon in 1676 which might possibly have succeeded but for the untimely death of its leader. The reactionary governor, Sir William Berkeley, whose relentless persecution of Quakers and Puritans had earlier driven over one thousand Dissenters out of Virginia, and who in a letter to the Lords Commissioners had thanked God that there were no free schools or printing presses in the colony (quite incorrectly, as there were in fact two excellent schools), confiscated the property of those who had taken part in the rebellion and executed a score of the leaders. Berkeley was recalled by Charles the Second, who exclaimed, "The old fool has killed more people in that naked country than I have done for the murder of my father," but the power of the popular party was broken. By gerrymandering the voting districts, the planters, though only a third of the inhabitants, kept the control of the assembly in their own hands. The small farmers were forced out of the richer lands of the Tidewater up into the hill country of the Piedmont. Two distinct classes were recognized: the "Tuckahoes" or gentry, and the "Cohees" or commoners. Thus Virginia repeated the pattern of England in developing on the one hand a ruling aristocracy supported by a conservative church, and on the other a discontented populace ripe for rebellion should favorable circumstances arise.

Yet it must be remembered that the gap between gentry and commoner, though clearly recognized, was much less than in England. The two social classes remained fairly fluid. It is significant that the nicknames "Tuckahoe" and "Cohee," applied to the residents of Tidewater and Piedmont, were territorial rather than class designations. There were poor as well as rich "Tuckahoes," and there were rich and poor "Cohees." The native aristocracy of Virginia had behind it no tradition of centuries of power and privilege; it was not fortified by any hereditary titles; it had arisen through its own efforts and could maintain its position only through constant manipulation of the suffrage and occasional timely concessions. And the populace of Virginia was an open-air populace, used to the physical freedom of the frontier, unacquainted with castles and palaces or the constraint of city walls, unbent to habits of servility or submission. The isolation of the separate plantations in the valleys and that of the small farms in the uplands were alike favorable to the development of individualistic ways of thought and behavior. Above all, planters and yeomen were equally indisposed to be exploited for the benefit of British merchants or aristocracy. By the beginning of the eighteenth century both "Tuckahoe" and "Cohee" were no longer Englishmen but Virginians, and in the sentiment of local loyalty they possessed a bond of union fully as strong as their class opposition.

CHAPTER 6 . *The First New England Colony — Maine*

THE FISHERMEN OF MAINE

THE Plymouth branch of the Virginia Company, organized, it will be recalled, at the same time as the London branch which colonized Virginia, was only five months behind the sister organization in getting under way. Headed by two Devonshire men, Sir Fernando Gorges and Lord Chief-Justice Popham, it sent over in May, 1607, two ships—the *Gift of God* and the *Mary and John*—carrying one hundred and twenty settlers, all men, to a spot which they called Popham Beach on the Sagadahoc River in Maine. Here they established the first settlement ever made in New England, preceding that of the Pilgrims by thirteen years. They built cabins, a church, a storehouse, and laid out fields and gardens. All went well until the severe Maine winter came on, during which they suffered that common misfortune of the early settlers—a disastrous fire, which wiped out the storehouse and a number of the cabins. The colonists managed to survive in great discomfort but with small loss of life until spring, when they all took advantage of the reappearance of the *Mary and John* to return to England. Had they had any impelling motive to stay, such as that of the Pilgrims and Puritans, had they brought their wives with them, or even had there been any Captain John Smith among them, the enterprise would not have been so quickly abandoned. But, as matters were,

99

one experience of a Maine winter was enough for these amateur colonists.

Without the necessary capital for further undertakings, the Plymouth Company was practically defunct until it was reorganized by Sir Fernando Gorges in 1620 under a new patent and with a new name—that of the Council for New England. Gorges was an aristocrat with the ideals of his class: his notion of what a colony should be was that of Lord Baltimore, the Carterets, the Berkeleys, the Earl of Shaftesbury, the Duke of York, and nearly all of the nobility and upper gentry, namely, that it should reproduce as closely as possible the feudal, manorial system of England. Had the plans of Gorges succeeded, New England would have suffered the trials and tribulations of Maryland, the Carolinas, and New York, in each of which the same fundamental form of a feudal society was to be set up, with bitter results for ensuing generations of American farmers. The Council for New England consisted of forty proprietors, who were granted absolute rights to divide up the territory as they pleased and to govern it as they pleased. It was a wholly aristocratic body including one duke, two marquises, six earls, one viscount, three barons, nineteen knights, seven esquires, and the dean of Exeter to add religious coloration. At a time when the future of feudalism in England was none too bright, these men were glad enough to stake out claims in the new world, but they had no desire to venture into that wilderness personally. Thus the chief business of the New England Council was that of making land grants on paper, which cost it nothing and brought in a considerable revenue. One must admit that these aristocrats, if benighted statesmen, were not bad businessmen.

Sir Fernando Gorges, however, was a more venturesome character than the others. As a distinguished naval and military commander, he was too much engrossed in home duties ever to have time to lead a colony to America, but in 1623 he sent over his son, Robert Gorges, at the head of a large company which effected a temporary settlement at Wessagusset (later Weymouth) on Massachusetts Bay. Here the Sagadahoc experience was repeated. The colonists returned ignominiously in 1624, leaving behind only a few bold, individualistic spirits who succeeded in making permanent homes for themselves at various points on the coast.

Meanwhile up in Maine a much humbler kind of colonization was slowly proceeding. Hardy fishermen from Devonshire, Holland, Brittany, and the Basque country had been frequenting those northern waters for more than a century. It was their custom to set stages on shore in the summer to dry their fish. Gradually a few men were found who preferred to stay through the winter rather than make the double journey across the Atlantic. Small semipermanent settlements grew up on Damariscove and Monhegan islands and at Pemaquid Point. Stations were established up the rivers for trade with the Indians. A certain camaraderie of the sea developed among these fisherfolk of many nations, which were often supposed to be at war with each other. Far from Europe, bound together by common perils, what to them were the struggles of rival potentates, monarchs or popes or bishops, three thousand miles away?

In 1622, when the Pilgrim settlement at Plymouth seemed likely to perish for lack of food, Edward Winslow made a trip to Maine in search of supplies. Among the fishermen he found "only entertainment and good respect with a willingness to supply all wants." They refused to "take any bills for the same, but did what they could freely, wishing their store had been such as they might in greater measure have expressed their own love and supplied our necessities, for which they sorrowed; provoking one another to the utmost of their abilities." Historians have usually refused the name of colonies to these Maine settlements which had no august charters or patents to justify their existence. Yet it seems rather strange to accord that name to the community of starving Pilgrims and refuse it to those which were able and willing to help them. The Maine settlements were small, but they survived, which would seem to be the true test of a colony.

During the sixteen-thirties the indefatigable Sir Fernando Gorges reappeared in the New England landscape. By successive charters of 1632 and 1639 he acquired proprietary rights to the "Province of Maine," and in 1640 he sent over his cousin, Thomas Gorges, to act as deputy governor. Near the Agamenticus River, where there was already a small farming settlement, the great cathedral city of "Gorgeana" was to be laid out on the plan of Bristol, with a mayor, aldermen, town clerk, serjeants of the white rod, and all the other official appurtenances of an English town. Markets and fairs were to be established; Gorgeana, in fact, was to be the wonder of all the American colonies. The reality that came out of these grandiose dreams was the small frontier settlement of York, with similar log cabin communities at Wells and Kittery. Though hampered by the instructions of the proprietor who continued to think of America as simply a slightly larger England, Thomas Gorges ruled his "province" with tact and discretion until his death in 1649. The inhabitants, left to their own devices, immediately showed that "Anglo-Saxon genius for self-government" which has been so often remarked upon by Anglo-Saxon historians. "With one free and unius animus consent," they bound themselves "in a body politick and combination to see thes partes of the cuntry and province regulated according to such lawes as formerly have bine exercised and such other as may be thought meet and not repugnant to the fundamentall laws of our nation and cuntry, and to make choyse of such governor or governors and majestrats as by most voysses they shall thinck meet." The proprietary of Sir Fernando Gorges was suddenly changed into a democracy.

Three months later, a Declaration of Religious Tolerance was adopted, reading: "That all gode people within the jurisdiction of this province who are out of a Church way and be orthodox in judgment and not scandalous in life, shall have full liberty to gather themselves into a Church estate, provided they do it in a Christian way: with the due observation of the rules of Christ revealed in his worde: and every Church hath free liberty of election and ordination of all her officers from tyme to tyme provided they be able, pious and orthodox." This declaration shows the inhabitants of Maine to have been, next after those of Rhode Island, the most liberal-minded of any of the English colonists. Once more the common people revealed themselves as the chief source and support of freedom of conscience. No such policy could have been adopted under the Anglican Gorges, and unfortunately, as the event showed, no such policy could be maintained in the immediate neighborhood of Puritan Massachusetts.

A governor and magistrates were elected, a general court was convened, jury trial was introduced, and for three years the people of Maine enjoyed self-government. But meanwhile Massachusetts was casting an increasingly envious eye at the fisheries and fur trade of its neighbor. And what Massachusetts wanted it could always justify by one kind of argument or another. A ground for the seizure of Maine was found in the ambiguous wording of the Massachusetts charter which allowed their territory to extend "three miles north of the Merrimac river." But the Merrimack River at its mouth or its source? The question had not mattered at the time the charter was granted, as everyone supposed that the course of the river throughout ran, as in the known part, from west to east. Actually, however, the source of the Merrimack was later discovered to lie far up in New Hampshire. Running a new line east and west from this point, Massachusetts accordingly claimed practically all the inhabited parts of both New Hampshire and Maine. (That portion of New Hampshire was nominally owned by Captain John Mason, a partner of Gorges, and some of it had been sparsely settled, as we shall see later, by refugees from the religious tyranny exercised in Massachusetts.)

The claims of Massachusetts were, of course, essentially fraudulent in view of the well-known intent of its charter, and they were later disallowed by the British government; but the inhabitants of Maine were too few in number to put up an effective resistance. A show of Massachusetts force was sufficient. So the simple Maine farmers and fishermen found themselves under the rule of a theocracy, obliged to recognize the authority of magistrates sent up from Boston and to attend a church in which few, if any, believed. Theoretically, at least, this was the case. But actually, although Massachusetts was able to maintain its hold on the territory by buying out the descendants of Gorges, the Puritan theocracy never took root in Maine. The manners of the frontier persisted. The people were not fond of churchgoing and they didn't go, no matter what the clergy and magistrates said or did. They were in the habit of swearing when they felt like it, and they continued to do so. Puritan laws to control drinking were disregarded. Maine continued to be a land of personal liberty where the only active religion was that of human association and friendliness. Together with New Hampshire and Vermont, it constituted a frontier fringe where the most practical kind of democratic equality lasted until long after the Revolution.

CHAPTER 7 · *The Pilgrim Experiment in Separatism*

THE PILGRIMS IN ENGLAND

THE Pilgrims are a name and a legend.[1] Many virtues have been attributed to them which they never possessed, and their limitations have been too often forgotten. Their heroic age was brief—twenty years at most; after that their life was inglorious. Yet America does well to cherish their memory. One cannot help feeling a peculiar warmth toward them. They were so poor and naïve and honest; when they tried to dissemble, they did it so badly; they were such a small group but with such mighty courage, never thinking of themselves as making history,[2] wanting nothing but to be able to live their own lives in their own way, essentially pure and unworldly. The power motive, present almost everywhere else, had no part here. They were more like the German Pietist groups to be considered later than they were like any of the other English colonists. For they had one idea, only one— that of the community of the faithful, covenanted together in a single local church for the worship of God. From this their self-

[1] The term "Pilgrim" apparently first came into use in 1798 and that of "Pilgrim Fathers" in 1799. The latter was a decided misnomer for a group nearly all of whose leaders at the time of emigration to America were remarkably young: Standish thirty-six, Allerton thirty-two, Bradford thirty-one, Winslow twenty-five, Alden twenty-one. Carver was forty-four and Brewster fifty-three.

[2] The *Mayflower* is probably the most famous single ship in history, yet Bradford did not consider it sufficiently important even to mention its name in his account of the Pilgrims.

104

government in politics was derived; from this everything was derived.

This basic Anabaptist conception of the church covenant, anglicized by Robert Browne and made the central principle of all later Congregationalism, was never so trenchantly stated as by the Pilgrim preacher, John Robinson: "In what place soever, by what means soever, whether by preaching the gospel by a true minister, or by a false minister, or by no minister, or by reading, conference, or any other means of publishing it, two or three faithful people do arise, separating themselves from the world into the fellowship of the gospel and covenant of Abraham, they are a church truly gathered, though never so weak—a house and temple of God rightly founded upon the doctrine of the apostles and prophets, Christ himself being the cornerstone." [3]

The Pilgrims, little dreaming that it would ever be their destiny to be cast as exiles on a barren shore three thousand miles from home, were originally merely a part of one of the numerous Separatist congregations that were beginning to dot the eastern counties of England in the opening years of the seventeenth century. Their first center was at Gainsborough, ministered to by John Smyth, the Se-Baptist of the future. Associated with Smyth was another unfrocked Anglican, John Robinson, also a Cambridge graduate, who had begun his preaching career in Robert Browne's old bailiwick at Norwich, where, however, the bishop, now on the alert for heretics, soon discovered in him Brownist tendencies and suspended him from the ministry. The Anglican, Joseph Hall, in an open letter to Robinson in 1610, reproached him for his early intimacy with Smyth, by that time a far more dangerous religious outlaw than Browne had ever been. Smyth, Hall wrote, was "your partner, yea, your guide, your oracle and generall"—which, considering that Smyth was much the older man, may well have been the truth. Still a third Cambridge graduate was drawn into their movement, Richard Clyfton, the nonconformist minister at Babworth a few miles distant. There was no lack of learning in the leaders of this Separatist group of artisans and yeomen. In Clyfton's congregation often sat a "puny boy" of twelve, one William Bradford, a farm

[3] Robert Ashton, *The Works of J. Robinson* (Boston: Doctrinal Tract & Book Soc., 1851), II, 232–233.

lad from the neighboring village of Austerfield, who was to transmit the story of the Pilgrims to posterity.

When Smyth led most of his Gainsborough congregation to Amsterdam in 1606, the village of Scrooby, eight miles from Babworth and twelve from Gainsborough, was selected as a convenient center for those left behind who, according to Bradford, included men from "sundry towns and villages, some of Nottinghamshire, some of Lincolnshire, and some of Yorkshire." Scrooby was an estate of the archbishop of York, and the archiepiscopal bailiff of the manor, as well as postmaster and innkeeper, was, somewhat amusingly, a Cambridge Separatist named William Brewster. During the week Bailiff Brewster collected rent and administered justice among no less than seventeen groups of tenant farmers who worked on the estate, while on Sunday, as Elder Brewster, he, with Clyfton or Robinson, met those of them who were Separatists together with the contingent from neighboring villages, for secret and illegal worship in the manor house. It was a situation fraught with peril, and in 1607 the congregation decided to follow Ainsworth and Smyth to Amsterdam. Their first attempt, undertaken too openly, was frustrated by the authorities, and Brewster, as the main leader of the movement, was in some danger of imprisonment, but before the government had made up its mind to take drastic action, he and about a hundred of the congregation safely escaped to Amsterdam.[4]

THE PILGRIMS IN HOLLAND

At this time there were already in Amsterdam two congregations of English Dissenters, bitterly opposed to each other—the conservative Ainsworth-Johnson group of Separatists and the Gainsborough group of radicals under John Smyth. The new arrivals from Scrooby held a position midway between the two. They could not but deplore the Mennonite influence that had led their old teacher Smyth into his Baptist and Arminian heresies. On the other hand, they disliked the authoritarianism of Ainsworth and Johnson, who in their pride of learning had lost faith in the com-

[4] In 1938 the Brewster tradition of independence was upheld by Bishop Benjamin Brewster of Maine, who resigned from the Society of Mayflower Descendants rather than yield to the demand of that shameless organization that he give up his membership in the American Civil Liberties Union.

mon people and held that the congregation, once it had elected its officers, should have no further control over them, whereas in the Scrooby group there was free discussion of the officers' conduct and these were subject to censure at any time by majority vote.

The aesthetic taste of the newcomers was not so developed but that they were glad to adopt as their hymnbook Ainsworth's rough translation of the Psalms into English doggerel. That much of ritual they were willing to tolerate. But the English Prayer Book continued to be anathema in their eyes. Robinson, in replying to Joseph Hall, wrote of it in fiery fashion: "What is the adoring of your truly human, though called 'Divine,' service-book, in and by which you worship God as the Papists do by their images? . . . Might not the Lord now be also purely and perfectly worshipped, though this printed image, with the painted and carved images, were sent back to Rome; yea, or cast into hell, from which both they and it came?"

Robinson was as disputatious as all good theologians were supposed to be. He later debated with Simon Episcopius, the leading Dutch Arminian, and wrote a rejoinder to Helwys' argument that it was the duty of Dissenters to return to England, pointing out that it was no part of the obligation of Christians to seek deliberate martyrdom. In spite of his prowess as a polemicist, however, he was, for a clergyman, remarkably ironic in disposition, welcoming the attendance of members of other sects at the religious services of his own congregation. A desire to escape from the heated theological atmosphere of Amsterdam soon caused the group under his leadership to withdraw to Leyden, where they could worship according to their own consciences undisturbed by the disputes of their fellow-countrymen.

In Holland they were free to live in their own way if they could manage to live at all. Their problem was no longer a religious but an economic one. These English yeomen were inevitably at a great disadvantage in a foreign industrial city where advancement in the handicrafts was dependent upon a guild membership which was open only to citizens. Had they been willing to renounce their English nationality and merge with the Dutch their economic difficulties could have been easily overcome, but this would have meant an abandonment of that corporate loyalty which was the central principle of their being. So they found what work they could as individuals. Isaac Allerton, a tailor in London, was a tailor in Leyden; Brewster and Edward Winslow became printers, Robert Cushman a wool comber, William Bradford a weaver. They were industrious and frugal, and even in their unfamiliar trades were able to make more than a bare living, being able in 1611 to buy a meetinghouse and grounds in the Klogsteeg or Bell Alley next the cathedral. Their relations with their foreign hosts were entirely amicable, as the Dutch had much respect for these quiet artisans, not one of whom was ever accused of the smallest crime.

Nevertheless, after a few years, they found that their condition seemed to grow worse rather than better. Bradford, in giving the reasons for the emigration to America, listed them in the following order: (1) the difficulty of making a living in competition with the Dutch, which prevented the church in Leyden from growing according to their hopes and expectations; (2) the precarious condition of their older members, no longer able to endure the strain of this competition, so that "within a few years more they would be in danger to scatter, by necessities pressing them, or sink under their burdens, or both"; (3) the sinister situation of their children, "so oppressed with their heavie labours, that though their minds were free and willing, yet their bodies bowed under ye weight of ye same, and became decreped in their early youth, the vigor of nature being consumed in ye very budd as it were," while others "were drawne away by evill examples into extravagante and dengerous courses, getting ye raines off their neks, & departing from their parents"; (4) "which was not least," a "great hope & inward zeall" to advance "ye gospell of ye kingdom of Christ" more effectively elsewhere than in Holland.

A further potent reason for departing from Holland was the fact that the twelve years' truce between Spain and the Netherlands would expire in 1621, with the likelihood of a renewal of the religious wars which would expose the Dissenters to the possibility of a Catholic persecution infinitely bloodier than any they could suffer in England.

The extent of their worry is indicated by the fact that in 1617 they entered into negotiation with the Virginia Company for a patent to lands in Virginia, even though their going thither would force them to acknowledge the lawfulness of the Church of England, the episcopal organization, the Thirty-nine Articles, and that prayer book which Robinson had said came from Hell. Such acknowledgment was now in fact made in seven articles drawn up by Robinson and Brewster and submitted to His Majesty's Council.[5] The Leyden congregation presumably justified this dissimulation as no more than a gesture in return for which they hoped to secure a private plantation with the right to elect their own local magistrates and pass their own laws under which they could continue their Separatist form of worship. As the nearly bankrupt Virginia Company was at this time willing to make extraordinary concessions to settlers, they actually succeeded, through the aid of the liberal Sir Edwin Sandys, in obtaining a patent in 1619 which was prudently made out, not to themselves, but to a friendly Anglican clergyman named John Wyncop.[6]

The Separatists were never very good at dissimulation; sooner or later, they were likely to throw caution to the winds and come out with their real opinions. At the very time that the negotiations for the Wyncop patent were approaching completion, William Brewster recklessly printed Calderwood's *Perth Assembly*, a work which roundly denounced King James for trying to force episcopacy on the Scottish Church. When the news of the publication reached England, it nearly wrecked the whole emigration scheme. The royal indignation was such that, though the Separatists had their patent, they dared make no use of it. All they could do was to wait for the incident to be forgotten, keeping Brewster discreetly out of sight in the meantime.

After some months, they were approached with an apparently liberal offer by a London trading firm known simply as the Merchant Adventurers, operating under a patent from the Virginia Company. The Adventurers proposed to take them into a joint-stock association in which each share of stock should be worth ten pounds to be contributed in the form of either capital or labor: the

---

[5] The "Seven Articles" may be found in Bradford, *History* (New York: A. Lovell and Company, 1896), I, 73–75.

[6] The Wyncop patent is lost, but C. M. Andrews believes, on the basis of other contemporary patents, that it contained the desired provisions for local self-government. See his *Colonial Period of American History* (New Haven: Yale University Press, 1936), I, 258–259.

Adventurers were to furnish transportation from England and necessary supplies, and for the first seven years were to own all houses, furniture, apparel, and food, to be distributed among the individual colonists from a common store; at the end of the seven years the property was to be divided among all the stockholders in proportion to the amount of stock owned, but until then the colonists were to devote four days out of each week to working for the Adventurers in order to repay them for their original outlay. The Separatists closed with this proposal and were making ready for their departure, when the London businessmen changed their minds and drew up a second agreement by which the emigrants should give all their time to the Adventurers for seven years, after which the property should be divided equally between the Adventurers and the settlers. This put a different face on the matter, and many of the Leyden congregation refused to take part in an enterprise which threatened to reduce them to the status of indentured servants. The choice of going or staying was left to the individual members, it being agreed that whichever way the decision went the majority should be under the charge of Pastor Robinson and the minority be led by Elder Brewster. Fatefully the vote determined that the clergyman should remain in Leyden and the colonists be led by the layman.

THE PILGRIMS IN AMERICA

OF the hundred and one passengers on the *Mayflower*, only thirty-five belonged to the original Leyden congregation, the others joining the expedition at Southampton and being, in Bradford's words, "a very mixed lot." After a weary voyage of sixty-five days, land was sighted on November 9, 1620. It proved to be Cape Cod, well beyond the limits of the Adventurers' patent. But as the autumn was now far advanced, the Pilgrims took the momentous decision to disregard the terms of the patent and settle illegally in New England instead of Virginia. Before landing, they drew up and signed the now famous Mayflower Compact in which the church covenant idea was extended for the first time to the civil government.

This celebrated document read:

"In ye name of God, Amen. We whose names are underwriten,

the loyall subjects of our dread soveraigne Lord, King James, by ye grace of God, of Great Britaine, France, & Ireland king, defender of the faith, &c., haveing undertaken, for ye glorie of God, and advancement of ye Christian faith, and honour of our king and countrie, a voyage to plant ye first colonie in ye Northerne parts of Virginia, doe by these presents solemnly and mutualy in ye presence of God, and of one another, covenant & combine ourselves togeather into a civill body politick, for our better ordering & preservation & furtherance of ye ends aforesaid; and by vertue hereof to enacte, constitute, and frame such just & equall lawes, ordinances, acts, constitutions, & offices, from time to time, as shall be thought most meet & convenient for ye generall good of ye Colonie, unto which we promise all due submission and obedience. In witnes whereof we have hereunder subscribed our names at Cap-Codd ye 11 of November, in ye year of ye raigne of our soveraigne lord, King James, of England, France, & Ireland ye eighteenth, and of Scotland ye fiftie fourth. An. Dom. 1620"

Thus was set up a government by consent with sovereignty residing in the whole male community, subject only to the ultimate authority of God and the King. The document was completely democratic in character: it made no distinctions of class or wealth or between the contingents from Leyden and London; and it was apparently signed by all the male adults, including four servants, except for a very few who were presumably too ill to attend the meeting or take any interest in the proceedings. The sentiment of religious equality was carried over into political equality, and the government that was set up was made morally responsible for promoting "ye generall good of ye Colonie."

Working with desperate haste under the lowering threat of approaching winter, the Pilgrims succeeded in erecting a comfortable "common house" by January 9th, only to have a serious fire break out in it at six o'clock in the morning of January 14th. A considerable number, including Carver and Bradford, were already ill as a result of the confinement and bad food on the voyage and subsequent exposure while they had no houses; these were successfully carried out of the burning building, and the fire was eventually extinguished with no further damage than the total destruction of the thatched roof, which left them, however, shivering all day under an icy downpour—for it was the Sabbath, so the roof could not be repaired, no matter how great the need. The piety of the Pilgrims cost them dearly. An epidemic of influenza, pneumonia, and galloping consumption, which had already started among them, was so accentuated by their exposure that seventeen died in February and thirteen in March, leaving only twenty-three of the adult members of the company still alive to greet their first New England spring. Among the dead was Governor Carver, who had apparently recovered but had gone out to work too soon, bringing on a relapse that was fatal. Somberly the survivors elected William Bradford in his place to save the colony if he could.

But it was the Indians who really saved the Pilgrims. In the middle of March a Mohegan from Maine named Samoset, who had learned English from stray fishermen along the coast, suddenly appeared at the settlement with offers of friendship, and soon afterward Chief Massasoit with sixty warriors paid the colonists a ceremonial visit. In the enfeebled condition of the Pilgrims, Massasoit could easily have annihilated them, but he chose instead the part of hospitality. An Indian called Squanto, the sole survivor of the Patuxet tribe, who had been carried off by an English expedition to London as a prize exhibit and there learned the language, spent much time teaching the Pilgrims how to plant twenty acres of Indian corn from which they reaped an abundant harvest in the fall.

The problem of subsistence might now have been mastered but for the arrival of thirty-five new colonists on the *Fortune* in November, 1621. These had been sent out by the Adventurers, but without any of the supplies promised by the latter. The arrival of the ship *Anne* in 1623 was a repetition of the same story. There were more mouths to feed without more food with which to feed them. For three years the Pilgrims literally fought off starvation in a grim yet ridiculous struggle. The ludicrous aspect of their situation was that their land was not unfertile, the harbors swarmed with fish, the woods were full of berries and of all sorts of game. What kind of people were these Pilgrims that in the midst of plenty they almost starved?

The more one knows of them the clearer it seems that they were stubborn and impractical idealists. After all their preliminary discussions they sailed from Holland without any of the things that they most needed: ex-farmers, they brought no cows or horses, no carts, no plows; supposed to make their living largely by fishing, they brought but one kind of hook and net, too large to catch the Massachusetts cod or other small fish; powder and guns they had but knew not how to use them and were slow to learn. They expected, according to their agreement with the Adventurers, to receive regular supplies from England; when these did not materialize, they found themselves in a situation they were unprepared to meet.

Most absurd of the provisions in that agreement had been the one by which they bound themselves to work seven years for the Adventurers irrespective of the proceeds of those years. Regardless of how hard they labored or how quickly they paid off their debt, they would receive nothing for themselves until the seven years were over. This was putting a more severe deterrent in the way of private initiative than anything ever contemplated by medieval communism.

For four years the Pilgrims strove loyally to fulfill the terms of their agreement with the Adventurers, in spite of the latter's having defaulted on their own obligations. But in 1624 they decided that it would be foolish to continue longer in such a course. Each family was given an acre of land and was henceforth responsible for its own sustenance but was also allowed to retain whatever profit it could make. An increased zeal for labor was immediately manifest. By this time, too, the colonists had learned how to fish and shoot and were beginning to adapt themselves to a diet different from that to which they had been accustomed in Holland. The betterment of their condition is shown by a second distribution of land in 1628 through which each family received a hundred acres apportioned by lot with some additional compensation to those receiving the poorer sections.

Bradford, neglecting the other factors involved, held that the Pilgrim experiment was sufficient to disprove the merits of communism: "The experience that was had in this commone course and condition, tried sundrie years, and that amongst godly and sober men, may well evince the vaniti of that conceite of Platos and other ancients, applauded by some of later times; that the taking away of propertie and bringing in communitie into a comone-wealth would make them happy and flourishing; as if they were wiser than God. . . . Let none object this is man's corruption, and nothing to the course itself. I answer, seeing all men have this corruption in them, God, in his wisdom, saw another course fitter for them."

The failure of communism at Plymouth was indeed even more striking than at Jamestown, as the colonists were of so much better caliber; yet it was hardly as decisive as Bradford supposed. In both instances, it was adopted as a temporary expedient without any particular devotion to it as a moral or economic ideal, and in both cases the increased prosperity that followed its abandonment was at least partly due to the growing adaptation of the settlers to their surroundings.

FROM COMMUNISM TO OLIGARCHY

THE principle of equality still held firm at Plymouth for some years after the giving up of communism. But in 1627 the lien which the Adventurers still legally possessed upon the Pilgrims' property was extinguished by an agreement whereunder the title passed into the hands of Bradford, as representative of the colony, in consideration of the assumption of an indebtedness of eighteen hundred pounds by eight of the leaders henceforth known as the Undertakers. These eight were Bradford, Standish, Allerton, Winslow, Brewster, Howland, Alden, and Prence, to whom a few others were from time to time added. In return for their assuming the total financial responsibility of the colony, it seemed but just that the Undertakers should be allowed a monopoly of the trade and fishing rights, control over prices and wages, and the general direction of the economic life of the community. This inevitably meant, however, the transformation of the government into an oligarchy.

Within the next decade a social hierarchy developed in the colony of Plymouth. Four groups are distinguished by Roland Usher in his careful study, *The Pilgrims and Their History* (Macmillan, 1918). At the summit of the social pyramid were the Undertakers, who "allotted themselves the best land, the best cattle, the best meadows for hay, and kept in their hands for nearly twenty-five years the entire trade with the Indians and all fishing rights." Below them was the great body of the church members, who were usually allotted desirable land and were admitted at the will of the Undertakers into the very flexible General Court erected by them in 1636 as the official governing body of the colony. A third group, called somewhat disparagingly "the Inhabitants," comprised those who were regarded as potential church members, to whom was allotted such land as remained after the higher groups had been satisfied. At the bottom of the social scale was the landless class of servants, apprentices, and a few slaves. All of this was a sad departure from the equalitarian promise of the Mayflower Compact.

The landowning and trading aristocracy also controlled the church and was careful not to allow heresy any footing. Plymouth followed in the footsteps of Boston by excluding the Quakers. Eventually the populace and even many of the freemen became impatient of the rigidity of church doctrine and discipline. In 1645, probably influenced by the example of Rhode Island, twenty-five freemen of Plymouth petitioned the General Court to "allow and maintaine full and free toleration of religion to all men that would preserve the civill peace and submit unto government." Edward Winslow wrote to John Winthrop of Boston, "You would have admired to have seen how sweet this carrion relished to the palate of most of the deputies." But orthodoxy was saved by the governor, Bradford's successor, Prence, through the simple expedient of refusing to put the question. As usual, it was the common people who pleaded for tolerance and the aristocracy who denied it.

In one respect, Plymouth failed to imitate Boston where it might well have done so. Nothing is more surprising than the utter neglect of education among the Pilgrims. During their twelve years in Holland they had seen at first hand a system of free public schools supported by taxation in a land where, in the glowing words of Motley, "every child went to school, where almost every inhabitant could read and write, where even the middle classes were proficient in mathematics and the classics and could speak two or more languages." [7] The Pilgrims had lived in Leyden, the center of learning, in the very shadow of the greatest university in Europe,[8] where

[7] Motley, *United Netherlands* (1868), IV, 432.

[8] Arthur Lord, *Plymouth and the Pilgrims* (Boston: Houghton Mifflin Company, 1920), p. 84. "The foremost university in Europe was in full view of their simple dwellings in Clock Street or Bell Alley."

John Robinson studied and debated. Brewster had a library of nearly four hundred volumes, Bradford had eighty, Miles Standish fifty. Yet these leaders of Plymouth seem not to have had the slightest interest in the promotion of education. Bradford's wife was illiterate, and Nathaniel Morton, the secretary and historian of the colony, never troubled to give his four daughters any education whatsoever. It was fifty years before the Plymouth Colony built a single school, either public or private.[9]

The morals of the community were thoroughly Calvinistic. Attendance at church was compulsory upon even nonchurch members, and a solemn demeanor during the service was obligatory, one of the alleged reasons for the expulsion from the colony of Samuel Gorton (of whom more hereafter) being that his wife's maid smiled in church. Laws governing the relations of the sexes were numerous: a suitor could not propose marriage to a woman without previously obtaining the consent of her parents or, in the case of a bond servant, that of her master; seduction was punished by flogging, and—to discourage any idea that one could atone for such a sin—if it were followed by marriage the husband was flogged again while the wife was put in the stocks. Smoking was prohibited on the street, although permitted within the house or in the fields— an illustration of the Calvinistic tendency to make morals a matter of outward conformity. As Charles Beard writes, "The most minute affairs of private life were subject to the searching scrutiny of the elders; prying, spying, and informing were raised to the height of prime diversions; swift and stern punishment was visited upon all who were guilty of blasphemy, drunkenness, sloth, or irregular conduct." With regard to drunkenness—the chief colonial vice— various degrees were recognized ranging from "excessive refreshment," "plain drunkenness," "beastly drunkenness," "filthy drunkenness," and "abominable drunkenness."

The Pilgrims, like all Calvinists, were inclined to mind other people's business. The trait came out especially in their treatment of Thomas Morton. This man, a well-trained English lawyer, became the first real American outlaw, the most colorful figure in early New England. He arrived in Massachusetts, shortly after the

[9] The first mention of any schoolteacher in Plymouth is in 1671. The first public school was established in 1673.

Pilgrims, in the company of one Captain Wollaston—"a man of pretie parts," said Bradford—to set up a trading post at a spot which they named Mount Wollaston (now Quincy). Wollaston quickly became discouraged with the enterprise, and having brought with him a number of indentured servants, he took most of them off to Virginia and sold them to the planters. But when he sent for the rest of them, Morton—by agreeing to accept them as partners— easily persuaded them to resist Wollaston's agent and take over the settlement, which they renamed Merrymount. There, according to Bradford, "Morton became lord of misrule, and maintained (as it were) a school of Athisme. And after they had got some goods into their hands, and got much by trading with the Indians, they spent it vainly, in quaffing and drinking both wine and strong liquors in great excess. . . . They also set up a Maypole, drinking and dancing about it many days togeather, inviting the Indean women for their consorts, dancing and frisking togethir (like so many fairies or furies rather)." Morton, in a word, united the two characteristics always most horrible to the Calvinist mind: he lived in a shockingly immoral manner and he was also a competitor in trade. The Pilgrims further alleged that he sold arms to the Indians, but the truth of that accusation is doubtful. When shipped back to England in irons, he was released soon after his arrival, indicating that the charges against him were not considered important. Later, he published *The New England Canaan* (1637), giving his own version of the proceedings at Merrymount and written in the style of university wit that had been popular in Elizabethan days. When, still later, he ventured to return and settle again near Boston, the Puritans of that city, more intolerant than the Pilgrims, burned down his house and put him in the stocks. He then fled to the wilderness of Maine, dying in Agamenticus as a citizen of the mythical Gorgeana. It was his misfortune to be a man of the Renaissance, born half a century too late in an age he could not understand.

In their accepted moral codes, there was no important divergence between the Pilgrims and the Puritans of Massachusetts Bay. Nevertheless, historians have been right in detecting a fundamental difference of spirit between the two groups. Plymouth was not a theocracy. There was no such tyranny of the clergy in Plymouth as was to develop in Boston; in fact, for the first nine years the Pilgrims were most of the time without a minister. Furthermore, the Pilgrim oligarchy never entirely lost their Separatist simplicity. To live in comfort and to be at the head of a small rural community satisfied them; they sought no unlimited gains in either wealth or politics. They still unconsciously thought in terms of the medieval subsistence economy rather than in those of the newer capitalism. The difference comes out strongly in the instance of Isaac Allerton, the only one of the Plymouth Undertakers who was ever accused of dishonesty. He was for a time the first man in the colony after Bradford, made several trips to England to arrange matters with the Merchant Adventurers, succeeded in bringing over the rest of the Leyden congregation in 1629, and secured a patent in 1630 which fully legalized the existence of the Plymouth Colony. Yet when he ventured on his own responsibility to contract heavy loans for the colony and went so far as to bring over a whole shipload of unauthorized goods for trade, Bradford declared he had "hoodwinckte" his fellows, and the Pilgrims repudiated him as their agent. Scornfully announcing that he would grow rich on the trade they neglected, Allerton departed to make good his word. He was essentially a modern capitalist, venturesome and unscrupulous; the others were timid, honest medievalists, who wished to pay off their old debts before contracting new ones.

Patiently, persistently, the Undertakers year after year reduced their obligations to the Adventurers until in 1648, in order to make the final payment of four hundred pounds, Bradford sold a farm, Alden and Standish each sold three hundred acres of land, Winslow and Prence sold their homes. This was not excessively brilliant financing, after twenty-two years of experience, but it was the sober, frugal, and honest Plymouth way.

The Pilgrims were almost the only English colonists who did not consciously seek to expand their territory. When, lured by more fertile land, Standish and Alden in 1631 moved to Duxbury to be followed later by Brewster and other leaders, Bradford regarded it as a kind of treachery to the original settlement. He realized better than they that the strength of the Pilgrims had resided in the community spirit that had held them together through the years of trial in Holland and the early heroic years in America.

They cared little for individual enterprise in affairs of either the flesh or the spirit, but as long as they kept together they preserved a certain staunch moral integrity of pattern. As town inevitably followed town—Scituate (1636), Sandwich (1638), Taunton (1638), Yarmouth (1649)—the old bonds were loosened with no compensating advantages. The colony still had no harbors comparable to that of Boston, and it was less advantageously located for trade either with Canada or the interior. Slowly it declined into the position of a mere political and commercial satellite of the Massachusetts Bay Colony in which it was finally absorbed in 1691. When Plymouth ceased to be Plymouth, it was nothing at all.

The Pilgrims exercised an important influence on American development, possibly in two respects, certainly in one. Roger Williams may well have derived from his residence in Plymouth, at a time when the Mayflower Compact still was remembered, the ideas of the popular basis of government that he transmitted to Thomas Hooker of Hartford; if so, Plymouth may be regarded as the parent of Providence and Hartford, of Rhode Island and Connecticut. If this is too hypothetical to count for much, the religious influence of Plymouth can hardly be questioned. When in 1628 the first Puritan settlement at Salem was attacked by the same disease that afflicted the Pilgrims on their landing, they sent to Plymouth for medical aid. A skilled practitioner and zealous Separatist, Samuel Fuller of the *Mayflower*, doctor and deacon, was dispatched to their assistance. Dr. Fuller did so well both medically and spiritually that he is credited with persuading the Salem church to adopt the Congregational form of organization. Thus, when the main body of Puritans arrived in 1630 they found Separatism already in their midst. This, together with the prestige of Plymouth as an older settlement, was a major factor in bringing about the unexpected acceptance of Congregationalism in the Bay Colony. John Robinson, who, had he lived to learn of it, would have been bitterly disappointed by the course of events at Plymouth, might nevertheless have received some consolation could he save foreseen that his little congregation of one hundred members would determine the ecclesiastical organization of the great state of Massachusetts and would through it influence the religious development of the United States of America.

CHAPTER 8 . *The Beginning of the Puritan Experiment in Theocracy*

VERY different in social status from the little band of outlawed Pilgrims, impoverished and unknown, who sailed secretly from Southampton on the *Mayflower*, was that great company of Puritans who in successive expeditions to Massachusetts Bay between 1627 and 1631 brought to their colony over one thousand inhabitants. The little advance guard of sixty persons under John Endicott, who in 1627 established the village of Salem, was followed the next year by a proud fleet of six ships carrying four hundred and six passengers, one hundred and forty head of cattle, forty goats, and an immense equipment of arms and tools. In 1630 John Winthrop's fleet brought to Boston, in the words of Moses Coit Tyler, "the greatest company of wealthy and cultivated persons that have ever emigrated in any one voyage from England to America." Subsequent expeditions raised the population of the colony to ten thousand in the first decade. No other of the colonial enterprises ever met with such immediate outward success, for behind the Puritan undertaking was the capital of a well-organized, single-minded, and powerful corporation.

The Massachusetts Bay Company was created in 1629 with about one hundred members, belonging to the Puritan wing of the Established Church. They represented the landed gentry and commercial classes, with a liberal sprinkling from the professions and a large number of prosperous tenant farmers. The Earl of Warwick, a dominant figure in the Virginia Company, was interested in the enterprise; Sir Richard Saltonstall, Sir John Young, and Sir Henry Roswell were members; the ablest among the first emigrants were the wealthy landowners, John Endicott and John Winthrop, the potential governors of Salem and Boston.

A charter was obtained from the King by somewhat crooked means as it infringed upon the prior rights of Sir Fernando Gorges, cutting a huge slice out of the center of his domain. Gorges was absent from England at the time but was certain to raise a storm on his return; hence, on the advice of Winthrop, the colonists took the precaution to carry the charter with them. This had the important consequence of transferring the actual seat of the corporation to America, vesting the real power in a minority of the members, not more than twenty of whom accompanied the expedition. The Puritan colony began, where that of the Pilgrims ended, as a strict oligarchy.

Nothing was further from the minds of the Puritans than any weakening of class distinctions. The antidemocratic sentiments of the ruling group were intense. "Democracy," said Governor John Winthrop, "is, amongst civil nations, accounted the meanest of all forms of government." "If the people be governors," queried the Reverend John Cotton, "who shall be governed?" The excuse often offered for the Puritan theocracy, that though the rulers treated the people harshly they treated themselves with equal harshness, is simply untrue. Throughout the seventeenth century the laws were class legislation of the frankest description. For example, an act of October, 1651, based its provisions on the following preamble: "We declare our utter detestation and dislike that men and women of mean condition, education and callings should take upon themselves the garb of gentlemen by the wearing of gold or silver lace, or buttons, or points at their knees, to walk in great boots; or women to wear silk or tiffany hoods or scarfs, which, though allowable to persons of greater estates, or more liberal education, yet we cannot but judge it intolerable in persons of such low conditions." Pews were assigned in church, and even scholastic standing was determined by social rank. Status rested upon wealth and education instead of upon birth, but it was none the less status.

Why were men of wealth and education especially willing to leave

England in the second quarter of the seventeenth century? Most of those who came shared the attitude of John Winthrop, who mentioned the increased cost of living as one of the chief reasons in his own case. "With what comfort can I live," he complained, "with seven or eight servants in that place and condition where for many years I have spent three or four hundred pounds [1] yearly and Maintained a greater chardge?" Similarly, the Reverend Thomas Shepard gave as the first of eight reasons for his emigration the fact that "I saw no call to any other place in old England nor way of subsistence in peace and comfort to me and my family." There was every prospect of a sharp increase in taxes under a king who had dismissed Parliament and was attempting to rule without it. For those who should venture to resist, confiscation and imprisonment were already on the horizon. In a word, just at that moment of history the economic outlook was black for the upper middle-class Puritans.

But if one leading motive in the establishment of the Massachusetts Bay Colony was unquestionably economic, this in no wise conflicted with a correlative religious motive. In seeking to better their worldly condition the Puritans quite naturally sought also to establish that cherished form of religion which justified their seeking to better their worldly condition. The Church of England, however Calvinistic it might be in far-off Virginia, was at home reverting, under the influence of Charles the First, to its traditional Anglo-Catholic attitude. Every day it became more clearly aligned with the aristocracy against the merchants and gentry. The number of clergymen who had been deprived of their charges or lived in well-grounded fear of that eventuality was now so great as to constitute, in the language of today, "an unemployed white collar class." In many parishes, especially in eastern England, the center of Puritanism, America beckoned equally to the clergy and to their leading parishioners.

King Charles was more than willing to see them depart, relieving his realm of a discordant element. Discordant, not rebellious. Charles Beard is most likely correct in his guess that "if they had not encountered obstacles, they would have made Massachusetts . . .

---

[1] Estimated in contemporary terms, this meant a yearly expenditure of considerably more than a hundred thousand dollars.

the home of an Established Church directed by a learned clergy according to the English forms, though 'purified' to suit the taste and temper of the emigrants." [2] The words of Francis Higginson, in his last sermon before the sailing of the second expedition to Salem, were possibly quite sincere, not only in their scorn of the lowly Separatists but in their expression of devotion to the Church of England: "We will not say, as the Separatists were wont to say at their leaving of England, Farewell Babylon, farewell Rome! but we will say, farewell, dear England! farewell the Church of God in England and all the Christian friends there." Whether sincere or otherwise, Higginson's words expressed the avowed position taken by all the Puritans, who were most eager to avoid every suspicion of Separatism lest they lose some of their most powerful supporters in England. Before the sailing of the emigrants to Boston, John Winthrop was deputed to write a tract on the subject, to be printed immediately after their departure.

Once they were safely established in America, however, the good opinion of their "Christian friends" at home seemed less important. Higginson of the brave words succumbed almost immediately at Salem, as we have seen, to the Separatist arguments of Dr. Samuel Fuller from Plymouth. And from Salem the Congregationalist heresy spread to Boston.

Besides the influence of Plymouth and Salem, there were other reasons that led to the adoption of the Congregationalist form of organization in Massachusetts. In addition to the main settlements at Boston and Salem, villages soon grew up in the neighborhood at Charlestown, Roxbury, Dorchester, Newton, Watertown, Ipswich, and Concord, each centering about its local church though all belonged to the single colony. As the situation in England became steadily worse under the arbitrary Charles the First and the bigotry of Archbishop Laud, the emigration to America rose by leaps and bounds. In many instances whole congregations arrived, each led by a favorite pastor. Within six years there were fifteen clergymen in the neighborhood of Boston, all of them Cambridge graduates, accustomed to the exercise of authority and to elucidating weighty points of doctrine, and none of them particularly disposed to give

[2] Charles Beard, *The Rise of American Civilization* (New York: The Macmillan Co., 1927), p. 54.

way to the opinions of his colleagues. Such a multiplicity of vicars of Christ created a *de facto* Separatism which led naturally to the Congregationalist type of organization. Unless Boston were to become the seat of a bishopric—something that none of the other towns would have accepted—Congregationalism, with a possible later development into Presbyterianism, was the only alternative.

But Congregationalism, Separatism, or Independency, adopted in Massachusetts for practical reasons to avoid local quarrels and jealousies, had nothing but its ecclesiastical organization in common with the movement originally started by Browne, Ainsworth, and Robinson. The New England clergy were wholly in sympathy with the political oligarchy of the Massachusetts Bay Colony. Two of the most prominent, John Davenport and Hugh Peters, were members of the Company; John Wilson, pastor of the First Church in Boston, was a nephew of Grindal, Archbishop of Canterbury; his colleague, John Cotton, had been Vicar of St. Botolph's in old Boston, one of the most pretentious Gothic churches in England, with a spire as high as that of Lincoln Cathedral, and with all the prestige of venerable antiquity fairly exuding from it. These were men to believe in order and authority—at least if they exercised the authority themselves. Knowing that they formed the intellectual elite of the colony, the clergy, in spite of individual wrangling, possessed a remarkable *esprit de corps*. This enabled them to become not only a part but the ruling part of the Massachusetts oligarchy. For fifty years, the important names in Massachusetts history were, with few exceptions, the names of clergymen.

Charles Andrews, while asserting that "the Massachusetts Bay Colony was founded primarily for religion and not for trade," [3] and admitting that there were times "when, in some respects, the functions of church and state would seem to have been interchangeable," [4] still insists that "Massachusetts was not a theocracy, as it has far too often been called, for the influence of the clergy was entirely unofficial and without the sanction of law," [5] since they acted purely in an advisory capacity sanctioned only by custom. This argument seems to the present writer a legalistic splitting of

[3] Charles M. Andrews, *The Colonial Period of American History* (New Haven: Yale University Press, 1934), I, 462.
[4] *Ibid.*, p. 450.
[5] *Ibid.*, p. 448.

hairs. Theocracy is, by definition, "the rule of God," as democracy is "the rule of the people," and in this, its literal and essential meaning, it was the avowed aim of both the clergy and magistrates in Massachusetts. The actual situation was a direct inheritance from medievalism. Formally, both Roman Catholics and Puritans accepted the separation of church and state—but only on the condition that "the temporal power" should carry out the aims of "the spiritual power." Obviously, government by the will of God would be the best of all possible governments, if the will of God could be surely known. That it could be so known, through the infallible Bible "properly" interpreted, was the common assumption of all Protestants except the radical continental sects who as yet had made little headway in England and none in America. The disputes were over the logically secondary though actually primary question as to who had the right to interpret the will of God, and here a century of warfare had brought little enlightenment. From "the divine right of the Pope" to "the divine right of the King" measured the progress of Anglican England; from "the divine right of the King" to "the divine right of the clergy and magistrates" measured that of Massachusetts.

The Calvinistic ideal of government,[6] realized in Massachusetts, was perfectly expressed by John Cotton: "It is better that the commonwealth be fashioned to the setting forth of God's house, which is his church, than to accomodate the church frame to the civil state. Democracy, I do not conceive that ever God did ordain as a fit government either for church or commonwealth. . . . As for monarchy and aristocracy, they are both of them clearly approved, and directed in scripture, yet so as referreth the sovereignty to Himself and setteth up Theocracy in both, as the best form of government in the commonwealth as well as in the church."

As early as 1631 in Massachusetts the church obtained a strangle hold on the state through the passage of an enactment reading, "For time to come no man shall be admitted to the freedom of this body politic but such as are members of some of the churches within the limits of the same." This measure indirectly gave the clergy a con-

[6] The New England Puritans were much more directly influenced by such English Calvinists as William Ames, John Preston, and Richard Baxter than by Calvin himself, but Calvinism, even at third hand, did not depart widely from the founder's fundamental positions.

trol of the vote, since in order to become a church member and thereby a voter it was necessary for the applicant, after a public confession of sin and conversion, to pass a rigid examination before the pastors and other church officials. In 1642 Thomas Lechford in his *Plain Dealing* attacked the theocracy in words that aroused in England much unfavorable comment on Massachusetts practices. "There is required," he wrote, "such confessions, and professions, both in private and in public, both by men and women, before they be admitted, that three parts of the country remain out of the church, so that in short time most of the people will remain unbaptized." The reply of the theocracy was simply to deny the facts. "It is not true," wrote John Cotton in his *The Way of the Congregations Cleared*, "that three parts of the country remain out of the church, if he mean three parts out of four, no, though he should take in those remote English who live a score of miles or more from any church." But it was Lechford, not Cotton, who was telling the truth. In actual fact, the discrimination was even greater than Lechford knew. Up to 1643, out of about fifteen thousand inhabitants only seventeen hundred and eight had been permitted to become freemen, and in that year in Boston there were, in a population of three thousand, only two hundred and thirty freemen. The inequity had been less objectionable at first when none but the freemen were taxed for the support of the clergy, but after 1638 every resident in the colony was taxed for that purpose.

One fatal concession, however, was made by the oligarchy in the very beginning. Following the example of Plymouth, lands were apportioned by the various towns to their members on the principle of ownership in fee simple. This seemed at the outset merely a prudent measure calculated to bring immigrants to the colony, and it took many years for the results to appear; yet this single measure determined the ultimate fate of New England. For eventually, men enjoying some degree of economic independence are certain to demand a similar independence in the religious and political spheres.

CHAPTER 9 . *The Rebellion that Became Rhode Island*

THE HERESIES OF ROGER WILLIAMS

DURING the decade from 1630 to 1640 the clerical oligarchy of Massachusetts carried on a determined campaign to increase its authority. The campaign was successful, but the clergy did not win without fighting many a costly battle.

In the first year the recalcitrants were few and unimportant. A man named Henry Lyon was flogged for blasphemy, and one Ratcliffe had his ears cropped for the same offense. Thomas Foxe threatened to appeal to England against the intolerant customs of Massachusetts Bay and was taught to bridle his tongue by exposure in the stocks. But such sporadic instances of discontent and harsh punishment might have been found almost anywhere.

In was different when in 1631 the newly arrived Roger Williams challenged the authority of the colony. Here was a man to be put in the balance against all the magistrates and clergy of Massachusetts and in the judgment of posterity to outweigh them all. The profoundest thinker that England gave to American history, one of the noblest and purest Christians that ever crossed the Atlantic, in him the Reformation justified and redeemed itself.

Unfortunately, little is known of Williams' early life or of the influences that molded his ideas. Born of poor parents in London in 1603, as a lad he attracted the attention of Sir Edward Coke by his skill in reporting the speeches of the Star Chamber and through Coke's patronage was enabled to attend the best of charity schools, Sutton's Hospital (later the Charterhouse), and to complete his academic education at the University of Cambridge. From Cambridge into the Anglican ministry as a Puritan was then the natural course, which led Williams to an attractive benefice in Lincolnshire. How far his ideas had developed at that time there is no means of knowing. He tells of being acquainted with John Cotton, John Eliot, and Thomas Hooker, with whom on one occasion he took an extensive journey on horseback. It would be interesting to have overheard their conversation. Gathered together were the future leader of Massachusetts Bay, the "Apostle to the Indians," the founder of Connecticut, and the founder of Rhode Island. What did they discuss as they rode on together? The plans for the impending emigration to America? The opportunity to spread the gospel among the Indians? The proper foundations of civil government? The nature of religious tolerance? A record of that lost conversation would be worth more to us than the Acts of Parliament for many a year.

Williams was the first of the four to give up his benefice and come to America, reaching Boston in February, 1631. He was at once invited to become teacher in the First Church as an associate of John Wilson—the position later held by John Cotton. But he found that the church had not yet been able to make up its mind definitely to abandon the Anglican communion, an action to which the conservative Wilson, nephew of a former archbishop of Canterbury, was strongly opposed. To the clear-thinking mind of Williams such shilly-shallying was offensive; when he had resigned his benefice and left the Anglican Church he had really left it. As he wrote later, "Being unanimously chosen teacher at Boston, I conscientiously refused, because I durst not officiate to an unseparated people."

The second most important clerical position in the colony was at Salem, where the teacher, Francis Higginson, had just died after finishing a book in praise of the healthfulness of the New England climate. Williams was called to the vacant position, and since there was no doubt about the Separatism of Salem he accepted and began his work there.

But more than the question of Separatism had arisen during Williams' stay in Boston. He had defied the oligarchy on a more fundamental issue, and it was now to be heard from. As we learn from Winthrop's journal, "At a court holden at Boston (upon information to the governor that they of Salem had called Mr. Williams to the office of teacher), a letter was written from the court to Mr. Endicott to this effect; that whereas Mr. Williams . . . had declared his opinion that the magistrate might not punish a breach of the sabbath, nor any other offense, as it was a breach of the first table; therefore they marvelled they would choose him without advising with the council, and withal desiring that they would forbear to proceed till they had conferred about it."

Perhaps Winthrop was writing carelessly, perhaps the letter from the General Court was intentionally misleading, or perhaps, as is most probable of all, none of them were able to understand Williams' position. Winthrop's phrase, "the magistrate might not punish a breach of the sabbath, nor any other offense," taken literally makes the absurd accusation that Williams held a completely anarchistic philosophy that denied the right of the magistrates to punish any crime. If Salem understood that these were Williams' views, it is not surprising that the interference of Boston was effective, forcing him to withdraw to Plymouth.

What were his real views? The first of the two tablets of stone on which the Ten Commandments were supposed to have been inscribed by Moses was assumed to have been covered by the first five; the "first table" therefore included the commandments against atheism, idolatry, blasphemy, Sabbathbreaking, and filial disobedience. Roger Williams held that the magistrates had no right to enforce any of these five commandments which concerned religious belief and private morals rather than matters of the public welfare. But he also held, like the earlier Cathars, Lollards, and Anabaptists, and the later Quakers, that to require or to give an oath was in itself to "take the name of the Lord thy God in vain" and was a form of blasphemy more harmful than ordinary profanity; for what could be more vain than an oath, needless if the taker of it were honest and useless if he were not, and what more likely to degrade the Bible than to use it as a legal stool-book with a hurried, formal oath ending in "selpmigod"? The Puritans were never quick at understanding their critics, and it was easy to become confused by the coupling of Williams' objection, on the ground of the first table, to the giving of oaths, with his objection to the enforcement of the same table. Yet to one who could follow Williams' reasoning, there was no inconsistency in asserting both that the magistrates had no right to enforce the first table and that they were themselves violating it by their manner of attempting to enforce it.[1]

Beneath the Biblical terms, one detects the real issue. Williams was striking at the central principle of the Massachusetts Bay oligarchy by demanding the separation of church and state. In reaching his convictions on this subject he was probably influenced by the writings of Anabaptists and Baptists, as they were the only sects who held his advanced position.[2] At Plymouth, Brewster expressed a fear that Williams might "run the course of rigid separation and anabaptistry, which Mr. John Smith, the Se-Baptist of Amsterdam, had done."

In moving from the Puritan oligarchy to the Pilgrim oligarchy, Williams exchanged a set of severe masters for a set of lenient ones, but he could not feel spiritually at home in Plymouth. The story of his two years' residence there is recounted briefly in Bradford's *History:* "Mr. Roger Williams (a man godly and zealous, having many precious parts, but very unsettled in judgmente) came over first to Massachusetts, but upon some discontente left that place, and came hither (where he was friendly entertained, according to their poor abilitie,) and exercised his gifts amongst them, and after some time was admitted a member of the church; and his teaching well approved, for the benefite whereof I still blese God, and am

---

[1] The great Puritan apologist, J. G. Palfrey, in his *History of New England* (1858), I, 407, imagined himself to have confuted Williams for all time by remarking that blasphemy and Sabbathbreaking "stand as penal offenses on the statute book of Massachusetts at the present day."

[2] Apparently, Williams was never in Holland, but he knew the Dutch language well, in addition to Hebrew, Greek, Latin, and French, and could have read the works of the Dutch Anabaptists in the original. That he was familiar with the English Baptist work, Busher's *Religious Peace* (1614), is shown by a parallelism of language too close to have been accidental:

Busher—"Persecution for religion is to force the conscience. . . . And herein the bishops commit a greater sin than if they force the bodies of women and maids against their will."

Williams—"A soul or spiritual rape is more abominable in God's eye than to force and ravish the bodies of all the women in the world."

Hansard Knolly Society, *Tracts on Liberty of Conscience, 1614-61.*

thankfull to him, even for his sharpest admonitions and reproufs, so farr as they agreed with truth. He this year begane to fall into some strang opinions, and from opinion to practise; which caused some controversie betweene the church and him, and in the end some discontente on his parte, by occasion whereof he left them some thing abruptly. Yet after wards sued for his dismission to the church of Salem, which was granted, with some caution to them concerning him, and what care they ought to have of him. But he soone fell into more things ther, both to their and the governments troble and disturbance. I shall not need to name perticulers, they are too well knowen now to all, though for a time the church here wente under some hard scensure by his occassion, from some that afterwards smarted them selves. But he is to be pitied, and prayed for, and so I shall leave the matter, and desire the Lord to show him his errors, and reduce him into the way of truth, and give him a setled judgment and constancie in the same; for I hope he belongs to the Lord, and that he will shew him mercie." This was as far as the Pilgrim Bradford could go in tolerance toward the true founder of American liberty and democracy: to pity him, pray for him, and hope, without great confidence, that he might not be damned.

Far from being "unsettled in judgmente," Williams was too consistent in his opinions for his own good. Back once more in Salem, he urged again his old demand for the separation of church and state. Discovering an incipient movement for the union of the churches into a presbytery, he declared that such a governing body would be "to the prejudice of the church's liberty." He was the same Roger Williams, still unbroken to the yoke of ecclesiastical discipline.

One new conviction, but one as obnoxious as his others to the Massachusetts rulers, Williams seems to have reached while he was at Plymouth, although he may possibly have arrived at it earlier: the conviction that the land rightfully belonged to the Indians and could not justly be taken from them without their consent. At Plymouth he had spent much time in visiting the neighboring tribes and had begun to learn their language, a difficult task which he eventually carried to completion, publishing the first work on the subject, *A Key into the Language of America* (1643). He was by no means an indiscriminate admirer of the Indians like Thomas

Morton, who declared that they were "more full of humanity than the Christians"; on the contrary, he described some of them as "wallowing in idleness, stealing, lying, whoring, treacherous, [and given to] witchcrafts, blasphemies, and idolatries"; others he referred to as "miserable drones of Adam's degenerate seed"; but he invariably treated them with justice and was probably the first white man to enjoy their full confidence. He, much more than John Eliot, was the true "Apostle to the Indians." They called him their "right hand, their candle and langthorne, the quencher of their fires." [3] Above all, he understood and sympathized with their attitude in regard to the ownership of the land.

To the majority of the English colonists, Williams' contention seemed as absurd as if he had maintained that the land rightfully belonged to the bears and wolves that infested it. How deep-seated was the Englishman's contempt for the natives may be seen from the words of Bradford, who, after the Indians had saved the colony of the Pilgrims from starvation by teaching them to plant corn, still referred to them as "savage and brutish men who range up and down, little otherwise than the wild beasts." The English recognized only one major duty toward the Indians: to Christianize them—which, since they were such poor Christians themselves, was a difficult task. The last of six items of farewell advice offered to Winthrop's party by John Cotton before their sailing was, "Offend not the poor natives, but as you partake in their land, so make them partakers of your precious faith; as you reap their temporals, so feed them with your spirituals: win them to the love of Christ, for whom Christ died." Williams, also, of course, desired to Christianize the Indians, but he did not propose to reap their temporals in exchange for his spirituals; he believed that he could have "baptized whole tribes" if he had cared to win merely formal converts; what he had in mind was a much more profound Christianization and mutual friendship which involved changing the attitude of the white man fully as much as that of the Indian. Had he, instead of John Eliot with his ephemeral Indian churches, been put in charge of the missionary enterprises of the colony, they might have had a less lamentable result.

[3] Charles M. Andrews, *The Colonial Period of American History* (New Haven: Yale University Press, 1936), II, 22.

The ideas of Roger Williams as to the proper treatment of the natives conflicted not only with those of the Massachusetts Bay Company but with the settled policy of every European government except those of the Swedes and the Dutch, who alone insisted upon something like adequate payment for the Indian lands, though their agents often failed to carry out the requirement. In order to maintain his position, Williams was forced to deny the finality of the Massachusetts charter. Here as elsewhere he refused to temporize. Consistent at all costs, he publicly proclaimed that it was not the act of a "Christian prince" to give away lands that did not belong to him, and further asserted that James the First was guilty of telling "a solemn public lie, because in his [Virginia] patent he blessed God that he was the first Christian prince that had discovered this land," whereas it had been discovered much earlier, as everyone knew, by Giovanni da Verrazano in the service of the King of France. With almost incredible idealism, he attempted to circulate among the clergy and magistrates a petition asking for the abrogation of that part of the charter which gave the colonists a right to the Indian lands; it is a marvelous testimony to his persuasive powers that he obtained any signatures at all to such a document before it was suppressed by the authorities. The latter had no great love for the memory of James the First, they were not particularly outraged by the spectacle of a subject giving the lie to a monarch, but they were determined to keep their Indian lands, and they went into action.

A summary demand was made upon the Salem church to dismiss its pastor. The Salem church refused. Williams, wrought to fighting mood, endorsed the sending of a letter from the Salem congregation to the other churches of the colony, protesting against Bostonian influence. But the Boston oligarchy had its best card still to play. Salem was engaged in a controversy over a certain district near Marblehead, the title to which was in dispute, and the General Court let it be known that if Williams were dismissed Salem's claim would be recognized, but not otherwise. The bribe proved effectual, Williams' following melted away, and he was obliged to resign.

But this time the oligarchy was not satisfied merely to have him out of the clergy; it felt insecure as long as Roger Williams remained in Massachusetts. A law was at hand, passed by the General Court with Williams particularly in view. It read: "If any person or persons within this jurisdiction . . . shall deny . . . their [the magistrates'] lawful right or authority . . . to punish the outward breaches of the first table . . . every such person or persons shall be sentenced to banishment." This sentence was passed upon Williams in October, 1635, but as he was ill at the time, his exile was postponed until spring on condition that he cease to promulgate his views. But the clerical spy system having discovered that he continued to express the same obnoxious opinions to various groups of friends that met in his house, the oligarchy decided in January, 1636, to ship him back to England to meet certain imprisonment and possible death. Doubtless his old friend John Cotton and others regretted what they considered the necessity of this step, but more important in their eyes than the fate of Roger Williams was the establishment of the principle that there must be no criticism, even within one's private house, of the Massachusetts system of government.

Forewarned by friends in Boston, Williams, too poor to own a horse, fled on foot into the wilderness, accompanied only by his relative, Thomas Angell.[4] It being the depth of winter, their chances of survival seemed slight; but happily they came upon a settlement of Narraganset Indians who hospitably took care of them until spring. The two then went on to the Seekonk River, where they were joined by five other fugitives from Massachusetts tyranny, and a plot of land was purchased from Massasoit. Soon, however, word came from Governor Winslow of Plymouth that they were trespassing on territory belonging to Plymouth under Bradford's patent of 1630. Ostracized from both colonies, the exiles wearily moved on to the shore of Narraganset Bay, where they founded the settlement of Providence, so named in thankfulness to God for having brought them at last beyond the reach of their vindictive fellow-countrymen.

Probably by means of mortgaging his house and lot in Salem, Williams was able to purchase from the Indians a considerable tract of land which he divided equally among the settlers at little more

---

[4] Ancestor of the noted presidents of the University of Michigan and Yale University.

than nominal rates. A covenant, drawn up by him and signed by all, vested the government—to deal with "civil things only"—in the heads of households with decisions reached by majority vote. Providence Plantations was from the outset a miniature democracy, the first in America aside from the halfhearted Pilgrim experiment in that direction. It was designed, in Williams' words, "For those who were destitute especially for conscience's sake," and it had few other attractions. The original settlers and those who came later were uniformly poor—as those who follow conscience are likely to be—and the colony progressed slowly with no mills, no cattle, and no plows for agriculture. But it was the one spot in America where a man could think his own thoughts, worship God in his own way, and enjoy an equal share in the government. Its single street of log houses, straggling along the bay, led to the future.

THE FEMINISM OF ANNE HUTCHINSON

THROUGHOUT the American colonies, but above all in Massachusetts, the family organization was patriarchal. The husband and father possessed property rights over wife and children; the correct wifely attitude was one of love and obedience, the correct filial attitude one of fear and obedience. During the early period of New England history, when large families were a great asset in working the land, the chief function of women was to bear as many children as possible. The normal history of the New England family was that of an early marriage productive of four or five children and the death of the first wife, followed by a swift second marriage of the widowed father to another young wife, four or five more children, and a second death, again followed by marriage, the now aging male taking a third young wife, with still more children before the end. In this economically useful scheme of living, the clergy were accustomed to set a meritorious example.

Occupying a subordinate place in the family and with no place at all in the body politic, women had little incentive to develop their intelligence and when they possessed native talents of leadership soon learned to suppress them. Considering the future importance of the sex in America, it is interesting to note how very few women are remembered from the colonial period. One mediocre poetess, one notable scalper of Indians, several diarists and letter writers, Priscilla Alden immortalized by a phrase, almost make up the list. The others shine, if they shine at all, in the reflected light of their husbands. But there is one exception, Anne Hutchinson, the second great American rebel, who, a year after the expulsion of Roger Williams, lighted so large a beacon fire that the united efforts of all the Puritan clergy were hardly enough to extinguish it.

Eighteenth and nineteenth century historians were loath to allow her any merits. Long after Roger Williams and William Penn were safely enshrined in their niches there was still no place for Anne Hutchinson in the American pantheon of liberty. The Reverend Leonard W. Bacon in 1897 expressed what was still the general view in his account of her: "Mrs. Anne Hutchinson, with a vast conceit of her superior holiness and with the ugly censoriousness which is a usual accompaniment of that grace, demonstrated her genius for mixing a personal controversy with personal jealousies and public anxieties, and involved the whole colony of the Bay in an acrimonious quarrel. . . . She seems clearly to have been a wilful and persistent nuisance in the little community, and there were good reasons for wanting to be rid of her." (*A History of American Christianity*, p. 101.) Whether, as is implied, the reasons were good enough to justify the conduct of the authorities, the reader may judge from the facts.

Niece of Sir Edward Marbury of the manor of Girsby, and of Sir Erasmus Dryden who lived at Canons Ashby in appropriate state, Anne Hutchinson belonged to one of the best families among the English gentry. More important, however, than her social status was the inheritance of intransigent temperament which she received from her father, the Reverend Francis Marbury, who had come into serious trouble through criticizing the laxity and indifference of the episcopacy in the matter of securing educated preachers. Tried for insubordination to his spiritual masters, he spoke out with astonishing recklessness: "I say the Bishops of London are guilty of the death of as many souls as have perished by the ignorance of the ministers of their making whom they know to be unable." For such words as these he was first imprisoned and was then unfrocked for a period of fifteen years, at the end of which time his vitality was sapped sufficiently to make him a safe candidate for an obscure living in London. Francis Marbury died defeated; but the gallant spirit of his youth was reborn in his daughter.

Much more a mystic than her father, Anne possessed a source of inner strength which he lacked. At the age of twenty-five, she underwent a religious crisis which she was to describe many years later in a defiant speech before her judges in Boston:

"When I was in old England, I was much troubled at the constitution of the Churches there, so farre, as I was ready to have joyned to the Separation, whereupon I set apart a day for humiliation by my selfe, to seek direction from God. Then God did discover unto me the unfaithfulnesse of the Churches, and the danger of them, and that none of these Ministers could preach the Lord Jesus aright, for He had brought to my mind that in I John 4:3 'Every spirit that confesseth not that Jesus Christ is come in the flesh is the spirit of Antichrist.' I marvelled what this should meane, for I knew that neither Protestants nor Papists did deny that Christ was come in the flesh; and are the Turks then the only Antichrists? Now I had none to open the Scripture to me, but the Lord. Then it was revealed to me that the ministers of England were these Antichrists, but I knew not how to beare this, I did in my heart rise up against it, then I begged of the Lord that this Atheisme might not be in my heart. After I had begged this light, a twelve moneth together, at last He let me see how I did oppose Christ Jesus, and how I did turne in upon a Covenant of works. From which time the Lord did discover to me all sorts of ministers, and how they taught, and to know what voyce I heard, which was the voyce of Moses, which of John Baptist, and which of Christ: the voyce of my beloved, from the voyce of strangers."

Incidentally, two years before this crisis, Anne Marbury had become Anne Hutchinson, marrying a rising young draper in the town of Alford, twenty-four miles from old Boston and almost within sight of the high tower of St. Botolph's beneath which preached the great John Cotton. In the handsome vicar who spoke with the tongue of angels, and boldly, as angels should speak, despising the vain pomp and ceremony dear to the timid, Anne Hutchinson thought she had found the minister of her own and her father's dreams. William Hutchinson was intelligent, true, and loyal, and Anne was a devoted wife, bearing him fourteen children without complaint; but spiritually she heard the voice of her beloved in the voice of John Cotton. And when he, like her father, was caught in the toils of the church, but was able to escape to America, the Hutchinsons decided to follow as soon as they could put their affairs in order. It seemed a happy omen that the ship which bore them was the same vessel, the *Griffin*, on which their adored pastor had crossed the year before. The only drawback was the presence on board of Zechariah Symmes and John Lothrop, two formal-minded ministers bound for Boston, with whom Anne Hutchinson had many a bitter argument over the Covenant of Grace and the Covenant of Works.

Once in Boston, their troubles seemed over. There was a slight unpleasantness at first when Symmes and Lothrop succeeded in delaying Anne's admission to the church for a week after that of her husband, but this was soon forgotten and the Hutchinsons were welcomed into the governing rank of the colony. They acquired a house and lot in the center of the town, a house and farm in Dorchester, and six hundred acres of land in Wollaston, while William Hutchinson was made a deputy to the General Court in 1635 and was appointed judge of the District Court in 1636. Could his wife have silenced the spirit of her father within her, all would have been well with them.

In the course of her many experiences in childbearing, Anne Hutchinson had acquired a considerable knowledge of midwifery. Finding that the one midwife in Boston, the well-meaning Jane Hawkins, was as ignorant and superstitious as were most of her trade, she undertook to assist her and thus soon earned the gratitude of the women of Boston, whose chief occupation was childbearing. From the treatment of physical difficulties, she went on incautiously to answer the questions of her neighbors in regard to spiritual problems. Soon she was holding weekly meetings of women, and when the curiosity of their husbands was aroused to the point of demanding participation, she instituted a second weekly meeting for both men and women. In these gatherings she set forth her favorite doctrine that church membership and the performance of ecclesiastical ceremonies were no evidence of inner righteousness or sanctification, which depended upon a union with the Holy Ghost: the former was the voice of Moses and the Covenant of

Works, the latter was the voice of Christ and the Covenant of Grace.

Here was the ultimate spirit of the Reformation speaking for the first time in America, and it swept Anne Hutchinson's audience before it. By October, 1636, as John Winthrop wrote in disgust, "All the congregation of Boston, except four or five, closed with these opinions." Young Harry Vane—who, as old Harry Vane, was to be, after Milton and Cromwell, the greatest of the English leaders in the Cromwellian period—had been elected governor at the age of twenty-four, and he was an ardent follower of Anne Hutchinson; another was Thomas Leverett, ruling elder of the Boston church; another, William Coddington, one of Boston's wealthiest citizens. But the rank and file also were with her, led by such humbler members of society as William Dineh, the barber-surgeon, and Thomas Marshall, the ferryman to Charlestown. When her brother-in-law, John Wheelwright, arrived during 1636 after being expelled from his living in Bixby, England, there was a general desire that he be installed together with John Cotton and John Wilson over the Boston church, but as this departure from tradition required the unanimous consent of the church members it was defeated by the single vote of John Winthrop. Wheelwright, however, received a church at Wollaston, near enough to make his influence felt in Boston. William Hutchinson was firm in his support of his wife and Wheelwright. Their party, including every liberal element in the colony, had all but overthrown the theocracy.

Then Anne Hutchinson's mystical belief that she was a touchstone of ministers led her into needless danger. Ever since her arrival she had sung the praises of John Cotton, and now she began to make invidious comparisons between him and the other Massachusetts clergymen, most of whom she had frequent opportunity to hear in Boston. Cotton's vanity was too highly gratified for him to ask his incautious admirer to be more discreet, as he could easily have done, but he saw that her attitude contained elements of peril for both of them. With some vain idea of effecting a reconciliation, he took the fatal step of inviting the leading clergymen to meet Mrs. Hutchinson at his house. As might have been anticipated, the meeting soon took on the aspect of a private trial. The questioning was led by Hugh Peters of Salem, not a wholly illiberal person but profoundly convinced that the world belonged to men and to ministers, not to women; he was assisted by Anne Hutchinson's old enemy, Symmes of Charlestown; by Nathaniel Ward, the crusty widower of Ipswich who despised the nugatory nature of women and proclaimed that whoever tolerated "divers religions or one religion in segregant shapes is either an Atheist or an Heretique or an Hypocrite, or at best a captive to some Lust"; by Thomas Shepard, the haunted witch-hunter of Newtown; by George Phillips of Watertown and Thomas Welde of Roxbury, both unsympathetic toward Mrs. Hutchinson; and by Welde's assistant, John Eliot, gentle-natured but a firm believer in the theocracy. John Wilson of Boston, by this time in a frenzy of jealousy over the continued invasion of his domain, took careful notes of the proceedings. Against this hostile array, Anne Hutchinson had on her side only Wheelwright, Cotton, and Leverett.

The ministers wished to know whether she accused them of preaching a Covenant of Works. To have admitted this would have been almost charging them with Catholicism, and Anne avoided the perilous issue by saying that none of them taught the Covenant of Grace "as clearly" as did John Cotton. The discussion waxed warm. Symmes goaded her into declaring that he was not properly "sealed" to his profession: an awful accusation. The meeting ended with all prospects of a truce abandoned.

From then on there was open war between the factions. At a stormy meeting of the General Court, Wilson attacked Cotton in an unseemly manner, for which he was put on trial by his own church and was saved from censure only by the vote of Winthrop. The unhappy rift between the two leading ministers of Boston was felt by the General Court to be a public scandal; God might well abandon a community in which such shameful goings on occurred, to obviate which a solemn Fast Day was proclaimed. Since for either Wilson or Cotton to deliver the sermon would be to invite further controversy, Wheelwright was asked, but he ungratefully chose to improve the occasion by denouncing the whole idea of Fast Days. Men fast because Christ is absent; if he were present, they would rejoice; the institution was itself a confession that they were following the Covenant of Works instead of the Covenant of Grace.

The conservative ministers now determined to give no quarter. By a bare majority, they carried a motion in the General Court to condemn Wheelwright's sermon as seditious. When Vane protested in writing against this action, the Court refused to receive his protest. A similar protest from sixty other Bostonians was rejected without a reading. In the gubernatorial election, with Vane running against Winthrop, it was certain that Vane would have a majority of the votes unless something were done to prevent it; so the election was transferred from Boston to Newtown, where the rural communities who had been unaffected by Mrs. Hutchinson's evil eloquence followed their pastors to the polls to vote back into power the oligarchical machine. Winthrop was elected governor, Dudley deputy governor, and Endicott a magistrate for life. The Hutchinsonians in Boston did their best by electing three deputies to the General Court, and although the election was declared illegal on the ground that two voters in Boston had not been properly notified, a second poll brought the same result. The Hutchinsonian party were counting on the arrival of fresh immigrants who would not be under the influence of the machine's control, but they were counting without their host. As the greatest stroke of his career, Winthrop put through the first American Alien Law, forbidding any town to receive an immigrant without the permission of the standing council composed of Winthrop, Dudley, and Endicott. Just at this juncture, Harry Vane was called back to England by the state of his family's affairs there, and with his departure the cause of Anne Hutchinson and liberalism was lost.

The first Massachusetts Synod was immediately called at Newtown. It fulfilled the usual functions of a synod by establishing a blacklist of eighty-two heretical opinions. The list was aimed especially at Mrs. Hutchinson. Four days later, Winthrop arbitrarily called a new election to the General Court, and so disheartened were the Hutchinsonians that out of thirty-three deputies they elected only the stalwart three, Coddington, Coggeshall, and Aspinwall. The rest was now easy. Wheelwright was sentenced to banishment on account of his seditious sermon; Aspinwall was banished for signing the petition which declared that the sermon was not seditious; for the same reason, Coggeshall was dismissed as a deputy and disfranchised; others of Mrs. Hutchinson's followers were disfranchised and sentenced to heavy fines. And then, with her party routed and broken, the archoffender was herself brought to trial.

At the outset, Mrs. Hutchinson asked to be told the charges against her. Winthrop, who acted both as presiding judge and as prosecutor, at once accused her of violating the Fifth Commandment to honor one's parents, for were not the magistrates and ministers the Fathers of the Commonwealth, even as John Cotton maintained in his *Spiritual Milk for Boston Babes, drawn out of the Breasts of Both Testaments?* Without disputing that subtle point, Anne demanded wherein she had failed to honor them. By supporting Wheelwright's sermon. She pleaded freedom of conscience. Winthrop replied plausibly: "Your conscience you may keep to yourself. But if your conscience comes into act, you must be called in question for it, and that is not for your conscience but for your practise." But Anne had not signed the Wheelwright petition; wherein then had her practice offended? Forced to shift his ground, Winthrop demanded what authority she had for teaching the women at the gatherings in her house. She flashed a text at him from the second chapter of Titus, and Winthrop abandoned that line also, saying scornfully, "We do not mean to discourse with those of your sex."

But it was necessary to discourse with her if she were ever to be convicted, so Dudley brought up the subject of the ministers' meeting at Cotton's house. The ministers were all there, eager to testify, but when Anne insisted that they be put upon oath they objected. A long wrangle ensued, but she was so clearly within her legal rights that her point was carried. One after another, Peters, Welde, Phillips, Symmes, Shepard, and Eliot swore that she had said they preached a Covenant of Works. Her own statement that she had said merely that they did not preach the Covenant of Grace as clearly as did Mr. Cotton was supported only by Cotton and Leverett. But she had stronger testimony. The notes taken at the meeting by John Wilson had come into the hands of Harry Vane, and before sailing he had entrusted them to her. She had in her hands the evidence that her ministerial enemies had perjured themselves. And then in the moment of her triumph a prophetic madness descended upon Anne Hutchinson. She believed, perhaps rightly, that no matter what the evidence she was certain to be convicted; but her unjust judges should at least be told how the case stood in the eyes of God.

She began with an account of her earlier religious experience and then went on rapidly to its dramatic climax just before her departure for America:

"Then the Lord did reveale Himselfe to me, sitting upon a Throne of Justice, and all the world appearing before Him, and though I must come to New England, yet I must not feare nor be dismaied. . . . It was revealed to me that they should plot against me, but the Lord bid me not to feare, for He that delivered Danieal and the three children, His hand was not shortened. And see this Scripture fulfilled this day in mine eyes, therefore take heed what ye goe about to doe unto me, for you have no power over my body, neither can you do me any harme.

"For I am in the hands of the eternall Jehovah my Saviour, I am at his appointment, the bounds of my habitation are cast in Heaven, no further doe I esteeme of any mortall man than creatures in His hand. I feare noe but the great Jehovah, which hath foretold me these things, and I doe verily believe that he will deliver me out of your hands, therefore take heed how you proceed against me; for I know that for this you go about to doe unto me, God will ruine you and your posterity, and this whole state."

It was the old rapture, the old appeal from man to God first heard in the hills of Palestine two thousand years before. But the Puritans were well-armed against any reappearance of the Prophets in their midst. They knew that Satan as well as the great Jehovah could inspire rhapsodic utterance; and if Anne Hutchinson claimed to be able to distinguish true from false ministers, the ministers and magistrates claimed to be able to distinguish true from false prophets. She had hardly finished before Dudley exclaimed, "I am fully persuaded that Mrs. Hutchinson is deluded by the Devil," and most of the Court echoed him in the cry, "We all believe it, we all believe it."

Cotton tried feebly to defend her, and Coddington pointed out that she had broken no law of either the Scriptures or the colony. But Winthrop refused to tarry longer. Knowing that he now had the Court with him, he pressed his advantage and put the matter to the vote: "If it be the mind of the Court that Mrs. Hutchinson is unfit for our society and should be cast off from us, let them hold up their hands." All but two, Coddington and a certain Colburn, held up their hands. And John Cotton, for whom Anne Hutchinson had crossed the waters, the one minister in Old England and New England in whom she had trusted, the friend and counselor of twenty years—how did John Cotton vote? That Anne Hutchinson was no longer fit for his society.

She made one more effort: "I desire to know wherefore I am banished." Winthrop's reply was short: "Say no more, the Court knows wherefore and is satisfied." The trial—or mistrial—was over.

As it was now November and Mrs. Hutchinson was pregnant, the magistrates mercifully postponed her actual banishment until the spring. But she was to be allowed no rest. The clergy had a further duty to perform: although it was their painful obligation to cast out Anne Hutchinson's body her soul might be saved. To this end, she was removed from her family and virtually imprisoned in Roxbury in the house of Joseph Welde, one of her most vehement accusers. Here she was subjected to daily visitations from the clergy in a prolonged inquisition which amounted to a four months' infliction of the third degree.

One instance will sufficiently illustrate the methods employed. In the course of explaining her beliefs for the thousandth time, Mrs. Hutchinson admitted that she had some doubts regarding the resurrection of the body. The grand inquisitor on that particular day, the Reverend Peter Bulkeley of Concord, an ancestor of Ralph Waldo Emerson chiefly noted for his "thunderous voice," thereupon demonstrated that to doubt the resurrection of the body was tantamount to the "Familist" belief in free love, for if there was no bodily resurrection, marriage was not a necessary or sacramental institution: so a belief in free love was added to the charges against Anne Hutchinson.

At last, a list of twenty-nine heresies was drawn up against her. Even her indomitable spirit gave way; weary unto death, she allowed herself to be persuaded by Cotton and Davenport to sign a retraction of all her errors. Had she thereby saved her soul? No, not even her church membership. For the clergy now decided that her guilt had been too monstrous to permit of atonement.

On March 15, 1638, Anne Hutchinson was formally excommunicated in the solemn words enunciated with dignity by the Reverend John Wilson: "Forasmuch as you, Mrs. Hutchinson, have highly transgressed and offended, therefore in the name of the Lord Jesus Christ and in the name of the Church, I do cast you out. I do deliver you up to Satan, that you may learn no more to blaspheme, to seduce, and to lie, and I do account you from this time forth to be a Heathen and a Publican; therefore I command you in the name of Christ Jesus and of this Church as a Leper to withdraw yourself out of this congregation."

Meanwhile, William Hutchinson had gone before with the rest of the family except little four-year-old Susanna to seek shelter with Roger Williams at Providence. Leading her daughter by the hand, Anne Hutchinson in her last month of pregnancy set out to walk on foot to Rhode Island, accompanied only by her brother-in-law, the shoemaker Richard Scott. With her departure the oligarchy could breathe freely once more. The "Modern Jezebel," as Peter Bulkeley called her, one "worse than Roger Williams," as Winthrop described her in his diary, was gone forever. And ere long came good news out of Rhode Island. Although Mrs. Hutchinson had safely rejoined her family in the hospitable settlement of Roger Williams, she had suffered a miscarriage—a visible mark of God's displeasure. Winthrop sent in haste to Dr. John Clarke, the physician who had attended her, to obtain all the details. They proved sufficiently gruesome to provide John Cotton with the material for an edifying sermon on God's punishment of Mrs. Hutchinson. Soon further evidence of the divine wrath came to light. It was discovered that Anne Hutchinson's friend, Mrs. Mary Dyer, had in October given birth to a monstrosity in the city of Boston, but this fact had been wickedly concealed so that God's warning had gone for naught. Once more the prurient Winthrop was able to learn all the details, this time from the terrified midwife, Jane Hawkins, and he promptly had the monstrosity disinterred and exhibited to a gaping populace. Jane Hawkins was banished, and she and the Dyers followed Anne Hutchinson to Rhode Island. There would be no more monstrous births in Massachusetts.

Neither would there be any more freedom of thought in that hapless colony for nearly a century. Mary Dyer was to see Boston once more and find it grimmer than ever when she returned years later as a Quaker missionary and was hanged on the Common. The Quaker executions and the witchcraft madness were expressions of the same spirit revealed in Anne Hutchinson's trial, that of a ruthless love of power on the part of clergy and magistrates who would brook no opposition. Anne Hutchinson, as she knew, was better off in the free poverty of Rhode Island than in the enslaving riches of Boston.

"ROGUES' ISLAND"

CODDINGTON, Aspinwall, Coggeshall, and a few other Hutchinsonians soon foregathered with those already at Providence to form a new settlement. Roger Williams negotiated for them the purchase from the Indians of the island of Aquidneck, whither the newcomers removed to set up a government of their own under Coddington, who was given the Biblical title of "Judge." The motto "Amor Vincit Omnia" was adopted by the colony, and a solemn declaration was made that "none shall be accounted a delinquent for doctrine." There were now two settlements in America, Providence, and Aquidneck or Portsmouth, which were devoted to the principles of religious tolerance and the separation of church and state.

In spite of its irenic motto, Portsmouth was not free from dissension. Coddington, who had been such an excellent fighter against the Boston autocracy, began to develop autocratic tendencies of his own as soon as he was in power. His judgeship lasted less than a year, when he was put out and William Hutchinson elected in his stead. Wrathfully, the ex-judge gathered his followers about him and founded a separate settlement at Newport.

Dissension was added to dissension by the presence in Rhode Island of that heretic of heretics and exile of exiles, Samuel Gorton. He was an Englishman of good family, learned in languages and the law, who, possibly under the influence of Henry Nicholas the Familist, developed an interesting mystical philosophy [5] based on the universal implication of the positive and negative principles, which led him to a complete individualism that recognized only the

[5] See Gorton's *Incorruptible Key* (1647). For his conflict with Massachusetts, see his *Simplicities Defense against Seven-Headed Policy* (1646).

authority of a personal union with Christ. He denied all the orthodox dogmas of Christianity, mocked at the clergy, and had no respect for the magistrates. Coming to Massachusetts in 1637, he was promptly banished; at Plymouth he met with a similar experience when he defended the right of his wife's maid to smile in church; he was expelled from Portsmouth and then from Newport for refusing to abide by their laws, since, as he wrote, "I thought myself as fit and able to govern myself and family as any that were then upon Rhode Island"; he was refused admission among the freemen of Providence for the same reason. Joining with four disaffected members of the latter colony, he founded a fourth settlement at Pawtuxet, but soon quarreling with them, withdrew to found a fifth settlement with other followers at Shawomet. The greedy Pawtuxites then laid claim to Shawomet and appealed to Massachusetts Bay to support them. The territory was clearly outside of the Bay's jurisdiction, but nevertheless the Massachusetts authorities decided to act, for reasons incautiously recorded for posterity by John Winthrop:

"Four of Providence, who could not consort with Gorton and that company, and therefore were continually injured and molested by them, came and offered themselves and their lands, etc. to us, and were accepted under our government and protection. This we did partly to rescue these men from unjust violence, and partly to draw in the rest in those parts either under ourselves or Plymouth. And the place was likely to be of use to us, especially if we should have occasion of sending out against Indians of Narragansett, and likewise for an outlet into the Narragansett Bay, and seeing it came without our seeking, and would be no charge to us, we thought it not wisdom to let it slip." In other words, the acquisitive magistrates of Massachusetts welcomed the pretext to obtain a foothold in Rhode Island—which, had the plan succeeded, would have led to the annexation of the whole district, as surely as similar pretexts did later with Maine and New Hampshire.

Gorton and his companions were seized and carried to Boston, where they were tried and convicted as "enemies of all civil authority." The General Court referred the question of the proper penalty to the clergy, who recommended death, but the Lower House of Deputies succeeded in having the sentence commuted to imprisonment at the Court's pleasure. Actually, owing to popular indignation, the men were released after only four months. Gorton then went to England, to return triumphantly four years later with an order from the Crown forbidding Massachusetts to molest him in the enjoyment of his legal rights, and with a safe-conduct from the Earl of Warwick which enabled him to pass triumphantly through the colony to repossess his settlement at Shawomet, renamed Warwick in honor of his protector.

The lesson of Gorton's experience was not lost on the other Rhode Islanders. Even before his release, the various towns banded together to form a united colony and sent Roger Williams to England to secure a charter. Known and respected by Cromwell, Sir Harry Vane, and John Milton, he had little difficulty in fulfilling the purpose of his visit.

Williams has been much but very unreasonably criticized for thus securing a charter for Providence Plantations after objecting to the charter for Massachusetts Bay. No real inconsistency was involved. His charter was a mere recognition by the British government of the right to land which had been already purchased from the Indians and settled, and it came from a parliamentary government which he supported. The charter of Massachusetts Bay had been given before settlement and by a tyrannical monarch who was busily persecuting the fellows of the Puritans in England. Williams was quite justified in thinking that there were charters, and charters.

During Williams' absence, his old friend, the Narraganset chieftain Miantonomo, fell on evil days. When a quarrel with Uncas, the Mohegan chief, led to war between the tribes, the Narragansets were defeated, and in their flight Miantonomo, weighed down by a suit of armor which was the gift of Gorton, was captured by the enemy. In ordinary circumstances, Uncas would simply have executed his victim without ceremony, but he knew that the Narragansets had long been the allies of the English and therefore sent his captive to Boston for the Bay Colony to decide his fate. Political policy dictated that the colony should now seek the friendship of the victorious Mohegans. The magistrates, however, sought to avoid the responsibility of betraying their old ally and left the decision to the clergy, who, with their views that all the Indians were children of the Devil, had no scruples in recommending that

Miantonomo be sent back to Uncas. This was done. He was killed immediately upon arrival, and the new ally of the colony celebrated the occasion by tearing off a part of the dead man's body and devouring it.

The favor shown the Mohegans by Massachusetts was distantly responsible for the tragic death of the much tried Anne Hutchinson. She had always been able to count on the aid of her ever faithful husband, and when he died she no longer felt safe so near to Massachusetts. Accordingly, she and her family sought shelter among the tolerant Dutch in New Amsterdam. Unfortunately, Director Kieft was a rogue who sold her a tract of land near Pelham Bay which he had never bought from the Mohegan Indians who owned it. Thus, when the Hutchinsons innocently moved to their tract they were unwittingly nestling in a den of angry lions, conscious of new power with Massachusetts behind them. Seeing a white family on their land, the aggrieved Mohegans avenged themselves on the wrong persons by massacring the intruders, with the exception of one little girl whom they carried off—but who, rescued years later by the whites, ironically became the ancestress of Thomas Hutchinson, the Tory governor of Massachusetts at the beginning of the American Revolution.

With the winning of the charter, Rhode Island's days of danger were over. Under the wise leadership of Roger Williams, the colony slowly grew and prospered. Coddington, to be sure, continued to make trouble, but Gorton, once established in his legal rights, forgot his anarchistic philosophy and became a constructive citizen. To his influence are ascribed two acts passed in 1652 during Williams' absence in England, which were a century and a half in advance of their time. The first abolished imprisonment for debt; the second enacted that slaves should be freed after ten years of servitude. Though the second law, unfortunately, was never enforced, it at least expressed an ideal elsewhere unrecognized.

With regard to religion, Rhode Island remained in both theory and practice true to the principles of Roger Williams. It was the only one of the colonies in which complete religious freedom existed for all, Quakers, Catholics, Jews, or any others. Until about 1680 its constituency was mainly Baptist, Williams himself having imitated the action of John Smyth in self-baptism soon after coming to Rhode Island—though he later withdrew from the church, not from any ill will but because he realized that he belonged, rather, with the unorganized sect of the Seekers vowed to the eternal search for new religious truth. After 1680 Rhode Island came under dominant Quaker influence.

Baptist or Quaker, it was always "Rogues' Island" in the eyes of the other New England colonies. When the New England Confederacy was formed by Massachusetts Bay, Plymouth, Connecticut, and New Haven for mutual protection against the Indians, Rhode Island was refused admission. As a result, it suffered severely in King Philip's War, brought on through the continued mistreatment of the Indians by Massachusetts. The horrors of this war might seem to have justified the philosophy of Roger Williams, but at the time no one apparently drew this conclusion. It was not in fact until the nineteenth century that Rhode Island gained the full respect of the rest of the nation. Then men turned back in surprise and realized that it had written the first chapter in the history of the American democratic movement.

CHAPTER 10. *Liberalism and Reaction in Connecticut*

THE founding of Connecticut, which took place shortly after that of Rhode Island, was due to a more moderate rebellion against oligarchic authority. In this case, we have once more the familiar combination of religious and economic motives. By 1636 the shores of Massachusetts Bay were already becoming overcrowded, and the communities on the outskirts of Boston, with their wealth chiefly in cattle, began to feel the need for more pasture land. They also feared and resented the dominance of the Boston magistrates in the General Court. Three of these outlying communities—Watertown, Dorchester, and Newtown—had already shown their independent spirit in 1632 by defeating an effort of Winthrop's political machine to rule without calling elections. Thomas Hooker, the minister at Newtown, had tried in vain to secure an extension of the franchise to all freeholders who were professing Christians. Much the ablest thinker in the colony after the banishment of Roger Williams, he was, quite possibly, jealous of the Boston prestige of John Cotton. At any rate, he was willing to lead an expedition into the west to escape from the neighborhood of Massachusetts Bay. When in 1634–35 reports of the extraordinarily fertile and beautiful valley of the Connecticut River began to reach Boston, the disaffected parishes succeeded in obtaining the permission of the General Court to form settlements there; and during 1636–37 all the more energetic members of the three insurgent communities, Newtown, Dorchester, and Watertown, led by their respective pastors, marched off en masse, men, women, and children, on the two weeks' trek through the forest to found the Connecticut villages of Hartford, Windsor, and Wethersfield.

The Connecticut settlements were nominally governed for the first year by a board of Massachusetts commissioners who set up a General Court with deputies from each of the towns. During 1637, however, Hooker visited the ostracized Roger Williams in Providence and began a religio-political correspondence with him which naturally strengthened his own liberal convictions. As a result, the hand of the Rhode Island outlaw had a part in framing the future government of Connecticut, for on May 31, 1638, at the meeting of the General Court, Hooker preached a sermon which was to determine the character of the new colony. He declared that "the foundation of authority is laid in the free consent of the people," that "the choice of public magistrates belongs unto the people by God's own allowance," and that "they who have power to appoint officers and magistrates have the right also to set the bounds and limitations of the power and place unto which they call them."

To enact this program into law, the freemen of the three towns met at Hartford on January 14, 1639, and drew up a formal state constitution. It contained no reference to either the King of England or the Massachusetts Bay Colony, but calmly set up an independent state as a federation of independent towns, each of which should have equal rights and equal representation in the General Court and should retain all powers not explicitly given to the Court. No general religious or property qualifications were made requisite for the exercise of the suffrage, the requirements for which were left to the individual towns.

These "Fundamental Orders" of the Connecticut Constitution have been somewhat overpraised. According to John Fiske, "they marked the beginnings of American democracy, of which Thomas Hooker deserves more than any other man to be called the father." There seems no good reason why the recognition of Hooker's merits should thus carry with it forgetfulness of the priority of Sir Edwin Sandys, Roger Williams, and the Mayflower Compact. The Connecticut system was less democratic than that of Rhode Island in permitting the establishment of the Congregational

Church, maintained by public taxation. In both his political and ecclesiastical theories, as seen in his *Survey of the Summe of Church Discipline* (1648), Hooker stopped at the principle of local self-government by the particular town or church instead of going on to the principle of individual representation, asserted by Sandys and Williams, which is the real basis of "American democracy." There was nothing in the "Fundamental Orders" to prevent the growth of local oligarchies, which indeed was what happened, so that twelve years after Hooker's death the suffrage was limited to those having estates of thirty pounds (in present values, nearly one thousand dollars). The principle of equal representation for every town, regardless of population, which has been practically followed in the Connecticut Assembly down to this very day, has resulted in a relative disfranchisement of the larger cities which is anything but democratic.

Thomas Hooker certainly should not be held responsible, however, for the failure of his descendants to carry on and develop his liberal principles by adapting them to changing conditions. He did permanently establish a state governed by settled law instead of by the arbitrary decisions of clergy or magistrates as in theocratic Massachusetts. John Winthrop, neither so good a man nor so deep a thinker but a far better writer than Hooker, had expressed the Massachusetts idea clearly enough: "Whatsoever sentence the magistrate gives, the judgment is the Lord's, though he do it not by any rule prescribed by civil authority." To this Hooker replied in his crabbed but on this occasion forceful style: "That in the matter which is referred to the judge, the sentence should lie in his breast, or be left to his discretion, according to which he should go, I am afraid it is a course which wants both safety and warrant. I must confess, I ever looked at it as a way which leads directly to tyranny, and so to confusion, and must plainly profess, if it was in my liberty, I should choose neither to live nor leave my posterity under such a government." Answering Winthrop's oligarchical argument that "the best part is always the least, and of that best part the wiser is always the lesser," Hooker roundly affirmed his belief that "a generall counsel chosen by all" was "most suitable to rule and most safe for relief of the whole."

Meanwhile, within the limits of the present state of Connecticut, there was being carried out an attempt to establish a government "by the best" which was seriously to interfere with the liberalism of Hooker's spiritual posterity. A group which came from London to Boston in 1637 included the Reverend John Davenport, former vicar of the wealthy church of St. Stephens, and his ex-parishioner the rich merchant Theophilus Eaton, both of them members of the Massachusetts Bay Colony and men of mark. Davenport, who was a friend of Hugh Peters and Cotton, took part in the trial of Anne Hutchinson and is believed to have influenced Cotton against her. Objecting to the Massachusetts code of laws, not because it was too strict but, incredible as this may seem, because it was too lax, Davenport and Eaton decided to found a colony to their own religious taste on the shores of Long Island Sound. With a group of followers, they established themselves at New Haven in 1638 and set up a government modeled on Cotton's *Moses his Judicials*, professing to find in the Bible, in Davenport's words, "a perfect rule for the direction and government of men in all duties." Under this dispensation, the franchise was, of course, as in Massachusetts, restricted to church members, and the famous New Haven "Blue Laws" were adopted, under which Sabbath observance was made compulsory, the death penalty was affixed to adultery, heavy fines were imposed for entertaining Quakers or other heretics, and trials by jury, being "unscriptural," were abolished. Thus, among the American colonies of little liberty there was rather less of it in New Haven than anywhere else.

CHAPTER II. *The Decline and Fall of the Puritan Theocracy*

THE PERSECUTION OF BAPTISTS AND QUAKERS

ROGER WILLIAMS once wrote, in winged words, to the Boston theocracy: "Yourselves profess freedom of conscience, but alas! it is but self, the great god self, only to yourselves." The same phrase, "freedom of conscience," carried entirely different meanings to Williams and to men like Winthrop and Cotton. This appears clearly in Winthrop's famous speech on liberty, delivered in 1645, in which freedom was transformed into its opposite with a verbal casuistry rarely surpassed: "There is a twofold liberty," Winthrop asserted, "natural (I mean as our nature is now corrupt) and civil or federal. The first is common to man with beasts and other creatures. By this, man, as stands in relation to man simply, hath liberty to do what he lists; it is a liberty to evil as well as to good. . . . The other kind of liberty I call civil or federal; and it may also be termed moral, in reference to the covenant between God and man, in the moral law, and the politic covenants and constitutions amongst men themselves. This liberty is the proper end and object of authority, and cannot subsist without it; and it is a liberty to that only which is good, just, and honest. . . . If you will be satisfied to enjoy such civil and lawful liberties, such as Christ allows you, then will you quietly and cheerfully submit unto that authority which is set over you, in all the administrations of it, for your good."

Winthrop's distinction between "a liberty to evil" and a "liberty to good" was very similar to the Catholic distinction in justifying persecution, between the "liberty to error" and the "liberty to truth." Obviously, neither evil nor error is desirable; Catholics, Protestants, and all others would agree that the moral law and the supremacy of truth are the objects to be promoted. The fallacy in Winthrop's plausible argument lay only in his identification, smuggled in unobtrusively, of the moral law with the absolute authority of the contemporary theocratic government "in all the administrations of it." Admit the possibility of evil or error in the government itself, and the argument falls to the ground. But this admission Winthrop could never make. The magistrates, being in a state of grace, were free from the natural corruption of the majority. Hence he could set up, in the name of liberty, an absolute authoritarianism.

It may possibly be an oversimplification to state, as does Hendrik van Loon, that "intolerance is always the result of fear," but it was certainly so in Massachusetts. The theocracy well knew that the finespun arguments of its leaders could never appeal to the plain-thinking populace untrained in the art of casuistry. Hence their especial dread of any sects, such as the Baptists and Quakers, who had a popular following.

There were, in addition, three particular reasons why the Baptists were outlawed in Massachusetts: their belief in the separation of church and state was a standing threat to theocratic government; their rejection of infant baptism was a standing threat to Puritan dogma; and finally, they came from the colony of the dangerous Roger Williams. Nevertheless, there were a few of them in Massachusetts, cherishing their beliefs in secret. In 1651 one of them, William Winter of Swampscott, nearly seventy years old and blind, wrote in his loneliness to friends in Rhode Island, praying for a visit from them. Accordingly, John Clarke, the Newport physician and pastor, Obadiah Holmes, the pastor of Seekonk, and John Crandall, a deputy from Newport in the Rhode Island General Court, decided to brave the perils of Massachusetts in order to fulfill their friend's request. They accomplished their visit but were seized at Winter's house, dragged off to church, where they refused to join in compulsory worship, and were then taken to the

Boston jail. Clarke challenged John Cotton to a public debate on the doctrinal points at issue, but Cotton, still staggering from the recent blows of Roger Williams, had no mind for further discussion. The three Baptists, men of the utmost distinction in Rhode Island, were sentenced to heavy fines, or, in default of payment, to severe flogging. When Holmes, on hearing the sentence, exclaimed, "I bless God I am worthy to suffer for the sake of Jesus," the Reverend John Wilson struck him in the face, crying out, "The curse of Jesus go with thee." The fines of Clarke and Crandall were paid by friends, but Holmes underwent the full rigor of the law, receiving thirty lashes—the same penalty as that decreed for rape, adultery, and counterfeiting. Being of the stuff of martyrs, Holmes bore the torture almost joyfully, telling the magistrates when it was over, "You have struck me as with roses."

In spite of the courage of Holmes, he presented so piteous a spectacle as he came all bleeding from the whipping post that several of the spectators spoke to him compassionately; for which expression of humanity they were arrested and two of them were fined. Holmes had been so badly beaten that for weeks afterwards, it is said, he "could take no rest but as he lay upon his knees and elbows, not being able to suffer any part of his body to touch the bed whereon he lay." Such was the treatment accorded by the Christian ministers of the Gospel in Massachusetts to the Christian ministers of the Gospel in Rhode Island.[1]

John Clarke fully described the incident in *Ill Newes from New England* (1653). "Let him that readeth it," he wrote, "consider which church is most like the Church of Christ (that Prince of Peace, that meek and gentle Lamb, that came into this World to save Men's lives, not to destroy them), the Persecuted, or Persecuting." His account of Massachusetts savagery added further fuel to the growing English hostility toward the colony.

In Massachusetts, the immediate result of the savage treatment of Clarke and his associates was to cause President Henry Dunster of Harvard College to examine what Cotton Mather called the

---

[1] The great nineteenth century apologists of the theocracy, J. G. Palfrey and H. M. Dexter, elaborated a finespun theory that the visit of the Baptists was deliberately arranged in order to provoke the persecution of which they were the victims. There is no evidence to support the theory, and even if correct it would not mitigate the cruelty of the Massachusetts authorities.

"comfortable doctrine" of infant baptism more closely than he had hitherto done, and two years after the Clarke episode he came out publicly against the practice. The amazement and horror of the theocracy was unbounded. To be sure, the colony was under great obligations to Dunster. He had rescued the college from an initial two years of mismanagement under its first president, the miserly and quarrelsome Nathaniel Eaton, and during his fourteen years of office had raised its standards of student life and scholarship, had turned his own house into a printing office for the first colonial press,[2] and had impoverished himself by the gift of one hundred acres to the college. But the theocracy had a short memory in matters of gratitude. Dunster was not only dismissed from the presidency but was brought to trial on the charge of disturbing the public worship by his remarks on baptism. Although the General Court voted for acquittal, it failed to provide for the prompt payment of forty pounds which the college owed him, and it ignored a recommendation of the Overseers that he be allowed one hundred pounds in recognition of past services. The ex-president retired in disgrace to Scituate, where he ended his career in the anticlimax of opposition to the "damnable opinions" of the Quakers.[3]

The laws against the Quakers, whose individualistic doctrine of the "Light Within" assailed in principle the very basis of the Puritan autocracy, were enforced with a self-defeating barbarity which aroused in the populace a great deal of sympathy for the victims. In the instance of William Brend, according to a contemporary account, the prisoner was "put into irons, neck and heels lockt so close together as there was no more room between each than for the horse-lock that fastened them on," and in this condition he was kept without food for sixteen hours, after which he was given ninety-seven lashes, "so that his flesh was beaten black and as into a gelly; and under his arms the bruised flesh and blood hung down, clodded as it were in baggs." When it seemed likely that Brend would die from his injuries, the indignation of the common people rose so high that a demand was made for the trial of the inhuman jailer. This was only prevented by the efforts of the Reverend John Norton, pastor of the First Church, who asserted that Brend had

[2] Set up in 1639.
[3] Norton Memorials.

"endeavored to beat our Gospel-Ordinances black and blue; and if he was beaten black and blue, it was just."

To suppress the popular support of the Quakers, laws were passed that anyone who should defend any Quaker belief should be banished on the third offense, and that anyone who should "revile" a magistrate should be fined or flogged. The laws against the Quakers themselves year by year became more terrible. To flogging and banishment, ear-cropping was added, and, in the case of Quakeresses, burning of the tongue with a red-hot iron; finally, at the instigation of the clergy led by Norton, the death penalty was decreed. There were four executions during 1659–60, and more would probably have followed but for the interposition of Charles the Second, who extended his royal hand to stay the Massachusetts madness. By his orders, the trials were stopped, and the imprisoned Quakers released. It was the *reductio ad absurdum* of Puritanism that the beginnings of tolerance should thus have been forced upon Massachusetts Bay by a reactionary feudal monarch.

THE PERIOD OF COTTON MATHER

The hysteria of the Quaker persecutions in Massachusetts marked the beginning of the slow decline of the theocracy. The first generation was now dead or dying—John Wilson was one of the last to go, in 1667—and their sons were less firm in the faith. Already in 1648 the voice of the second generation had been heard in the Cambridge Platform which discontinued the requirement of public confession for admission to church membership, even from those baptized at birth; and a further step in the same direction was taken in the Halfway Covenant of 1662, adopted over the opposition of Mather, Davenport, and Charles Chauncy, Dunster's successor at Harvard, whereby baptized noncommunicants were allowed to be counted as members without any recital of religious experience. Had they been asked to exhibit the experience they could hardly have done so. The Massachusetts sermons of the latter half of the seventeenth century are full of somber references to the growing religious laxity. A statute of 1675 sounds singularly modern in its reference to the "loose and sinful habit of riding from town to town, men and women together, under pretense of going to lectures but really to drink and revel in taverns." Festivities abhorrent to the stern spirit of early Puritanism were springing up everywhere. In 1681 the law forbidding the observance of Christmas was repealed. By this time, Cotton Mather informs us, "gynecandriacal" or mixed dancing had become common. In the presence of such sins Increase Mather declared in the bitterness of his heart that "in the glorious times promised to the church on earth, America will be Hell."

Meantime, the clergy was suffering an internal moral decay, well illustrated in the pathological case of its best-known representative, Cotton Mather. Belonging to the third generation of the most influential family in Massachusetts, Cotton Mather had almost at birth an overwhelming sense of his own importance. Genuinely precocious, at eighteen already an important figure in the colony as assistant of his father, Increase Mather, in the First Church, he became an incredibly assiduous scholar and writer, amassing an unequaled fund of pedantic knowledge and publishing no less than four hundred and thirty-seven books, tracts, and pamphlets. Yet the source of this energy was an almost monstrous desire for admiration and praise. He is revealed by his diary—a treasure for psychoanalysts—to have alternated constantly between moods of inconceivable self-righteousness and fits of depression during which he would grovel on the floor in abject appeals to God, regarding himself as the most miserable sinner on earth. He devised moral precepts to bear in mind at every hour of the day, never paring his nails or satisfying the needs of the toilet without drawing farfetched religious analogies. An incurable hypochondriac, he recommended in one of his works as an "unparalleled remedy" for disease, approved by his own experience, the drinking of urine and the eating of human ordure. He has been much praised for his early endorsement of inoculation for smallpox, but one may doubt whether he was guided in this by the as yet unproved effectiveness of the remedy or by its nastiness.

At the same time that the theocracy was gradually falling into moral decadence and losing the moral support of even the upper classes, it was becoming deeply embroiled with the home government. During the civil wars in England, no British statesman had

had much time to give to colonial affairs, and Massachusetts had profited by this neglect to set up what amounted to being almost an independent state, with its own established church hostile to the Church of England, its own legal system based on the Book of Leviticus instead of the English common law, and its own system of trade pursued with entire neglect of the British navigation laws and the commercial interests of the mother country. With the Restoration, the British government had leisure to take stock of the situation. Massachusetts was from the first marked out for special and unfavorable attention. Probably nothing that the colonial government could have done would have sufficed to preserve the peculiar institutions which Massachusetts had developed, but the colonial magistrates and clergy, long used to the exercise of absolute authority, made matters worse by treating with studied contempt the royal commissioners who were sent over. The result was that whereas Rhode Island and Connecticut were able to obtain liberal charters which granted them a great amount of local autonomy, Massachusetts by stubbornly clinging to the special privileges granted under its fifty-year-old original charter brought about a situation which resulted in the revocation of that charter in 1684.

In 1686 the British government adopted one of those grandiose projects dear to the hearts of statesmen at a distance from the localities with which they are dealing. This was nothing less than to combine all of the colonies north of the Delaware in one regional district, to be known as "The Dominion of New England," under a single governor. The attempt would have been fraught with insuperable difficulties in any case, but the government deliberately courted disaster by appointing to the delicate office of administrating this vast domain the most unpopular man in the colonies, Sir Edmund Andros, the brutal and tyrannical governor of New York. With his new capital in Boston, Sir Edmund devoted himself to the task of crushing the independent spirit of Massachusetts, abolishing the General Court, depriving the town meetings of their power of taxation, and levying arbitrary taxes himself. For protesting against these measures, John Wise, the courageous pastor of Ipswich, was imprisoned, fined fifty pounds, and suspended from the ministry.

The governor's factotum, Joseph Dudley, was appointed censor of the press, to prevent expression of the popular discontent. The indignation of all classes of the people needed but the news of the landing of William of Orange in England to flame up in open insurrection. Andros was seized and sent home, and "The Dominion of New England" was a thing of the past.

Through the diplomatic efforts of Increase Mather a new charter was obtained from the Whig government; it was the best he could get, but it was far from satisfying either the people or the theocracy. By it, Massachusetts became a crown colony similar to Virginia, the governor to be appointed by the King and all laws to require the royal approval, although the colonial legislature was allowed to retain the exclusive right of imposing internal taxes. But its most terrible feature, in the eyes of the clergy, was a clause which abolished the religious qualification for suffrage.

THE WITCHCRAFT CRAZE

THE witchcraft craze, following close upon the Andros regime and the promulgation of the new charter, and directly fomented, as the records show, by the clergy, must be attributed primarily to the hysterical wrath of a ruling class suddenly threatened with the loss of power. The Reverend Cotton Mather might write delightedly in his diary on the appointment of Sir William Phipps as governor that "the time for Favour" was "now at hand" and that "all the Councellors of the Province are of my own Father's Nomination; and my Father-in-law, with several related unto me, and several Brethren of my own church, are among them"; it was evident to all, none the less, that the influence of clerical fathers and fathers-in-law was almost over, and that the long declining theocracy was now approaching its end. Put in terms of Puritan ideology, this meant that Satan had triumphed over the righteous, and to the mind of the Mathers the sudden outbreak of witchcraft was a natural evidence of the Satanic victory. As Cotton Mather commented, "Before I made any such Reflection myself, I heard this Reflection made by *others*, who were more considerate; that this Assault of the *evil Angels* upon the Countrey, was intended by Hell, as a particular Defiance, unto my poor Endeavours, to bring the Souls of Men unto Heaven."

Explanations of the witchcraft craze in terms of social psychology have not been popular with New England historians. For among the flowers of New England, Puritan apologists seem to be hardy perennials. Even in the twentieth century we have had such distinguished examples as Edward Channing, Stuart Sherman, Samuel Morison, and Kenneth Murdock. The last-named is the most intransigent. With courage worthy of a better cause, he upholds both the Quaker and witchcraft persecutions. In his *Increase Mather, the Foremost American Puritan* (1925), he writes: "We must remember that for a Boston citizen of the year [1657] to punish a Quaker was not mere idle cruelty, but necessary defense of the integrity of his state. Placed in the shoes of a leader of the time, believing as he did, and equipped with his understanding of his position in the community, and the purposes of that community, any one would have acted much as he did." With regard to the action of the clergy in the witchcraft cases, he says: "They did what most good citizens, divines or not, would do to-day—urged the prosecution of criminals." The former passage seems to say little more than that if one believes in persecution he will be a persecutor, and the latter passage ignores the point that the so-called witches were not well-known criminals but were merely accused of crime and that on the flimsiest evidence. Laboring heavily to prove the universality of the witchcraft delusion, Professor Murdock continues: "I find no record of any New England minister who disbelieved in witchcraft." Yet it was only necessary to look among the victims themselves to find the Reverend George Burroughs, one of the charges against whom was that he had publicly denied the possibility of witchcraft, and who vainly sought during his trial to be allowed to introduce evidence to show that the "witches" mentioned in the Bible were not "witches" in the New England sense of the word. And, as we shall see in a moment, there were numerous others who, without denying the possibility of witchcraft in the abstract, were utterly skeptical of its actuality in the cases under consideration.

The belief in witchcraft, it is true, followed logically enough from the medieval presuppositions that had never been discarded from Puritan theology. Granted the existence of a Prince of Evil permitted by God for His own mysterious purposes to tempt men and women to their destruction, what more certain than that some would yield to his wiles and enter into covenant with him? It never occurred to Thomas Aquinas, with all his rationalism, to doubt the existence of anything so entirely natural as witchcraft. But in the hierarchy of magic wherein such medieval aristocratic heroes as Dr. Faustus and Don Juan obtained by their compacts with the Devil all worldly wisdom, power, and love, ordinary witches stood at the bottom, essentially plebeian, creatures of popular folklore, embodying the petty malice of *Poltergeisten* and lubber fiends. Their stigmata were well known. A witch was usually a malignant old woman who lived in a hovel with a broomstick, a black cat, and an imp or two whom she suckled from diabolical teats, that were believed, with Puritanic obscenity, to grow on her privy parts. Whether she was able to assume the forms of other people was a question fiercely debated but never entirely settled.

However natural and reasonable the existence of such beings might seem, it was in actual fact impossible to find any who met the rather difficult requirements. Hence, the belief, first attacked by Reginald Scott in 1584, had long been slowly dying in England and America when the Mathers chose to revive it. Only six alleged witches had been executed in England during the Protectorate and only two since that time, while in the colonies there had been no executions outside of New England. In 1684 when a Pennsylvania woman was accused of riding on a broomstick, William Penn dismissed the case with the contemptuous remark that there was no law in Pennsylvania against riding on broomsticks. No instances had occurred in Plymouth, only one in Hartford fifty years before, and but two in New Haven, the last in 1653. Massachusetts was far ahead of all the other colonies, with a record of eleven cases between 1647 and 1691, but even there interest in the subject was waning, and in one of the latest trials the accused, although he confessed, was dismissed because of the contradictions in his own statements.

But in 1684, the year of the loss of the charter, Increase Mather, "the foremost American Puritan," brought the superstition back into favor through the publication of his *Remarkable Providences Illustrative of the Earlier Days of American Colonization*, about one third of which was devoted to a collection of old wives' tales in proof of witchcraft. The fact that the book was particularly praised by Richard Baxter for its "convincing evidence" indicates that disbelievers were already numerous enough to need refutation. In 1688 the malicious pranks of the Goodwin children in Boston led to the execution of a poor washerwoman, Goody Glover; Cotton Mather delightedly took one of the Goodwin children into his own household for observation, and publicized the whole affair in his *Haec Ipse Miserrima Vidi*. There can be no doubt that the girls in the family of the Reverend Samuel Parris, who started the Salem agitation in 1692, were directly inspired by the example of the young Goodwins. When the character of the trials seemed likely to arouse public indignation, Cotton Mather published an official defense of them in his *Wonders of the Invisible World*. His personal attitude is shown by these words written earlier: "Our Good God is working of Miracles. Five Witches were lately executed, impudently demanding of God, a Miraculous Vindication of their Innocency. Immediately upon this, Our God Miraculously sent in Five Andover-Witches, who made a most ample, surprising, amazing confession. . . . Since those, there have come in other Confessors; yea, they come in daily. About this prodigious matter my Soul has been Refreshed with some Little short of Miraculous Answers of prayer."

Our amazement at the number of confessions may be less than that of Cotton Mather when we learn that none of those who confessed was executed. That punishment was reserved for those whose personal integrity was too great to allow them to take the easy refuge of self-defamation. The first victims in the Salem trials were poor people, Goody Good, a beggar, and Goody Bishop, the keeper of a cheap tavern. Soon, however, the disease spread to include all and sundry. The magistrates, accustomed for half a century to dispense with careful legal procedure, hurried on the trials,[4] dismissing in one case the verdict of the jury for acquittal, brow-

---

[4] The apologists make much of the fact that the clergy of Boston, led by Cotton Mather, advised caution in the admitting of so-called "spectre evidence," testimony that the accused appeared in the form of apparitions. But in the same statement the clergy urged "the speedy and vigorous Prosecution" of the cases. No suggestion was made as to just how to reconcile speed and caution. See *The Return of Several Ministers Consulted by His Excellency and the Honourable Council, upon the Present Witchcrafts in Salem Village.*

beating and terrorizing witnesses, and after a parody of justice securing the desired condemnations.

For five months, from May to October, 1692, the trials and executions went on with an average of one death a week. The slightest opposition to the proceedings was likely to bring charges of witchcraft against the critic. The Reverend Mr. Burroughs, who dared to make the assertion that "there neither are nor have been witches," was tried and condemned, his execution being watched by Cotton Mather, the while he harangued the crowd on the virtuous lessons to be drawn from the occasion. John Procter was convicted and executed because he refused to allow his maid-servant to attend the trials. When Martha Corey, wife of the aged Giles Corey, expressed disapproval of her husband's attendance, this was taken as evidence of her own consciousness of guilt as a witch and she followed the others to death. Then the eighty-year-old Giles Corey, who had approved the sentencing of his wife, himself fell into disfavor and was executed with a consummation of cruelty by pressing to death between heavy weights, the process involving several days of continuous agony. Sadism itself could go no further. After the execution of Giles Corey, the frenzy began to abate, and the governor at last intervened to stop the series of horrors by terminating the Special Court which had been set up for these cases. Of the fifty-three accused who were still in prison, fifty were acquitted by the Superior Court in January, and the remaining three were reprieved.

Although no one else had been so imprudent as Burroughs in openly assailing the basic belief in witchcraft, a great many had been opposed to the trials. Among them were John Wise of Ipswich, always to the front in every liberal cause, who signed a petition on behalf of Procter; Willard and Moody of the Old South Church, who helped two suspects to escape; Nathaniel Saltonstall, who resigned from the Special Court of Oyer and Terminer rather than sit on these cases; Thomas Brattle, the wealthiest merchant in Boston, who characterized the trials as "Ignorance and folly" in a letter of October 8, 1692; Thomas Wilkins, John Tarbell, and Samuel Nurse, all three excommunicated for attempting to stop the proceedings. But the Mathers stuck by their guns. A year after the collapse of the trials, Cotton Mather attempted to start a further witch scare in Boston with his *Another Brand Pluckt out of the Burning,* an account of his efforts to exorcise the Devil out of one Margaret Rule, but this time he found few supporters. Eventually he confided to his journal a vague fear of "Divine Displeasure" for his "not appearing with *Vigor* enough to stop the proceedings of the Judges" during the Salem episode. Not even to his own diary would he admit that he had been the chief instigator through his books, sermons, and personal influence with the judges. Well might Parrington write, "Candor flew out at the window when a Mather entered the door."

In 1697 Justice Samuel Sewall made his noble public confession of having given unrighteous judgment when he joined his colleagues in the witchcraft sentences. The jury made a similar confession, and in the same year Robert Calef, a liberal-minded Boston merchant, finished writing his *More Wonders of the Invisible World,* a full and detailed reply to Cotton Mather's defense of the trials. The Mathers still had sufficient influence in Boston to prevent the book's publication there, and after it came out in a London edition Increase Mather, as president of Harvard, had a copy burned with appropriate invectives in the Harvard Yard. None the less, *More Wonders* accomplished its mission. There may be exaggeration in Charles W. Upham's assertion that "Calef's book drove the Devil out of the preaching, the literature, and the popular sentiment of the world," [5] but at least in New England it achieved that result. The belief in Hell was not immediately affected, but the first step toward loosening the sway of Hell over men's imaginations was achieved in this dethronement of the monarch of Hell. Time would show that Hell itself could not endure when deprived of its ruler.

The ultimate reason for the decline of clerical power was that the clergy had lost the allegiance of the merchants. Calvinism could not possibly survive indefinitely in an era of commerce. It had helped to create such an era through its idealization of acquisitiveness as a part of one's calling. But the time had come for the camel to swallow the tent. One cannot successfully sell goods to another or buy goods from him if he insists upon continually pointing out

[5] Charles W. Upham, *Salem Witchcraft and Cotton Mather* (Morrisania, N. Y.: 1869), p. 83.

the other's sinfulness. As the seventeenth century grew old it discovered, at first with amazement, then with relief, that tolerance, not intolerance, is the life of trade. Nowhere else was this discovery more welcome than in mercantile Boston. The merchants, who had once been the main support of the clergy in keeping the lower classes in their due place, now joined the latter, for the time being, in attacking the rule of the clergy; and they brought to the attack resources which the lower classes never had had.

It was the merchant class represented by the Brattles and Calef which at long last rescued Massachusetts from ecclesiastical tyranny. The final conflict was between the Brattles and Mathers over the control of Harvard College. William and Thomas Brattle had been classmates of Cotton Mather. William first became a tutor in Harvard, where his heroism during a smallpox epidemic earned him the affectionate name of "Father of the College," and later he became pastor of the Cambridge Church, the first in Massachusetts since the time of Roger Williams to have the opportunity of listening to sermons that emphasized God's love and Christ's universal mission of salvation. His brother, Thomas, the merchant, was the chief organizer in 1698 of the liberal Brattle Street Church in Boston which discarded the relation of religious experience as a requirement for membership. Both were members of the Harvard Corporation, and it was war to the death between them and the Mathers. The first battle was won by the conservatives when Increase Mather obtained a new charter for the college from the General Court giving him despotic powers which he used to appoint his personal friends (whose first act was to confer the degree of D.D. upon him), and to exclude from the Corporation the two Brattles and John Leverett, the most progressive teacher in the college. But victory later inclined to the other side when the charter was nullified in England, and the campaign closed decisively with the resignation of Increase Mather in 1701.

This was really the end of the theocracy in Massachusetts. When, after losing control of the political government, the clergy also lost control of the seat of learning its autocratic power was a thing of the past. The Mathers made a desperate attempt to retain at least the clerical rule in the church itself, but even here they were defeated. When in 1705 Cotton Mather launched a "Proposal" for a "consociation of the churches" on the Presbyterian model so as to give greater influence to the ministerial association, its only importance in Massachusetts was to occasion the writing by John Wise of the two most memorable and influential works on ecclesiastical government ever to come from a New England pen— *The Churches Quarrel Espoused* (1710) and *Vindication of the Government of the New England Churches* (1717), both reissued in 1772 and during the long interval accepted as the most authoritative statement of the principles of New England Congregationalism.

Wise, who was versed in political doctrine as well as in theology and was much under the influence of the theory of natural rights as put forth in Pufendorf's *De Jure Naturae et Gentium* (1672), showed how the various kinds of civil government had been paralleled in the government of the churches: monarchy under the Pope and the Anglican King, aristocracy in Presbyterianism and the Massachusetts oligarchy, and democracy in the original form and intent of Congregationalism. Wise met the theocratic argument advanced by Winthrop and others in support of "government by the best" with a realistic appeal to experience:

"Though we should rely upon the best of men, especially if we remember what is in the hearts of good men (namely, much ignorance, abundance of small ends, many times cloaked with a high pretense in religion; pride skulking and often breeding revenge upon a small affront, and blown up by a pretended zeal, yet really and truly by nothing more divine than interest or ill nature), and also considering how very uncertain we are of the real goodness of those we esteem good men . . . it cannot consist with the light of nature to venture again upon such perils, especially if we can find a safer way home.

". . . If there be any of the regular forms of government settled in the church of God, it must needs be . . . a democracy. . . . Government was never established by God or nature, to give one man a prerogative to insult over another. . . . The end of all good government is to cultivate humanity, and promote the happiness of all, and the good of every man in his rights, his life, liberty, estate, honor, etc., without injury or abuse to any."

Thus the principles for which Anne Hutchinson, Roger Williams, the Baptists, and the Quakers had struggled and suffered were at last accepted in the land of their oppression, accepted and given clearer expression than had been possible for the early leaders themselves, immersed as they were in the thick of the conflict. And not only were the former outlaws alive again and triumphant in John Wise, but Thomas Jefferson and the Declaration of Independence were already foreshadowed.

CHAPTER 12. *Tolerance and Intolerance in Maryland*

THE essentially experimental nature of American colonization is well brought out by the amazing adventure of Roman Catholic Maryland, which would be quite incredible if it had not actually happened. At a time when Catholics were not allowed to hold public office in England and no open celebration of the mass was permitted, a Catholic nobleman was nevertheless able to become, with the royal approval, the virtually independent ruler of a vast domain in America and to set up peacefully a government under Catholic control with a local church directed by that most hated and feared of all groups, the Jesuits. And this government and church proved themselves more tolerant than any Protestant group had yet been when once established in power. For a time, at least, Maryland was the one place in the world where Catholics and Protestants could and did live peaceably side by side with mutual forbearance. This was the great lesson of the Maryland experiment, and as a lesson it was more significant than certain other features of the enterprise that were thoroughly reactionary and anachronistic.

The idea of creating a place of refuge in America for the persecuted Catholics of England was not original with Lord Baltimore, the founder of Maryland. It had previously occurred to his relative, Sir Thomas Arundell, who with the aid of Shakespeare's generous patron, the Earl of Southampton, sent an expedition under

171

George Waymouth in 1605 to explore the country with this end in view. Waymouth charted the coasts of Massachusetts and Maine, but accomplished no more in the way of religion than to set up crosses wherever he landed and to kidnap five Indians whose subsequent exhibition as a sort of strange animal in England helped to add to the general interest in the new continent. From that time the Catholic project seems to have slumbered until it was taken up by Lord Baltimore twenty-five years later.

Sir George Calvert, the first Baron Baltimore, was a Protestant already well launched on a political career as a member of Parliament and one of the chief secretaries of state before his conversion to Catholicism. That he chose to change his religion when it was highly disadvantageous and even somewhat dangerous to do so is sufficiently eloquent testimony to his sincerity. But it did not mean that he was without personal ambition. As a nobleman of great wealth, keenly aware of the opportunities across the Atlantic, he early became interested in colonization, invested in the stock of both the Virginia Company and the Council for New England, and in 1622 started his own personal colony of "Avalon" in the island of Newfoundland. On visiting his settlement in 1627–28, however, he was sorely disappointed because, as he wrote, "from the middle of October to the midst of May there is a sadd face of wynter upon all this land . . . the air so intolerable cold as it is hardly to be endured." Seeking a more favorable seat for a colony he visited Virginia but was not allowed to remain, since he refused to subscribe to the Act of Supremacy denying both the spiritual and temporal authority of the Pope. Pleased with the climate, he now conceived the idea of a major Catholic colony to be carved out of the territory of the defunct Virginia Company. He accordingly applied to the King for a charter to the land next north of Virginia, a princely domain of some ten to twelve million acres between the Potomac and Susquehanna. Unfortunately dying before the technical terms of the grant were completed, he had the satisfaction of knowing that his efforts were about to be crowned with success and that they would be carried out by his competent and devout son and heir, Cecilius Calvert.

By the terms of the charter which created the first of the proprietary colonies the second Baron Baltimore became the personal owner and absolute ruler of a territory larger than that of many a European principality. He had the right to apportion the land as he wished, to govern it as he wished, to enact laws, to levy taxes, to control trade; he was the chief justice of whatever colonial courts he might choose to set up, he was the commander in chief of whatever colonial troops he might choose to raise; he was everything. The King of England did not begin to exercise the authority over his realm that the uncrowned king of Maryland had over his province. The feudal privileges of the Bishop of Durham in the fourteenth century, extreme even in that period, had been taken as the basis for the extraordinary powers granted to Lord Baltimore in exchange for the annual payment to the Crown of "two Indian arrows."

The Baltimores proposed nothing less than to transfer the most antiquated features of the old world bodily into the new world. Their ideal was to establish a feudal Catholic palatinate held by them in fief to their monarch and ruled autocratically with only the smallest possible concessions to the rising principle of popular government. The bulk of the population would undoubtedly prove to be Protestant but beyond granting them freedom of worship no power was put in their hands. The deputy appointed by the proprietor was in turn to appoint his own council as a distant equivalent to the House of Lords, while a shadowy substitute for the House of Commons was created in an elective assembly to act only in an advisory capacity without the right of either initiating or rejecting legislation. In addition to the usual freeholds paying an annual quit-rent, there were set up by special patents some sixty great manorial estates, each owned by a lord of the manor as an immediate tenant of the proprietor. All the inhabitants must take an oath of allegiance to the proprietor and were to regard themselves as his subjects. Leonard Calvert, twenty-eight years old, the deputy of Cecilius in Maryland, was given dictatorial powers, being made chief magistrate, chief justice, and chancellor with authority to appoint all officers—nearly always chosen from among the Catholic gentry— and to make all necessary regulations for trade and commerce.

There was only one progressive feature in the whole scheme— the toleration of Protestants. Something too much has been made of this by Catholic writers. The Calverts could hardly have been otherwise than tolerant of Protestants if they wished to obtain a charter from a Protestant government or secure an adequate supply of Protestant settlers. The famous Maryland "Toleration Act" of 1649 was undoubtedly adopted for "home consumption" in England, where anti-Catholic feeling ran high at the moment and charges were rife that Baltimore's colony was a hotbed of "popery." The amount of tolerance in the act has been overemphasized. It was much less liberal than the declaration adopted in Rhode Island a decade earlier or than that passed six months later in the province of Maine. Tolerance was extended only to Trinitarian Christians; any non-Christians or Unitarian Christians were subject to the death penalty. Fines and whipping awaited all who spoke disrespectfully of the Virgin or of any religious organization as well as those who profaned the Sabbath by blasphemy, drunkenness, disorderly recreation, or unnecessary work. The most that can be said of the Maryland Toleration Act is that it was much less intolerant than the legislation of most of the other colonies. Freedom of conscience meant only freedom of religious worship; it did not imply any political freedom of speech. By a law initiated by Cecilius Calvert in the same year of 1649, with later laws of the same character, anyone who denied the rights of the proprietor was liable to a variety of punishments ranging from nose-slitting, tongue-boring, ear-cropping, up to imprisonment at the proprietor's pleasure, banishment, or execution.

The illogical combination of political autocracy with religious liberty was essentially unstable. The Calverts, no doubt, intended to be benevolent in their rule; they desired a colony of peaceful, contented inhabitants. Cecilius Calvert specifically warned the Catholics on the first voyage against any attempts to propagandize, and he consistently refused to allow the Jesuit order to acquire corporate property in Maryland. His ideals were aristocratic but not theocratic. None the less, the Protestants, who soon came to form the great majority of the population, found themselves under the rule of a small minority of Catholic gentry. No less than eighteen relatives of the proprietor, all but two of them Catholic, held high office in Maryland during the early years of the colony. The one resource of the commonalty lay in the popular assembly which struggled gallantly year after year to obtain some real power of legislation; but in the face of this popular opposition the proprietor refused to modify any of the privileges conferred by his charter.

All this must be borne in mind when judging the later conduct of the Protestants. The repressed Puritans of Virginia, rejoicing to find the freedom denied them there obtainable so near at hand in Maryland, came into the colony in large numbers to form a Protestant settlement at Portsmouth (later Annapolis). Like all Puritans, they were fighters, and after the overthrow of Charles the First they were able, with some parliamentary assistance, to put themselves at the head of a Protestant movement which obtained control of the government in 1654. In ungrateful return for the Catholic hospitality which they had enjoyed, they at once passed a law depriving "Papists and Prelatists" of civil rights, including the right of religious worship. The Restoration brought the Calverts back into power, but after the Revolution of 1688 there was a second popular rebellion headed by the ambiguous John Coode, a renegade priest concerning whom little is known except through the obviously biased reports of his enemies. Power was lodged for a brief period in the Assembly, but then the British government took it over and for the rest of the colonial period Maryland was ruled as a crown colony. In 1716 the last proprietor's son was able by turning Protestant to recover the rights to his annual quitrents, but the days of proprietary and Catholic powers were gone forever. As in all the other royal colonies, the Church of England was nominally established, and the Catholics were once more subjected to the same discriminations that had originally led to the founding of the Maryland colony. On the other hand, the powers long sought by the Assembly were granted, the royal governor's authority was limited as that of the proprietor had never been, and a far greater approach toward popular government was made than would ever have been possible under the Calverts.

CHAPTER 13. *The Rise and Rule of the Quakers*

FROM Cathars to Waldenses—from Waldenses to Lollards—from Lollards to Moravians—from Moravians to Anabaptists—from Anabaptists to Baptists—from Baptists to Quakers. The line of descent is perfectly clear. It does not matter that there are broken links in the chain where direct influence must be inferred rather than proved. One may, if he wishes, argue that the whole chain is merely a striking example of the truth that similar conditions produce similar results. Fox, the Quaker, would certainly have said that the likeness of ideas among all these groups of radical Protestants testified to a common source and that that source was God. The important point for us is that century after century the same cluster of ideas appeared and reappeared, now in one country, now in another, but always in the same lowly social class and always representing the extreme left wing of the Reformation.

In all this movement the germinal idea never perished: that religion is not a matter of external ritual or ecclesiastical organization but an inner attitude of the individual spirit. This attitude, believed to be directly inspired by God, again and again issued in a similar code of ethical conduct. Both the attitude and the code were too exalted to be maintained continuously; time after time there was relapse into formalism, to be followed by a fresh emergence of the original spirit in some other group. The Quakers represented the last high point of the movement. As William James well said: "So far as our Christian sects to-day are evolving into liberality, they are simply reverting in essence to the position which Fox and the early Quakers so long ago assumed. . . . In a day of shams, it was a religion of veracity, rooted in spiritual inwardness." [1]

GEORGE FOX, THE FOUNDER

GEORGE Fox, the itinerant shoemaker who founded Quakerism, was one of those unusual men who must discover reality for themselves. Although both his parents were strict Puritans, and his father, Christopher Fox, was known as "Righteous Christer" because of his exemplary piety, the boy could not take his religion at second hand even from his father. To his direct, simple mind it seemed obvious that if one were really concerned with God nothing else could matter, yet he saw his fellow-townsmen in the village of Drayton-in-the-Clay, while professedly religious, greatly taken up with worldly pursuits and enjoyments. At nineteen, he seemed to hear a voice saying, "Thou must forsake all and be as a stranger unto all." There followed three years of journeyings and returnings, with reading of the Bible, visits to churches, hearing of sermons, and long earnest conversations with the ministers, but all to no purpose. "I went to many a priest for comfort," he wrote, "but found no comfort from them." Then suddenly one day there came to him the typical mystic experience, as told in his published journal (where the style was revised, but without changing the content, by friends better able to use correct grammar):

"When all my hopes in them [the clergy], and in all men was gone, so that I had nothing outwardly to help me, nor could tell what to do; then, O then I heard a voice, which said, 'There is one, even Christ Jesus, that can speak to thy condition,' and when I heard it my heart did leap for joy. . . . And then the Lord did gently lead me along, and did let me see His love, which was endless and eternal, and surpassing all the knowledge that men have in the natural state, or can get by history or books. . . . And I saw all the world could do me no good. If I had had a king's diet, palace, and attendance, all would have been as nothing; for nothing gave me comfort, but the Lord by his power."

[1] William James, *Varieties of Religious Experience* (New York: Longmans, Green and Co., 1903), p. 7.

Fox was truly a mystic, subject to the hearing of strange voices, to visions and trances, one of which lasted for fourteen days, but his intuitions were logical. He saw at once that God's love for men, of which he now felt assured, was incompatible with the Calvinistic notion of predestined damnation. To quote again from the journal: "the priests had frightened the people with the doctrine of election and reprobation, telling them that God had ordained the greatest part of men and women for hell. . . . I was led to open the falseness and folly of their priests' doctrine, and showed how they, the priests, had abused those Scriptures they quoted. Now, all that believe in the Light of Christ, as He commands, are in the election, and sit under the grace of God, which brings their salvation."

The unlettered shoemaker had recovered the essential spirit of the teachings of Jesus of Nazareth with their triune conception of God's love of man, man's love of God, and man's love of man. From these three ideas, inseparably united, flowed all of the Quaker doctrines. The limited class of the Calvinistic elect was broadened to include all believing Christians who truly loved God, the gates of salvation were opened, the nightmare of unavoidable endless torture dispelled. As sharers in God's promise, all men were brothers, who should not go into courts of law against one another, far less make war on one another. The only valid distinctions among them were those of personal merit; rank or wealth entitled no man to reverence, and to doff one's hat in their presence would be a constantly repeated outward betrayal of these convictions. So also it was not permissible to recognize class distinctions in speech; why should the members of one class be addressed by the respectful "You" and those of another by the familiar "Thou"? Brothers should all use the familiar term as a matter of course. (In this instance, the incalculable permutations of language, by eliminating "Thou" and "Thee" from ordinary speech, have reached by an opposite road the Quaker ideal of a uniform term—at least in England and America, more class-conscious Europe still holding to the distinction.)

In Fox's teachings, spiritual liberty and spiritual equality were united. The individual who followed the "Light Within" owed no obeisance to any other religious authority, even that of the Bible itself. When a clergyman at Nottingham maintained in a sermon that the Bible was the "light that shineth in a dark place" spoken of by Peter, Fox could not refrain from crying out, "Oh no, it is not the Scriptures, but the Holy Spirit, by which the holy men of God gave forth the Scriptures." God was not to be found in a printed book or through the ceremonies of any church, He was not the God of the dead but of the living, speaking to them directly through their inner experience. And one who had thus found God knew that all men were equal before Him.

Immediately after his illumination in 1646, Fox set out to preach the gospel of salvation to his fellows and at once began to obtain followers among the Baptists and scattered groups of Seekers in the north of England. In 1652 he was fortunate in gaining the adherence of Judge Thomas Fell and his wife, Margaret, of Swarthmore Hall, which became the center of the early movement. Its growth was now rapid. By 1653 there were thirty traveling Quaker preachers in the field; and a year later there were seventy. With his individualistic approach, Fox had not had the remotest idea of founding a sect or a church, but one grew up naturally among his followers. As soon as meetings became regular a congregation actually existed, and as soon as representatives of these congregations came together for advice and assistance, a church organization was already begun. These tendencies were recognized by calling a General Meeting in London in 1660, which may be taken as the date when the Society of Friends came into formal existence.

The radical equalitarianism of Fox worked immediately for the advantage of the suppressed half of humanity, women. From the outset, Fox welcomed women preachers among his disciples, and they well rewarded his faith in them. Such women as Margaret Fell, Mary Camm, and Anne Audland were among the most effective proponents of the new doctrine. They were the direct spiritual ancestors of the nineteenth century American emancipators of women—Susan Anthony, Elizabeth Stanton, Lucretia Mott, Lucy Stone, Frances Willard, and the whole host of women prominent in nineteenth century public life. Before the time of the Quakers, the only escape from domesticity open to women of the lower class was through prostitution. The reputable pursuits of literature, art, and political intrigue were closed to all but the wives and daughters of the aristocracy. Quaker feminism portended one of the profoundest changes in modern civilization, a change to be produced almost entirely by peaceful methods.

THE EARLY QUAKERS

ORIGINALLY, the Friends had called themselves the "Children of Light," later the "Publishers of Truth" and the "Friends of Truth"; the more modest title finally adopted best fitted the character of the movement. The popular term "Quaker" had by now come into general use, but its origin is disputed. So far as is known, a certain Justice Bennett first applied the word to Fox, as early as 1650, but we do not know the exact sense in which he used it. William Penn thought that the name referred to the trembling of the Friends under religious emotion in their meetings (in the same way that the more orgiastic Shakers came by their popular title), but perhaps the stout beef-eating judge merely made the common mistake of confusing pacifism with cowardice.

Never was such an imputation more unjust than in the case of the Quakers. For two decades, every prison in England bore witness to their courage and constancy. For the peace-loving Quakers were persecuted beyond all other sects: Fox himself was again and again mobbed and beaten and was constantly in and out of prison; a large number of his early disciples died as a direct result of their prison treatment. But none recanted. The testimony of Fox's close friend, William Dewsbury, was the usual one. When he went into his first prison he was a hardy ex-soldier of Parliament and when he emerged from his last confinement twenty years later he was a shattered wreck cast out to die, yet dying he could say: "I can never forget the day of God's great power and blessed appearance, when he first sent me to preach the everlasting Gospel and proclaim the day of the Lord to the people . . . this I can say, I have never since played the coward, but as joyfully entered prisons as palaces, telling mine enemies to hold me there as long as they could, and in the prison-house I sang praises to my God; and esteemed the bolts and locks put upon me as jewels."

The early Quakers had a fullness of religious faith and joy much like that of the Primitive Christians, and more idealistic than theirs as it was not inspired by expectation of any earthly millennium. Nothing could better show how far the other Christian churches, always excepting the Baptists, had drifted away from any understanding of Primitive Christianity than their amazing misconceptions of the Quakers. For no other reason than that the Catholics were also unpopular in England, the Quakers, further from Catholicism than any other group, were nevertheless accused of being in league with the Pope. Richard Baxter, who debated with Penn, could nevertheless write with complete self-assurance: "The Quakers among us are the ignorant, proud, giddy sort of professors, first made Separatists . . . and then drawn further by Popish subtlety, and now headed with some secret dissembling Friars, and by them and by the devil enraged against the ministers of Christ, and set upon the propagating of the substance of Popery." [2]

One must remember that the early Quakers were not the mild-mannered men that their prosperous descendants later became. They were fully as eager as the Puritans to reform the world. The very fact that they relied upon persuasion rather than force made them incessant propagandists. There can be no doubt that the first Quakers were quite as much of a nuisance in ordinary life as the Hebrew prophets or early Christians had been in their time. Comfortable citizens who followed easygoing accepted standards of business or pleasure were naturally annoyed by the perpetual intrusion of the idealistic demands of the Quakers. In reading such a passage as the following in Fox's journal, one gets a certain fellow feeling for the miserable worldlings whom he rebuked:

"About this time I was sorely exercised in going to their courts to cry for justice, in speaking and writing to judges and justices to do justly; in warning such as kept public houses for entertainment that they should not let people *have more drink than would do them good;* in testifying against wakes, feasts, May-games, sports, plays, and shows, which trained up people to vanity and looseness, and led them from the fear of God; and the days set forth for holidays were usually the times wherein they most dishonored God by these things."

Although Fox was far in advance of the other religious leaders

---

[2] Quoted in Elizabeth Braithwaite Emmott, *A Short History of Quakerism* (New York: George H. Doran Company, 1923), pp. 107–108.

of his time in rejecting the Calvinistic theology as well as its theocratic ideal, he accepted like them the Calvinistic asceticism. No faintest cultural interest was aroused among the early Quakers. They were as hostile as the Puritans themselves to drama, music, and art. They were equally humorless, equally intolerant of all forms of amusement. Their simple theology did not require the severe intellectual training which Calvinism imposed on its defenders, and they were suspicious of education beyond the primary grades. If their internationalism and pacifism could be taken to imply a general political program, the same could not be said of their economics, in which their reforms went no further than to attempt, like Baxter but with more success, to subject current business practices to moral control.

Fox took a justifiable pride in the business honesty of his followers: "At the first convincement," he wrote, "when Friends could not put off their hats to people, nor say you to a particular, but thee and thou; and could not bow, nor use the world's salutations, nor fashions, nor customs—and many Friends being tradesmen of several sorts—they lost their custom at the first, for the people would not trade with them nor trust them . . . but afterwards, when people came to see the Friends' honesty and truthfulness and yea and nay at a word in their dealings, and their lives and conversations did preach and reach to the witness of God in all people, and they knew and saw that they would not cozen and cheat them for conscience' sake toward God, and that at last they might send any child and be as well used as themselves at any of their shops, so then the things altered so that all the inquiry was where was a draper or shopkeeper or tailor or shoemaker or any other tradesman that was a Quaker: then that was all the cry, insomuch that Friends had double the trade beyond any of their neighbors: and if there was any trading they had it, insomuch that then the cry was of all the professors and others, If we let these people alone they will take the trading of the nation out of our hands."

Great would have been Fox's dismay could he have foreseen that prosperity would work with his people, even as it worked elsewhere, to weaken the very religion that caused it.

Persecution rather helped than hindered the spread of Quakerism. Six years after Fox began his preaching the new religion was introduced into Ireland and two years later into Wales and Scotland. It was carried to Barbados in 1655 by Mary Fisher and in the following year to Rhode Island. In 1671 Fox himself, with five followers, visited Barbados, where he made the first recorded efforts on behalf of the slaves, urging the owners "to cause their overseers to deal mildly and gently with them" and "after certain years of servitude" to free them entirely.

After three months in Barbados, the party went on to Jamaica, thence to Maryland, overland to Rhode Island, and back down the coast to South Carolina, where they took ship once more. It was the longest missionary journey in colonial times and was fruitful of permanent results. Entertained on the way by numerous Indian "kings" and "emperors," Fox inspired a confidence in the Quakers that the natives never had reason to lose. In North Carolina he found that he and his party were the first clergymen ever to visit that remote colony. The Quakers accordingly were able to establish the first organized religious community there. Fortunate, a few years later, in the appointment of a Quaker governor, John Archdale, the colony formulated a policy of friendship with the Indians, passed liberal land legislation, and enacted the first recorded liquor law. Over a hundred years later the North Carolina Quakers converted the young Bronson Alcott from a peddler into an idealistic social reformer; through him the long dead George Fox had a part in the rise of New England Transcendentalism.

Largely through the missionary efforts of Fox himself, Quakerism through its expansion was entering new fields of political and educational action quite uncontemplated in the beginning. In this new sphere, Fox was unfitted to be a leader. With all his intelligence, he had remained nearly illiterate; the mysteries of syntax and rhetoric continued to baffle him; and he never entirely overcame his early distrust of schools and colleges. He was decidedly opposed to any attempt on the part of the Friends to exercise political influence. The government in his experience was always wrong, a thing to be fought rather than controlled; power, in his view, always corrupted. He was, to the end of his life, the inspired peasant. No one can say what would have happened to Quakerism if Fox had had no successor of equal caliber or a successor merely of his own type. But by supreme good fortune it was to have in William Penn the very man to meet the new needs, and to develop and direct the new tendencies.

WILLIAM PENN, THE STATESMAN

No ONE seeking a religious leader to carry on Fox's work would have been likely to look for him in the family of the aristocratic Admiral William Penn, that stout navigator interested in seamanship, not in souls, who was a favorite with Cromwell and an equal favorite with Charles the Second. Nor could any Quaker in 1664 have looked with approval on the Admiral's tall, handsome, fashionably dressed young son, just back from two years on the Continent, where he had studied at the Protestant College of Saumur in France, traveled in Italy, gained the friendship of Algernon Sidney, become an accomplished swordsman, and been presented at the court of His Catholic Majesty, Louis the Fourteenth. "I perceive something of learning he hath got," wrote flat-spoken Samuel Pepys, clerk in Admiral Penn's naval office, "but a great deal, if not too much, of the vanity of the French garb and affected manner of speech and gait." Yet the foppish Francophile was no weakling. He set himself to master the law at Lincoln's Inn, then accompanied his father to the Dutch war, was entrusted with personal dispatches to King Charles, and from London was sent to Ireland to clear up the title to estates claimed by the Admiral, where he showed noted gallantry in helping the Duke of Ormond's son suppress a dangerous mutiny. By all appearances, here was a belated Elizabethan of the Raleigh type, destined for an adventurous, many-sided career as soldier, courtier, scholar, and man of the world.

He was indeed destined for adventure, but on quite a different plane. As a boy of twelve he had listened to Thomas Loe, the Oxford Friend, and while at the university had again been impressed by the Quaker's eloquent preaching. At that time, when the authorities of Christ Church ordered the students to wear surpliced gowns, Penn was a ringleader among those who resisted and who tore the gowns off the backs of the mean-spirited students who donned them—for which he was duly suspended and, on arrival at home, soundly thrashed by his father. But those days were now six years in the past, and the Admiral was comfortably feeling that his impetuous son was safely launched on the smooth tide of courtly success when suddenly he received the worst of all possible news. That son was become a Quaker!

The Admiral had reckoned without Thomas Loe. In Ireland, Penn went for the third time to hear the preacher, the meeting was interrupted by a riotous soldier who was roughly ejected, and, for this act of disrespect to the military, Penn with some others was sent to prison. A letter from him to Lord Orrery, president of Munster, in defense of freedom of conscience, promptly brought his release, but he then at once publicly joined the Friends, deliberately sacrificing his career, his aristocratic connections, and the favor of his father, who immediately disinherited him.

The fiery young convert was at this time as far as Fox himself from the meek and lowly Quaker of later tradition. In the spirit of a religious knight-errant, he began an exciting career of preaching, debating, and pamphleteering—varied by imprisonment—which lasted for more than a decade. Gifted with an extraordinary flow of words, copious powers of invective, the keenest reasoning ability, when he chose to exercise it, and a scholastic learning new to the Friends, he educated them in the art of persuasion and made their opponents at last give some heed to their arguments.

In this cause he counted no time or energy wasted. He went out of his way to challenge all comers—Anglicans, Presbyterians, Baptists, Ranters, and Levellers, in the purlieus of the court or in the slums of East London. He even sought out the shop of the madman, Lodowicke Muggleton, leader of the Muggletonians, vulgarest of the vulgar, who could hardly speak without oaths or obscenity. This visit was an unpleasant duty but one Penn deemed strictly necessary—for Muggleton and a certain John Reeve had announced themselves as the "two witnesses" mentioned in the Revelation of St. John the Divine 11:3, who should "prophesy a thousand two hundred and threescore days, clothed in sackcloth." Reeve had fallen and died in mid-course, but Muggleton was still in his sackcloth a-prophesying and must be refuted. To him Penn went, but when his simian-faced opponent declared with many oaths that God was the size of a man and Heaven exactly six miles from earth, the young Quaker was so outraged that he could only exclaim,

"Well, L. Muggleton, God will blast thee for ever, thou presumptuous and blaspheming wretch, if thou turnest not from thy wickedness." Later he devoted to the madman a special tract, *The New Witnesses Prov'd Old Heretics*, which Muggleton answered in a long volume of windy obscenity. Were such verbal conflicts the expense of spirit in a waste of shame that they seemed? Penn, always willing to cast his pearls before swine, never asked the question.

Thrown into prison for writing *The Sandy Foundation Shaken*, an attack on the dogmas of the Trinity and the Atonement which was rather an exercise in clever dialectic than an expression of his considered opinion, Penn proceeded immediately to write two more works while in prison, *Innocency with Her Open Face* and *No Cross No Crown*, the latter the most eloquent of his many pleas for freedom of conscience. Released after nine months, he was soon back in prison again, charged with inciting to riot at an open-air meeting in London. His trial proved to be a landmark in English constitutional history, as the Court sentenced the jury itself to prison for bringing in a verdict of acquittal. Penn, who had studied at Lincoln's Inn to some purpose, defended himself and his jury so ably that the case was carried up to a higher court whose decision established the important principle that no jury could be penalized for its opinion.

Admiral Penn, in spite of himself, could not help being proud of his son's gallant behavior, and a full reconciliation took place, through which Penn was to inherit on the death of his father an estate of fifteen hundred pounds a year and a claim against the Crown for sixteen thousand pounds owed as unpaid salary and for money advanced by the Admiral to the British fleet.

Meanwhile, in 1671 an unexpected opportunity came to Penn to draw up a form of government for West New Jersey, an almost uninhabited wilderness recently purchased from the proprietor, John, Lord Berkeley, by a group of Quakers headed by one Edward Byllinge. The "Laws, Concessions, and Agreements" of March 3, 1671, mainly Penn's handiwork, outlined a more democratic scheme of government than had yet been put in practice anywhere on earth. In West New Jersey, Penn wrote, "we lay a foundation for after ages to understand their liberty as men and Christians, that they may not be brought in bondage but by their own consent, for we put the power in the people." Legislation was vested in a single assembly elected by all the inhabitants; the elections were to be by secret ballot; the principle of "No taxation without representation" was clearly asserted; freedom of conscience, trial by jury, and immunity from arrest without warrant were guaranteed; a generous system of land grants was adopted, with insistence upon the recording of deeds (one of Penn's special innovations). Theft was to be punished, ingeniously and rationally, by restitution either in money or labor of twice the amount that was stolen. The three great aims—personal liberty, popular government, and community prosperity—were united in this remarkable document. The sincerity of the promoters was vouched for by their submitting the "Concessions" for signature to the more than two hundred colonists who made up the first expedition to the new province.

After several years there were five hundred West New Jersey Quakers comfortably settled in the flourishing towns of Salem and Burlington on the Delaware. But unfortunately Byllinge went bankrupt, leaving the colony without the financial backing for larger expansion. Had the Quakers had sufficient wealth they might at this time have bought East New Jersey and consolidated both regions in a single important province—for the proprietor, Sir George Carteret, was in trouble with the inhabitants, who, having purchased their farms in fee simple from Governor Nicoll of New York when New Jersey had been a part of that province, naturally resisted the payment of an additional quitrent imposed by Carteret. The best the Quakers could do was to organize a stock company of twelve, later twenty-four members, in which they had only a minority voice. Under these circumstances, the "Laws, Concessions, and Agreements," which Byllinge himself had failed to live up to entirely, remained only as a kind of dead-letter tribute to Penn's statesmanship.

THE HOLY EXPERIMENT OF PENNSYLVANIA

THE failure of the Quaker hopes in New Jersey gave added significance to a much more ambitious enterprise which Penn had long had in mind. Inheriting, on the death of his father, the latter's claim of sixteen thousand pounds against the Crown, in exchange for relinquishing this Penn obtained from Charles the Second a charter to the vast territory between the Delaware and Ohio rivers. Charles the Second could never resist an opportunity to be generous at no cost to himself and in this instance he was also motivated by real affection for Penn's dead father in whose honor he insisted the region be named "Pennsylvania." Penn, on his part, was inspired by the ideal of establishing on a suitably grand scale a Quaker colony in the new world. "There may be room there," he wrote, "though not here, for such a holy experiment."

It must be admitted that the frame of government which Penn drew up for his own province was considerably less democratic than the one which he had helped to devise seven years before for New Jersey. But it should be remembered that Penn had seen how those excellent "Laws, Concessions, and Agreements" had failed to function, and he was determined first of all to establish a system of government strong enough to survive. Thus he made its original constitution unamendable except with the consent of the proprietor and six sevenths of the colonial legislature. It was an early instance of that dread of amendments which was later to haunt the framers of the United States Constitution. Within this rigid scheme of government, a bicameral legislature was instituted, to consist of a council of seventy-two members (soon reduced to eighteen), one third to be elected each year—to whom was given the right to initiate all legislation and who were to be presided over by the proprietor in the capacity of governor (or his deputy), entitled to a triple vote; and a popular Assembly of from two hundred to five hundred elected annually—to whom was given the right of a veto on all legislation. The suffrage was limited by a property qualification, fixed at the possession of fifty acres or fifty pounds, in which respect the system of government, though conforming to what was now the general custom, was actually less liberal than that inaugurated by Sir Edwin Sandys and the Virginia Company in 1619.

Penn hoped to attract men of wealth to the province through his land policy. Estates of five thousand acres were offered for a hundred pounds with fifty additional acres for every indentured servant brought over. But at the same time Penn was not forgetful of his humanitarian aims, making provision that on the completion of the term of indenture every servant should be entitled to fifty acres of his own, carrying with them the right to vote. And, what turned out to be the most important provision of all, he offered to small investors blocks of five hundred acres at a penny an acre. Both large and small estates were made subject to an annual quitrent— the least justifiable feature of the whole scheme but one strictly in harmony with the proprietary custom of the day. As a matter of fact, the whole idea of the quitrents proved a delusion since, even had they been paid, which they weren't, they would have been too small to have recompensed Penn for his expenditures on behalf of the colony. The anticipated large investors never arrived. Instead came the tradesmen, yeomen, and peasants who gave Pennsylvania its distinctive character.

Religious tolerance was granted to "all who confess and acknowl- edge one Almighty and eternal God to be the creator, upholder, and ruler of the world and that hold themselves obliged to live peaceably and justly in civil society." The vote was, however, re- stricted to those who also professed belief in the divinity of Jesus Christ, and political office was not open to Catholics. Penn's tol- erance, great though it was, fell far below that of Roger Williams.

Other civil liberties were guaranteed as under the New Jersey code, the death penalty was restricted to murder and treason, and the penal system was inspired by the radical idea that punishment should be reformatory in its purpose instead of merely preventive.

Having sent over his cousin, Colonel Markham, in advance, to select a site for his capital, Penn set sail on the *Welcome* in Sep- tember, 1682, for a voyage which proved to be one of unusual duration and hardship. In an epidemic of smallpox which carried off one third of the crew and passengers, he showed his Quaker courage and tenderness in nursing the sick, but it was a weary shipload which landed after nine weeks at Newcastle on the Dela- ware. Undiscouraged by this luckless beginning, Penn energetically set out to organize his province. The first General Assembly, meet- ing in December, 1682, took only three days to pass the forty laws submitted by the proprietor, with the addition of twenty-one others; the three Delaware counties of Newcastle, Sussex, and Kent —to which Penn laid claim by lease from the Duke of York—were taken in as part of the province; and the resident Finns, Swedes, and Dutch were naturalized. The projected capital, Philadelphia, was carefully planned and laid out in four sections with an eight-acre park in the middle of each "for the comfort and recreation of posterity." In the teeth of a distant sardonic future not his, Penn expressed what then seemed a rational hope that the city would remain "a greene country town, which . . . might never be burnt and might always be wholesome."

Even before the trees were cleared, Penn set up a printing press —in contrast to the eighteen years' delay in Massachusetts, the seventy-three years' neglect in New York, and the actual hostility of the government to learning in Virginia and Maryland. In the first year, Enoch Flower's private school was opened, and a public school followed a few years later. Pennsylvania in its birth was a planned society and while still in its swaddling clothes was the most civilized of the colonies.

Not the least of Penn's achievements was his treaty of friendship with the Indians, described by Voltaire as "the only treaty between these people and the Christians never confirmed by an oath and never broken." Penn met the Indians with a complete absence of spiritual condescension, took part in their sports, beat them all in the long-distance jump, and aroused in them an enduring devotion. At the death of their beloved "Onas" seven years after his last departure from the colony, the Indians sent a sympathetic gift of furs to his widow, and for eighty years longer honored his memory by an annual ceremony wherein his words to them were reread. Had Penn's example been followed elsewhere, the Indians might have been peacefully absorbed—to the enrichment of the American nation—instead of exterminated, and the extraordinary development of brutality in the later American pioneers might have been largely avoided.

PENN'S DANGEROUS GAME

IN 1684 Penn returned to England to defend successfully his title to the Delaware counties against the claims of the third Lord Baltimore. He expected to go back in a few months, but it was to be fifteen years before he would see Pennsylvania again. The Anglican Church had begun to indulge in a renewed persecution of Dissenters and Quakers, and Penn felt that his continued presence was needed in England. After the accession of James the Second, who had always by some queer attraction of opposites had a personal liking for Penn, the Quaker leader was able to obtain the release of some fourteen hundred imprisoned Friends. Then, to the amazement of all, Penn rose to become almost the chief royal favorite. A daily visitor at Whitehall, he would spend long hours closeted alone with the King while the proudest nobles were kept waiting in the antechambers. Rumor said he was offered and declined a peerage. His levees at Holland House in Kensington became famous for the number of suitors in attendance; a contemporary, Gerard Croese, averred that he saw as many as two hundred there at one time, and Penn himself tells us that had he been disposed to use his influence selfishly he could have made as much as twenty thousand pounds for himself and a hundred thousand pounds for his province during this period.

Naturally, the old stories of Quaker Jesuitry were revived, to be later presented very plausibly by Macaulay in his *History of England* with a mass of ugly charges which were, however, adequately refuted through the researches of Penn's biographers, Janney, Dixon, and Falkner. Penn was a bad judge of character, and really trusted the unworthy monarch; his vanity was flattered by the royal favor, and he found the resumption of his early life as a courtier exceedingly pleasant; but beyond these errors of judgment and very human weaknesses, he had the most solid of reasons for cultivating an intimate relationship with the King. Each needed the other for the furtherance of his dearest ideal. With Penn that ideal was tolerance for the Quakers; with the King it was Catholic supremacy, to be gained through the granting of universal tolerance as a first step. Penn had no objection to tolerance for Catholics if it were coupled with tolerance for Dissenters and Quakers; the King was willing to tolerate Dissenters and Quakers, if under that cover he could bring in the Catholics. Each was playing a dangerous diplomatic game, and the stakes were high; as it turned out, they included the proprietorship of Pennsylvania and the throne of England.

Unable to obtain the consent of Parliament, James issued his Declaration of Tolerance on his own insufficient authority and under its cover appointed Catholics to high positions in the army and in Oxford University; finally, when he ventured to imprison six Anglican bishops, the nation rose against him, William of Orange was invited to assume the throne, and the last of the Stuarts fled to Ireland. Penn, together with a Dissenter named Stephen Lobb, both of whom had vainly tried to guide the untrustworthy monarch to more moderate courses, came in for more than their share of popular execration. A Whig ballad of the new reign chanted triumphantly:

> "Lobb, Penn, and a score
> Of those honest men more
> Will find this same Orange exceedingly sour."

Penn was arrested time and again, and although he always succeeded in answering the charges of Jacobitism that were brought against him, he at last grew weary of this petty persecution and went into hiding. Then came the heaviest blow of all, enough to have broken any weaker heart than his: he was deprived of the proprietorship of the colony he had created, which was annexed temporarily to New York under Governor Fletcher.

"THE FRUITS OF SOLITUDE"

THE greatness of Penn never shone more brightly than in this distressful period. Impoverished, disgraced, all his hopes and mighty plans shipwrecked, he now composed that one of his works which rose above contemporary issues to be a permanent contribution to the literature of the world. *The Fruits of Solitude*, two collections of short, pithy maxims on life and conduct, partly reminiscent of Bacon, partly suggestive of the future Franklin, but on a much higher plane of thought than either, summarized the serene philosophy of the mature William Penn. The closing of the world of action to him seemed to set his spirit free from all its immediate limiting urgencies, from all bonds of party and sect, and allow him at leisure to distill into words the very essence of his varied experience. And this essence proved to be surprisingly close to that of the French Enlightenment a century later.

The Fruits of Solitude revealed how far Penn had outgrown that inconsistent condemnation of Nature which had lingered on in the

Puritanic aspects of George Fox's teachings. He now, like the future Deists, sought in Nature a revelation of the purposes of its creator. "It were happy," he wrote, "if we studied Nature more in natural things; and acted according to Nature; whose rules are *few, plain and most reasonable* . . . the World wearing the *Mark* of it's Maker, whose stamp is every where *visible*, and the Characters very *legible* to the *Children of Wisdom*." It was no small matter that Penn here spoke of the "Children of Wisdom" rather than the "Children of Light." He had left the seventeenth century behind him and was speaking the very language, thinking the very thoughts, of eighteenth century Deism.

Consistently with these principles, Penn worked out a theory of education which looked forward to Rousseau and Pestalozzi: "The first thing obvious to Children is what is sensible; and that we make no Part of their Rudiments. We press their Memory too soon, and puzzle, strain and load them with Words and Rules; to know *Grammar* and *Rhetorick*, and a strange Tongue or two, that it is ten to one may never be useful to them; leaving their natural Genius to *Mechanical* and *Physical* or natural Knowledge uncultivated and neglected; which would be of exceeding Use and Pleasure to them through the whole course of their Life. To be sure, Languages are not to be despised or neglected. But Things are still to be preferred. Children had rather be making of *Tools* and *Instruments* of Play; *Shaping, Drawing, Framing*, and *Building*, &c. than getting some Rules of Propriety of Speech by Heart."

In his ethics, Penn anticipated John Dewey's emphasis on harmony of means and ends. One can see the fruit of sad reflection on his own mistakes under James the Second in such words as these: "If we are but sure the End is Right, we are too apt to gallop over all Bounds to compass it; not considering that lawful Ends may be very *unlawfully* attained. Let us be careful to take *just ways* to compass just Things; that they may *last* in their Benefits to us."

During this same period of outward defeat and inward victory, Penn wrote his *Essay toward the Present and Future Peace of Europe by the Establishment of a European Dyet, Parliament, or Estates*. At a time when Europe was rent apart by religious and political dissension, this undaunted believer in the power of reason pled unheeded for the establishment of a federation to outlaw war, and became the first proponent of a League of Nations, as of so many other idealistic movements far in the future. Closer to that future was Penn's similar suggestion, fifty years before Franklin, of a federation of the American colonies for mutual advice and assistance.

PENN VERSUS PENNSYLVANIA

EVENTUALLY cleared of the absurd charges of Jesuitry and Jacobitism, and with his province restored to him, Penn returned to Pennsylvania in 1699. It would have been better for his reputation had he never done so. During his fifteen years of absence he had fallen out of step with his colony. To him it seemed merely fitting that the owner, proprietor, and governor of the province should live in state on his eight thousand acres at Pennsbury Manor and that, being elderly and grown somewhat portly, he should have his own coach-and-four and his barge on the Delaware. But had he not been away so long he would have realized that such ostentation was very untactful, as well as indefensible on Quaker principles. Many a Friend shook his head in regret as he remembered the simple ways of George Fox and the early Quaker insistence on human equality. As for the non-Quakers in his province, they were frankly scornful or envious.

Much more important, and unfortunate, was Penn's conflict with the popular branch of the legislature. During his absence, the Assembly, led by David Lloyd—an able Quaker more consistent than Penn in squaring his acts with his principles—had steadily encroached upon the powers of the Council, first winning the right to advise on the laws passed, next the right to amend, then the right to initiate, until it now demanded the virtual abolition of the Upper House, which would make Pennsylvania the most democratic of all the colonies. The proposal, which foreshadowed the reform of the British Parliament two centuries later, was strictly in harmony with Quaker equalitarian ideals, but Penn, incited by his authority-minded agent, James Logan, resisted it bitterly. His experience at the time of James the Second's overthrow had not increased his respect for the people. In *The Fruits of Solitude* he had written with unwonted cynicism, "Let the people think they govern, and they will be governed." And now in the stress of his conflict with the

Assembly, he descended to the point of violating his own most fundamental ideal, that of freedom of speech. He had one of his opponents publicly whipped, censured another for reprinting Penn's own original "Frame of Government" for the colony, suppressed Atken's hostile *Almanac*, and confiscated the printing press of William Bradford. The trial of Bradford for libel, won for the defendant through a divided jury, was very important, preceding the similar and better known case of Peter Zenger, as the first in which the American principle was asserted that "truth is a defense" against libel charges.[3] Alas, and incredible but true, this great principle was first maintained against, of all men, William Penn!

It would be easy to conclude from all this that Penn was a progressive statesman only in theory while in fact he had become a stubborn reactionary. Yet this would be far from true. His betrayal of his own deepest principles was a temporary aberration due to a hysterical sense that he had gotten himself into an impossible position. Once he had recovered his wonted equanimity, he yielded gracefully on the whole question. The Constitution of 1701, mainly the work of David Lloyd, legalized the unicameral legislature, and Pennsylvania, alone of the colonies, lived under this ultrademocratic form of government until the American Revolution. Penn's final acceptance of popular rule in practice as well as in theory saved Pennsylvania from the class struggles that rent every other colony outside of New England.

In the case of William Penn versus the Assembly, virtue and wisdom were by no means wholly on the side of the representatives of the people. Two of his most enlightened laws were rejected by the assemblymen: a statute prohibiting the sale of rum to the Indians, and another providing for the marriage of Negro slaves. In a later session, prudence did overcome greed sufficiently to pass the former, but the assemblymen stood irremovably against the latter. A slave brought a higher price in the market unmarried than married, and, as Dobree puts it, "The Assembly preferred them immoral and profitable rather than moral and of less value." The same avaricious spirit appeared in the colonists' attitude toward Penn's

---

[3] For a detailed account of Penn's conflict with the Assembly, see V. F. Calverton's *The Awakening of America* (1939), ch. 16. Mr. Calverton's position is much more wholly pro-Assembly and anti-Penn than is my own.

own finances. Although by this time he had sunk over a hundred thousand dollars in the Holy Experiment and the payment of his quitrents had for years been little more than nominal,[4] the Assembly demanded that, at a time when land values were rising everywhere in the colony, Penn should continue to sell his own lands at the original price. He, not unnaturally, refused, saying firmly, "I think this an unreasonable article, either to limit me in that which is my own, or to deprive me of the advantage which time gives to other men's properties."

There remained one final problem, the hardest of all. Ever since the beginning of the first war with France in 1689, Quaker pacifism had involved the colony in a difficulty which no logic could solve. Called on to furnish contingents to the army, the Quakers had refused to do more than equip their Indian allies, a concession dubiously defensible on the ground that the Indians had no moral scruples against warfare but none the less exposing the Quakers to the ugly charge that they were willing to let others fight for them while unwilling to endanger themselves. Called on now by the Crown to do more than this in preparation for another war, the Quakers refused to budge from their principles. And without their moral excuse, the non-Quakers in the province were equally recalcitrant through narrow self-interest. Penn himself was, of course, a pacifist, but he believed that in a rough world it was often necessary to sacrifice one good principle for the sake of other good principles, and he was unwilling that Pennsylvania should live like a parasite on the Crown and the rest of the colonies. Fearing lest the attitude of the province should lead to a new attack on the charter, he felt it necessary to return once more to England in 1701.

Penn succeeded in keeping the charter, but new misfortunes befell him in England. Always careless in business matters—in itself a sufficient refutation of the charge of avarice brought against him—he had incautiously allowed the title to his property to fall into the hands of a knavish agent, one Ford, who milked the estate for thousands of dollars. After Ford's death, his widow, seeking for more of this easy loot, brought suit for an enormous sum which

[4] In 1698 he asserted that in twelve years he had not received "one sixpence" from his quitrents.

Penn was quite unable to pay. He was imprisoned for debt in the Old Bailey during eleven months of the year 1707 while he vainly appealed to Pennsylvania for the aid which, still smarting over his land policy, it denied him. Bitterer to bear even than this was the prospect that his three sons, who had forsaken his Quaker faith and were mere dissipated snobs, would, when they succeeded to the proprietorship of Pennsylvania, utterly degrade the reputation of the Penn family by trying to wring the uttermost farthing out of the province for their own selfish enjoyment.

Betrayed on all hands, infinitely perplexed, Penn began tentatively to broach the idea of selling to the Crown that charter which he had struggled so long to defend. Under the circumstances, that would undoubtedly have been the best solution—the very solution that the colony itself years later came to demand. But at the moment it met only with an angry response from the province that the suggestion savored "first of fleecing and then of selling."

At last, when men had abandoned him, the Nature in which Penn had trusted brought him release. A paralytic stroke, by destroying his reason and memory, gave him a few years of happiness. Able to move about, he enjoyed his garden and found endless delight in chasing bright-colored butterflies—as if his organism retained some ironic, symbolic sense of his life's endeavors. Visitors were made welcome—he did not know who they were, but he always greeted them with a friendly smile. Only when he happened to pass his desk or his bookshelves would he hesitate and frown slightly while a vague look of unhappiness came over his face as though from some dim memory of work left unfinished. He would stop and try to remember and then go on—there were always the butterflies—until death came, on July 30, 1718, to all that was left of one who had been among the foremost political thinkers of modern times.

THE LATER QUAKERS

No OTHER modern religious movement has ever developed such strength in so short a time as did the Quakers'. Theirs is the supreme example of the futility of persecution and the power of passive resistance. Within fifty years from the time of Fox's first preaching, this most persecuted of all sects had become the largest and strongest of the dissenting groups in both England and the colonies. At the date of Fox's death in 1691 there were, according to the estimate of the Quaker historian, Elizabeth Emmott, no less than sixty thousand Quakers in England—more than the combined number of Roman Catholics, Presbyterians, Independents, and Baptists.[5] In the colonies at this time they were in political control of Rhode Island and Pennsylvania, with a strong foothold in West New Jersey and in North Carolina. Any historian in 1700, judging of the future in terms of apparent tendencies, would have been likely to forecast a Quaker America.

But the Quaker America never materialized. There was not even to be a Quaker Pennsylvania. By the end of the eighteenth century the Friends no longer guided the ethics or politics of a single state. Those who had started out to convert the world in the dream of winning Sultan and Pope to their cause, were now apparently content to accept the position they have ever since occupied of a minor sect among many sects. The decline of the Quakers in external power was almost as rapid as their spectacular rise.

Numerous reasons may be given for this relative failure of the most humane and idealistic of all the Protestant sects. The growing economic prosperity of the Quakers lifted them from the lower middle class into the upper middle class, and, as with the Puritans, religious zeal tended to decline in proportion as wealth increased; the tolerance of the Quakers opened their settlements to outsiders who thronged in in such numbers that the Friends were soon a minority even in their own colonies; the indifference of the Quakers to higher education left them without the trained leaders that came out of Harvard, William and Mary, Yale, Princeton, and Brown; their extreme individualism prevented the development of an adequate ecclesiastical organization; their religious radicalism, and especially their opposition to war, put them at a disadvantage in competing with the otherwise not unsimilar sects of Baptists and Methodists who were more willing to compromise with the Devil

[5] Elizabeth Braithwaite Emmott, *A Short History of Quakerism* (New York: George H. Doran Company, 1923), p. 322. Other estimates are even higher. Herbert Hensley Henson, Bishop of Durham, in *The Oxford Group Movement* (New York: Oxford University Press, 1933), p. 26, states that "At the close of Charles II's reign it was estimated that there were as many as 100,000 Quakers in a population, of, perhaps, six millions. To-day, in a population over six times as numerous, the number does not exceed 20,000."

when it seemed necessary; finally, their ideals were too far in advance of their times and too universal in scope to provide a suitable doctrinal basis for any one sect to the exclusion of others.

The Quakers were inspired by an active benevolence which made them eager to act as hosts to the world. While the Puritans were still striving to exclude all but Puritans from New England, William Penn had been on his third trip through Holland and Germany inviting persecuted Protestants to make their home in his colony. The German Catholics had learned nothing from two centuries of religious warfare, and persecution flamed as fiercely as ever across the Rhineland when Penn invited these victims of bigotry to take refuge in Pennsylvania. Among them, the worst sufferers were the mystical Pietistic sects of the Palatinate, descendants of the original Anabaptists and like them frequently persecuted by the Lutherans as well as the Catholics. Coming to Pennsylvania in great numbers in the first quarter of the century, these devout Germans settled in the valleys of the Delaware, Lehigh, and Susquehanna, where they found at last under Quaker rule the peace they had so long sought in vain. Tenacious of their language and local customs, they formed separate communities of their own, strange and picturesque, diversifying the cultural landscape: the Women in the Wilderness, the Neugeborene, the Dunkers, the Spiritual Brethren of Ephrata, the Moravian Brethren, the Mennonites, Amish, and Schwenkfelders. In spite of the racial and linguistic barriers, it was relatively easy for the Quakers to keep on good terms with these "Pennsylvania Dutch" because of their community of ultimate purpose. Plainness of living, distaste for ceremonies, belief in mystical experience, and hatred of war—these characterized equally the ideals of the German Pietists and the English Quakers.

It was very different when the Scotch-Irish Presbyterians came, representing an alien tradition. Devoted to the harsh dogmas of Calvinism, driven out of Scotland to Ireland and then out of Ireland, they had reacted to persecution by adopting much of the vindictiveness of the persecutors. Arriving late on the Pennsylvania scene in the second quarter of the century when the best land was already pre-empted, they were obliged to settle on the western frontier, squatting on land still ostensibly held by the proprietors, or intruding into the hunting grounds reserved for the Indians. Constantly exposed to physical hardships and dangers unknown to those in the eastern part of the colony, they developed into a strong, lithe, muscular type, extraordinarily independent and aggressive, fiercely determined to assert their own rights and little concerned with the rights of others. When the proprietors demanded their quitrents the Scotch-Irish answered that "It was against the laws of God and of Nature that so much land should remain idle while so many Christians wanted it to labor on." That quarrel did not concern the Quakers; all good Pennsylvanians hated the proprietors. But the question of the Indians was different. At the time of the conspiracy of Pontiac a group of the Pennsylvania frontiersmen crossed into Ohio and massacred all the inhabitants in a peaceful Indian settlement of Moravian converts who had taken no part whatever in Pontiac's movement, and a few years later another frontier gang of Scotch-Irish, known as the "Paxton Boys," massacred another group of Christianized Indians. By such acts the fruits of the enlightened Indian policy which the Quakers had pursued for eighty years were utterly destroyed. Between the pacifistic ideals of the Quakers and the militaristic conceptions of the Scotch-Irish there could be no possible truce.

The Quakers themselves, it is true, had not succeeded in squaring all of their political activities with the fundamental principles of their faith. Though a minority group, they kept political control of the colony through the property limitation of suffrage. If this could perhaps be defended as conforming to the practice in all the colonies, the inequality was made greater in Pennsylvania than in some other places through skillful Quaker manipulation of the county representation whereby their own three counties obtained twenty-four votes as against eleven votes for the much more populous five Scotch-Irish counties. Meanwhile, the affairs of the colony were financed mainly by a poll tax, of which the Germans and Scotch-Irish paid the larger part, and by an excise tax which bore more heavily on the hard-drinking frontiersmen than on the temperate Quakers. Certainly the latter gave little heed to the principle of "No Taxation Without Representation": their taxation fell heaviest where the representation was least. In the hostility between the Quakers and Scotch-Irish, each party had sufficient grounds for complaint.

But while in these ways the Quakers of Pennsylvania seemed to have degenerated into an unprincipled political oligarchy, on the question of war and peace they stood firm. Not only did they refuse to give any assistance to the frontiersmen, harassed by Indian attacks which the frontiersmen themselves had provoked, but they also refused to support the wars between the British Empire and the French. Rather than yield on this point, their delegates left the Assembly in 1756, and Quaker rule in Pennsylvania was over. Unfair as had been their methods of retaining political power, when the final test came the Quakers gave up the power rather than give up their principles.

It was only in the sphere of economics that the Quakers were able to sail continuously forward over smooth seas. But there all the winds were indeed favorable, and few problems arose save as to the nature of the cargo which it was permissible to carry.

In an age when the shopkeeper and merchant were known personally by their customers, honesty was indeed, as Benjamin Franklin maintained, "the best policy." We have seen that George Fox early noted that in this respect the personal integrity of the Quakers brought economic advantages in its train. What Logan Pearsall Smith writes of the English Friends has always been equally true of the Friends in America: "The confidence they everywhere inspired, by making others trust them filled their pockets with worldly pelf: they really couldn't help it. As tradesmen who were the first to place fixed prices on their goods, as honest manufacturers, as brewers and trusted bankers, families like the Barclays, the Gurneys, Buxtons, Lloyds and Hoares and Peases, have founded those dynasties of English Quakers, whose names, redolent of wealth, are familiar to us all on the signs of public houses, on the great portals of breweries and banks. So inevitable, indeed, has been the accumulation of wealth among these pious people, that an impecunious Quaker is now a *rara avis*, like a white blackbird, in the social scheme of things." But if this accumulation of wealth was "inevitable" it was perhaps equally inevitable that many of the Quakers should come to cherish their wealth as dearly as they cherish their religion. Herman Melville's satiric portrait in *Moby Dick* of the Quaker whaling master, Captain Bildad, was something more than satire—that immortal Captain Bildad who is represented as thus addressing his crew:

"God bless ye, and have ye in His holy keeping. Be careful in the hunt, ye mates. Don't stave the boats needlessly, ye harpooners: good white cedar plank is raised full three per cent, within the year. Don't forget your prayers, either. Don't whale it too much a' Lord's Day, men; but don't miss a fair chance either; that's rejecting heaven's good gifts. Have an eye to the molasses tierce, Mr. Stubb; it was a little leaky, I thought. If ye touch at the islands, Mr. Flask, beware of fornication."

Yet, after all, this desire to unite worldly and spiritual advantage, to insure at the same time both a good life on earth and a better one in heaven, was the common driving force of all the Protestant sects. The Quakers were in this regard no exception. And, to do them justice, they were more ready to sacrifice pecuniary gain to religious principle than were any of the others.

Captain Thomas Chalkley, half-merchant, half-missionary, Whittier's "gentlest of skippers, rare sea-saint," was probably as typical as Melville's imaginary Captain Bildad. Much of his time was spent as an itinerant preacher on long journeys up and down the coast, but when the need for money became too pressing he would make a highly profitable commercial trip to Bermuda or the West Indies. He was shot and seriously wounded in Barbados for expostulating with some of the inhabitants on their cruel treatment of their slaves. On another occasion when his becalmed ship ran out of provisions and the crew was ready to resort to cannibalism, he offered himself to be the first victim in a sacrifice that was averted only by the providential capture of a large dolphin. Chalkley's *Journal* (1749) should rank next to Woolman's more famous one as the record of a life of good will.

Anecdotes of Quaker honesty are legion. One of the most delightful is the tale of that ancestor of Logan Pearsall Smith who, after buying a plot of ground from a neighbor and on later reflection deciding that he had paid too little for it, was riding over the next day with additional money when he met the neighbor coming in his turn to report that he had put too high a price on the land and wished to give back a considerable part of the sum.

Another pleasant story of the quality of Quaker honesty is that of John Warder. He was a Quaker merchant of Philadelphia who was living in London during the Revolution. The captain of one of his ships, without his knowledge (so, at least, Warder claimed), took out letters of marque as a privateersman and brought in a fine Dutch prize named *Holland's Welfare*, worth about two thousand pounds. Warder, on the remonstrances of other Friends, was induced to put this money aside as a trust fund for the benefit of the original owners whenever they should be discovered. In the unsettled conditions of the period, it took a long time to find them. Warder died; the trust fund, well invested, continued to grow; and eventually when all the claims, amounting to thirty-three hundred and forty-five pounds, had been paid, there was still an equal amount left in the fund. What to do now? The Friends decided that complete restitution demanded the spending of the money for the good of Holland, and accordingly the fund was used to establish a free public school in Amsterdam— the first in the city—which was appropriately named "Holland's Welfare." [6]

The acid test of Christianity was its attitude toward slavery, and here the Quakers were the only Christian sect to acquit themselves with much credit. The British slave trade hardly became important before 1680, as up to that time the business had been virtually monopolized by the Dutch, the Spanish, and the Portuguese. And as early as 1688 the German Quakers of Germantown, led by Franz Daniel Pastorius, protested against the trade and the whole institution of slavery to the Philadelphia Yearly Meeting and in the Assembly. Although William Penn possessed a few slaves, he emancipated them all in his will, which read: "I give my blacks their freedom, as is under my hand already, and to old Sam one hundred acres to be his children's, after he and his wife are dead, for ever." In 1712 the Friends of Nantucket passed a minute to the effect that "It is not agreeable to Truth for Friends to purchase slaves and keep them a

---

[6] *Bulletin of Friends' Historical Society*, vol. 7, no. 1 (May, 1916), and from William Warder Norton, the direct descendant of John Warder, and the publisher of this book.

term of life." From then on individual Quaker voices were raised against the institution almost continuously, as in William Burling's *Address to the Elders of the Church* (1719), Ralph Sandiford's *Mystery of Iniquity, in a Brief Examination of the Practice of the Times* (1729), Elihu Coleman's *Testimony against the Anti-Christian Practice of Making Slaves of Men* (1733), and Benjamin Lay's *Treatise on Slave-keeping* (1737). But it was not until the greatest of the later Quakers, John Woolman, entered the lists with *Some Considerations on the Keeping of Negroes* (1754), soon followed by Anthony Benezet's *Caution and Warning to Great Britain and Her Colonies on the Calamitous State of the Enslaved Negroes* (1766), that really effective action began to be taken.

John Woolman was well acquainted with the horrors of slavery through his extensive preaching tours throughout the South. But he did not indulge in any diatribes against the slaveowners. With sweet reasonableness, he based his whole argument on the brotherhood of man which was to him not merely a religious dogma but also an empirically observable fact: "When we remember that all nations are of one blood (Genesis, 3:20), that in this world we are but sojourners, that we are subject to the like afflictions and infirmities of body, the like disorders and frailties in mind, the like temptations, the same death, and the same judgment, and that the all-wise being is judge and lord over us all, it seems to raise an idea of a general brotherhood, and a disposition easy to be touched with a feeling of each others afflictions."

By such appeals Woolman succeeded in inducing the Philadelphia Yearly Meeting to repudiate slavery in 1758, and in 1776 that body dissolved all connection with Friends who had refused to emancipate their own slaves. In 1780 a system of gradual manumission was adopted by the state of Pennsylvania, but long ere that time slavery had ceased to exist among the overwhelming majority of the Quakers.

What no one of the antislavery Revolutionary leaders, Washington, Jefferson, Patrick Henry, was ready to do—emancipate his own slaves—hundreds and thousands of Quakers willingly did. One of the popular sophisms of the present day is that "No ruling class ever voluntarily relinquishes its power over others." Americans might at least remember the American Quakers.

BOOK 3. *From Religion to Politics*

CHAPTER 14. *Jonathan Edwards and the Great Awakening*

JONATHAN EDWARDS, THE PURITAN SAINT

THE all-important characteristic of the eighteenth century was that it registered a change from the religious to the secular viewpoint. Worldly interests: commerce and industry, the cultivation of polite literature, a genial indulgence in all kinds of philosophical theories—these began to take the place of the former concentration upon religion. The evidences of change were too overwhelming not to be forced upon the attention of the religious-minded equally in Old England and in New England. And in both lands there were men who girded up their loins to meet the danger with new weapons forged in the new situation itself. Wesley and Whitefield of Oxford, Jonathan Edwards of Yale, three men of utterly different temperament, strove with a common desperation to bring back to the world the waning religious spirit.

Of the three, the American was by far the deepest thinker and scholar. Already possessing a knowledge of Greek, Latin, and Hebrew when, at the age of thirteen, he entered Yale College—founded in 1701 by conservative Calvinists to replace fair but false Harvard—by the time he was fifteen Edwards had mastered the works of John Locke and at nineteen he sketched out a philosophy somewhat similar to the subjective idealism of Bishop Berkeley although he was apparently quite unacquainted with the latter's writings. Sub-

207

jectivism and idealism always remained the keynotes of Edwards' thought. With a temperament both exceedingly mystical and extremely logical—a combination less unusual than is often supposed—he was able on the basis of presuppositions supplied by his mysticism to build a remarkably logical metaphysical system, the first, and almost the last, American so to do. It took in the objective world but in a visionary manner, as seen from a mountain top, the general pattern of hills and valleys quite plain but with detailed perspectives distorted and the dwellings of men lost to view. A Platonist in the manner of his thinking, without Plato's Humanism, Edwards was a lover of perfection, of supernal beauty, of form and order and absolute distinctions. He drew Calvinism up out of the murk of this world into an atmosphere high above considerations of politics and earthly advantage, while in rising into this realm of universal principles he unconsciously deprived Calvinism of that urge to righteous power which was its actual basis. He moved back and forth between the two poles of the individual and the universal, and in neglecting the intermediate stages of social activity he facilitated the withdrawal of religion into the limited field of individual conduct to concern itself above all with the subjective conscience.

It was Edwards' deep conviction that the true church was an association of the genuine elect. And he knew only too well that the world had turned against those Children of Light. His *History of the Work of Redemption* (1739) contained not a word about the political theocracy. There was no question now of establishing the Kingdom of God on earth. There must first be a day of judgment after which the Kingdom of Heaven would be established not on earth but truly in Heaven:

"Then shall the whole church be perfectly and for ever delivered from the present evil world; shall take their everlasting leave of this earth, where they have been strangers, and which has been for the most part a scene of trouble and sorrow; where the devil has reigned as God, and has greatly misled them, and which has been such a scene of wickedness and abomination; where Christ their Lord has been cruelly used; and where they have been so hated, reproached, and persecuted. They shall leave it, and shall never set foot on it again. And there shall be an everlasting separation made between them and wicked men. Before, they were mixed together, and it was impossible in many instances to determine their characters, but now all shall become visible; both saints and sinners shall appear in their true characters and forms. Then shall the church be seen ascending to the right hand of God. . . ."

As in logic A can never be Not-A, so to the mind of Edwards the class of Saints must be eternally separate from the class of Sinners. In the corrupted currents of this world, as he was fain to confess, the Saint often seems to merge into the Sinner until all moral distinctions become blurred and confused; but, reason seemed to tell him, this must be an illusion, and "in their true characters and forms" each is known for what he is by the deity. That in his "true character" one might be a mixture of Sinner and Saint Edwards could never admit, for this would have belied his basic conviction that the world was, in spite of its moral evil, none the less a logical order.

Edwards was as profound a believer in reason and science as any eighteenth century rationalist. Far above seeking for proofs of God's existence in miracles or special providences, he would have looked for them in the laws of Nature, had he needed to look beyond his own flaming intuition. His deity was a Supreme Being, almost pantheistic, an infinite harmony of goodness, truth, and beauty, the perfect union of all positive qualities. His idealism at times strangely reminds one of Emerson's, save for its more determined wrestling with the problem of evil and its denial of human goodness. The universe was God's universe—what other source could it have?—an emanation of His glory rather than a literal creation—a shadow of God, partly divine as being His shadow, partly undivine as being only a shadow and not ultimate reality itself. In the universe an element of negation was necessarily present, the logical Not-A implied by A and known to men as ugliness, error, and sin. Yet in being rejected of God these elements enhanced His glory as light is enhanced by contrast with darkness. Evil necessarily existed, sinners sinned of necessity, their bodies subject to natural laws, and their moral choices always determined "by the apparent good as seen by the mind"; yet in their suffering the eternal torments appropriate to sin, moral distinctions were preserved and justice was done. In the aesthetico-logical system of

Edwards the static divine harmony incorporated even the negative aspects of the universe, and the goal of philosophy seemed attained. Man as man was sacrificed, but what mattered that in comparison with the glory of God?

This imposing system of thought which did violence to every natural instinct of human kindness was not reached by Edwards without personal agony. His was naturally a peculiarly delicate and sensitive temperament, delighting in physical beauty and quickly responsive to beauty of character. His intense mystical faith in the reality of perfection made every instance of human depravity something utterly shocking and unforgivable. He was filled with love toward man, Nature, and God; but constrained by his logic to sacrifice the lesser to the greater, he did not hesitate; nevertheless his personality was wrenched and distorted in the process. All this depth and bitterness of personal experience welled up in his sermons, perhaps the only ones out of the millions of sermons preached in America that have an enduring place in our literature.

Even an unbeliever cannot read his words on "Sinners in the Hands of an Angry God" without shuddering. What wonder that many in the congregation shrieked or fainted or were thrown into convulsions? The wonder is that there were any there who could sit quietly till the end.

"O Sinner! Consider the fearful danger you are in. 'Tis a great furnace of wrath, a wide and bottomless pit, full of the fire of wrath, that you are held over in the hand of that God, whose wrath is provoked and incensed as much against you as against many of the damned in hell. You hang by a slender thread, with the flames of divine wrath flashing about it, and ready every moment to singe it, and burn it asunder; and you have no interest in any mediator, and nothing to lay hold of to save yourself, nothing to keep off the flames of wrath, nothing of your own, nothing that you have ever done, nothing that you can do, to induce God to spare you one moment. . . .

"How dreadful is the state of those that are daily and hourly in danger of this great wrath. . . . If we knew that there was one person, and but one, in the whole congregation, that was to be the subject of this misery, what an awful thing would it be to think of! If we knew who it was, what an awful sight would it be to see such a person! How might all the rest of the congregation lift up a lamentable and bitter cry over him! But alas! instead of one, how many is it likely will remember this discourse in hell? And it would be a wonder if some that are now present should not be in hell in a very short time, before this year is out; and it would be no wonder if some person that now sits here in some seat of this meeting-house, in health, and quiet and secure, should be there before to-morrow morning."

The effect of such sermons, continued week after week, driving home their appeal to the elemental fears present in all men, was naturally to multiply conversions. Between 1734 and 1739, Northampton under the impulsion of the Edwardsian fervor was in what might be called a condition of chronic revivalism. From Northampton the contagion spread to other towns and villages until all of western New England was ablaze. The movement, euphemistically named by theologians "The Great Awakening," swept over New England, New York, New Jersey, into Pennsylvania, and southward. Edwards had unleashed forces far beyond his control and little to his liking. His sermons were imitated and vulgarized everywhere by parrot-preachers who lacked his inner experience to ennoble what with them became a kind of hell-mongering. Typical of the crowd was a popular preacher named Davenport, one of whose meetings was attended by Charles Chauncy of Harvard, who described it as follows:

"At length he turned his discourse to others, and with the utmost strength of his lungs addressed himself to the congregation under these and such like expressions, viz: 'You poor unconverted creatures, in the seats, in the pews, in the galleries, I wonder you don't drop into hell! It would not surprise me, I should not wonder at it, if I should see you drop down now, now, now, this minute, into hell! You Pharisees, hypocrites, now, now, now, you are going right into the bottom of hell. I wonder you don't drop into hell by scores and hundreds, etc.' And in this terrible way he ended his sermon. . . . After a short prayer, he called for all the distressed persons (who were twenty) into the foremost seats. Then he came out of the pulpit, and stripped off his upper garments, and got into the seats, and leaped up and down for some time, and clapped his hands, and cried out in those words: 'The war goes on, the fight goes on, the devil goes down, the devil goes down,' and then betook himself to stamping and screaming most dreadfully." [1]

This was not what Edwards had intended. The most intellectual of American theologians had unwittingly made himself responsible for initiating a religion of sheer emotionalism on which the church would come increasingly to rely. For the church was now far from those palmy days in early New England when church membership was a privilege jealously guarded. The church needed members, and Edwards had shown it a way to secure them. Henceforth, the technique of revivalism would always be at hand to be used by those who judged the effectiveness of religion in terms of the quantity, not the quality, of the converts.

With all this tendency Edwards himself had no sympathy. He felt no slightest temptation to substitute the multiplication table for standards of excellence. As the Great Awakening went on he withdrew from the movement and publicly expressed his disappointment with the results, which indicated no permanent improvement in conduct but rather an extreme moral laxity that too often followed in the wake of the religious excitement. Edwards' disappointment caused him to attempt an impossible revival of the inquisitorial attitude of earlier times. Calvinism in its own abstract terms is sublime; enthroned over the actual world, it is tyrannical and horrible; but if it merely pecks at the actual world it becomes ridiculous. This was Edwards' fate when for once he descended to the level of Cotton Mather. The story is fully narrated in Dwight's biography:

Learning that certain "licentious books" were circulating from hand to hand among the younger members of his congregation, Edwards laid the matter before the elders of the church, who most heartily agreed that disciplinary action ought to be taken. But when at a subsequent meeting Edwards read forth the names of the lascivious young people whom he had ferreted out, it appeared, in the words of his biographer, Sereno Dwight, "that there were but few of the considerable families in town, to which some of the persons named, either did not belong or were not nearly related." The sad result was that "a great number of heads of families altered

[1] Charles Chauncy, *Seasonable Thoughts* (1747).

their minds . . . and little or nothing could be done further in the affair." [2]

Edwards now realized that the severest scrutiny was necessary to distinguish the sheep from the goats even in his own flock. Accordingly, he came out openly against the Halfway Covenant under which his Northampton church had hitherto operated. Long and earnestly, he strove to persuade his congregation to return to the practice of restricting church membership to those who could show evidence of having had genuine religious experience. But he strove in vain. He himself was perhaps the only one in his parish who could have passed such a test. In 1750 he was dismissed on the ground that the separation was necessary to "the peace of the Church and Town."

Thus ejected from his parish with a large family to support and no means of doing so, the foremost theologian of America considered himself fortunate to secure after a year the pastorate of a tiny church in the village of Stockbridge with the additional duty of acting as missionary to the remnants of a tribe of Housatonic Indians in the neighborhood. Though they heard his discourses only through an interpreter, the Indians understood him better than the white men had done and gave him unstinted admiration and love. Neglected by the world, continually ill with fever and ague, Edwards during his first years at Stockbridge put his theology in its final form in his three great works: *An Inquiry into the Freedom of the Will* (1754), the less well known but still more significant *Dissertation Concerning the Nature of True Virtue* (1754), and *Dissertation Concerning the End for Which God Created the World* (1754). In 1757 he was called to the presidency of the College of New Jersey at Princeton, but five weeks after inauguration he died from inoculation for smallpox.

Akin to Roger Williams and William Penn in his love of moral excellence, and a much better writer than either, Edwards fell below them in being unable to construct any bridge, as they did, from God to man. He was the one great absolutist in American thought, who sacrificed the world and himself to an abstract ideal that would have been barren and colorless but for the elements

[2] Sereno Edwards Dwight, *Life of Edwards* (1829), p. 30.

which he unconsciously projected into it from the depths of his own personality.

For two generations, the mighty mind of the dead Jonathan Edwards continued to rule the Connecticut clergy. His influence was directly perpetuated through his son, Jonathan Edwards, Jr., and even more through his pupils, Joseph Bellamy, pastor of Bethlehem, and Samuel Hopkins, pastor of Great Barrington. John Smalley, pupil of Bellamy, had in his turn as pupils Nathanael Emmons and Ebenezer Porter. Timothy Dwight, president of Yale, was a grandson of Edwards. These men constituted a veritable intellectual bureaucracy. All of them were scholars accustomed to spend fourteen hours a day over their study tables, all wrote voluminous theological works, and all enjoyed in their own day an enormous respect and reverence. The slight modifications of Edwards' views introduced by Samuel Hopkins gained him the credit of being the founder of a new "Hopkinsian" school of theology. Yet anyone who attempts today to peruse their almost unreadable works will find these Connecticut scholastics tiresome writers and trivial thinkers. Infinitely subtle formulators of meaningless technical distinctions, they struggled helplessly with the old problems, reemphasized by Edwards, of reconciling man's freedom with God's omnipotence and of differentiating between the true and the merely apparent elect.

Reading these stiff-necked theologians, one might easily get the impression that Connecticut was immune to new ideas. But this was true only of those in the seats of the mighty. While they held the old fort with no thought of surrender and busied themselves with repairing every tiny hole in the walls, their garrison was deserting. More slowly than in Massachusetts and much less vocally, the people of Connecticut were giving up the cherished beliefs in original sin and all but universal damnation. Odell Shepard in his recent work, *Connecticut: Past and Present* (1939), has traced the change in an interesting and convincing manner through the study of graveyards. The memorial stones were at first grimly marked by skulls and crossbones, fitting emblems of the death of the soul as well as the body; later, the skulls sprouted wings as resurrection symbols; then, as the hope of salvation became more general, they were replaced by cherubs; finally, toward the end of the eighteenth century, when the whole problem had become unreal, the Christian emblems disappeared entirely to make way for the secular urn and branch of cypress borrowed from paganism.

THE HEIRS OF THE GREAT AWAKENING

MEANWHILE, the Middle Colonies presented a much more violent scene of religious strife than anything in New England. The heavy Scotch-Irish immigration in the eighteenth century swelled the number of American Presbyterians with new members to the manner born, stern Calvinists, independent, intolerant, disputatious, who became the most active and vociferous religious force from New Jersey to North Carolina. But when George Whitefield arrived on his oft-repeated evangelistic tours, thirteen in all, and the Great Awakening swept over the Middle Colonies, it created a popular turmoil that boded ill for the rule of the elders. Whitefield was a Calvinistic Methodist, associated in England with Wesley, but since Methodism was almost unknown in America he preached wherever he could get a hearing and to Protestants of every denomination. His was a most contradictory character: a large slaveowner, he eulogized slavery for its temporal blessings to the masters and its spiritual blessings to the slaves; yet, born a man of the people, he excoriated the luxury and formalism of the clergy. Everywhere that he went he created an emotional fervor, a desire to go out and convert the world as he was doing. He and his disciples were so eager to redeem the multitude that they quite forgot the traditional role of the elect in a Calvinistic community.

Following in Whitefield's footsteps, Gilbert Tennant, a passionate Presbyterian, carried the sword and wrath of the revivalist gospel again into New England and back through New York and New Jersey. The conservative Presbyterians of Pennsylvania became alarmed, seeing that theological dogmas were being forgotten in the popular excitement, and the Synod of Philadelphia expelled whole presbyteries for using revivalist methods. The result was to split the sect into two parties, known as "Old Side" and "New Side," meeting in separate synods. The New Sides, having a preponderance of ability, in 1746 established the College of New Jersey (later Princeton) as a center of more liberal Presbyterianism.

When the smoke of battle had cleared away and the two parties were reunited in 1759, it was seen that the victory had gone to neither, but to an entirely different sect, the Baptists. Although they, like the Presbyterians, split on the revivalist issue, becoming "Old Light" and "New Light" Baptists, the distinction was merely one of the degrees of revivalism, both groups responding to the Great Awakening and reaping its fruits in an increased membership drifting in from the other sects.

The true heirs of the Great Awakening were the Baptists. This unforeseen result, deplorable in the eyes of those who initiated the evangelistic movement, was a natural consequence of the technique employed. That technique consisted in arousing in the breast of the sinner an agonized feeling of utter unworthiness combined with a mounting terror of eternal torture until at last the unbearable emotion would break in surrender of the individual consciousness to the common will, accompanied by a sense of release and purgation, all easily interpreted as a belated reception of the grace of God. This was the immediate effect sought by the evangelists, but the permanent effect was quite different. They had suddenly converted a multitude of sinners into a body of the elect. These newly sanctified souls, conscious of an immediate, personal relationship with God, were less likely than before to submit to clerical advice or ecclesiastical discipline. Instead, they were headed for whatever sect was most willing to recognize and encourage their individual temperaments. This sect, with the decline of the Quakers, was now represented by the Baptists.

In 1740 there were only twenty-one Baptist churches in New England; by 1768 there were sixty-nine; in 1790 there were two hundred and eighty-six. This rapid development was greatly accelerated after a Baptist academy established at Hopewell, New Jersey, in 1756 was removed eight years later to Warren, Rhode Island, and later became Brown University—the first entirely liberal American educational institution. Brown's charter provided that "sectarian differences of opinion shall not make any part of the public and classical instruction." Although Baptists were given a majority on the Boards of Fellows and Trustees, there was a provision that Episcopalians, Congregationalists, and Quakers must also be represented. For this magnificent lesson in religious tolerance four

Baptist clergymen were responsible: James Manning, the first president of the college, Morgan Edwards, Hezekiah Smith, and Isaac Backus—all of them worthy spiritual descendants of Roger Williams.

The Baptists, the first sect to represent the English yeomanry, still represented the descendants of that yeomanry in America. With little of the canniness possessed by the Quakers, they had not acquired many worldly possessions. They were the smallest of small farmers, individually the poorest of all the sects. In that condition they felt more than others the pinch of taxation to support the established Congregational Church. The political battle cry now increasingly heard—"No Taxation Without Representation"—was quickly applied by them in the field of religion. In 1774 Isaac Backus sent a vigorous protest against the injustice of sectarian taxation to the patriot leaders in Boston. But consistency was as yet no part of the patriotic program. John Adams replied contemptuously that Backus might as well look forward to an alteration of the solar system as to expect any such change as he demanded in the laws of Massachusetts. And in fact the Baptists were obliged to wait fifty-nine years longer for the disestablishment of the Massachusetts church. Neither Adams nor Backus lived to see it. Backus died in 1806, still strong in hope, knowing that the Baptist agitation for justice would continue unabated. Adams died in 1826, having learned to his cost that the stability of the solar system was not to be paralleled in American politics. In 1833 the church was disestablished. The American Revolution, like the Great Awakening, led eventually to results most unanticipated, most undesired, by some of its early leaders.

CHAPTER 15. *The Rise of Deism*

NATURAL RELIGION VERSUS REVEALED RELIGION

THERE were two diametrically opposite courses open to the churches in dealing with the growing secularism of the eighteenth century. The first was simply to react against it in sharp opposition, as did the American Calvinists—a response that turned out to be self-defeating, since in concentrating on religion alone it abandoned the whole field of social conduct, limiting religion to private domestic life, and sacrificing intellectual leadership for the sake of gaining an untrustworthy emotional following. The reverse course was to make peace with the enemy, revise theological formulations to bring them into harmony with scientific knowledge, and work out new systems of ethics and politics on a rational basis—in other words, to attempt to infuse religion into the entire cultural movement, though with the risk that religion itself might get lost in the process. This, much the more interesting of the two modes of response, was the method chosen by liberal leaders in England and America. It led first to the development of Natural Religion and then on to Deism.

In the early part of the seventeenth century it had not been necessary to prove the existence of God. That had been taken for granted. His direct providential government of the world had also been taken for granted. The only questions had been as to the exact nature of God, the exact rules to be followed in carrying out His will on earth, and for those questions the Bible had afforded the answers. With the advance of seventeenth century physics, however, it became necessary to reconcile the existence of God with newly discovered natural laws unknown to the Biblical writers. This task at first did not seem particularly difficult, except to the stubborn Calvinists. Resort was had to the cosmological and teleological arguments of Aristotle which seemed to prove the necessity of a First Cause (not temporally but logically first) behind the derivative phenomena of Nature, and to guarantee the beneficence of this First Cause by pointing to the evidences of design present throughout the universe. Modern biology, with its story of the struggle for survival, was still undreamed of; Nature seemed to be adequately described in terms of astronomy and mathematical physics, supplemented by obvious examples of the adaptation of life to environmental conditions. The harmony of Nature revealed by the scientist was also contemplated by the poet under the aspect of perceptual beauty. Surely, in all this new conception of the world there was nothing for the Christian to fear. The God discovered by Natural Religion was wholly perfect, and the world was more than ever His world. The reasonableness of religion seemed proved beyond the possibility of doubt. And the Anglican Church, especially, could see in the reign of law everywhere further justification for its own claims to exercise orderly lawful authority.

Thus, for those eighteenth century Americans who were repelled both by the narrow rigidities of conservative Calvinism and by the emotional extravagances of the Great Awakening, there was a well-trodden religious highway recommended by British example. It led back to the now renovated and liberalized Church of England, engaged in reconciling its dogmas with science and in building up a new ethical code in harmony with the secular trends of the day, while still endeavoring to retain the authority conferred by tradition and embodied in a ritual of great aesthetic appeal. This road to Canterbury seemed safe and well-guarded, offering a pleasant escape from the turmoil of the American sects. It led to bishops' palaces and aristocratic country houses where philosophy, science, and politics were discussed with an absence of rancor that was strange to American ears. The elite of the Church of England was immeasurably more cultured and tolerant than any to be found in

America. Why could not its spirit be brought to the colonies? Must the Anglican road run only in one direction? Here was a new dream offered to reflective American minds in the middle of the eighteenth century.

Young Samuel Johnson of Yale was perhaps the first American of note to feel the lure of that old world culture which was to draw so many thousands of his countrymen across the ocean in the century to come. He was primarily interested in philosophy, but the only gateway to philosophy in America was still theology, and the only way for a philosopher to make a living was as a clergyman. Johnson went to England to be ordained as an Anglican minister, mingled in the life of the wits of London, met Alexander Pope, then at the height of his career, and his own greater British namesake still struggling in Grub Street, and at last returned to America, equipped as both a philosopher and a man of the world, but a stranger to the Yale of his upbringing. The doctrines of Calvinism were abhorrent to his kindly Humanism. They were, he asserted, "contrary to the nature and attributes of God"; they were logically inconsistent and morally unworthy, for they pretended that an omnipotent and benevolent deity could have created a human being who immediately fell into total depravity, and that then He could find no better way of dealing with this unfortunate being than to consign him to an irretrievable Hell. Assisted by Bishop Berkeley's idealistic philosophy, Johnson held that the Calvinistic doctrine of grace was a perversion and limitation of the truth that all men were assisted by the inward light of reason "perpetually beaming forth from the great fountain of light."

Johnson changed the basis of ethics from the sense of sin to the desire for happiness. If man was not a hopelessly selfish creature but came into the world already endowed with impulses of brotherhood and co-operation, his salvation did not necessitate a complete conversion but rather a development, an arranging and ordering of his life in accordance with universal laws which his reason could recognize. Had Johnson's *Elementa Philosophica* (printed by Benjamin Franklin of Philadelphia) been published in England, its fundamental approach would have seemed neither new nor startling, though the treatise was well worthy to rank with the numerous ethical works of Cudworth, Clark, Shaftesbury, Hutcheson, or Adam Smith; but in America it opened up an entirely new world of thought. While nothing could have been further from Johnson's intention than the promotion of a purely secular ethics divorced from dogmatic Christianity, the tendency of his work, like that of its British prototypes, was clearly in that direction.

To Johnson himself, a well-ordered inner life seemed to demand a well-ordered outer life under the mild discipline of the Anglican Church. But his efforts on behalf of the church came to naught. The British turned a deaf ear to his pleas for the appointment of American bishops, while at home the loyalty of the colonial church to the Crown made it decreasingly popular. Elected president of New York City's recently founded King's College, chartered by Parliament in 1754, "to prevent the growth of republican principles which already too much prevail in the colonies," Johnson was too keenly aware of the trend of the times to be able to derive much enjoyment from his official eminence. Unable to dissociate his cultural ideals from their British background, he saw in the growing alienation of the colonies from the mother country a moral and intellectual cataclysm. When his wife, eldest son, and son-in-law all died in an epidemic of smallpox, he developed a morbid terror of the disease and became a pitiable object haunted by fears of death that were unbecoming to him either as a Christian or as a philosopher. Finally, he succeeded in compensating for his loss of personal dignity, and the approaching defeat of his cause, through a mystical conviction that the end of the world was at hand. Thus at last Johnson's seemingly well-reasoned Humanism proved to have been only the escape of an amiable but essentially weak character who had turned his back upon native sources of strength to seek them abroad, only to find that they failed him in his hour of need.

The contemporary Humanists of Harvard took a different path. Scornfully repulsing the emotionalism of the Great Awakening, and passing by the alluring compromises of the Church of England, they pushed on into the field of rationalistic speculation and entered on the course which was to lead to the Unitarian and Universalist movements of the nineteenth century.

The Reverend Ebenezer Gay of Hingham, emphasizing the distinction between Natural and Revealed Religion, seems to have been the first preacher in America to cast doubt upon the infallibility of the Bible. "No pretense of revelation," he stoutly asserted, "can be sufficient for the admission of absurdities and contradictions. The manifest absurdity of any doctrine is a stronger argument that it is not of God than any other evidence can be that it is." He talked of a "spiritual gravitation" which drew men toward God in the same way that physical gravitation operated to draw objects together, the conscience of man causing him to feel joy for his virtuous acts and pain for his evil ones. Gay, however, refrained from carrying his leveling doctrines into politics, clinging there to the high Tory platform.

The connection that Gay declined to make between religion and politics was easily established by Jonathan Mayhew, a patriot of the patriots, in his *Discourse Concerning Unlimited Submission and Non-Resistance to the Higher Powers* (1750). The syllogistic chain was unbroken from the doctrine of a natural conscience to that of self-government in morals, and from self-government in morals to self-government in politics. For the rest, Mayhew sought the revelation of God in the universal laws of Nature and human conduct, he rejected the Nicene and Athanasian creeds, and he declared the dogma of innate depravity to be a dishonor to God and a libel on man.

Charles Chauncy, the most important of the Harvard group, after many campaigns against revivalism, Calvinism, and episcopacy, closed his career with three works—*Salvation for All Men* (1782), *The Benevolence of the Deity* (1784), and *Five Dissertations on the Fall* (1785)—in which he cautiously drew the Unitarian and Universalist conclusions implicit in all this mass of liberal doctrine. The goodness of the Creator, he argued logically, implies the goodness of the creation and involves a natural goodness in man as a part of creation. In Chauncy's benevolent universe there was no place for Hell. But Chauncy was well aware that the privilege of being damned, or at least of seeing one's neighbors damned, was too dear to men to permit the dogma of Hell to be attacked with impunity. He discreetly published the most radical of his later works, *Salvation for All Men*, anonymously.

The Natural Religionists, through these strayings from orthodox dogma and veiled attacks upon the authority of the Bible, made it fairly evident that they were a transitional party. It began to be clear that in calling upon the aid of Natural Religion the churches had brought an unreliable ally into the fray.

The trouble was that Natural Religion proved too much. If men could discover the laws of God through the study of science, what need to pore over the Bible or mingle in the strife of the sects? Revelation tended to become merely a kind of desirable supplement to Natural Religion. This was virtually admitted by the entirely orthodox Samuel Johnson: "Because some parts . . . of Natural Philosophy and the whole of Moral Philosophy are of the greatest concern to us, God has of his special kindness to us, given us, relating to them a particular and express revelation of his mind and will, and how we (having offended Him) may yet secure his favor, through the mediation of his son. Here, therefore, belongs the Christian Philosophy which is only theology and morality more clearly and perfectly revealed to us." [1] This might satisfy a philosopher, but it was far from making Christianity the absolutely necessary thing it had formerly been considered. Instead of being the very basis of morality and theology, Christianity had now become only a clearer and more perfect form of them. If man was able through his own reason to grasp the essential principles of religion, why was it necessary for revelation to step in at just the point that it did or, indeed, to step in at all? The concessions made to reason and science by eighteenth century Christianity were, it is true, hardly greater than those of medieval Scholasticism, but at that time the Catholic Church had had at its disposal the powerful arguments of the rack and the thumbscrew to keep reason within its due limits. In the eighteenth century such restraints were no longer available.

THE PRINCIPLES OF DEISM

NATURAL RELIGION thus tended to supplant Christianity instead of reinforcing it as intended. Under the name of Deism, it developed a positive content with definite ethical and political implications. Whereas, after the time of St. Paul, orthodox Christianity was always divided between its original millennial hopes that looked toward the future and its later emphasis on the lost paradise of the

[1] Samuel Johnson, "A General Idea of Philosophy" (an early outline of his *Introduction to Philosophy*), first published in Isaac Woodbridge Riley's *American Philosophy: The Early School* (New York: Dodd Mead & Co., 1907), pp. 64-67.

Garden of Eden far in the past, the eighteenth century religion of Deism represented a new orientation of thought which was almost entirely futuristic. In this dynamic quality, Deism differed still more from the older static religions of Nature. Logically, a world view derived from astronomy and physics should have pictured man as a wholly insignificant part of a mechanical order the same yesterday, today, and forever. It should have been as pessimistic as later paganism. Actually, however, Deism was much less purely scientific than it supposed itself to be. Commercial aspirations and unconscious religious traditions combined to make the cosmos of Deism even more moral and purposive than that of Christianity. For the latter had always recognized an element of destruction and evil as somehow an intrinsic part of the natural order. This was exactly what Deism denied. God was all-wise and all-good; He was admittedly the creator of man and the universe; how could these be other than fundamentally good? Such evils as existed in human society must be temporal and accidental, due not to man's wicked will but to ignorance, or at worst to the wicked will of a small minority of priests and aristocrats who had managed to perpetuate their power through tyrannical institutions that were out of harmony with the laws of God and Nature. Destroy these institutions, set man free to develop his real inner being, his mind, and his reason, and perfection would lie just around the corner.

Deism was neither profound nor consistent. It underestimated the power of the dark, abysmal forces in Nature and man, and it took over from Christianity the dogmas of personal immortality and salvation to which it had no right on its own premises. There were even materialistic Deists who believed the mind to be a form of material energy and yet contrived to accept the immortality of the soul. But the illusions of Deism were generous illusions. If it overrated the goodness of humanity, it at least succeeded in making some part of humanity better and wiser than it had been before.

In its time Deism was a gospel of intellectual and spiritual liberation more far-reaching than anything in previous history. Its strength lay in its universality. It gave men a broader outlook on the world, freeing them from the parochialisms to which they had been accustomed. It dissolved the bonds of national and class loyalties, substituting for them a devotion to the good of humanity. The

Deists were not wrong in asserting that in this they were much nearer to the real spirit of Christ than were any of the so-called Christian churches. Like the earlier Humanists, they remained unorganized, functioning merely as individual writers and teachers, without the exclusiveness of the sectarian elites. If, as they believed, reason, the supreme faculty, was present in all men, even though in varying amounts, individual thinking and speculation could be safely encouraged.

In ethics the Deists were hedonistic or eudaemonistic, regarding virtue on its individual side as a kind of enlightened self-interest which practiced restraint as the means to secure more permanent satisfaction; while, on the social side, the same enlightenment, recognizing the individual's intimate ties with his fellow-men, could be trusted to enlarge his instinctive sympathies into an attitude of general benevolence and philanthropy. Most of the Deists never doubted that man had an innate sense of right and wrong, but they tended to regard this as a function of reason, insisting that conscience must also be intelligent. Thus they enlarged the older religious demand for freedom of conscience into the wider modern demand for freedom of thought in every field.

In the American colonies, the clergy, absorbed in sectarian quarrels, were rather slow to realize the danger of Deism. For example, Thomas Clapp, the rector of Yale, who refused to accept for the college library a gift of Baptist books offered by Thomas Collins, a Rhode Island merchant, nevertheless did accept a larger donation from Bishop Berkeley which contained a number of Deistic works. The more liberal Ezra Stiles, who succeeded Clapp, having saved himself, as he believed, from the errors of Deism by a wide course of reading, encouraged the students not to be afraid of heretical writings, with the result that most of them soon became Deists. If this was true at Yale, it was still truer at Harvard. In 1755 the authorities were content to establish the Dudleian lectureship to explain the principles of Natural Religion, but by 1789 they felt called upon to create the Alvord professorship "to prove the compatibility of revelation with reason." Even in orthodox Princeton the situation was little different, while at William and Mary, where an avowedly secular and nonsectarian policy was pursued, Deism was virtually the accepted college religion.

Thus, by the time of the Revolution, Deism was fairly well on the way to being naturalized in America. Its intellectual arguments and its devotion to science were of interest primarily to educated groups, but it also possessed distinct elements of mass appeal. Its individualism was congenial to the frontier, its democracy recommended it to the city tradesman, and its humanitarianism allied it with Quakerism.[2] Ultimately, it might prove to be too narrowly rational for all but the educated, but that remained to be seen.

Nearly all the leaders of the American Revolution were Deists, not orthodox Christians. Samuel Adams, Roger Sherman, and John Jay were almost the only exceptions, while the Deists numbered among them Benjamin Franklin, John Adams, Ethan Allen, Washington, Hamilton, Jefferson, Madison, and the Revolutionary poets, Joel Barlow and Philip Freneau. Of these American Deists, two of the earliest demand special consideration in this connection: Benjamin Franklin, the city tradesman; and Ethan Allen, the Vermont frontiersman.

THE DEISM OF BENJAMIN FRANKLIN

BENJAMIN FRANKLIN has been called "the first civilized American." He seems to us at this distance to have been the first American to stand entirely on his own feet, self-made, revealing the new native pattern, shrewd, kindly, honest, courageous but prudent, inventive but no dreamer, frugal and practical, with a realistic humor that seemed hardly more than applied common sense, essentially a man of good will, infinitely tolerant, the very embodiment of the Deistic gospel of enlightened self-interest.

His conversion to Deism came at an early age. "I was scarce fifteen," he wrote, "when, after doubting by turns of several points, as I found them disputed in the different books I read, I began to doubt of Revelation itself. Some books against Deism fell into my hands; they were said to be the substance of sermons preached at Boyle's Lectures. It happened that they wrought an effect on me quite contrary to what was intended by them; for the arguments of the Deists, which were quoted to be refuted, appeared to me much stronger than the Refutation; in short, I soon became a thorough Deist."

---

[2] William Penn and Robert Barclay were both accused of Deism in their day.

Franklin's early attitudes were also much influenced by those of his elder brother, James Franklin, printer and publisher of the first radical American newspaper, the *New England Courant*, largely devoted to attacks on the clergy. Soon after the publication of Cotton Mather's *Essays to Do Good*, articles by a Mrs. Silence Dogood began to appear in the *Courant*, ridiculing in homely language the pretentiousness of the clergy, the idleness and extravagance of the gilded youth at Harvard, the stupidity and class bias of the magistrates. Mrs. Dogood, the creation of the editor's young brother, already exhibited most of Franklin's characteristic qualities, being a kind of early sketch of Poor Richard. As a vernacular mouthpiece of popular wisdom, she was the first representative of a new and distinctively American literary type, the distant ancestress of Josh Billings, Artemus Ward, Finley Peter Dunne, and almost innumerable others.

The career of the *New England Courant* was short, as it was soon silenced by the magistrates and its editor jailed. Ere that time, however, it had lost the services of its most brilliant contributor. James Franklin's liberality stopped at the front door; he was a believer in political freedom and domestic tyranny, and proved a harsh taskmaster to his apprenticed brother. But Brother Benjamin was not a fighter by temperament: when he encountered stupidity and intolerance, he preferred, if possible, simply to move into a more peaceful and enlightened environment. At the beginning of the eighteenth century, there was only one choice for such a person to make in America; as a matter of course, the rebellious young printer went to Philadelphia.

The role of printers in the development of American culture deserves a special study. At a time when they often combined the functions of printers, publishers, newspaper editors, and librarians, they were, more than any other group, in direct touch with the contemporary thought of the world. The literature of the past was to be found in the colleges; the center of living literature was the printing shop. The printers formed a kind of mediating group between the upper and lower classes. They usually, like Franklin, sprang from the common people, yet their clientele was drawn from the educated minority; in spirit they were half-commercial, half-professional; as printers engaged in earning a precarious livelihood, they were tradesmen; as publishers, they sought to secure as wide a patronage as possible; as editors, they enjoyed a sense of public responsibility. In all their varied activities, they were, almost of necessity, interested in the spread of education.

Coming at the very beginning of this development, Franklin was one to appreciate all of its opportunities. Very early in his career he went, like any modern publisher, to England, both to purchase books and to find out what was happening in the literary and scientific worlds. Through his Library Company he introduced to the American reading public such radical works as those of Wollaston, Hume, and Spinoza, and such French authors as Buffon, Cabanis, Condorcet, and Lavoisier.

Never, in these early years, did Franklin forget his religio-philosophical interests. While in London, he published *A Dissertation on Liberty and Necessity, Pleasure and Pain*, written to refute Wollaston's *Religion of Nature Delineated*, and proving, to its author's momentary satisfaction, that under a God of combined omnipotence and benevolence, the world must be a perfect deterministic order, and the distinction between virtue and vice an illusion. Then, after he had given away a few copies, he very characteristically destroyed the remainder under a sudden moral compunction that they might "have an ill effect." On his return to Philadelphia, he organized among his fellow-printers a "Junto Club" for the study of religious and ethical principles. The personal creed which he composed at this time is interesting:

"I believe there is one supreme, most perfect Being, author and Father of the Gods themselves. . . .

". . . When I stretch my imagination thro' and beyond our system of planets, beyond the visible fix'd stars themselves, into that space that is every way infinite, and conceive it fill'd with suns like ours, each with a chorus of worlds forever moving round him, then this little ball on which we move, seems, even in my narrow imagination, to be almost nothing, and myself less than nothing, and of no sort of consequence.

"When I think thus, I imagine it great vanity in me to suppose that the Supremely Perfect does in the least regard such an inconsiderable nothing as man. More especially, since it is impossible for me to have any positive clear idea of that which is infinite and incomprehensible, I cannot conceive otherwise than that he the Infinite Father expects or requires no worship or praise from us, but that he is infinitely above it."

Thus far, aside from the mention of plural gods, Franklin's "First Principles" followed the straight course of Deism, but at this point they suddenly swerved to a tack of their own, highly characteristic of their ingenuous author:

"But, since there is in all men something like a natural principle, which inclines them to devotion, or the worship of some unseen power . . .

"Therefore I think it seems required of me, and my duty as a man, to pay divine regards to SOMETHING.

"I conceive then, that the INFINITE has created many beings or Gods, vastly superior to man. . . .

". . . I conceive that each of these is exceeding wise and good, and very powerful; and that each has made for himself one glorious sun, attended with a beautiful and admirable system of planets.

"It is that particular wise and good God, who is the author and owner of our system, that I propose for the object of my praise and adoration.

"For I conceive that he has in himself some of those passions he has planted in us, and that, since he has given us reason whereby we are capable of observing his wisdom in the creation, he is not above caring for us, being pleas'd with our praise, and offended when we slight Him, or neglect his glory."

One may smile at all this youthful exuberance of theological fancy, at Franklin's determination to worship "Something," and at his belief that he could attain the necessary inner conviction and emotional warmth by so tenuous a process of reasoning. Nevertheless, his frank recognition of the fact that religion was not derived from external evidence but from an inner need of man to worship some power in which he could find security enabled him in his common sense manner to put his finger on the central weakness of Deism: the remoteness of the Deistic Deity from all mundane affairs. He was not alone in his attempt to fill the infinite space between God and man with a crowd of polytheistic subdeities; the same device was adopted by Wollaston (from whom Franklin derived it), and by Thomas Jefferson, while Franklin's conception of a local, finite deity was to be revived in the twentieth century by William James and H. G. Wells.

The prudential character of Franklin's ethics has often enough been attacked. Poor Richard's emphasis on moneygetting has sadly overclouded the issue. Thus Max Weber, probably Franklin's severest critic, regards his philosophy as simply a continuation of Puritan acquisitiveness, essentially Transcendental in spite of its Deistic pretensions: ". . . The *summum bonum* of this ethic, the earning of more and more money, combined with the strict avoidance of all spontaneous enjoyment of life, is above all completely devoid of any eudaemonistic, not to say hedonistic, admixture. It is thought of so purely as an end in itself, that from the point of view of the happiness of, or utility to, the single individual, it appears entirely transcendental and absolutely irrational."

In answer, it may be pointed out that Franklin never regarded "the earning of more and more money" as the *summum bonum;* that his table of virtues was a modification of the list in Aristotle's "Ethics"; that only a few of them had anything to do with moneymaking; that they represented personal ideals which Franklin actually achieved, except, perhaps, in the case of his rather peculiar conception of chastity: "Rarely use venery but for health and offspring"; and that, if by happiness be meant inner serenity, few men in history seem to have been as happy as Franklin. True it is that he regarded wealth, like virtue, as a means to happiness, exactly as did the eudaemonistic Aristotle, but that he ever considered it an end in itself is contradicted by a lifetime more completely devoted to the aim of social service than that of any other American of his generation. The original founder of the Philadelphia Public Library and Fire Department, of the University of Pennsylvania, of the American Philosophical Society; the man who spent unrewarded years in England to defend Pennsylvania against the proprietors; the philosophical envoy to France who could meet Voltaire as an intellectual equal and yet remain so persuasive an example of simple manhood and obvious worth as to arouse among the French such enthusiasm for the colonial cause that this became a potent influence in bringing on their own Revolution;[3] the American patriot who, for all his "prudential ethics," risked his life as the most prominent signer of the Declaration of Independence; the septuagenarian who was the only person in the Constitutional Convention to say a word for the claims of labor—this man was not a moneygrubber but a genuine Humanist, and a very great one.

THE DEISM OF ETHAN ALLEN

ETHAN ALLEN of Vermont, the frontier philosopher, was a homespun thinker who suffered from none of the cautious inhibitions of Franklin. His *Reason the Only Oracle of God* (1784) was angrily characterized by Timothy Dwight as the first open attack on Christianity ever published in the United States. It was hardly that; but it certainly was a remarkably bold assault on the Christianity of the churches. As to whether he was a Deist or not, Allen professed to be in some doubt, as his philosophy was his own creation, but he was very sure that he was no Calvinist. Nor was he a believer in any of the compromises by which orthodox Christianity was striving to preserve its revealed religion by harmonizing it with the new religion of Nature. The two, Allen held, were fundamentally incompatible. Appealing to common sense and making much use of a homely frontier wit, he pointed out inconsistency after inconsistency in the orthodox doctrines. The clergy, he maintained, were mystery mongers who pretended to a higher knowledge of the nature of the universe than that vouchsafed to the plain man by the light of his own reason. The alleged revelations were either incomprehensible, in which case they were no true revelations, as they made nothing clearer, or else they were comprehensible, and in that case they offered no explanations that reason could not achieve without them. The notion of miracles or any other acts of Special Providence implied some imperfection in the laws of Nature, else why should God find it necessary to contravene them in particular instances? Yet God was acknowledged to be the creator of Nature and was proclaimed to be perfect; how then could He be the author of imperfection? The orthodox view degraded God to the level of a kind of cosmic watch-

---

[3] For Franklin's influence on the French Revolution, see Bernard Faÿ, *Franklin, the Apostle of Modern Times* (Boston: Little, Brown and Company, 1929).

maker who so bungled his original job that he had to be perpetually tinkering with it ever after. The same difficulty appeared still more strikingly in the Calvinistic doctrines of predestination and original sin which made God the actual creator of moral evil. The argument that human reason was depraved except among the elect was refuted by observable facts that showed great relative differences in the amount of reason possessed by individuals but never showed that the faculty was monopolized by the elect. As to the unjust and fundamentally immoral ideas of transmitted sin and an atonement by Christ, it was enough to point out that every tub ought to stand on its own bottom.

Thus in crude, vulgar, but not unforceful fashion, Ethan Allen derided the clerical dogmas. And in the opinion of orthodox Christians, Divine Providence interposed in an effective manner to prevent the circulation of his impious work. A fire destroyed most of the copies soon after its publication. Nor did Providence neglect to pursue the impenitent author still further and inflict upon him the righteous punishment he deserved. The "awful death of Ethan Allen" by a stroke of apoplexy at the age of fifty-two afforded the text for many a sermon. Even the relatively liberal Ezra Stiles committed to his diary a sardonic comment on Allen's death: "13th Inst. died in Vermont the profane and impious Deist General Ethan Allen, Author of the Oracles of Reason, a Book replete with scurrilous Reflections on Revelation.—'And in Hell he lift up his Eyes being in Torments.'" The incorrect title, from so good a scholar as Stiles, suggests that he had never read the book, but that would not have kept him from certainty as to the author's merited fate.

The majority of Americans would quite possibly have agreed with the Reverend Ezra Stiles. It must not be forgotten that the Deists were important through the quality, not the quantity, of their adherents. Herbert Morais, in his monograph on *Deism in Eighteenth Century America* (1934), cites two noteworthy examples suggestive of the general attitude. John Leland, a Baptist clergyman living during the Revolution in a parish only forty miles from Boston, had never heard of "Deism or Universalism," while Joseph Clark of Northampton, writing to his Boston bookseller for some Deistic works, cautioned him to send them very secretly because of "the bigoted attachment of the people in this part of the country to the particular principles in religion that they had been educated in." Leland, it is true, must have been unusually dull, and Clark may have been unnecessarily timorous, but it is also true that in many parts of America at the time of the Revolution Deism was either practically unknown or was considered immoral. Religious and political radicalism should logically have gone together in America as in France; actually, however, the low level of intellectual culture prevented the conjunction except in the minds of an influential minority. The synthesis of religion and politics was begun but was far from completed.

CHAPTER 16. *European Political Theory and American Political Fact*

ONE. EUROPEAN THEORY

AS AMERICAN religion was originally an importation from Europe, so, it might seem, was American political democracy a European product. Prior to the actual Revolutionary period, American thinkers had produced little or nothing of strictly political import. Long after secular political philosophy was well developed in England and France, colonial writers still moved in the shadow of theology; Calvinism was an issue in Connecticut, Quakerism and Pietism were issues in Pennsylvania, up to the very time when the guns began to speak at Lexington and Bunker Hill. The colonists began to fight before they were very clear in their minds as to just what they were fighting for, and when clarification came at last it came in the light of foreign theory. But while this was true enough in the realm of explicit formulation of doctrine, it was not at all true in the realm of behavior. In their actual practice the colonists were well on the way to democracy without knowing it—much further on the way, in fact, than the English or the French. When they finally began to concern themselves with political theory they already had amassed a fund of political experience by which to test and criticize it. This explains their almost incredible advance in this field of thought between 1760 and 1790—thirty brief years that determined the political ideals and the political forms of the hundred and fifty years to follow.

At the beginning of that critical period, democratic theory and democratic fact were separated, the theory being in England and France, the fact in America. At the end of the period the two were united—so far as theory and fact are ever united—in a well-defined body of doctrine implemented by a well-defined government.

THE THEORY OF NATURAL RIGHTS

THE explicit theory of political democracy was logically derived from the larger philosophy of Nature already discussed. That philosophy, traced to its distant origins, is an interesting example of the way in which theories are turned inside out in response to social needs. The conception of Nature as the embodiment of divine reason, advanced by the Stoics and upheld by the medieval Scholastics, was originally a highly conservative doctrine. A static Nature fitted in beautifully with a static government and a static church. Nevertheless, there were revolutionary implications to be found in the theory as soon as men cared to look for them. If any particular government could be shown to be out of harmony with the fundamental constitution of things, then that government was demonstrably "unnatural," a temporary human aberration from the universal order, a government whose laws were intrinsically null and void.

Furthermore, the theory of Nature could easily be given an individualistic cast. For it seemed obvious that Nature had endowed men as individuals with certain capacities that were quite independent of social organization or governmental laws and enactments. The exercise of each of these capacities was therefore a natural right, guaranteed by "Nature and Nature's God." As long as the sense of individual personality remained as feeble as it was during the Middle Ages the theory of natural rights remained undeveloped, but with the growth of individual self-consciousness fostered by the Reformation, and, above all, with commerce and industry established on an individualistic basis, the new conformations found in the theory an admirable sanction for their desires and aims.

It was undoubtedly the utility rather than the logical necessity of the new way of thinking that caused it to be acceptable just at this time. For the logical question at once arises: granting the existence of natural rights, how many and what are they? But there was no systematic treatment of this problem by any of the liberal philosophers of the period, no attempt to determine the number of natural rights or to present them in schematic form. As late as the classic American statement of them by Jefferson in 1776 there was still no definite enumeration or close definition; instead, he referred to "certain unalienable rights" and to particular ones "among these."

The actual rights selected for emphasis were clearly those that had come to be generally accepted or that were regarded as especially valuable. As set forth in the famous Bill of Rights of 1688, these seemed to be little more than the traditional privileges which Englishmen had enjoyed, in theory, ever since the Magna Charta. With regard to them, the conservative Blackstone asserted, quite correctly, in 1765: "The Great Charter protected every individual of the nation in the free enjoyment of his life, liberty, and property unless declared to be forfeited by the judgment of his peers or the law of the land." The weakness of this position lay in the little word "unless." If the law of the land could abrogate these rights at the will of the rulers, which, of course, was what actually had happened constantly through war and taxation, then the rights enjoyed a very tenuous existence. Life, and the freedom of personal movement (which seems to have been the chief meaning attached to "liberty"), and even the acquisition of property by individual labor, might all be independent of any government in their origin; but if the government, though it could not create them, was entitled to destroy them, the rights remained essentially theoretical. The degree to which one could enjoy them depended upon governmental tolerance and upon one's personal ability to enforce them. John Locke, the chief English exponent of natural rights, was thus a shrewd thinker, as well as a good bourgeois, when he emphasized the right to private property as the base of the others: for if one had sufficient property he could usually protect his life and liberty. Locke, with some effort, convinced himself that the ownership of property was, like the others, a natural right. Does not a man create his property through his own labor, and has he not a right to that which he has himself produced? That the larger part of actual property is not thus directly produced by the owner did not trouble Locke greatly in a period when the type forms of industry were considered to be those of agriculture and handicraft, to which other forms, by a bit of intellectual sophistry, could easily be assimilated.

Through the parliamentary debates of the seventeenth century the middle class had learned the importance of free speech, and this also, with more reason, was now considered a natural right. True, the very words that one uses reach him through social tradition, few of us making any notable individual additions to the language; but the meaning expressed through these words is, we fondly think, a matter of individual thought. Even though our original ideas may be much fewer than we suppose, it can hardly be denied that new ideas have somehow arisen in the course of history. Freedom of speech thus rests upon a freedom of thought actually guaranteed by Nature to a much greater extent than are the supposed rights of life, liberty, and property. One may be easily deprived of any of these three, but no outward force can prevent one from thinking his own thoughts as long as he remains alive and in possession of his faculties. The assault upon freedom of thought can be made only indirectly by destroying the thinker, or through restricting his freedom of speech to such an extent that his thought cannot be fructified by social intercourse. Both methods had been tried repeatedly by the Catholic Church during the Reformation, and the Protestant triumph seemed to demonstrate their futility.

THE THEORY OF THE SOCIAL CONTRACT

ALTHOUGH the various natural rights could thus be grounded, with varying degrees of philosophical cogency, upon the native capacities of man, not one of them was self-enforcing. The belief that they were derived ultimately from Nature's God lent an added religious fervor to their support, but it did not of itself secure their recognition from stubborn monarchs or aristocrats. The rights would still have remained theoretical had not another theory of partially independent origin been united with the theory of natural rights to give it revolutionary force. This was the doctrine of the so-called "Social Contract."

The conception that government rests upon some kind of implied contractual obligation was of late medieval origin, a natural outgrowth of the recognition of mutual responsibilities involved in feudalism, but it was also much affected by the rise of commercial interests, the very idea of "contract" being an intrusion into politics from the business world. There was a good deal of confusion as to the exact nature of the contract involved: it was at first often considered as one between rulers and subjects; later, as with Locke and Rousseau, it came to be regarded as a many-sided contract among all the individuals in the state of Nature, whereby they gave up their individual rights in exchange for the protection afforded by government, although as late as 1830 Robert Hayne, in his famous debate with Daniel Webster, half-reverted to the earlier notion.

In 1576 Jean Bodin attempted to turn the doctrine to the advantage of French absolutism, arguing in his *De la République* that the social contract between ruler and people transferred the power irrevocably to the former, whose sovereignty became thereby "supreme and perpetual, absolute, and subject to no law." This doctrine of transference involved the admission that sovereignty originally resided in the people, an admission which the opponents of absolutism were not slow to seize upon as carrying with it an implied right of revolution if the ruler failed to fulfill the terms of the contract that had bestowed the authority upon him in the first place. The argument raged for a century, both sides admitting the contractual character of government but reaching opposite conclusions, depending upon whether the original contract was regarded as inviolable or as subject to abrogation if its purposes were not fulfilled. The conservative interpretation was supported by Hugo Grotius (1585–1643), Samuel Pufendorf (1632–1694), and Thomas Hobbes (1588–1679); while the radical position was upheld by Johannes Althusius (1557–1638), Richard Hooker (1553–1600), and the Jesuits, Robert Bellarmine (1542–1621) and Juan Mariana (1537–1624), who, however, attacked the absolutist conception of royalty only in order to uphold the absolute authority of the Papacy.

Logic and the spirit of the times favored the radicals. The doctrine of natural rights early came into the discussion, and when Grotius and Pufendorf admitted the existence of a *jus naturale* precedent to the *jus civile* their conservative conclusions were nullified in advance. Influencing the development of the theory was the practice of the radical Protestant sects in organizing their congregations by a mutual covenant, the final form of the contract theory being in essence an enlargement of the covenant principle to include all social and political organization. This was the definitive form which the doctrine received in John Locke's *Two Treatises on Government* (1690).

The theory of the social contract is often misinterpreted today as having been based upon the false assumption that men originally lived in a lawless condition from which they saved themselves by coming together and forming a deliberately organized society to preserve the natural rights strangely imperiled in the state of Nature. The eighteenth century philosophers were neither such bad historians nor such bad logicians as this would imply. References to the mythical history do occur a few times in Locke and in the earliest work of Rousseau, but the main argument was never based upon them. The social contract theory, which had come to include that of natural rights, rested upon logical, not historical assumptions.[1] Natural rights were held to be logically prior to those granted by social enactment in the sense that they were based upon permanent and unchanging qualities in human nature, whereas the civil law, notoriously varying from age to age and land to land, owes what validity it possesses to its protection and organization of these inherent natural rights. Similarly, the social contract did not mean anything so absurd as the contention that governments had actually been created, save in exceptional and minor instances, by contract, but that they ought to have been so created, or rather that their moral justification depended upon the acceptance of such an implied contract as their foundation. The gist of both theories, in combination, was never presented more succinctly or clearly than in a single sentence of the Declaration of Independ-

[1] See Morris R. Cohen, *Reason and Nature* (New York: Harcourt, Brace and Co., 1931), pp. 402–404. Those interested should read the entire chapter on "Natural Rights and Positive Law." It is by far the ablest discussion of the whole subject that is available in English.

ence: "To secure these rights [natural rights], governments are instituted among men, deriving their just powers from the consent of the governed." [2]

JOHN LOCKE: POLITICAL REVOLUTIONIST

THE American theory of political democracy, as it was formulated at the time of the Revolution, was derived mainly from Locke. And the political philosophy of Locke was double-edged. As the first to gain wide acceptance for that "right of revolution" which was expressly set forth in nearly all the early American state constitutions, Locke was more radical than the majority of modern democratic thinkers are ready to be. On the other hand, in upholding an individual inherent "right to property," he ranged himself among the conservative supporters of an established order based upon property. These apparently divergent trends were harmonized by him with considerable skill in his statement of the basic principles of society.

The possession of property he regarded as the *fons et origo* of ethics and social morality. "Where there is no property there is no injustice, is a proposition as certain as any demonstration in Euclid." Justice and injustice do not depend, as Plato and Aristotle supposed, upon the nature of man; they depend upon the nature of property. And it is the nature of property, unfortunately, to be easily stolen or taken by violence; hence, though the majority of men, as Locke believed (in this reflecting the new optimistic thought appearing in England after 1688), were naturally governed by "the law of good will, mutual assistance and preservation," a few powerful rascals could in the state of Nature do a great deal of harm. To protect the interests of the majority, therefore, a civil society was formed and government was organized. In return for this protection the individual tacitly agreed to accept the majority will, expressed through a system of laws. The so-called "ruler" (whether monarch or president) was merely the executive agent to carry out and enforce these laws. Such in its essential principles was Locke's famous and fairly elaborate theory of "government by consent."

[2] See Carl Lotus Becker, *The Declaration of Independence* (New York: Harcourt, Brace & Co., 1922), pp. 68 ff.

Manifestly, in this scheme the "sovereign" was no longer sovereign; above him was "the law" or, concretely, the legislature, and above the legislature was "the people." Not only was the monarch now made, in principle, subject to the authority of that Parliament which had begun in the thirteenth century to be a restraining brake on its will, but the Parliament itself was, at least in principle, subject to the will of those who elected it. If either the executive or the legislative misused its powers, the sovereign people would clearly be justified in removing them, either peacefully or, if necessary, by violence.

But by the people Locke meant the property owners. Clearly, those without property could not in logic make any part of a society formed for the purpose of protecting property, and so they could not claim any legal or moral right to the suffrage. This, as we have seen, was what the term also meant in actual practice throughout the eighteenth century, both in Great Britain and in all the colonies.

It is difficult for the contemporary mind to be quite fair to John Locke. We have been told again and again in recent years that his social philosophy was oriented equally toward a vindication of the bourgeois revolution that had already occurred and toward prevention of any other kind of revolution in the future—much in the same way that the Puritans justified their own rebellion against the authority of others and condemned rebellion against their own authority. But such an interpretation is not only somewhat unjust to Locke; it distinctly obscures the nature of his historical influence. In the first place, the victory over absolute monarchy was not securely established for all time by the Revolution of 1688: not when Locke was writing immediately afterward, nor yet a hundred years later when absolutism, still triumphant in Germany, Russia, and France, was reasserted in England by George the Third and his Tory ministers with sufficient strength to bring on the American Revolution and to cause an undeclared civil war at home. Events in our own time have shown but too clearly that in warring against absolutism in government Locke was fighting against an attitude to which reversion is always possible. In the second place, Locke did not simply vindicate the Revolution of 1688 but went far beyond it in demanding the responsibility of Parliament to the electorate, as well as the responsibility of the King to Parliament. Only the latter was gained in 1688, the former not until more than a century later.

Furthermore, there was another radical principle, set forth in Locke's epistemological theories, which he himself never attempted to apply in the political sphere—not, at least, in any thoroughgoing manner—but which had important implications there, nevertheless. His theory of knowledge began with the assumption that the mind of every individual is at birth a *tabula rasa*, on which subsequent sensations organized by reflection write all the items of knowledge that humanity ever attains. On this assumption all men are clearly born equal, and their later divergence is most easily explained by the differences in their social position which expose them to different types of experience. This environmental theory was a splendid weapon against aristocratic pretensions of hereditary merit, but it could evidently, if it fell into violent hands, be used much more extensively and to ends that would have shocked and grieved unutterably its first propounder.

FRENCH POLITICAL THEORY

THIS was exactly what happened in France. For the French had not yet had *their* revolution. Hence the same theories which, being developed in England after the fact, were there turned to relatively conservative ends, became in France, before the fact, flaming prophecies of radical change. In England, economic control was definitely centered in the upper middle class, which shared its power with an aristocracy by now mainly composed of ennobled members of the bourgeoisie, and with an established church also upper middle class in personnel and sympathies. In France, the aristocracy was still feudal, the church was Catholic, and the bourgeoisie derived its potential power mainly from the overwhelming numbers of its lower middle-class constituency. So whereas in England men were inclined to defend their democratic leanings by appeals to religion and the citation of scriptural texts, in France the democratic movement quickly became antireligious. The British philosophers usually stopped short at sensationalism; or if, as in the case of Hobbes and Priestley, they ventured to advance a frank materialism, they still managed to harmonize a belief that the mind is merely a form of material motion with further beliefs, real or avowed, in "God, freedom, and immortality." In France, where social considerations made for consistency as definitely as in England they made for inconsistency, a thoroughgoing scientific materialism was developed by La Mettrie, Holbach, Diderot, d'Alembert, and other Encyclopedists, and this scientific materialism, vulgarized and popularized by the Deistic Voltaire, exercised a wide influence throughout the nation.

Horace Walpole, traveling in France, was shocked by the carelessness with which members of the upper class expressed irreligious sentiments in the presence of their servants; once the lower orders lost their reverence toward God, he rightly felt, they might soon lose their reverence for their earthly superiors.

Of course, no such result was contemplated or desired by most of the contributors to the *Encyclopédie*. Of that many-volumed, monumental work, Charles Beard writes judiciously, "Though associated in the common mind with attacks on religion, its real import was the meager space which it gave to that ancient monopoly as compared with the pages and tomes dedicated to man's understanding of the material universe, his place in it, and the society of which he was a part." The *Encyclopédie* was primarily a gigantic attempt to substitute the world view of science for that of religion, and in the thoroughness with which it accomplished that aim, it represented the most important revolution in men's thoughts that had occurred in human history. But its immediate implications for political change were all of bourgeois character, looking toward the gradual overthrow of church and nobility in favor of the rule of an educated and enlightened middle class. The Encyclopedists, in a word, constituted a self-conscious "intelligentsia," the first since the decline of the classical schools of philosophy, an intellectual aristocracy, proud of their own erudition and little interested in the lot of the common man. Thus Voltaire, the wealthy notary's son, constantly insulted by the nobility on the score of his birth, was quite willing to indulge in similar taunts of Rousseau, the lowly watchmaker's son. Like all intellectuals, the Encyclopedists shrank from translating their theories into emotion and action. That part of their task remained to be completed by a latecomer among them, the intellectual parvenu and renegade, Jean Jacques Rousseau.

ROUSSEAU: SOCIAL REVOLUTIONIST

JEAN JACQUES ROUSSEAU was the first man to take the theory of natural rights with entire seriousness. What had been a useful academic construction became in his hands a fiery gospel, transferred from the field of intellectual assent to that of passionate conviction. Poetically sensitive to the beauty of Nature, swept without great resistance by waves of sensuality, acquainted through his vagabond youth with those despised and rejected by society because of their poverty, vice, or crime, and finding in them most admirable qualities thwarted and stunted by their environment, he took up the cause of Nature against civilization, as the latter was understood by his contemporaries. Man was naturally good, he proclaimed, until corrupted by the injustice of society. The awakening of this conviction, which came to him suddenly at the age of thirty-seven upon reading the subject assigned for the Dijon Academy prize essay—Has the revival of the sciences and the arts helped to purify or corrupt morals?—had for him all the force of a religious conversion. And well it might. For although the assertion of the natural goodness of man had been the underlying basis of the theory of natural rights from the first, and had indeed been openly maintained by Locke, no one before Rousseau had dared to develop its implications as he did. These involved nothing less than the frank acceptance of human desires, the recognition that anything is a value if someone values it, and the building up of a new system of ethics on the foundation of human needs and aspirations instead of upon religious fiat. In a word, it set the moral task of the next two centuries and one knows not how many more.

Rousseau's thinking was mainly intuitive, yet when his prize essay, *A Discourse on the Arts and Sciences*, became immediately the talk of all France and was praised or attacked on every hand, he proved himself a keen enough logician in defending his position. That this position was recognized as being on the whole consistent with the general natural rights philosophy is indicated by Diderot's and d'Alembert's approval of the essay and by the fact that Rousseau was at first universally numbered among the Encyclopedists. He was clearly with them in his naturalistic philosophy, even though he misprised the scientific analysis of Nature and re-created the poetic myth of the pure and noble primitive so vividly that he almost seemed to believe it with unbecoming literalness. The emotional sympathy of humanitarianism which he added to the philosophical reasonings already in vogue supplied a motive power for group action. Liberty capped by fraternity became a social ideal, appealing to the sentiment of solidarity as liberty alone could never do. That sentiment was strongly developed among the Encyclopedists themselves, and, while they might be a little distrustful of thus precipitately broadening out their own blessings among all mankind, they could hardly do otherwise than support Rousseau's attitude.

But Rousseau with increasing distinctness now attempted to base both liberty and fraternity on the natural right of equality. To the question, "Whence the alleged injustice of society by which the natural man is corrupted?" he returned the ready answer: "The first source of evil is inequality." This, the Encyclopedists thought, was going much too far, and they turned against him.

The role of equality as a natural right had usually been veiled in a discreet haze. Of course, a transcendental, metaphysical equality of all men had been asserted by Christianity, but this equality in the eyes of God was not only compatible with human inequality, it could even be appealed to, as by Martin Luther, as the chief reason why men should not strive to change their earthly state, since the latter was entirely unimportant. Equality as a natural right was manifestly something very different from a mere transcendental assumption, but its status was still so undetermined in 1753 that the Dijon Academy offered as its prize subject for that year the question: "What is the origin of inequality among men, and is it authorized by natural law?" Possibly the authorities chose the subject with the deliberate design of tempting their former prize winner to compete; if so, they were successful. Rousseau's response, the *Discourse on Inequality*, disposed of the question so completely that henceforth in France, and eventually in England and even America, liberty and equality were accepted as a single concept, though Rousseau's meaningful interpretation of the term was whittled down into something much less significant. By equality, Rousseau meant frankly economic equality:

"So long as men were content with their rustic hovels, so long as they confined themselves to stitching their garments of skin, to decking their bodies with feathers and shells and painting them in different colors—in a word, so long as they only applied themselves to works that single persons could do, and to arts that needed no more than one pair of hands—then they truly lived, free, healthy, good, and happy, enjoying among themselves always the sweetness of independent intercourse. But from the moment that one man had need of the help of another, as soon as they perceived it to be useful for one person to have provisions for two, then equality disappeared, *property was introduced*, labor became necessary, and the vast forests changed into smiling fields which must be watered by the sweat of men, and in which they ever saw bondage and misery springing up and growing ripe with the harvests."

Rousseau had no illusions about the origin and purpose of government; it had been developed in order to perpetuate the power of the rich and mighty; the peace and order maintained by it were for the benefit of a small class; its pretended laws of justice were calculated to divert the minds of the poor from their sufferings and to reconcile them to the oppression under which they labored. It was nonsense to pretend that the ruler owed his position to the loyal support of his subjects. "Force maintains him; only force may overthrow him." Such had been the reality of all governments hitherto.

It is evident that Rousseau had traveled far from the position of Locke. Private property, instead of being considered a natural right, was now regarded as destructive of natural rights. A social revolution, instead of being something safely consummated in the past, was something to look forward to as the hope of the future.

As to just what the nature of the society after the revolution would be, Rousseau, like most revolutionists, was decidedly vague. Anarchism, socialism, and democracy were all to derive fuel from his doctrines during the nineteenth century. But in any event, whatever the exact political complexion of the ideal society, it must be decisively agrarian; men must enjoy direct contact with the soil, and their way of life must be characterized by simplicity. Urban luxuries, urban vice, could not be permitted. And this ideal society was still to be nourished upon religion. In Rousseau's Utopian state, belief in the existence of God and in the reality of future rewards and punishments was to be enforced on pain of banishment for any miserable unbelievers. Good as man was, in Rousseau's philosophy, he was not deemed good enough to be virtuous without the threat of eternal torment if he were otherwise.

Such were the varieties of liberal theory already developed in Europe before the American Revolution. There was abundance of diversity: the religious middle-class republicanism of Locke; the antireligious middle-class republicanism of the Encyclopedists; the radical equalitarianism of Rousseau. Almost any kind of revolution could find justification in one or another of these systems of thought. What more was needed to complete the theories was merely the actual revolution. This, the American colonists were now ready, in their own way, to supply.

TWO. THE AMERICAN FACT

ONE permanent characteristic of the American nation was by this time definitely apparent: an all but complete indifference to theory apart from its practical consequences. In emerging from the theological twilight, the colonists were inclined to throw both metaphysics and abstract logic out on the ash heap. The clergy themselves, led by the most redoubtable of the logicians, Jonathan Edwards, had come to rely on immediate emotional experience as a substitute for doctrine. The merchants were much less interested in discovering unknown laws of trade than in avoiding the navigation laws which they knew. The farmers, with scientific agriculture far in the future, planted and reaped in accordance with the rules which they worked out for themselves. Even the lawyers, rapidly coming to be the most intellectual and aggressive class in the colonies, were chiefly concerned with adapting the common law of England to the very different kind of society that had grown up in America. John Locke and Rousseau were left on the shelf; America would use them when it had need of them, not before.

But if Americans cared little for political and social theory, they cared enormously for political and social fact. And political fact in the colonies was much closer to John Locke's ideal than was political fact in England; indeed, in some ways the colonies were closer to Locke than the United States government was to be later. In both England and America the struggle between the executive and legislative bodies was still continuing, but while at this time in England George the Third was recovering some of the lost royal power by alliance with the ruling Tory party in Parliament, the governors of the various colonies almost always had the majority in the Assemblies against them. As the King was dependent on Parliament for his supplies, so the governors were dependent on the Assemblies for their salaries in most of the colonies; and even in the exceptional cases where the gubernatorial salary was derived from duties and quitrents the governors had not been able to escape from Assembly control. In spite of the property qualification of suffrage, alike in both countries, the colonial Assemblies were, as a whole, much more broadly representative than Parliament and were much more honest than Parliament. There were, as yet, no "rotten boroughs" in America, and the loot of India had not been used to corrupt American statesmen.

"The Freest of Peoples were the First to Revolt," as C. H. Van Tyne has well put it.[3] As we shall show, the revolt was very largely a defensive revolt to preserve liberties that had been long enjoyed. In many ways the actual (as contrasted with the theoretical) form of government was more democratic than that later adopted in the American Constitution. Just as the Bolshevist battle cry in the Russian Revolution was "All power to the Soviets," so the American cry might well have been "All power to the Representative Assemblies," unhampered by executive or judiciary—for that was very nearly the condition the Revolutionists sought to defend. Thus, for example, in 1754 the Privy Council informed His Majesty that the New York Assembly had "taken to themselves not only the management and disposal of such publick money but have also wrested from Your Majesty's Governor the nomination of all offices of Government, the custody and direction of the publick military stores, the mustering and direction of troops . . . and in

[3] Claude H. Van Tyne, *The Causes of the War of Independence* (Boston and New York: Houghton Mifflin Co., 1922), p. 18.

short, almost every other executive part of government." Or, as the Tory chief justice of New York, William Smith, was fain to declare after the Revolution: "The truth is the country had outgrown its government and wanted the true remedy (i.e. a strong executive and judiciary) for more than half a century before the rupture commenced. . . . An American Assembly, quiet in the weakness of their infancy, could not but discover in their elevation to prosperity that they themselves were the substance, and the governor and Board of Counsel were shadows in their political frame."

In many of the colonies, local self-government was developed to an extent undreamed of in England. Wherever the original settlement had been made by separate religious congregations, parishes, or well-integrated religious groups of any kind, these had naturally tended to develop their own organs of local government, such as the famous New England town meetings. That the colonists had thoroughly acquired the habit of ruling themselves through a system of laws is shown by the ease with which, during the Revolution and after, frontier communities organized themselves into separate states: Vermont, with its private "Declaration of Independence"; the state of Franklin in Tennessee; the republic of Transylvania in Kentucky; the republic of Indian Springs in northern New Hampshire.

The colonial social structure differed still more from that in England. In colonial society hereditary titles were unknown, or known only through the unpopular British officials and a few baronial lords who were mostly absentee owners. Birth carried with it no political privilege. There was, to be sure, even in the North, a mild aristocracy of gentility: the students at Harvard were still ranked according to their social standing, not according to scholarship (John Adams ranking only seventeenth in a class in which he was the outstanding member), and all Harvard graduates, and indeed all college graduates, were, of course, "gentlemen" never to be confused with the rabble. But this gentility rested only on family wealth and prestige, so that anyone might hope, with a bit of luck, either to become a gentleman himself during his lifetime or, at least, to become the father of gentlemen.

Except in New York and South Carolina, the amount of unencumbered private wealth was not great. There were, it is true, genuinely rich Philadelphia bankers and Virginia planters, but their number was few. In the colonies as a whole, judged by modern standards, the rich were ridiculously poor, and the poor were ridiculously comfortable. Aside from the institution of slavery, there was undoubtedly more economic equality in most of the American colonies between 1750 and 1850 than anywhere else in the civilized part of the globe.

The general equality of manners in America, which, persisting into later times, has deceived so many modern observers into overlooking the economic inequalities concealed beneath it, was, at the outset, a much more genuine expression of actual conditions. There is abundant testimony, also, to lead one to believe that the standard of manners was itself on a much higher level of taste than it is today. The Comte de Ségur, newly arrived from the court of France, could write:

"An observer, fresh from our magnificent cities, and the airs of our young men of fashion—who has compared the luxury of our upper classes with the coarse dress of our peasants, and the rags of our innumerable poor—is surprised, on reaching the United States, by the entire absence of the extremes both of opulence and misery. All Americans whom we met wore clothes of good material. . . . Indigence and vulgarity nowhere; abundance, comfort, and urbanity everywhere. The inhabitants, each and all, exhibited the unassuming and quiet pride of men who have no master, who see nothing above them except the law, and who are free from the vanity, the servility, and the prejudices of our European societies."

And to similar effect, Lafayette: "Simplicity of manners, the desire to oblige, and a mild and quiet equality are the rule everywhere."

With such facts in mind, Thomas Jefferson, who knew France well and loved it well, was driven to make the following striking comparison: "Of twenty million people supposed to be in France, I am of opinion there are nineteen million more wretched, more accursed in every circumstance of human existence, than the most conspicuously wretched individual in the United States."

It was obviously only a question of time and occasion as to when a people so self-sufficient and so self-reliant would break the ties which still bound them to what was, by now, an essentially foreign nation.

All things, however, are relative. What, in contrast to England or France, looked like equality was often, from the closer viewpoint of the colonists themselves, gross inequality. Everywhere an internal struggle had been going on between the upper and lower classes from the beginning, a struggle that differed greatly in intensity from region to region: relatively mild in New England and Pennsylvania, more bitter in Maryland and Virginia, and approaching a chronic state of class warfare in the Carolinas and Georgia, and in that colonial anomaly and anachronism, New York. Since this was to be of the greatest importance in the approaching Revolution, the conditions in these last four exceptional colonies demand at this point some special consideration.

THE CAROLINAS AND GEORGIA

The Carolinas had been founded as a single proprietary colony under a frame of government drawn up by no other than John Locke—but in his younger aristocratic days when he was secretary to the Earl of Shaftesbury. Charles Beard well describes Locke's "Fundamental Constitutions" for the Carolinas as "one of the most fantastic documents now to be found in the mouldering archives of disillusionment." [4] They envisaged the establishment, in the Carolina forests and swamps, of a landed aristocracy, with hereditary titles, ranked in a strict hierarchical pattern. At the top, of course, were the proprietors (eight in number), each of whom reserved to himself a "seignory" of twelve thousand acres in every county; next to them, a group of "landgraves" ruling over "baronies"; then came "caciques," [5] as lords of manors; and, at the bottom, mere yeomen, who must possess fifty acres in order to vote. Final authority was to rest with the proprietors, but in the colony itself was to be located a grand council of fifty members to initiate laws, and an assembly sitting in two houses—an upper house of the colonial noblemen and a lower house of elected deputies who must have estates of five hundred acres.

[4] Charles Beard, *The Rise of American Civilization* (New York: The Macmillan Co., 1933), p. 66.
[5] A Spanish word for the chief of an Indian tribe.

Although the Lockean hereditary titles could not survive in the American atmosphere, the aristocracy survived and, through the intermarriage of merchants and planters, formed a ruling class that governed the colony without effective opposition except such as came from the absentee proprietors or, later on, from the Crown. Great indigo and rice plantations were developed through slave labor, first Indian, later Negro, which proved so profitable that the slaves came to outnumber the whites. Trade with England flourished, and the established Church of England was held in high honor; the gentry sent their sons to England and the Continent for education and travel; the richest of them owned houses in London. South Carolina was by far the most British and the most aristocratic of all the colonies.

On the other hand, North Carolina, given separate recognition in 1729, was one of the most democratic and most American. With poor, shallow harbors which the heavy-draft British ships could not enter, and cut off from its neighbors by almost impassable forests and swamps, North Carolina became a rough, independent community of small tobacco planters whose trade was carried almost entirely by New England ships of light tonnage able to pass the dangerous shoals that environed the coast. The proprietors had little interest in it, and it had less interest in the proprietors. On three occasions the Assembly deposed the proprietary deputy governor and imprisoned him in a log cabin until he either bent to its will or went back to England. Although the Church of England was nominally established, and until 1769 no marriages were legal unless performed by an Anglican clergyman, few Anglican clergymen were willing to come. In 1769, indeed, there were only six in the whole colony, so that most of the North Carolinians were legally bastards. During the eighteenth century the population came to be overwhelmingly composed of Scotch-Irish Presbyterians, Baptists, and German Lutherans, disunited but ready to fight for their rights.

Meanwhile, the east-west sectional cleavage, normal everywhere south of the Potomac, had developed in both of the Carolinas. The older, wealthier, and better established Tidewater region manipulated the votes, levied taxes, and controlled the judiciary in its own interests as against the more recently settled Piedmont. In South

Carolina the Piedmont was too weak to offer effective resistance; but in North Carolina, shortly before the Revolution, actual civil war broke out between the government and the "Regulators" from the frontier land of the "Sky Blue Mountains." The defeat of the Regulators in the battle of Alamance in 1771 caused thousands to emigrate over the mountains into the Watauga and Holston valleys in Tennessee, where, under the leadership of "Noluchucky Jack" Sevier, they set up the "independent state of Franklin"—named after Benjamin Franklin, who, however, ungraciously declined the honor merely because he did not approve of Sevier's habit of massacring the Indians whenever he had nothing else to do.

Georgia, the last of the thirteen colonies, had been founded in 1732 by the idealistic Sir James Oglethorpe as a home for imprisoned debtors under a remarkably progressive set of laws which forbade the importation of either slaves or rum. But the corruption of good manners by evil communications was peculiarly easy in Georgia. It was too much to expect of human nature that the Georgians be content with poverty and hard labor while in prosperous, leisurely South Carolina the heavy and disagreeable work was performed by slaves. Similarly, liquor prohibition could not be enforced in Georgia when it was unknown elsewhere. Both rum and slavery were soon introduced, and Georgia became a kind of cruder South Carolina. Oglethorpe's liberal legislation was followed by the most reactionary penal policy to be found anywhere in America, under which, according to contemporary testimony, there were more whippings and imprisonments in Georgia than in all of the rest of the colonies put together.

THE STRANGE COLONY OF NEW YORK

NEW NETHERLAND had been established by the Dutch West India Company wholly as a commercial enterprise in which the settlers enjoyed none of the political or educational advantages of the home country with the single exception of religious liberty. That one factor, however, had sufficed to bring into the colony such a varied population that as early as 1643 Director Kieft reported that eighteen different languages were spoken on Manhattan Island. New York City that was to be came into existence with the cosmopolitan character it was always to have. Far from being the sleepy town of Washington Irving's description, New Amsterdam was the gayest, most lively, most hard-drinking, and morally irresponsible settlement on this side of the Atlantic. The Quakers, to be sure, were able to take advantage of Dutch religious tolerance to the extent of creeping up through the hill country along the Connecticut line until they covered a considerable region, where the well-kept Quaker farms, schoolhouses, and quiet peaceful communities furnished an example of the blessings to be found in a simple equalitarian life. But their influence was of little weight compared with that of the system of "patroonships," great estates along both sides of the Hudson River, which was established by the Dutch and taken over and developed by the British when they gained control of the colony. In 1688 there was a lower-class rebellion, led by Captain Jacob Leisler, in New York City, but after an initial success the movement was broken and Leisler was executed.

Before the end of the seventeenth century Governor Bellomont could declare that the "whole province" had been "given away to thirty persons." Three of these grants embraced more than a million acres apiece; several were for more than two hundred thousand acres; the least of them ran to fifty thousand acres. As in South Carolina, the leading families increased their power through intermarriage among themselves, or with the wealthiest of the merchant group in New York City. Thus there grew up a landed oligarchy of a few families—chiefly the upstate Van Rensselaers, Schuylers, Livingstons, and Morrises, and the downstate De Lanceys, Van Cortlandts, and Philipses—who, as long as they stood together, had no difficulty in controlling the Assembly or obtaining such public offices as they wished. Under these conditions the population grew slowly. At the time of the Revolution, New York was still numerically below frontier North Carolina. The potential wealth of the whole colony, as contrasted with the individual wealth of the few, remained undeveloped. In 1764 Lieutenant Governor Cadwallader Colden wrote that the greater part of the acreage of the large estates was still uncultivated and "without any benefit to the community."

By the middle of the eighteenth century the tenant farmers were desperate and ripe for revolt. In 1754 a fighting Irishman of Dutchess County, William Prendergast, discovered that the quitrent—four pounds and eight shillings—which he paid Frederick Philipse for his tiny farm was exactly the same as that which Philipse paid the British government for all of his holdings. A few days later two tenant farmers of Dutchess County were carried off to prison in New York for nonpayment of rent. Prendergast called for volunteers to march on New York to release them, and a thousand men flocked to his standard. They initiated their undertaking by giving a neighboring justice a ducking; when the outraged official exclaimed that he was a representative of the King, Prendergast, seized with the spirit of prophecy, replied, "If the king were here I would serve him the same way. Mobs have brought kings to before now and will again." His army then marched on New York and actually reached Kingsbridge just across the Harlem from the terrified city. But after inspecting the defenses of Fort George and learning the strength of its garrison, the rebel leader wisely decided not to risk an assault. Instead, he turned back up the Hudson and marched from estate to estate, everywhere declaring that manor rents were abolished and restoring dispossessed tenants to their farms, ending his spectacular campaign with a successful attack on the jail at Poughkeepsie. Then, after the manner of farmers, his forces broke up and went to look after their crops. The Twenty-eighth Regiment of British Grenadiers under General Thomas Gage, who was soon to have George Washington as an antagonist, now set out to capture the eighteenth century Wat Tyler. Prendergast, who had married a Quaker girl named Mehitabel Wing, fled to the meetinghouse on Quaker Hill with a few followers and prepared to defend it. Eventually, however, his Quaker wife persuaded him to surrender in order to avoid useless bloodshed. During his trial for treason she pleaded his hopeless cause with remarkable skill in the courtroom, and, immediately after his condemnation to death, mounted her horse for a wild ride to New York to obtain a reprieve from the governor, with which she returned to Poughkeepsie just in time to forestall an attempt at rescue by Prendergast's followers. Through the aid of the governor, who seems to have been utterly charmed by the demure

Quakeress, Prendergast was pardoned.[6] The antirent revolt failed, but it was more than a gesture, being a prerevolutionary symbol of events that were soon to come.

New York moved into the shadow of the Revolution disunited. There were greater extremes of wealth there than in any of the other colonies. The landed class, which had long sent its sons to England to be educated, was held to Great Britain by ties of sentiment and self-interest, but within that class there was bitter conflict between the upstate and downstate aristocrats. Among the common people there was the mass of rebellious tenant farmers in the Hudson valley, the group of pacifist Quakers on the eastern border, another group of rugged frontiersmen beyond the western mountains, and down at the tip of the colony in the city which had still preserved its roistering, riotous character there were rich conservative merchants, poor, discontented merchants, tradesmen still poorer, more discontented, and artisans and workmen, poorest and most discontented of all.

In general, it can be said that the ruling classes in New York and in the extreme southern colonies were favorably disposed toward Great Britain. The same might have been true in Virginia save that there the planters were hopelessly in debt to British merchants and so themselves suffered under what might be called an upper-class peonage. In the other colonies, upper-class sentiment was divided, while the lower classes everywhere were ready for battle, both to defend Lockean democracy and to extend it.

[6] This romantic story is told in interesting detail by Carl Carmer in *The Hudson* (New York: Farrar and Rinehart, 1939), ch. 9. Mehitabel Wing is still a legend on Quaker Hill, where there is a monument to her memory. The reader will be glad to learn that her husband and she lived to a good old age, dying peacefully in western New York, within a year of each other, in 1811–12.

CHAPTER 17 . *The American Revolution as a Popular Movement*

THE BIRTH OF THE REVOLUTION

THE birthplace of the American Revolution may be rightly located, not at Lexington or Concord, but on the Plains of Abraham at Quebec. The defeat of Montcalm and the collapse of the French colonial empire rendered the colonies independent *de facto* seventeen years before they became so *de jure*.

The colonial policy of Great Britain, as of other nations, was directed by what is known as the "mercantile theory," according to which colonies represented an original investment of capital and energy by the mother country, and the profit from the investment therefore naturally belonged to the mother country, which in turn was obligated to provide for the defense of the colonies. The possibility of industrial competition between the home nation and the colonies was eliminated in advance by the understanding that the colonies should furnish the raw materials needed for home manufactures, but should not develop manufactures of their own. With the colonies enjoying a monopoly of raw materials and the home nation enjoying a monopoly of manufactures, assuming that neither traded with any other country, a kind of static system of barter for mutual advantage was envisaged. The actuality, of course, did not correspond very closely to the abstract logic of the theory, either with the British or any other colonial system. The mother country continued to produce such raw materials as it could, the

257

colonies developed such manufactures as they could, and both were eager to sell to foreign nations. During the eighteenth century Great Britain found it necessary to promulgate the ever-lengthening series of Navigation Acts to restrict the industrial development of the American colonies within the strict limits contemplated by the mercantile theory. The weak point of that theory was that it hinged upon the provision of defense by the home country. Whenever such defense should cease to be required, it would be necessary for the mother country either to give up the theory or to give up the colonies.

After 1759 that was exactly the situation with regard to Great Britain and her American possessions. Once the French menace was removed, no foreign power threatened the colonies. Spain, in the far South, was too weak to be dangerous, and the colonists were abundantly able to handle the scattered Indian tribes along the western frontier. Colonial shipping had developed to the point where, if free trade were permitted with Europe and the West Indies, American ships could supply all the American needs that were not already satisfied by home production. The importation of British manufactured goods was still highly desirable but no longer essential. After 1759 the colonists were in the position to dictate terms to the mother country. But, naturally, it took them some time to learn this, and the British statesmen were never to learn it until the American Revolution was over.

At the very moment when it behooved Great Britain to show the tenderest consideration toward the colonies if she desired to retain their loyalty, the British statesmen were driven by financial difficulties into adopting the exactly opposite policy. The French war had been won, but it had not been paid for. A great part of its expense had gone into the defense of the American colonies. True, the British had defended the colonies for the sake of British, not American, merchants; still, from whatever motives, the American merchants had been protected. Would it not be eminently fitting, then, for the colonies to contribute to the very utmost toward defraying the expense of the war? Every pound obtained from America would be a pound saved for the British.

On the other hand, the colonies themselves had already contracted a war debt of over two million dollars, part of which had been remitted by the generous action of Parliament but with enough still remaining to constitute a heavy drain on colonial resources. Why, then, the colonists asked, should they contribute further? Did the British expect to wring blood from a turnip or draw water from an empty well? The colonial militia had fought as bravely as—and sometimes better than—the British regulars, for all the supercilious airs assumed by the latter. The colonial trade was estimated by William Pitt to bring in an annual profit of more than two million to the British merchants. Could they not be content with that?

The statement of J. Franklin Jameson in *The American Revolution Considered as a Social Movement* (1926) is not likely to be challenged by any future historian: "Of the deep underlying causes which for a generation had been moving the American mind in the direction of independence none was so potent, according to all the best testimony, as the parliamentary restrictions on the trade of the colonies." The Revolutionary war was, like others, an economic war. Put in purely economic terms, it meant simply that in order to determine who should bear the expense of one war, the British and Americans went to the further expense of a second war. In such a statement there would seem to be little place for any ideology of "liberty" and "natural rights." But, as always, to isolate the economic motive in this manner would give an erroneous picture of the whole situation. The Revolution was not only an economic war; it was also, just as the colonists insisted, a war for liberty and natural rights.

This came about through the fact that the British could not enforce the parliamentary restrictions without invading established political rights and thereby raising the ideological issue. No one in Great Britain was better disposed toward the colonies than William Pitt, yet when in 1761 he attempted to revive the Molasses Act, passed in 1733 but never enforced, he unintentionally created a situation pregnant with insoluble political problems. By forbidding the colonial molasses trade with the French and British West Indies, the Act struck at New England's chief commercial asset. It was, in consequence, so widely evaded that enforcement legislation seemed necessary, and in an evil hour the royal customs collector in Massachusetts petitioned the Superior Court to issue "Writs of Assistance," i. e., blanket search warrants.

As so often happens, the question of the means immediately became much more important than that of the end which they were supposed to serve. Opinions might differ as to whether the Molasses Act in itself infringed upon fundamental American rights, but there could be little doubt that the legalization of blanket search warrants did. Empowering the customs officials to enter any office or house whatsoever and without any specific evidence that dutiable goods were concealed there, the issue of Writs of Assistance plainly violated one of the most cherished "traditional rights of Englishmen," guaranteed in the inviolability of domicile proclaimed by the Bill of Rights of 1688 and never assailed since that time. Were the colonists entitled to the rights of Englishmen, or could these be denied them by every petty customs official?

The King's advocate-general in Massachusetts was the brilliant young lawyer, James Otis, heir to two generations of legal talent through his grandfather, Judge Otis, and his father, Speaker Otis of the House of Deputies. Called upon to support the petition for Writs of Assistance, he resigned his office and argued the case against them in the first great speech of the Revolution. "Otis was a flame of fire!" said John Adams, who heard the speech and took down the only notes of it which we have. "American independence was then and there born; the seeds of patriots and heroes were then and there sown."

What were the forces that rallied behind Otis and later Samuel Adams in resisting the oppressive British measures in the early years of the conflict? As usual, the first to protest were those who suffered most from these measures, namely, the common people. The merchant class, though affected injuriously by the Navigation Acts, could still exist under them, since, of course, American merchants did not wait until the nineteenth century to learn the art of passing on tariff charges to the consumer. There was no such relief for the common people. To them, the duties meant merely higher prices, an increase in the cost of living. They realized perfectly well—what the confused American mind has since often forgotten—that a tariff is also a tax. And a foreign tariff did not even bring with it the doubtful compensation of wider employment. It meant less employment and at the same time it lowered real wages. Hence, as we have had occasion to observe with the beginnings of the Reformation, it was the lower class that first took the lead in revolutionary measures. In the crucial years from 1761 to 1774 the mechanics and artisans, petty tradesmen, and small farmers formed the backbone of the patriotic party; after that—and again the parallel with the Reformation holds good—their program was taken over by the merchants, large planters, and lawyers.

In Boston, the lower class already had an effective organization in the "Sons of Liberty," originally formed to fight, not the rule of the British, but that of the Boston merchants. The Sugar Act of 1764, a revision of the Molasses Act and enforced by the hated Writs of Assistance—granted in spite of the efforts of Otis—was essentially a tax on a necessity of life, and it at once brought the Sons of Liberty to the fore and gave them an incomparable leader in Samuel Adams. The "Liberty Boys," as they were scornfully called by the merchants, had a similar organization in New York City with several fearless men at their head: Isaac Sears, a stout young sea captain; John Lamb, the owner of a small wine shop; Alexander McDougall, the son of a humble New York milkman; and John Moran Scott, a lesser Adams, the theoretician of the group. In Virginia, where there were no real cities, the struggle was carried on by the farmers of the Piedmont under the leadership of the backwoods lawyer, Patrick Henry. Meanwhile, the merchants backed and filled, unable to take a firm stand until the Tea Act of 1773 shut them out of the tea trade.

The tea dumpings in Boston, New York, and elsewhere, together with the enforced return of the tea ships with unlanded cargoes from the other American ports, were open and general acts of resistance which, if punished at all, called for general punishment. But the British ministry understandably shrank from so large an order and decided to make an example of Massachusetts by closing the port of Boston while leaving the rest of the ports open, so that Boston's loss would be the others' gain.

The temptation to profit by Boston's disaster was almost irresistible. It was strongest in Boston's nearest rival, New York, where the struggle that followed was one more illustration of the general principle that the class least capable of disinterestedness, least capable of making any sacrifice for the common good, is the class that already possesses the most.

On May 12, 1774, when the news of the Boston Port Bill reached New York, the Sons of Liberty, guided by Isaac Sears and John Lamb, at once held a meeting, appointed a committee, and three days later dispatched a letter to the Boston committee in which they announced: "We have received the shocking and detestable Act of Parliament, that shuts up your Port the first of June. . . . We want Language to express our Abhorrence of this additional Act of Tyranny to America . . . a great number of our citizens wish our Port to be in the same state with yours . . . we have stimulated the Merchants to appoint a Meeting tomorrow evening at seven o'clock to agree upon a general Non-importation and Non-exportation Agreement of Goods."

As Frank Monaghan remarks in his life of John Jay, "the merchants had been more 'stimulated' than Sears and McDougall suspected." Gouverneur Morris began his dishonorable record as a wirepuller with a letter to Proprietor Penn happily announcing the formation of a conspiratorial plot among the merchants. "The heads of the mobility grow dangerous to the gentry, and how to keep them down is the question . . . to trick them handsomely a Committee of patricians was to be nominated." The merchants managed to pack the meeting of the Sons of Liberty to such good effect that they succeeded in enlarging the Committee of Twenty-five by electing twenty-six additional members of their own choosing. Rivington, the Loyalist editor, wrote jubilantly to his friend, Henry Knox, the Maine landowner: "You may rest assured no non-im nor non-exportation will be agreed upon. . . . The power over our crowd is no longer in the hands of Sears, Lamb and such unimportant persons who have for six years past been the demagogues of a very turbulent faction in this city: but their power and mischievous capacity expired instantly upon the election of the Committee of Fifty-one, in which there is a majority of inflexibly honest, loyal and prudent citizens." [1] Rivington could not

---

[1] Frank Monaghan, *John Jay* (New York and Indianapolis: The Bobbs-Merrill Company, 1935), p. 52. The other quotations in this paragraph are taken from the same excellent work.

foresee the day two years later when, with war already under way, his shop would be destroyed by a crowd of angry patriots led by the despised Isaac Sears.

Fortunately, there were men in every colony and in each social class who could see beyond the immediate interests of their group and section to the larger issues involved; men whose spirit of determination rose to meet the increasing dangers. The humiliating example of the New York merchants was not followed. Even in New York their political representatives, led by the farseeing John Jay, proved willing to collaborate with "the mobocracy" in all necessary measures of general defense. The Committees of Correspondence established by Samuel Adams saved the day, and when a call went out from Virginia for a Continental Congress one colony after another swung into line. American resistance was not to evaporate, as the British ministers had hoped, in a squabble between social classes.

The other colonies deliberately made the cause of Massachusetts their own. Within less than six months of the day when Rivington had exulted because "no non-im nor non-exportation" agreement would be passed by New York, not New York alone but the whole Continental Congress adopted the measure which the Sons of Liberty had proposed. This meant that all the colonies were now united in an open economic rebellion; that, in effect, they were seeking to impose what in the language of today would be called "economic sanctions."

Any nation in history might well have been proud of the Continental Congress. It represented the best in character and intelligence that the colonies had to give, and this best was of a high order. Included in one or the other of the first two Congresses were nearly all of the great American Revolutionary leaders: Franklin, Washington, Jefferson, the two Adamses, Patrick Henry, Richard Henry Lee, John Jay, James Wilson, Joseph Galloway, John Dickinson, John and Henry Rutledge. Of this body, Lord Chatham, conversant with its addresses, petitions, and resolutions, declared that "for solidity of reason, force of sagacity, and wisdom of conclusion under a complication of difficult circumstances, no nation or body of men can stand in preference to the general Congress at Philadelphia." Naturally, at a time when higher education was so narrowly limited to the upper classes, they were the ones chiefly represented, but there was no question of the general patriotism of these representatives or of their usual willingness in the hour of emergency to sink their immediate interests in the common welfare. Even the temperamentally censorious John Adams could write to his wife, "There is in the Congress a collection of the greatest men upon this continent in point of abilities, virtues, and fortunes. The magnanimity and public spirit which I see here make me blush for the sordid, venal herd which I have seen in my own Province."

During the next few months while the Congress was not in session Adams had occasion to think better of venal Massachusetts, for during the interval were fought the battles of Lexington, Concord, and Bunker Hill. Emerson was an accurate historian as well as good poet when in his "Concord Hymn" he stressed the point that the "shot heard round the world" was fired by the embattled farmers of Massachusetts. The actual Revolution was begun by the common people, the same class that had been most uncompromising in their resistance from the beginning and that would continue until the end to furnish the mass power necessary for the Revolution's success. The British troops were already besieged in Boston by the popular army, and Fort Ticonderoga had been taken by the Green Mountain Boys "in the name of the Great Jehovah and the Continental Congress"—at least, that was the story —before the Continental Congress reconvened. The religious mood in which the people went into their war for freedom is well illustrated in the astonishing popular battle song, "Bunker Hill," written and composed by two Rhode Islanders, Nathaniel Niles and Andrew Law:

> "Why should vain Mortals tremble at the Sight of
>   Death and Destruction in the Field of Battle,
>   Where Blood & Carnage clothe the Ground in Crimson,
>   Sounding with Death-Groans?
>
> "Death will invade us by the Means appointed,
>   And we must all bow to the King of Terrors;
>   Nor am I anxious, if I am prepared,
>   What shape he come in . . .

"Life, for my Country and the Cause of Freedom,
Is but a Trifle for a Worm to part with;
And if preserved in so great a Contest,
Life is redoubled."

When the Congress met, it confronted a fait accompli. But it lost no time in giving its sanction to what had been done and in putting all its energy behind what remained to do. It devoted itself to the task of raising an adequate army. It gave the command to the one person in the colonies most fitted for the position—for Colonel George Washington, though his military experience was practically confined to his single campaign under General Braddock, had nevertheless in that disastrous retreat showed a courage and cool resourcefulness that had given him an intercolonial reputation, while he had learned to know as none other the weaknesses of the British regulars and the strength, as well as the weakness, of the colonial militiamen. Only in two vital matters did the Congress fail of efficiency, and in both instances the failure arose chiefly from the fact that it did not have a united country behind it. Being essentially a revolutionary organization without legal authority, it dared not venture upon the imposition of taxes; instead, it issued continental bills of credit supposed to be redeemable in specie in the several states, but when the time for redemption arrived the states merely issued their own bills of credit, and all this paper money, continental and state, was left hanging in the air and sure to depreciate, as it did. The second failure of Congress was shown in the long delay in issuing the Declaration of Independence, without which there could be no alliance with France or Spain, no foreign military aid, no foreign loans. It was certainly a ridiculous situation to be engaged in open warfare for fifteen months before admitting the fact. But again the Continental Congress had no authority to act on such a matter without special instructions from its constituents, and the separate colonies were slow to make up their minds on the issue.

LOYALIST AND PACIFIST SENTIMENT

In GENERAL, aside from the beleaguered merchants of Boston and the debt-ridden planters of Virginia, the richest merchants, the largest landowners, and the lawyers with an upper-class clientele, were Loyalists. Even in patriotic Boston, James Otis and John Adams are said to have been the only important lawyers who espoused the popular cause. The Episcopal clergy and those of the nascent Methodist Church, which was still a part of the Anglican body, were nearly all Loyalists. And, of course, the royal officeholders, including Benjamin Franklin's natural son, William Franklin, the governor of New Jersey, were Loyalist to a man. These various groups probably constituted an actual numerical majority in New York, Georgia, and South Carolina.

The sections in which the Quakers were strongest were naturally centers of pacifism. In Rhode Island, the Quaker influence was counteracted by that of the militant Baptists, who had already come back into political power, but in certain districts of New Jersey and North Carolina the Quakers were still a force to be reckoned with, while in eastern and central Pennsylvania, where their pacifism was re-enforced by that of the German Pietists, they were sufficiently powerful to keep that important region in a practical state of neutrality whatever its political representatives might decide upon. This was a body blow at the cause of the patriots, since Pennsylvania was not only the richest of the colonies but it occupied a strategic position between the North and the South which made Philadelphia the natural location for the national capital. It was inevitable under the circumstances that the attitude of the Quakers should be misjudged by the patriots and bitterly attributed to mere cowardice and lack of patriotism. It was, of course, neither. Unfortunately, however, there was only too much ground in many individual cases for the suspicion that the Quaker and Pietist pacifism was not entirely pure. The richest Quaker merchants had the same ties with Great Britain as the Loyalist merchants elsewhere, while the German-speaking Pietists could hardly fail to remember that George the Third was personally more German than English. But that, fundamentally, the racial motive was not the controlling one is shown by the fact that the German Lutherans were easily rallied by the Muhlenbergs to the patriot cause, and years later the ultimate sincerity of both Quakers and Pietists was proven by their still remaining true to their pacifist principles in the Civil War, when it was greatly to their disadvantage to do so.

There was no resisting the realistic irony of a situation which forced the Quakers for all practical purposes into the same camp with their original Anglican enemies. The result of their love of peace at any price was to discredit them as a sect in the eyes of the majority of Americans and to hasten the numerical decline that had already begun from the internal causes earlier discussed. The loss to the Quakers was great, but the loss to America was tragic. The virtual exclusion of the Quakers as a group from the national councils made it much easier to pursue those policies of exterminating the Indian, retaining the southern Negro in permanent slavery, and neglecting the rights of the northern workingmen, all of which were to darken the face of American democracy in the decades to come.

With the exception of the Anglican, Methodist, Quaker, and German Pietist groups, the various Protestant sects stoutly supported the patriots. The British government was itself largely responsible for this. The Quebec Act of 1774 not only granted religious toleration to the Roman Catholics in such liberal terms as virtually to constitute it the established church in that province but, by extending the boundaries of Quebec to include the Ohio land west of the Alleghenies, brought the threat of a Catholic establishment under French direction all along the colonial border. The Act made the loyalty of Canada certain, as it was intended to do, but at the same time it aroused a natural fear and resentment among the American Protestants. A wave of anti-Catholic feeling swept over the colonies. The Continental Congress attempted to go over the head of King and Parliament with an *Address to the People of Great Britain*, written by John Jay, who had been brought up among the intensely anti-Catholic Huguenots of New Rochelle, in which he expressed the colonial "astonishment that a British Parliament should ever consent to establish in that country a religion that has deluged your island in blood, and dispersed impiety, bigotry, persecution, murder, and rebellion through every part of the world." Anti-Catholic propaganda was circulated in the army at Cambridge, and the old custom of burning an effigy of the

Pope on "Pope Day"—the equivalent of Guy Fawkes Day—was resumed throughout the colonies. Patriotic versifiers warned of the danger of toleration:

"If Gallic Papists have a right
To worship their own way
Then farewell to the Liberties,
Of poor America . . ."

and taverns echoed to the rollicking song:

"Then heigh for the penance and pardons,
And heigh for the faggots and fires,
And heigh for the Popish church wardens,
And heigh for the priests and the friars;
And heigh for the raree show relics
To follow my Canada Bill-e
With all the Pope's mountebank tricks;
So prithee, my baby, be still-e.
Then up with the Papists, up, up,
And down with the Protestants down-e
Here we go backwards and forwards
And all for the good of the Crown-e."

Suddenly the picture changed almost overnight. The unexpected victory at Ticonderoga led the Congress to consider General Benedict Arnold's suggestion of an invasion of Canada, and in that event it would be highly desirable to gain the support of the Canadian Catholics against the British. With what seems almost incredible tactlessness the same John Jay who had written the address to the people of Great Britain was now commissioned to write another, "To the Oppressed Inhabitants of Canada," which contained the rather surprising announcement that the Congress "perceived the fate of the Protestant and Catholick colonies to be strongly linked together" and therefore invited the Canadians to join with them "in resolving to be free, and in rejecting, with disdain, the fetters of slavery, however artfully polished." In pursuance of the new policy, Washington gave strict orders forbidding the "ridiculous and childish custom of burning the effigy of the Pope." The whole anti-Catholic agitation died away even more quickly that it had begun.

"FREE AMERICA WITHOUT HER THOMAS PAINE IS UNTHINKABLE"

IT WAS not unfitting in a conflict that was, in one aspect, really a double civil war in both England and America, that the man who finally aroused the colonies to assert their independence was an Englishman and the son of a Quaker. Thomas Paine's *Common Sense*, published in January, 1776, was certainly the most influential piece of propaganda ever brought out in America prior to the appearance of *Uncle Tom's Cabin;* it was probably the most influential work of its kind that had ever been published anywhere in the world. Contemporary opinion was unanimous in recognizing Paine's book as the determining factor that at last brought the hesitating American mind to its irrevocable decision. John Adams, who detested the author, calling him "the filthy Tom Paine," was yet compelled in all honesty to admit that history would "ascribe the revolution to Thomas Paine," and Lafayette declared that "free America without her Thomas Paine is unthinkable." *Common Sense* turned what had hitherto been a rebellion into a revolution and clarified, if it did not determine, the basic principles for which it was to be fought.

Paine was able to exercise the influence which he did because he was a man of the people, accustomed to thinking in terms of concrete reality unembarrassed by scholastic subtleties or legal technicalities. He could speak to the people in their own language, as Franklin had done when Franklin was younger. The great Benjamin, whose friendly advice in London led to Paine's coming to America in the first place, recognized at once on the appearance of *Common Sense* that his successor had arrived and with the utmost generosity acclaimed him enthusiastically. "Others can rule, many can fight," he said, "but only Thomas Paine can write for us the English tongue." And only Thomas Paine could express the thoughts which the common man, coming upon them written out in clear, direct words, would perceive to be those which he himself would have had if he had been capable of such resolute thinking.

Paine's father, a humble corsetmaker of Thetford, had given his son something more valuable than wealth or position: an early acquaintance with the principles of the Quaker religion. But much water had gone under the mill since the time of George Fox. Born into an age whose chief interests were philosophical and political, Paine could no longer hold to Quakerism in its older Biblical and dogmatic form. As he grew into manhood, with only a grammar school education but reading widely and with quick intelligence, his half-Unitarian Quaker theology became transformed into Deism—of which both Barclay and Penn had been sometimes accused. There was in his temperament no slightest trace of mysticism or quietism: all that side of the Friends' religion escaped him, and with it went their devotion to pacifism, their unworldliness, their reluctance to deal with affairs of state. But the humanitarian side of Quakerism and its lower-class sympathy with the lot of the common man met with the fullest possible response from Paine, whose own long familiarity with poverty as he struggled to gain a precarious livelihood, first as a corsetmaker, then as a badly paid excise officer, gave him a sense of the economic realities underlying religion and politics. And religion and politics were to him inextricably intertwined. He denominated his Deism "the religion of humanity," being the first to use the phrase, and he could equally well have defined his political views as "the politics of humanity." The ideal state was described by him in these words: "When it shall be said in any country in the world, 'My poor are happy; neither ignorance nor distress is to be found among them; my jails are empty of prisoners, my streets of beggars; the aged are not in want, the taxes are not oppressive; the rational world is my friend, I am a friend of its happiness'—when these things can be said, then may that country boast of its constitution and its government."

Two unhappy marriages, the first terminated by death, the second by separation, left him without domestic ties to interfere with his absorption in the public welfare. When he was dismissed from office for organizing his fellow-excisemen in a demand for higher wages, the premature labor unionist was quite ready to follow the advice of Benjamin Franklin. There was no place for such as Paine in England; there might be in America. It was the old call to the land of opportunity for idealists—the call that had been heard by Roger Williams, Penn, and Oglethorpe, and that was now heeded by one of their truest descendants.

Paine arrived in America in November, 1774, thirty-seven years old, poor and unknown, a failure by all worldly standards. Aided by a letter from Franklin to his son-in-law, Richard Bache, he was able almost immediately to obtain employment as the editor of a new monthly magazine, and his real career had begun. From the first he was delighted with his adopted country, loving its newness and its lack of binding traditions. He did not feel that he was an Englishman in a remote part of England, but a citizen of the world in one of its most important centers. (In *Common Sense* he was to ridicule the idea of England as *the* mother country, pointing out that representatives of every European nation were here, sometimes far outnumbering, as in Pennsylvania, the original English stock.) A single blot on the picture perturbed him: the existence of slavery; and he had already begun to attack it in his magazine when he came to see that the growing conflict with England must be settled first. To that task he devoted all his efforts in *Common Sense*.

For over a year the American patriots had been in the anomalous position of declaring that they were still King George's "most loyal subjects" at the same time that the King himself was denouncing them as rebels and traitors. In January, 1776, when Paine's *Common Sense* appeared, the officers in George Washington's army still toasted the King every night. But the fiction that the colonists were merely resisting the illegal acts of Parliament but not the King was wearing desperately thin when everyone knew that the King had Parliament in his pocket. What was needed was for someone to call attention to the realities of the situation and restore the possibility of clear thinking. The greatest obstacle in the way was the attenuated sentiment of loyalty to the monarchy that still survived in speech though it was no longer a matter of genuine conviction. Paine's English background was here an advantage. If he, an Englishman born, could speak with contempt of King George, surely Americans might express their own real beliefs on the subject. Paine brought the latent hatred of monarchy to full self-consciousness, and in doing so established the first tradition of the nascent republic.

With broad muscular strokes he swept King, Parliament, and half of the English Constitution into the dustbin: "The nearer any government approaches to a Republic, the less business there is for a King. It is somewhat difficult to find a proper name for the government of England. Sir William Meredith calls it a Republic: but in its present state it is unworthy of the name, because the corrupt influence of the Crown, by having all the places in its disposal, hath so effectually swallowed up the power, and eaten out the virtue of the House of Commons (the republican part in the constitution) that the government of England is nearly as monarchial as that of France or Spain. For 'tis the Republican and not the Monarchial part of the constitution of England which Englishmen glory in, viz., the liberty of choosing a House of Commons from out of their own body; and it is easy to see that when republican virtue fails, slavery ensues. Why is the constitution sickly, but because monarchy hath poisoned the republic? The Crown hath engrossed the Commons. . . . Of more worth is one honest man to society, and in the sight of God, than all the crowned ruffians that ever lived."

To call George the Third a "crowned ruffian" was crude and unjust, if one will, but it was the most effective way possible of challenging all reverence for hereditary rank and title.

Paine went on to point out the practical advantages that would come to the colonies from independence: " 'Tis not in the power of Britain to do this continent justice; the business of it will soon be too weighty and intricate to be managed with any tolerable degree of convenience by a power so distant from us, and so very ignorant of us; for if they cannot conquer us, they cannot govern us. To be always running three or four thousand miles with a tale or a petition, waiting four or five months for an answer, which, when obtained, requires five or six more to explain it in, will in a few years be looked upon as folly and childishness." As long as the colonies remained a part of the British Empire they would inevitably be involved in European wars with which they had no concern. Foreseeing and advocating the isolationist policy that would govern the future nation in the first century of its existence, Paine declared that by nature England and America belonged to "different systems": "England to Europe, America to itself."

This appeal to self-interest was not made in any parochial spirit; rather, the direct opposite. Having no local ties with any particular colony, Paine could think of them more easily as a united nation and could glimpse their future importance more clearly than if he had been a citizen of any one of them. The immediate issue acquired a new dignity and grandeur from the sweep of his vision:

"The sun never shined on a cause of greater worth. 'Tis not the affair of a city, a county, a province, or a kingdom; but of a Continent, of at least one-eighth part of the habitable globe. 'Tis not the concern of a day, a year, or an age; posterity are virtually involved in the contest, and will be more or less affected even to the end of time, by the proceedings now."

Cutting under specific questions of direct and indirect taxes and the merits of this or that particular law, Paine claimed the sanction of natural right for what had always been implicitly, and what was henceforth to be explicitly, the fundamental American demand and conviction: "A government of our own is our natural right."

THE DECLARATION OF INDEPENDENCE

WITHIN two or three months after its publication, *Common Sense* was read by practically every American who was able to read. Discussed in a thousand village stores, blacksmiths' shops, public conveyances, everywhere in fact that two or three were gathered together, its arguments were soon familiar to the illiterate as well as the literate. The popular response was immediate and unmistakable. "Every Post and every Day rolls in upon us Independence like a Torrent," reported John Adams. In March, North Carolina took the decisive step of setting up its own independent government; in May, Congress advised every state to do the same; and in June, Virginia adopted a constitution which included in its famous Bill of Rights a definite statement of the philosophical and legal principles that were henceforth to be accepted as the fundamental basis of the American theory of government.

George Mason, the author of this tremendously important document, composed by him with some slight assistance from James Madison and Patrick Henry, is today almost forgotten save by historians. Yet few Americans have better deserved to be remembered. Born in 1725, he was the oldest of that extraordinary group of liberal Virginia statesmen which included Henry, Jefferson, Madison, George Wythe, and John Taylor of Caroline, and he was in many respects their leader. Like Jefferson, and unlike Patrick Henry, he was much more interested in legislation than oratory. Although one of the richest of the planters and one of the highest in social position, he was a firm believer in the general principles of popular sovereignty. How far he was ready to go, and how far Virginians were ready to follow him, was made clear in the opening sections of the Bill of Rights:

"A declaration of rights made by the representatives of the good people of Virginia, assembled in full and free convention; which rights do pertain to them and their posterity, as the basis and foundation of government.

"1. That all men are by nature equally free and independent, and have certain inherent rights, of which when they enter into a state of society, they cannot by any compact deprive or divest their posterity; namely, the enjoyment of life and liberty, with the means of acquiring and possessing property, and pursuing and obtaining happiness and safety.

"2. That all power is vested in, and consequently derived from, the people; that magistrates are their trustees and servants, and at all times amenable to them.

"3. That government is, or ought to be, instituted for the common benefit, protection, and security of the people, nation, or community; of all the various modes and forms of government, that is best which is capable of producing the greatest degree of happiness and safety, and is most effectually secured against the danger of maladministration; and that when any government shall be found inadequate or contrary to these purposes, a majority of the community hath an indubitable, unalienable and indefeasible right to reform, alter or abolish it, in such manner as shall be judged most conducive to the public weal."

After thus formulating the general principles of popular government, the Virginia Bill of Rights went on to apply them through provisions for rotation in office, freedom of elections, and the preservation of fundamental liberties through insistence upon jury trials, moderate bail, humane punishments, freedom of the press, religious toleration, and prohibition of general warrants and standing armies.

It would be difficult to overestimate the importance of the Virginia Bill of Rights. Both its substance and language were copied in most of the state constitutions adopted during the Revolution;

they were paraphrased by Jefferson in the opening sections of the Declaration of Independence; they formed the basis of the first ten amendments to the Federal Constitution; and they served as the immediate model for the French Declaration of Rights in the beginning of the French Revolution.

Considering the close parallelism between the Virginia Bill of Rights and the Declaration of Independence, it might seem as if George Mason, rather than Thomas Jefferson, were the real author of the Declaration. But in actuality there was no real question of "authorship" in either case. What John Adams said testily of the Declaration was equally true of both documents: "There is not an idea in it but what had been hackneyed in Congress for two years before." This, however, instead of detracting from the merit of these great state papers was precisely what gave them their representative value. Otis, Samuel Adams, John Adams himself, Patrick Henry, James Wilson, and countless others, had combined to build up the system of thought that found its final expression in the Declaration of Independence.

Nevertheless, Jefferson's particular part in it should not be minimized. He was responsible for most of the splendor of its phraseology, and for the rhythmical march from clause to clause. He formulated the long list of charges against George the Third, which, though of little interest today, was of great importance at the time it was written. And on two particular points, he departed, more significantly than is often realized, from previous statements of the natural rights position.

Jefferson placed as the first of the "self-evident truths" to which he appealed the fact that "All men are created equal," thus laying even more stress on equality than on liberty itself, a relative emphasis made still more striking in his original draft by the clause that followed: "and from that equal creation they derive rights inherent and unalienable, among which are the preservation of life and liberty and the pursuit of happiness." Jefferson's recognition of equality as the more inclusive concept upon which that of liberty depends was philosophically sound and was absolutely fundamental to a democratic interpretation of liberty. It is evident that if all men are equal no one of them can control another, whereas, without such equality, "Liberty for the pike is death for the minnow," as R. H. Tawney remarked. When Jefferson's more conservative colleagues struck out the six words, "from that equal creation they derive" and substituted the high-sounding phrase, "they are endowed by their Creator with," they broke the all-important connection between liberty and equality, separated the former from the condition of its universal attainment, and paved the way for the nineteenth century laissez-faire degradation of liberty which virtually made it equivalent, during the age of the industrial robber barons, to the right of the strongest.

Jefferson's second important change in formulating the theory of natural rights was much less felicitous. The most important of those rights were customarily considered to be, as we have seen, the rights to "life, liberty, and property." All three had been united and given additional ethical meaning by George Mason in his words, "the enjoyment of life and liberty, with the means of acquiring and possessing property, and pursuing and obtaining happiness." By omitting all mention of property and the attainment of happiness, leaving a mere "pursuit" of the latter as the right that was to be defended, Jefferson and his fellows cut the theory of natural rights free from its economic moorings. Jefferson may have felt that in so doing he was making the theory more purely idealistic and humanitarian by relieving it of its mercantile implications, but this would hardly have weighed with most of his colleagues. More likely, the determining reason with all of the signers was that the revolting colonies were about to confiscate the great Tory estates and that under such circumstances it would be more prudent, as well as more honest, not to mention the subject of property at all.

It would be a mistake, however, to say with Thomas Skidmore that the third of Jefferson's natural rights was entirely meaningless. The mere recognition of the pursuit of happiness as something legitimate and natural for all men meant a final rejection of the theocratic program and set up the humanitarian ideal of general happiness as the ultimate aim of the government.

THE SLAVERY ISSUE

THERE was one contradiction between American theory and American practice that was so palpable, so utterly indefensible in either logic or morals, that the Tories were quick to seize upon it. Thomas Hutchinson was able to point out with scorn the discrepancy between the rhetorical devotion to liberty in the Declaration of Independence and the actual American practice of depriving "more than a hundred thousand Africans of their right to liberty." [2] Other Tory writers made the most of a point that seemed unanswerable. What defense of American sincerity could be offered as long as they chose to maintain the institution of slavery in the midst of their land of freedom?

Eighty years later, Chief Justice Taney in his Dred Scott decision offered on behalf of the framers of the Declaration of Independence an excuse which none of the Revolutionists themselves ever mentioned: "It is too clear for dispute," he said, "that the enslaved African race were not intended to be included. . . . They had for more than a century before been regarded as beings of an inferior order, and altogether unfit to associate with the white race, either in social or political relations; and so far inferior, that they had no rights which the white man was bound to respect; and that the Negro might justly and lawfully be reduced to slavery for his benefit. He was bought and sold, and treated as an ordinary article of merchandise and traffic, whenever a profit could be made by it. . . . This opinion was at that time fixed and universal in the civilized portion of the white race. It was regarded as an axiom in morals as well as in politics, which no one thought of disputing, or supposed to be open to dispute; and men in every grade and position in society daily and habitually acted upon it in their private pursuits, as well as in matters of public concern, without doubting for a moment the correctness of this opinion."

In thus endeavoring to bring the Declaration of Independence to the support of his own illiberal views, Taney must have been quite aware that he was constructing a mythological history. At the time of which he was writing, most of the Quakers had already emancipated their slaves, the northern French Huguenots were strongly opposed to the institution, and nearly all of the great Revolutionary leaders openly condemned it. Among those most

---

[2] Actually the figures were much larger. J. F. Jameson, after a careful estimate colony by colony, gives half a million as the total number. *The American Revolution Considered as a Social Movement* (Princeton: Princeton University Press, 1926), p. 31.

outspoken in this condemnation were Christopher Gadsden of South Carolina, Washington, Jefferson, Madison, Mason, and Henry of Virginia, Franklin and Dickinson of Pennsylvania, Jay of New York, and even Timothy Dwight of Connecticut. Such apologies for slavery as were offered by liberals like Willie Jones and Nathaniel Macon of North Carolina took the form of admitting the injustice of the system but holding that it was necessary for southern prosperity. Rarely, indeed, was there any wholehearted defense of the institution during the Revolutionary period. In England, while the opposition was not so acute, it had already found leaders in Clarkson and Wilberforce. The civilized portion of the white race was very far from upholding the uncivilized view attributed to it by the chief justice.

In 1774 the Continental Congress temporarily prohibited the slave trade, and in July of that year Rhode Island passed a law freeing all slaves thereafter brought into the colony, pointing out in the preamble the relation between this and the colonial struggle for liberty: "The inhabitants of America are generally engaged in the preservation of their own rights and liberties, among which that of personal freedom is the greatest, and . . . those who are desirous of enjoying all the advantages of liberty themselves should be willing to extend personal liberty to others." Similar in tone was the preamble to the constitution of the first antislavery society in America, formed on April 14, 1775, in Philadelphia, which declared that "Loosing the bonds of wickedness and setting the oppressed free is evidently a duty incumbent on all professors of Christianity, but more especially at a time when justice, liberty, and the laws of the land are the general topics among most ranks and stations of men."

In 1776, Thomas Jefferson had the opportunity to draft the Declaration of Independence of the United States, and in it there is no overt condemnation of slavery. Was Jefferson then, after all, as insincere as the planters who had voted against him in the Virginia convention? Some modern historians have been tempted to defend his position by resorting to casuistry, as, for instance, Morison and Commager, who flatly assert that "Jefferson did not mean to include slaves as men," thus identifying his stand with that of the Dred Scott decision of 1856. But Jefferson's intellectual integrity was of a different order from that of Chief Justice Taney. Had these historians ever troubled to read his original draft of the Declaration they would have found in it a denunciation of the slave trade in which he used every device of language, italics, and capitalization to emphasize the precise point that he *did* "mean to include slaves as men." This is the suppressed passage, intended to have been the culminating charge against George the Third, and regarded by John Adams as one of the ablest parts of the original Declaration:

". . . He has waged cruel war against human nature itself, violating its most sacred rights of life and liberty in the persons of a distant people who never offended him, captivating and carrying them into slavery in another hemisphere, or to incur miserable death in their transportation thither. This piratical warfare, the opprobrium of *infidel* powers, is the warfare of the *Christian* king of Great Britain. *Determined to keep open a market where MEN should be bought and sold*, he has prostituted his negative for suppressing every legislative attempt to prohibit or to restrain this execrable commerce. . . ."

According to Jefferson's own statement, which there is no reason to question: "The clause . . . reprobating the enslaving of the inhabitants of Africa was struck out in complaisance to South Carolina and Georgia, who had never attempted to restrain the importation of slaves, and who on the contrary still wished to continue it. Our Northern brethren also I believe felt a little tender under those censures; for tho' their people have very few slaves themselves yet they had been pretty considerable carriers of them to others."

Frustrated by Congress in his first attempt to make a national issue of what he characterized as the "abominable crime" of slavery, Jefferson immediately renewed his attacks on the system in his native state. Within four months of the adoption of the Declaration of Independence he had introduced in the Virginia Assembly, along with much other radical legislation, a bill which provided for gradual emancipation. Defeated once more, the best he could do was to secure the enactment of a law in 1778 forbidding the slave trade within the state. Six years later he seized an opportunity to revive the issue as a matter of national policy by presenting in Congress a plan to organize the frontier territories under a legal code forbidding slavery—a measure which was defeated by a single vote. "Few more dreadful calamities have occurred in the history of America," writes Virginius Dabney of Virginia [3] with no exaggeration. Jefferson himself was well aware of the fateful consequences involved. "Thus we see the fate of millions unborn hanging on the tongue of one man," he wrote of the vote, "and Heaven was silent in that awful moment."

It is hardly too much to say that Jefferson three times nearly succeeded in saving his country from the ghastly tragedy of the Civil War. Had his indictment of the slave trade been included in the Declaration of Independence, the compromises on that subject in the Federal Constitution could not have been adopted without a self-stultification that the framers of the Constitution would hardly have dared to risk. Had his bill for the gradual abolition of slavery in Virginia been passed, it is highly probable that the other southern states would have followed the lead of the Old Dominion; but even had they not done so, Virginia, together with the Virginian-settled Kentucky and Missouri, would have been aligned with the North, leaving the rest of the South in a hopeless minority. Had Congress accepted his proposed ordinance of 1784, Kentucky, Tennessee, Mississippi, Alabama, and Florida would all have come into the Union as free states, and slavery, confined to the Carolinas and Georgia, could hardly have lingered for long. Thus, had any one of Jefferson's three measures been adopted, the entire future of America would have been altered.

Or had Washington seen fit to bring his enormous prestige to the support of Lafayette's scheme for a general emancipation of the slaves immediately after the Revolution, the same result would probably have been accomplished. Washington approved of the purpose of his friend's idealistic enterprise but felt that he himself could not afford the financial loss involved, and, since he was one of the richest men in the country, how could he ask others to undertake a sacrifice from which he shrank himself? So he postponed the emancipation of his slaves until his death, leaving the financial problem to his heirs; and the force of what might have been a compelling example was almost wholly lost.

[3] Virginius Dabney, *Liberalism in the South* (Chapel Hill: University of North Carolina Press, 1932), pp. 64–65.

Much the same was the attitude of Patrick Henry, who wrote to a friend: "Is it not amazing that at a time, when the rights of humanity are defined and understood with precision, in a country above all others fond of liberty, that in such an age and such a country we find men professing a religion the most humane, mild, gentle and generous, adopting a principle as repugnant to humanity as it is inconsistent with the Bible and destructive to liberty? . . . Would anyone believe I am the master of slaves of my own purchase! I am drawn along by the general inconvenience of living here without them. I will not, I cannot justify it. However culpable my conduct, I will so far pay my devoir to virtue, as to own the excellence and rectitude of her precepts, and lament my want of conformity to them. I believe a time will come when an opportunity will be offered to abolish this lamentable evil— Everything we can do is to improve it, if it happens in our day, if not, let us transmit to our descendants, together with our slaves, a pity for their unhappy lot, and an abhorrence of slavery."

The opportunity for which Patrick Henry professed such desire existed at the time he was writing, and would never return; the sacrifice which would then have been only an "inconvenience" would later entail the destruction of the whole economic system of the South. But the easy solution chosen by Henry was only too attractive to others as well: to transmit to their descendants both real slaves and a theoretical abhorrence of slavery, thus preserving both their unrighteous wealth and their inner feeling of righteousness, was the sort of compromise with conscience to which the majority of men have always been prone.

Nevertheless, the rise of the revolutionary spirit did result almost at once in eliminating slavery in the northern states, where the economic motives for its continuance were less powerful than in the South. Vermont, unrecognized by the Continental Congress, issued its own declaration of independence in 1777 and adopted a state constitution which was the first in America to prohibit slavery. In 1780 gradual emancipation was proclaimed in Pennsylvania; in 1783 the Massachusetts courts held that slavery was inferentially prohibited by the declaration of rights, similar to that of Virginia, in its new state constitution; in 1784 the example of Vermont was followed by New Hampshire, and that of Pennsylvania was followed by Rhode Island and Connecticut. Although Jefferson declared disconsolately in 1785 that opponents of slavery were as rare south of Chesapeake Bay as they were numerous to the north of it, some progress was made even in the South while the impetus of the Revolutionary spirit persisted. In 1787 both North and South Carolina laid prohibitory duties on the slave trade, and the latter was totally abolished in Georgia in 1798. It was not until the effects of Eli Whitney's cotton gin, invented in 1793, began to be manifest that the cause of antislavery was wholly lost in the South.

WAS THE REVOLUTION WORTH FIGHTING FOR?

ONE final question remains: were the results of the Revolution worth fighting for? Benjamin Franklin asserted, "There is no good war and no bad peace," but short of that absolute principle, which Franklin himself did not follow, there is ample reason to believe, with the English and French liberals of that day, that the Revolution was well worth the cost. It brought in its train five permanent results without which America would not have been the America we have known.

The first was, of course, political. The sovereignty of the people was established as the basic principle of American government. This advanced position had not yet been taken anywhere else in the world. It has been often maintained that the same principle was established in England by the Revolution of 1688, but the contention will not hold water. The Revolution of 1688 established the sovereignty of the British Parliament, which was a very different thing. No American could ever imagine that the sovereignty resided in Congress—the American analogue of Parliament—any more than it rested with the executive. Both were henceforth regarded as the agents of the sovereign people. The Revolution transformed Americans from subjects into citizens.

The second result was social. Hereditary rank was tacitly abolished. This did not mean the elimination of social distinctions nor did it establish a classless society; it did not prevent—nothing ever could—a reverence for titles among the more snobbish; but it did create a situation in which, broadly speaking, public respect would be given, not necessarily to individual merit, but at least to individual ability, whether military, political, financial, or what not.[4] The American standards of achievement were often crude, and would unfortunately become even cruder, but within those standards, whatever they were, it was necessary for the individual to achieve something himself in order to rise very far in general favor. This attitude has become so ingrained in the average American that it is difficult for him to regard the retention of hereditary rank in Europe as anything more than a picturesque anachronism like the survival of ruined castles and dismantled abbeys. The Revolution broke the American's connection with the limiting past and oriented him toward an apparently ever-widening future.

The third result was religious. At the beginning of the Revolution, four of the colonies—Rhode Island, New Jersey, Pennsylvania, and Delaware—were, as they had always been, thanks to the Baptists and Quakers, free from the burden of an established church. But for a century they had been on this point the exception, the outlaws, among the colonies. The Revolution brought the others, quickly or slowly, to adopt the Baptist and Quaker policy. Maryland and North Carolina voted for disestablishment in 1776, and South Carolina followed in 1778. In the intervening year Vermont came into political existence under a constitution which forbade the union of church and state. Elsewhere there was more reluctance to carry religious liberalism to its logical end. It took what Jefferson called "the hardest struggle of his life" before he was able, with the aid of Lee, Mason, and Madison, to secure the adoption of the Virginia Statute of Religious Liberty in 1786. This was followed by the prohibition of a national establishment in the First Amendment to the Federal Constitution in 1790. There the liberating movement was halted for a number of years. It naturally proved much more difficult to disestablish the patriotic Congregational Church in New England than it had been to overthrow the unpopular Anglican Church in the South. But New Hampshire yielded in 1817, Connecticut in 1818, and Massachusetts in 1833. As with the question of hereditary rank, the separation of church and state has come to seem so much a part of the natural order to most Amer-

---

[4] Note the typically American remark of Abraham Lincoln to Herndon, "I don't know who my grandfather was, and I am much more concerned to know what his grandson will be."

icans that one easily forgets the facts that when it was first adopted by the Revolutionists it was a wholly unprecedented experiment outside of America, that it was not adopted anywhere in Europe until the twentieth century, and that it still does not exist in England.

The fourth and fifth results were economic. Three months after the adoption of the Declaration of Independence, Jefferson introduced in the Virginia Assembly a bill for the abolition of the system of entail and primogeniture. The liberal Piedmont and conservative Tidewater once more closed in conflict over this issue, not only in Virginia but up and down the coast as far as Georgia. And eventually the Piedmont won. Though this did not prevent the maintenance of large plantations in the hands of single families, it did remove the legal obstruction to decentralization wherever economic conditions permitted the latter.

Finally, and of more immediate economic importance, the confiscation of the great Tory estates accrued to the benefit of the small landowners. The vast domains of the Pepperell, Philipse, Penn, and Fairfax families, embracing hundreds of square miles in Maine, New York, Pennsylvania, and Virginia, were divided up in small holdings to nourish a new race of independent farmers. The estate which had once belonged to Roger Morris of New York now supported two hundred and fifty separate owners. So with the lands of the De Lanceys and Calverts, of Governor Wentworth in New Hampshire, of Sir William Johnson in New York, of Henry Harford of Maryland, of James Wright of Georgia. It is rather idle today to debate the justice or injustice of these proceedings. The American peace commissioners, Franklin, Adams, and Jay, rather than insist on some dubious legal justification, found it easier to agree that Congress should request the states to make restitution, but both they and the British government knew that the states never would do so. Most of the confiscated land had been originally acquired through favoritism or bribery; all of it had long benefited the few at the cost of the many; the legal owners could be held to have forfeited their rights by adhering to the cause of what had become a foreign power; there were plenty of moral arguments to justify the course of the states even though it worked hardship upon many individual owners of the highest personal character. The result was, at any rate, that the right of the state—under certain circumstances—to confiscate private property for the sake of the general welfare was recognized in practice by the American nation at its very beginning. On the other hand, nothing like a final definition of those "circumstances" has even yet been achieved.

Other equally important but less direct results may be safely attributed to the impetus given by the Revolution. The example of Vermont in establishing universal white manhood suffrage was not immediately followed elsewhere, but Pennsylvania adopted a low taxpaying requirement which was a long step in the same direction. Though the custom of indentured servants was still legally recognized, it began to fall into disuse. The large amount of social equality which already existed in America, as compared with other countries, at the beginning of the Revolution, was immeasurably greater at its conclusion. The Revolution initiated by the common man had not betrayed him.

CHAPTER 18 . *The Democratic Compromise*

THE POST-REVOLUTIONARY CRISIS

THE American Revolution did not create the American nation. It created thirteen new nations, each theoretically sovereign in its own right. The Articles of Confederation adopted in 1781 merely established a loosely knit confederacy in which the Continental Congress was given the right of legislation but no powers of enforcement. Washington, when retiring from the command, sent a farewell letter to the governors of the states, advocating three much needed measures: creation of a federal government with authority to enforce its decrees; the payment of the public debt; the reorganization of the militia on uniform principles. No attention was paid to these statesmanlike suggestions. The laws passed by Congress, the taxes levied by it, its advice and appeals were disregarded; its revenue, mainly dependent upon state quotas, was highly precarious. The states erected interstate tariff barriers and neglected to pay their state debts, while the Congress had no power to pay the national debt. Under these conditions, all classes suffered; foreign and domestic trade declined, foreign and domestic credit collapsed; merchants and lawyers were unable to transact business under thirteen different sets of laws; soldiers paid in depreciated paper had nothing to show for their services in the war.

The traditional account by nineteenth century American historians was that in this grievous situation a group of noble, disinterested patriots succeeded in having a Constitutional Convention

286

called and that the Federal Constitution which resulted was a further carrying out of the principles of the Declaration of Independence, making them the law of the land. Doubt was cast upon some phases of the tradition in the sixties by Henry B. Dawson, a New York historian, who was roundly abused for his pains by descendants of Jay and Hamilton. But it was not until the beginning of the twentieth century that the epoch-making works of J. Allen Smith and Charles Beard proved conclusively that what the Constitution carried out was rather a counterrevolution, a Thermidorean reaction, in the interest of the wealthier classes. Interpreted from a radical point of view, the Constitution checked the natural development of democracy toward further democratic equality; interpreted conservatively, it saved the country from anarchy. Both interpretations are probably true.

Rather symbolically, the American nation was born of the first great American depression. It does not seem to have occurred to anyone at the time, or indeed during the dozen large or small crises that followed in the next century, to seek the cause in the lack of mass purchasing power. Nevertheless, the farmers, who were the worst sufferers, did succeed in obtaining measures of relief in all but four states—measures strikingly similar to some of those of the New Deal, consisting as they did of stay laws (moratoriums on debt) and deliberate inflation of currency. But just in proportion as the large class of debtors was relieved, the small class of creditors was alarmed. The planters of Virginia, the manor lords of New York, and the merchants of Massachusetts and Connecticut refused to make the slightest concessions. Massachusetts, in fact, went so far as to prohibit the practice of barter to which the hard-driven farmers were beginning to resort.

Daniel Shay, or Shays,[1] was a Revolutionary captain who had been cited for valor at Bunker Hill, had served at Ticonderoga, Saratoga, and Stony Point, and had come out of the war with nothing except a sword presented to him by Lafayette, which poverty soon forced him to sell. Beholding most of the other ex-soldiers in the same condition, his soul was filled with a sense of injustice. Had they fought the Revolution for this—to be denied aid even when

[1] Historians have usually preferred the spelling Shays, but his marriage record gives the name as Shay.

starving? Organizing a force of eight hundred militant farmers, he attempted to prevent the sitting of the courts to give judgments for debt. His "army" was easily defeated and dispersed by the state militia; it was the old story of the Peasants' Revolt—farmers armed with scythes and pitchforks against the most modern weapons of warfare.

"Shay's Rebellion" thoroughly frightened the upper classes. Samuel Adams, grown old and conservative, begged Congress for federal aid to protect "property rights," and Congress did go so far as to authorize a small force, to be used ostensibly against the Indians but actually designed to prevent any further rebellion of the farmers. The most exaggerated ideas were promulgated as to the revolutionary intentions of such men as Shay. General Henry Knox, who owned enormous estates in Maine, was speaking for his entire class when he wrote to Washington as follows:

"The people who are the insurgents have never paid any, or but very little taxes— But they see the weakness of government; They feel at once their own poverty, compared with the opulent, and their own force, and they are determined to make use of the latter, in order to remedy the former. Their creed is 'That the property of the United States has been protected from the con-fiscations of Britain by the joint exertions of all, and therefore ought to be the common property of all. And he that attempts opposition to this creed is an enemy to equity and justice, and ought to be swept from off the face of the earth.' In a word they are determined to annihilate all debts public and private and have agrarian laws, which are easily effected by means of unfunded paper money which shall be a tender in all cases whatsoever."

THE COUNTERREVOLUTION

A WAVE of antidemocratic feeling swept over the ruling groups. John Adams undoubtedly expressed the attitude of the legal profession in desiring a government by "the rich, the well-born, and the capable." Ezra Stiles and Noah Webster voiced probably the views of most of the better educated in the community. Stiles roundly declared: "An unsystematical democracy and an absolute monarchy are equally detestable. An elective aristocracy is preferable for America." Still more violently, Noah Webster asserted, "The very principle of admitting everybody to the right of suffrage prostrates the wealth of individuals to the rapaciousness of a merciless gang, who have nothing to lose, and will delight in plundering their neighbors."

Taking advantage of a local dispute between Maryland and Virginia, the conservative leaders, through the skillful generalship of their great legal representative, Alexander Hamilton, succeeded in 1787 in inducing Congress to call a convention to revise the Articles of Confederation. There can be no doubt of Hamilton's intentions. He who said, "The people, sir, is a great beast," made no concealment of his belief that only the wealthy and educated were fit to rule. It is usually stated that Hamilton's great achievement was to bring the men of wealth to the support of the new nation, but it could equally well be stated that he brought the new nation to the support of the men of wealth. Indeed, it might be said that the new nation was created largely for that very purpose. As Charles Beard writes, "The overwhelming majority of members, at least five-sixths, were immediately, directly, and personally interested in the outcome of their labors at Philadelphia, and were to a greater or less extent economic beneficiaries from the adoption of the Constitution."

The chance of the moment played into the hands of the wealthier classes by the removal of the former popular leaders: Sears and McDougall were dead, Benjamin Franklin was too old to be any longer effective, personal prosperity had killed all the radicalism in Samuel Adams and Patrick Henry, and Thomas Jefferson, in this hour of his country's need, was in France.

The members of the Constitutional Convention were, and knew that they were, an elite of wealth, education, and intellect. All that has ever been said in praise of their ability was well deserved; and much might also be said in praise of their public spirit. They were elite-conscious, aware of the responsibilities as well as the privileges of their office. They never dreamed that there could be any conflict between their devotion to the interests of their own class and devotion to the public welfare. In their view, the public welfare demanded that they or men like them should be at the head of the nation, but they meant to create a system in which this could be done in a perfectly constitutional, legal manner, insuring tranquillity and public order, and so in the long run conducing to the benefit of all.

To some extent, they represented the same groups that had subscribed to the Declaration of Independence, and a few of the signers were actually present, but they were now in a very different mood. They were not meeting to frame a statement of ideal principles, but to form a practical government. Disregarding their explicit instructions, they proceeded to forget the Articles of Confederation and to create an entirely new fundamental law for a new nation. Feeling that the majority of their ignorant fellow-countrymen would mistakenly disapprove of their purposes if they were allowed to follow the debates, they secured absolute freedom of action by adopting the strictest rules of secrecy.

George Washington, president of the Convention, set the keynote at the outset. "It is too probable that no plan we propose will be adopted. Perhaps another dreadful conflict is to be sustained. If, to please the people, we offer what we ourselves disapprove, how can we afterward defend our work? Let us raise a standard to which the wise and honest can repair; the event is in the hands of God."

With all their class interests, they were acutely aware of their historical present and knew that the common people must have a share in the government. When Hamilton made a five hours' speech advocating a kind of constitutional monarchy with a president elected for life and empowered to appoint the governors of the separate states, he won no adherents. What the overwhelming majority favored was the Aristotelian ideal of a "mixed government," partly aristocratic, partly democratic.

The political philosophy of the convention was mainly shaped by James Madison. It was founded on the most explicit economic realism. "Those who hold and those who are without property," argued Madison, "have ever formed distinct interests in society. Those who are creditors, and those who are debtors, fall under a like discrimination. A landed interest, a manufacturing interest, a mercantile interest, a moneyed interest, with many lesser interests, grow up of necessity in civilized nations, and divide them into different classes, actuated by different sentiments and views. The regulation of these varying and interfering interests forms the principal task of modern legislation. . . ." [2]

The more one studies American history, the larger becomes the role of "little Jimmy Madison," the rather pale Virginia liberal and Deist. He has been overshadowed by the more dramatic figures of Hamilton and Jefferson, yet he rather than they was the true founder of the American system of government. They represented extremes, neither of which was adopted; he stood for the mean between them, which was actually put into practice.

The economic realism of Madison differed from that of Karl Marx in envisaging a perpetual conflict of groups instead of a temporary conflict of classes, and in finding the political solution in a balance of forces instead of in the triumph of one class as preliminary to a totally classless society. Marx, in comparison with Madison, was a Utopian. Seeing that politics always had been a scene of factional strife, Madison concluded that it always would be. He analyzed the concept of "the people" into its constituent elements, resolving it into a pluralism of almost any number of forces which were still sufficiently interdependent to form a semi-organic unity. Political health was like physical health: something normally attainable to a high degree through long periods of equilibrium, but never perfect, always carrying within it the germs of disease, always liable to collapse.

Madison's conception of society clearly prescribed that government must be sufficiently flexible to allow for changing conditions of economic production and the rise of new groups of interest. The ideal of balance clearly prescribed concession and compromise as the appropriate method of political action. Government was bound to be largely a matter of experimentation in its details.

Considering their conservative economic bias, the members of the Constitutional Convention went at their self-chosen task of devising an entirely new system of government in a remarkably free spirit, taking what they wanted from the institutions of the past and combining them as they wished, subject only to the ultimate limitation as to how much "the people" whom they were supposed

[2] *The Federalist*, No. 10.

to represent would stand for. Almost every conceivable combination of executive, legislative, and judiciary was at one time or another discussed in the convention.

Their sureness of their ends was only equaled by their hesitation as to means. Living before the topic had been smothered in a hundred years of cant, they were not in the least ashamed to avow their economic motives. No Marxist could have stressed these more than did the members themselves. Again and again it was asserted that property was "the primary object of society" or "the main object of government," and that the Constitution was to be the basis of "a government instituted principally for the protection of property." And it was the preservation of property, not its wise or equitable distribution, with which the members were concerned.

Fear of "the people" was expressed on the floor of the convention as often and as strongly as was regard for property. And in the final result, of the three branches of the government the people were allowed to elect only one half of one third, the House of Representatives. Of all the various methods of choosing the President, popular election was the only one that was never discussed. Could the founding fathers have foreseen what the Constitution would become, with slavery (recognized by it) abolished, and with the executive and Senate elected by the people, they might have made the difficulties of amendment even greater than they are. The impossibility of such foresight is well illustrated by the fact that while the members of the convention spent weeks in discussing the powers of the legislative and executive, they spent relatively little time on the judiciary, the one branch of the government that has remained outwardly unchanged.

Whether the Constitutional Convention intended to give the Supreme Court the right of "judicial review" over acts of Congress as well as state laws is a moot question on which agreement is perhaps never likely to be reached. It is admitted that no such power is explicitly given to the Court anywhere in the Constitution, but the defenders of judicial review argue that it is implied in certain phrases. The matter came up for debate only incidentally in connection with the veto power of the President, when six members spoke in favor of the Supreme Court's having the final authority over Congress and five spoke against it. Since the courts were exceedingly unpopular at the time, it seems probable that the members of the convention, whatever their personal inclinations, did not wish, or dare, to give open adherence to the principle of judicial supremacy.

Practically, however, silence was equivalent to consent. Too late, James Madison realized the true situation in 1788 when he wrote: "In the state constitutions and indeed in the federal one also, no provision is made for the case of a disagreement in expounding them [the laws], and as the courts are generally the last making the decision, it results to them, by refusing or not refusing to execute a law, to stamp it with its final character. This makes the Judiciary Department paramount in fact to the Legislature, which was never intended and can never be proper." [3]

Madison's whole theory was one of divided sovereignty in accordance with his economic pluralism. It was a further development of the idea of the federal state expounded by John Adams, Wilson, and Jefferson just before the Revolution. The chief distinction of the American system of government from all others lay in its theory of dual sovereignty, as enjoyed by the states and the nation, supplemented by the triple sovereignty of executive, legislative, and judiciary within each division, as advocated in Montesquieu's *Esprit des Lois*. Faction, Madison believed, might obtain control of one department of the government, but it was hardly likely to secure control of all of them at the same time.

THE SLAVERY ISSUE AGAIN

THE most severe struggle in the Constitutional Convention was indirectly over the question of slavery. How should slaves be counted, if counted at all, in enumerating the population as a basis for representation? The question had already arisen in the Continental Congress in connection with the apportionment of taxation, when a proposal that the taxable population should be considered to include three fifths of the slaves had been bitterly opposed by the southern states. Now when the same suggestion—a typical Madisonian compromise—was offered with regard to rep-

---

[3] If any statement as to the intent of the Constitutional Convention can be considered final, it would seem to be this one by Madison.

resentation, the shoe was on the other foot, and the southern delegates were as eager for it as they had formerly been opposed to it. A prolonged debate ensued. Wilson, the logician of Pennsylvania, pertinently asked: "Are they [the slaves] admitted as citizens—then why are they not admitted on an equality with white citizens? Are they admitted as property—then why is not other property admitted into the computation?" Paterson of New Jersey queried: "Has a man in Virginia a number of votes in proportion to his slaves? And if Negroes are not represented in the States to which they belong, why should they be represented in the general government?" Gouverneur Morris of New York was on his feet a number of times in opposition to the measure, and presented the issue in realistic terms when he declared it to be evident that "the Southern gentlemen will not be satisfied unless they see the way open to their getting a majority in the public counsels." Either, he asserted, the distinction between the North and the South was fictitious or it was real: "If fictitious, let it be dismissed, and let us proceed with due confidence; if it be real, instead of attempting to blend incompatible things, let us at once take a friendly leave. . . .

Encouraged by their victory in the matter of representation, the southern delegates next refused to grant to the federal government immediate power over the slave trade. In this, they were able to appeal directly to the cupidity of New England. "Religion and humanity," declared Rutledge of South Carolina, "have nothing to do with this question. Interest alone is the governing principle with nations. The true question at present is, whether the Southern States shall or shall not be parties to the Union. If the Northern States consult their interest, they will not oppose the increase of slaves, which will increase the commodities of which they will become the carriers." This argument immediately converted the Connecticut delegates. Oliver Ellsworth, later chief justice of the United States Supreme Court, said complacently, "Let every State import what it pleases. The morality or wisdom of slavery are considerations belonging to the States themselves. What enriches a part enriches the whole." He was supported by his Connecticut colleague, the pious Roger Sherman, who, however, insisted on reconciling his vote with his conscience by declaring that the federal government ought to prohibit the slave trade if it were in its power to do so, but since the South would not consent to this, there was nothing to do but refuse to grant the government that power. Discouraged by this defection in the northern ranks, the opponents of slavery accepted the so-called "compromise" which prohibited the federal government from interfering with the slave trade before 1808, by which time the southern states imagined that they would be sufficiently well supplied.

By this time the northern opposition was so thoroughly broken that when Pierce Butler of South Carolina introduced a measure making compulsory on the several states the return of fugitive slaves, described as persons "held to service or labor," the clause was approved without a single dissenting voice. And when the Constitution embodying all these obnoxious measures came to final vote, the blustering Gouverneur Morris signed it with the rest.

The completeness of the slaveholders' victory was well summed up by C. C. Pinckney of South Carolina: "By this settlement we have secured an unlimited importation of Negroes for twenty years; nor is it declared that the importation shall then be stopped; it may be continued. We have a security that the general government can never emancipate them, for no such authority is granted. . . . We have obtained a right to recover our slaves, in whatever part of America they may take refuge, which is a right we had not before. In short, considering all the circumstances, we have made the best terms, for the security of this species of property, it was in our power to make."

THE CONSTITUTION

ALL in all, it would be difficult to deny the truth of a recent statement in M. L. Wilson's *Democracy Has Roots* (1939) that the Constitution was "a remarkable achievement in the avoidance of majority rule." A balance of powers in which the majority of the people could elect only one sixth of the government would seem to be a somewhat unbalanced balance. Granted that in a large modern nation the people cannot possibly participate directly in all the affairs of government as they sometimes did in the Greek city-states, it still remains true that the amount of political democracy in a nation can be judged by the degree to which the representatives are directly responsible to the majority of the people. From this point of view the American Constitution was an extremely undemocratic document. It gave more power to the President than has ever been accorded to any European constitutional monarch. It set up an irresponsible federal judiciary. In these respects, it was less democratic than even John Locke's system of government, later adopted in England, under which the actual sovereignty was exercised by elective Parliament. Practically, it was less democratic than most of the colonial governments had been in their final stages. The most that could be said for it from the point of view of democracy was that it explicitly recognized the principle of popular sovereignty in its eloquent Preamble, that it implicitly sanctioned the methods of peaceful compromise, and that it established a system of government under which a real democracy could be secured, with difficulty to be sure, but without shattering the fundamental form of the state. It was typically American in its very inconsistencies and relativistic character; it retained no traces of absolute monarchy; it outlawed hereditary ranks and titles.

The Constitution was really not completed by the Constitutional Convention. Popular opposition to ratification led to the concessional promise that a Bill of Rights, consisting of proposed amendments, would be adopted by the first session of Congress. In some respects, these first ten amendments, of popular origin, were the most important part of the Constitution, as in them are to be found nearly all of the "constitutional rights" which Americans are supposed to enjoy: the separation of church and state; the maintenance of free speech, free press, and "the right of the people peaceably to assemble and to petition the government for a redress of grievances"; the prohibition of general warrants, excessive bail, and the infliction of "cruel and unjust punishments"; the right to "a fair and speedy" trial by jury. But for these popular amendments, all that Roger Williams, Penn, Otis, and Jefferson had fought for, all that two centuries had accomplished for individual liberty, would have been complacently sacrificed, so far as the federal government was concerned, by the elite of education and wealth in the Constitutional Convention.

With the addition of these amendments, personal liberty was

made secure, at least to the extent that this can be done by written documents. They further established the fundamental democratic principle of peaceful discussion as the method of initiating social change. After their adoption, the Constitution was to remain essentially unaltered [4] for three generations.

[4] The eleventh and twelfth amendments were not unimportant, but they introduced no major changes.

CHAPTER 19. *The Federalist Elite*

THE supporters of the Constitution were naturally the ones elected to put it into practice. The Federalist party entered upon a decade of almost unlimited power with every branch of the government in its control. A hundred years after the overthrow of the Puritan theocracy, America was to experience a second example of rule by an elite.

It turned out, like the first, to be a government of the people, by an elite, for the elite. To the extent that the interests of the few coincided with those of the many, it was a very good government. It did establish the nation on a definitely permanent basis. The hopeful expectations of Frederick the Great that the American Confederacy would soon drift into anarchy were evidently not to be realized. The achievement of Alexander Hamilton, as Secretary of the Treasury, in paying off the foreign debt was a notable financial accomplishment which restored national credit. Commerce, freed from the burdensome and conflicting state laws, began to revive. Americans began to recover their momentarily lost faith in the American future. As a crisis government, the strong Federalist rule was perhaps justified as the quickest means of putting the nation on its feet.

Nevertheless, all this was done primarily in the interest of a class rather than in the interest of the nation. In the very first session of Congress, when Madison introduced a tariff measure for revenue only, it was immediately transformed, under the influence of the Philadelphia merchants, Fitzsimmons and Clymer, into a tariff for specially favored manufacturing and commercial groups. At the same time, the operation of the law was postponed until the late summer, thus enabling the merchants to raise prices in anticipation of the duties and yet get in their spring importations duty free, thereby depriving the government of over a million dollars of revenue and mulcting the public of an almost equal amount. A twenty years' charter was conferred on a so-called national bank under private control, and for private profit, but insured by a government contribution of one fourth of the stock. During these years of budding American capitalism, the last thing that businessmen desired was to have the government keep out of business; they were willing to have the government in business up to its ears, provided that they, not the government, received the profits.

The payment of the domestic debt, owed chiefly to the Revolutionary soldiers, was so manipulated that it redounded solely to the benefit of speculators, mainly Federalist senators and congressmen who bought up the depreciated paper certificates in anticipation of their own action to raise them to their original value. The deal was so raw that it drove James Madison, "the Father of the Constitution," to form a small but desperately earnest Anti-Federalist party, which was greatly strengthened by Jefferson's return from France to become a minority member of Washington's cabinet—a position which he resigned when he found that the President, with all his personal magnanimity, still remained under Federalist influence.

To have the author of the Declaration of Independence back at large on American soil was not something that any true Federalist could look on with pleasure. A thoroughgoing man of the world, interested in philosophy, science, architecture, engineering, invention, discovery, appreciative of almost every form of humanistic endeavor, Jefferson had been much at home in France. His house in Paris had been a rendezvous for Lafayette and other moderate revolutionists, whom he had urged to form a popular bloc, headed by the King, against the aristocracy and the clergy. In religion, he was an advanced Deist, calling himself at various times "an Epicurean" and "a materialist." In politics, he was still, as in the Revolution, much more of an equalitarian democrat than any other American leader. His basic principle, "Equality for all, special privilege for none," was utterly opposed to everything the Federalists stood for.

But a much more important temporary ally of the suppressed American democracy than any individuals, even a Jefferson or a Madison, could possibly be, now appeared. France, once inspired by American example, was advancing while America had retreated. As the French Revolution moved on to the overthrow of the monarchy and the establishment of the First Republic, its course was followed in the United States with growing enthusiasm. Everywhere "Democratic Clubs" sprang up, whose members made valiant efforts to remember to address each other as "Citizen Jones" or "Citizeness Smith." In New York, King Street was renamed Liberty Street, and in Boston, Royal Exchange Alley became Equality Lane. It was useless for the Federalists to try to make capital out of the execution of Marie Antoinette. Americans refused to be shocked. A queen so brainless as to ask, "If they can't find bread, why don't they eat cake?" deserved to be executed.

It turned out, however, that in becoming the tail of the French Revolutionary kite, the Anti-Federalists had made a mistake. The insolence of the envoy Genêt, the excesses of the Terror, and the rise to power of the reactionary Directorate completely reversed the American view of the French. When, in Adams' administration, Talleyrand refused to continue diplomatic relations with the United States except on the basis of a loan to France of $12,800,000, sweetened by a *douceur* of $240,000 for the Directors, it was the last straw. No distinctions were made between the French government and the French people; the latter were evidently the dishonest, giddy, licentious folk that the Federalists had always proclaimed them to be! It was easy for Hamilton and his followers to rush Americans into the mood of a moral crusade which took form in preparations for war.

Natural as was this result, it was a cultural disaster of major importance. The discrediting of the French Revolution carried with it a repudiation of the whole French Enlightenment and its scientific spirit. America was thrown back upon British and later upon German models, both of which intensified the national tendency to overemphasize the practical, domestic, and emotional at the expense of the theoretical, social, and rational. They served to strengthen the American will, which needed no strengthening, whereas the French influence would have helped to invigorate the rather feeble American reason. Aside from the temporary vogue of Fourierism in the forties, French influence did not creep back into the stream of American life until the latter half of the nineteenth century, and then it was felt only in the relatively isolated field of the plastic arts, the relatively unimportant field of costume, or the relatively trivial field of amusement and pleasure. "Good Americans when they die go to Paris" became a popular adage long before the close of the nineteenth century, but it would have been better for the country if more good Americans had chosen to go there, and to go more seriously and frequently, before they died.

Had the Federalists possessed the slightest political wisdom, had they been capable of the least moderation, there was no reason why they should not have retained the advantage which Talleyrand's action had given them. But they were in a feverish and hysterical state, their nerves raw and ragged. In their new role of patriots, they became the first typical American jingoists. In their heated imaginations they were already at war not only with the French but with every foreigner on American soil, and with a large part of the native population as well. In this vindictive mood, they passed the Alien and Sedition Acts, the former empowering the President at his own discretion to deport any alien whose presence he might consider dangerous "to the peace and safety of the United States," and the latter making it a criminal offense "to write, print, utter, or publish" any "false, scandalous and malicious" criticism of the government. The first put irresponsible power in the hands of the President, and the second threw the door wide open for the persecution of political enemies.

Thus, within ten years after the adoption of the Constitution, the constitutional guarantees of free speech and free press were torn into shreds. Under the Sedition law, no fewer than ten prominent Anti-Federalist editors were fined and imprisoned merely for criticizing the government. Among the victims of the Act were Thomas Cooper, physician, chemist, and philosopher, considered by Thomas Jefferson to be the profoundest thinker in the United States; Matthew Lyon, United States congressman from Vermont; and James Callender, one of the most vigorous of the Anti-Federalist group of popular journalists. An editor was imprisoned for printing in his paper an appeal for money to pay Lyon's fine. A Pennsylvania farmer named Fries, who incited a mob to resist the local tax collectors in the good old American style, was indicted not for riot but for treason, and during the trial Justice Chase was so unfair in his rulings and so bullyragged the attorneys for the defense that they withdrew from the courtroom. Fries, sentenced to death, was promptly pardoned by President Adams; the Federalist leaders began to suspect that they had a traitor in the White House; and the miserable tragicomedy ran on. When George Logan, the Quaker, paid a private visit to France to interview various French leaders on behalf of peace and returned with the story that neither Talleyrand nor anyone else wanted a war with the United States, he was denounced as a conspirator. To prevent a repetition of the offense, Congress, influenced by Secretary of State Pickering, made it a high misdemeanor for any American citizen to correspond with officials of a foreign government with intent to influence their conduct in any dispute with the United States. The Federalists were determined to have their war, whether the French wanted one or not.

It took Talleyrand some time to become convinced that the Americans were really serious. He had regarded his helpful suggestion to the American envoys as merely a little business proposal among gentlemen, never expecting it to become public property and never imagining that in any case the Americans would get so excited about it. But since they did take the affair in such a humorless spirit, he was quite willing to make concessions. Adams was notified indirectly that the French government was more than ready to resume negotiations.

Disregarding the objections of his Hamiltonian cabinet and those urged by a special committee from the Federalist Senate, the President sent over a set of commissioners who were properly received, and an amicable agreement was soon reached between the two nations.

John Adams had saved his country from war, but the members of his own Federalist party were furious. They watched the Anti-Federalists come back into popular favor as defenders of civil liberties, they perceived a growing movement in support of Jefferson for president, yet they wasted their energies in intrigues against Adams. The organizational unity which had been the chief strength of the Federalist party was broken, but it had been too long in power to be really able to imagine the possibility of defeat. To the accompaniment of its utter rout and confusion, Thomas Jefferson was elected president of the United States in the opening year of a new century.

CHAPTER 20 . *The Secondary Jeffersonian Revolution*

THE COLLAPSE OF DEISM

IT IS almost impossible for us to realize today the magnitude of the fears with which many Federalists regarded the election of Jefferson. They could hardly have been greater had a madman been installed in the White House. Timothy Dwight, president of Yale, accused the new incumbent of having a fixed purpose to root out of the world "civil and domestic government, the right of private property, marriage, chastity, and decency . . . all under pretense of giving man liberty and equality." One could confidently anticipate, Dwight thought, that his election would be the prelude to a second French Revolution and Reign of Terror. In fact, Dwight was inclined to believe that the Reign of Terror had already begun: "We have a country governed by blockheads and knaves," he wrote; "the ties of marriage with all its felicities are severed and destroyed; our wives and daughters are thrown into the stews; our children are cast into the world and forgotten; filial piety is extinguished, and our surnames, the only mark of distinction among families, are abolished. Can the imagination paint anything more dreadful on this side of hell?"

What lay behind these wild and whirling words was simply the fact that Jefferson was a Deist and that his election coincided with a luckless attempt on the part of a few of his followers to implant the principles of Deism among the masses. The leader in this hope-

304

less enterprise—for the cause of Deism had become so intertwined with that of the French Revolution that it was already lost in America—was Elihu Palmer, Connecticut born, honor graduate of Dartmouth, ex-Baptist minister expelled for heresy, and a true, though belated, Deistic missionary. He succeeded in converting a few small groups of mechanics and printers in the Atlantic Coast cities, edited a Deistic paper, and published a semiphilosophical work entitled *Principles of Nature, or a Development of the Moral Causes of Happiness and Misery Among the Human Species* (1802). But he should have been warned of the uselessness of his labors by the care which the Deistic groups took to avoid the dreaded name, preferring titles redolent of Masonry, such as the "Society of Ancient Druids" or the "Order of Illuminati." Palmer's attempt to carry Deism to the masses merely hastened its final defeat. Men like John Adams, Gouverneur Morris, and Chancellor Kent might remain Deists in their private thinking, but their dread of popular movements always led them to support the orthodox church in their actions. For every illiterate follower gained by Palmer, Deism lost two or three from the groups of "wealth and education." The true situation was revealed in the general outburst of conservative wrath which in 1802 greeted President Jefferson's invitation to Thomas Paine to return from France to America on a government ship.

Paine was coming back after fifteen years' absence to a nation that no longer knew him. His services to the Revolution in *Common Sense* and *The Crisis* had been forgotten; forgotten, too, his telling refutation of Burke's sentimental *Reflections on the French Revolution* by the logical arguments of *The Rights of Man*, in regard to which Jefferson had written the author, "The printers season every newspaper with extracts from your last" and "Our people love what you write." The religious revival to be discussed in a subsequent chapter was already under way in America, and "our people" now chose to see in Paine only the author of his latest work, *The Age of Reason*, which attacked the authority of the Bible. Yet that work stemmed from the same source as the others. *The Age of Reason* might have been prefaced by the following passage from *The Rights of Man*: "There never did, there never will, and there never can exist a parliament, or any description of men, or any generation of men, in any country, possessed of the right, or the power of binding and controlling posterity to the end of time, or of commanding how the world shall be governed, or who shall govern it. . . . The vanity and presumption of governing beyond the grave is the most ridiculous and insolent of all tyrannies." The belief in the infallibility of the Bible was the most striking of all possible examples of the conception of an inviolable constitution capable "of binding and controlling posterity to the end of time." Worthless as *The Age of Reason* is from the historical viewpoint of modern higher criticism, in terms of its own day it was an effective presentation, marshaling the Biblical errors, inconsistencies, and sheer absurdities with a good deal of skill; as against his critics who merely denied the facts in the case, Paine was a thousand times right. He was immeasurably more honest than they; he was immeasurably more concerned with moral standards and human welfare. He was, even, more concerned with religion: the True Word of God, he thought, was not the Bible but the Book of Creation; he was striving to dethrone the pretender in order to make way for the legitimate monarch. But the majority of Americans in the year 1802 were in no mood to understand either Paine's work or its purpose.

"What!" cried the *New England Palladium* of Boston, "invite to the United States that lying, drunken, brutal infidel, who rejoices in the opportunity of basking and wallowing in the confusion, devastation, bloodshed, rapine, and murder, in which his soul delights!" John Dennie, America's leading literary critic, wrote in the *Portfolio:* "If during the present season of national abasement, infatuation, folly and vice, any portent could surprise, sober men would be utterly confounded by an article current in all our newspapers, that the loathsome Tom Paine, a drunken atheist and the scavenger of fashion, is invited to return in a national ship to America by the first magistrate of a free people. A measure so enormously preposterous we cannot yet believe has been adopted, and it would demand further nerves than those possessed by Mr. Jefferson to hazard such an insult to the moral sense of the nation." Jefferson's nerves were stronger than Dennie imagined, and Paine duly returned on the government ship, but America's subsequent treatment of one of its foremost patriots was a long-enduring national disgrace. Taking up his residence in the New Rochelle house donated to him by Congress during the American Revolution, Paine was denied the right to vote, caricatured in the press, denounced from a thousand pulpits, and mobbed when he attempted to speak. The myth of his "atheism" became generally accepted, persisting even into the twentieth century in the "dirty little atheist" of Theodore Roosevelt's oft-quoted phrase, in which that ignorant American President managed to put three misstatements into three words.

Paine was the perfect symbol of Deism, and his treatment indicated the collapse of the movement. So complete, indeed, was this collapse that the hysterical Timothy Dwight of 1802 became the complacent Timothy Dwight, who in 1822 could dismiss Deism with the contemptuous remark that "the common people caught it up . . . but found that the liberty of infidels was not the liberty of New England." Neither was it the liberty of America. The final discomfiture of Deism was accomplished by the revival of orthodox religion. The effects of that revival, so far as Deism was concerned, were well summarized by Woodbridge Riley: "A saying of the day that the battle in behalf of infidelity had been the desultory attack of a barbarian, not of a civilized soldier, might with more truth be applied to the onset against the free-thinker, for that onset was carried on by all sorts of irregular recruits, by the Methodist and his saddle-bags education, by the Campbellite and his new light, by the Spiritualist and his celestial rapping, and even by the Mormon and his gold bible. . . . Among the people the majority were drawn off by an emotional substitute for thought; among the colleges those who were not affected by revivalism were held in check by circumscribed courses presenting the similarities between natural and revealed religion; finally, among the clergy the greater part stood for orthodoxy." [1]

Yet it should be remembered that it was these very groups that stood behind the Jeffersonian and Jacksonian revolutions, that guided the frontier democracy, and that in the end, however ignorantly and unconsciously, did establish, on a lower cultural level, many of the principles for which the Deists had struggled.

---

[1] Isaac Woodbridge Riley, *American Philosophy: the Early Schools* (New York: Dodd, Mead & Company, 1907), p. 319.

THE AGRARIAN VICTORY

WHEN it was found that under Jefferson's administration none of the anticipated evils occurred, that "civil and domestic government, the right of private property, marriage, chastity, and decency" still endured, the conservatives breathed very audible sighs of relief. Nor were they entirely wrong. For perhaps the greatest significance of the so-called Jeffersonian revolution was this: that it showed conclusively that the American system of government permitted a peaceful shift of political power. There had been nothing surprising in the fact that the system had survived under the direction of those who had first established it—that was to be expected; but when the most violent opposition party came into power and still the fundamental forms of the system were unassailed, it meant that they were not likely to crack in the future. Once this was clearly perceived, a new sense of confidence pervaded all classes. The American experiment was not destined to go the way of the all-too-brief French endeavor in the same field of democracy. Whatever its imperfections, the American system of government was here to stay.

Why, then, speak of the Jeffersonian "revolution"? The term was perhaps first applied by Jefferson himself, many years after the event, when he wrote: "The revolution of 1800 was as real a revolution in the principles of our government as that of 1776 was in its form." In his first inaugural he had stated that the chief aim of his administration would be "the encouragement of agriculture and of commerce as its handmaid." This, of course, directly inverted the position of these two interests under the Federalist economy. In transferring political power from the mercantile to the agricultural class—in other words, from the minority to the majority—the Jeffersonian agrarian program implicitly established the principle of majority rule, within the limits fixed by the Constitution, as the political basis of the American system. The abolition of religious and property qualifications for the franchise in the various states was greatly expedited. The unexpected opportunity to purchase Louisiana from Napoleon, which was eagerly taken advantage of by Jefferson, in extending the national territory to the Rocky Mountains, created what seemed like an unlimited field for agricultural expansion, a genuine "new world" wherein all individuals starting from scratch could, theoretically, and to a very considerable extent practically, enjoy that union of liberty and equality prophesied in the Declaration of Independence.

Jefferson was profoundly influenced by the French physiocrats, Quesnay, Turgot, Mirabeau, DuPont de Nemours. His ideal society, like theirs, was strictly agrarian: "Those who labor in the earth," he exclaimed, "are the chosen people of God, if ever He had a chosen people, whose breasts He has made his peculiar deposit for substantial and genuine virtue. It is the focus in which He keeps alive that sacred fire, which otherwise might escape from the face of the earth. Corruption of morals in the mass of cultivators is a phenomenon of which no age nor nation has furnished an example."

This was perhaps all very well as far as the free West was concerned. But what of the South? The South was agrarian, but the slaveowners of Virginia and the Carolinas and Georgia could only be said to labor in the earth in a metaphorical and vicarious sense. Intrinsically, agrarianism was no more equalitarian than capitalism. In fact, feudalism itself had been agrarian. What was there in the Jeffersonian practical program, as distinguished from its underlying moral ideals, to prevent the growth of an American agrarian feudalism? The abolition of primogeniture and entail had been a noble beginning, but only a beginning. It had destroyed the landed aristocracy of the North, but it had not unseated the economically rooted plantation aristocracy of the South. What more did Jefferson propose to do about slavery?

And what of the East? The factory system was already planted in New England in its most oppressive form based on the cheap labor of women and children. Had not Hamilton urged as one of the chief advantages of manufacturing over agriculture the fact that the labor of women and children in the factories would always keep wages low and production costs down? That was a realistic view of the situation. What did Jefferson propose to do about that?

The answer to both questions was simply: Nothing.

With regard to slavery, Jefferson had already shot his bolt before he became president. He had done his best and had failed. The loathsome system was established beyond his power to shake it.

As for the industrial proletariat, there was no place for it, no function which it could exercise, in the Jeffersonian scheme of things. The urban mechanics were to Jefferson, as to Hamilton and Washington, "the mob." Washington's words, "The tumultuous populace of large cities are ever to be dreaded," were echoed in Jefferson's metaphor that "the mobs of the great cities" were "sores on the body politic."

It must be remembered that in the natural rights philosophy, especially as this was developed by the physiocrats, the conception of government was a wholly negative one. The problem, as they saw it, was to keep the government from becoming tyrannical and interfering with the conditions of liberty and equality prescribed by Nature. The events of the eighteenth century seemed to demonstrate the correctness of their view, and nowhere more clearly than in America. What had been the outstanding evils against which the mass of Americans had struggled? Navigation laws and Stamp Acts under the British, funding bills, internal taxes, sedition laws under the Federalists—one and all the products of oppressive governments. Brissot de Warville, traveling through the United States, expressed not only his own but the sentiment of the American people when he declared that liberty "is always in inverse proportion to the extent of the powers of the government." No utterance of Jefferson was more popular than the statement in his first inaugural that good government consists in "a wise frugality, which does not take from the mouth of labor the bread it has earned, and which, restraining men from injuring one another, leaves them otherwise free to regulate their own pursuits." To keep taxes low, to refuse to pass injurious tariffs, to refrain from building up a strong and expensive military establishment, to maintain public order without infringing upon the rights of free speech, free press, and free assembly—if a government did all this, it did all that it should do.

The whole conception reminds one a little of the farmer's definition of good people as those "who don't do no harm to nobody." It seems absurd that in a democracy, where the government is supposedly an agent of the people, it should not be required to render more positive services. To employ an inevitably expensive agency on condition that it do little or nothing is, from a logical point of view, simply ridiculous. But when political democracy was first struggling into being it could not be expected to develop more than an insurgent philosophy. The gospel of natural rights made excellent rebels but inadequate rulers. Its advocates had never really decided just what they would do when they came into power. They would, of course, undo what their predecessors had done, but beyond that lay an unexplored region. In this respect, the early philosophy of democracy at the beginning of the nineteenth century was similar to the philosophy of Marxism at its close. Each was much more conscious of evils to be overcome than of positive goods to be achieved.

CHAPTER 21. *The Tertiary Jacksonian Revolution*

THE essential politics of the Silver Age that succeeded the Jeffersonian revolution was a politics of evasion. The fundamental and still unsolved problems of democracy were never raised if it was possible to avoid them. Until the stubborn insistence of Calhoun made the issue of chattel slavery inescapable, Congress did its best to avoid the unpleasant topic and pretend that it was buried forever by the Missouri Compromise of 1824. The New England representatives became past masters at concealing the analogous evil of wage slavery in their midst. And the West was too thrilled by the glowing expansion of its territory to worry about the ignorance and cultural barbarism that accompanied it.

Only once during the period did the political situation take on reality for the average American voter. That was in the so-called Jacksonian revolution of 1828. Four years before, the election had been thrown into the House through the lack of a majority for the leading candidate, Andrew Jackson, over three others who were in the field, and Henry Clay, as Speaker of the House, had succeeded in defeating the will of the people by using his potent influence to throw the election to John Quincy Adams, who was fifteen votes behind Jackson in the electoral college. Clay, the idol of Kentucky, whose career up to that time had been one continuous political triumph, did not dream that the people would really

312

object to his highhanded action. Had the king maker not gone on to accept the office of secretary of state from the monarch whom he had created, the storm might not have broken. But that was too much. The cry of "Bargain and Corruption"—whether well or ill based has never been proven—was henceforth to haunt Adams and Clay all the days of their life. The Kentuckian might just as well have abandoned his presidential ambitions then and there; the New Englander was wasting his time in seeking re-election; the people, for once genuinely aroused, swept their candidate overwhelmingly into office in 1828, and the Jacksonian revolution was on.

It was primarily, though not wholly, a symbolic revolution. The moral effect of Jackson's victory can scarcely be overemphasized. It registered the westward movement of population, installing a pioneer in the White House and a horde of his grammarless followers in public office. Henry Clay, Virginia born and educated in the law by Chancellor George Wythe, had carried his aristocratic intellectual baggage with him when he moved to Kentucky to begin his legal practice where the competition was less keen than in his native state. He was at most only a pseudo-westerner. But Andrew Jackson, product of the Tennessee frontier, was the real thing. All of his predecessors in the presidency had been "gentlemen" by birth or education, whereas Jackson had had no external advantages whatever. He was the first self-made American in national politics since Benjamin Franklin. True, had the phrase "natural aristocracy" been used sincerely, Jackson would have been at once admitted to that august body. By nature he was quite as much of a gentleman as any earlier President, possessing in fact a native dignity and chivalry that were rarely matched, and, although no reader of books and weak in his spelling, he was better able than most of his forerunners to cut through webs of sophistry to the central core of an argument. When in the saddle, leading his troops, he had exhibited a remarkable command of profanity, but so had George Washington under similar circumstances. Profanity is doubtless a vice in a clergyman, but it has never been deemed a fault in a soldier. And as a soldier, Jackson in the Seminole War and again in 1812 had shown himself to be an extraordinarily able commander. By his victory at New Orleans over twice the number of British veterans, he had become the one great military hero that the unfortunate War of 1812 had produced. But he was not elected as a military hero. He had mastered enough law to become a judge in Tennessee, but his legal attainments were laughable in comparison with those of Webster and Clay. His political experience, derived from one obscure term in Congress, was practically negligible. He was elected as a man of the people whom the people believed they could trust, one of themselves, yet unquestionably worthy through integrity and force of character to hold the highest office in the Republic. And the people did not choose wrongly. Their representative proved the ablest President between Thomas Jefferson and Abraham Lincoln.

Jackson had absorbed the political philosophy expounded by the clearest thinker among the old Jeffersonians, John Taylor of Caroline, who in his *Inquiry into the Principles and Policy of the Government of the United States* (1814) had gazed prophetically down the future and had seen it dominated by a finance capitalism under the rule of bankers able to control the economic system of the country through the manipulation of credit. That twentieth century development seemed close at hand when the question of rechartering the Bank of the United States (a successor of the original Hamiltonian Bank) came up for decision in 1836. Its president, Nicholas Biddle, was a preliminary sketch of the Morgans. The Bank was a monopoly, governed secretly by a subcommittee of the board of directors, using the funds of the government for private profit, and maintaining, through an elaborate system of special loans at low rates of interest, a kind of legalized bribery of newspaper editors and members of Congress. It was the very embodiment of special privilege, a threat to the very existence of an independent democratic government. Unable to obtain the necessary congressional support, Jackson, with the approval of the country, overthrew the obnoxious institution by executive action in withdrawing the public funds on his own authority.

All in all, the Jacksonian revolution did represent a further carrying out of Jeffersonian agrarianism and decentralization. The forces of industrial capitalism had encountered a definite setback, which was not unimportant. Clay's "American System" had been thrown on the ash heap. Nothing of ultimate significance had been accomplished, but the country was able to return to the comfortable conviction that it would remain safely agrarian for an indefinite time to come. Henceforth, the West was clearly a power to be reckoned with; no one would be tempted to repeat Clay's mistake of ignoring it; homespun and coonskin must be at least cajoled and flattered by every politician who hoped to succeed.

Unfortunately, cajolery was not difficult. The frontier faith in untutored human ability and the unimportance of education or specialized training had been happily justified in the exceptional instance of Jackson himself, but the notion that all frontiersmen were potential Andrew Jacksons had little foundation in fact. The democratic ideal of equal opportunity was exaggerated on the frontier, and to a considerable extent throughout the country, into the absurd dogma of equality of ability. This meant in practice a decreasing regard for the personal merit of candidates and an increasing tendency to vote according to party. When the period of Jacksonian prosperity was followed by a financial panic in 1837 the American voter reacted, as he has always done since, by simply blaming the party in power. Through the mere myth that he had been born in a log cabin and brought up on cider, General Harrison, the Whig candidate of Webster and Clay, was able to carry the allegiance of shouting frontiersmen in the most meaningless campaign that ever disgraced American history. And Harrison was followed by a long succession of mediocre Presidents under whom the real political leadership passed to the southern planter minority, who specialized in political training as the first line defense of slavery.

Thus, if the election of Jackson seemed to prove that the American people were intelligent enough to vote according to their own interests, subsequent elections equally well proved the opposite. In reality, neither of these broad generalizations was proved. What seemed to emerge, if anything, was that the people could occasionally become sufficiently wrought up to use their own judgment in voting, but that normally they would be content to accept the stereotypes handed them by political leaders. In other words, the American people, after as before the Jacksonian interlude, did not habitually take politics seriously. The shouting mobs that went from village to village yelling "Tippecanoe and Tyler too" in the Harrison campaign did not really believe that birth in a log cabin and a fondness for hard cider were determinants of political merit, but they were getting an emotional katharsis out of the hubbub they made, very similar to that furnished them by the religious camp meetings.

BOOK 4. *The Faith Romanticized*

CHAPTER 22. *The Creedless Frontier*

THE opening of the nineteenth century witnessed an unexpected revival of supernaturalistic, as opposed to humanistic, religion throughout the western world. The explanation usually offered is that the discrediting of the supernatural had been confined to the educated classes and so lacked the mass support necessary for continuance. This was quite true, but it hardly explains why the educated classes themselves returned to a position which they seemed to have permanently outgrown. There were profounder, more universal causes at work. The situation was by no means a new one. When the educated classes of Greece and Rome lost faith in their pagan mythologies, they did not abandon the supernaturalistic outlook; they either deified the Roman Emperor, or embraced the Christian mythology. When the Scholastic philosophers, starting out in the thirteenth century to supply rational proofs of the Christian dogmas, discovered that the proofs were inadequate, the Scholastics did not lose faith in the dogmas; they merely lost faith in reason and turned to mysticism. So, too, with the corrosive action of science in the seventeenth and eighteenth centuries. It was one of the greatest of European scientists, Emanuel Swedenborg, who became the most mystical of all mystics. At the end of the eighteenth century, Immanuel Kant, driest of logicians, after annihilating the so-called rational proofs of supernaturalism in his *Critique of Pure Reason,* reinstated the same supernaturalism on moral grounds in the *Critique of Practical Reason.*

319

Nineteenth century romanticism was in essence a reassertion of transcendental values on a far greater scale than ever before. The philosophic idealism of Germany was a disguised theodicy, showing that the universe was an objectification of the Fichtean "Will" or the Hegelian "Idea," while romantic art glorified in detail what romantic philosophy glorified in principle. Both gave a cosmic status to human values, an infinite extension to human desires. The common man, who was neither philosopher nor poet, found an analogous exaltation in personal religion. Faith in emotion and intuition was to replace, for the next fifty years, faith in logic and science.

The conclusion seems to be that what men sufficiently desire to believe they will usually find justification for believing, if not by one kind of proof then by another. As long as reason seems helpful in solving immediate problems men will follow it gladly, but if reason dares to turn its weapons against man himself by denying him any stake in the universe, men will simply say, "Away with reason!" At the beginning of the twentieth century this pessimistic conclusion might plausibly have been doubted, but the reassertion of supernatural, or at least subrational, values under the thin disguise of "dialectic materialism" or inviolate "racialism," accompanied by the emperor worship of Stalin and Hitler, lends it renewed force today. Franklin was not a fool when he recognized that he must have "SOMETHING" to worship. Even the strongest of men has but a precarious hold upon life; man is still confused in a world he does not understand, and still less does he understand himself; so until humanity achieves more self-mastery and a fuller adaptation to environment than it has ever yet attained, habits of reason will not become so generally integrated with organic behavior as to prevent perennial relapses to the instinctive level, no matter how imposing the forms of outward civilization.

Nevertheless, at the beginning of the nineteenth century, there were certain differences between the situations in America and in Europe which gave the American return to supernaturalism a distinct character of its own. Desperate and hard-fought as was the seven years' struggle of the American Revolution, seven years are a short time in comparison with the full twenty-five years of European embroilment after the French Revolution. And, what was still more important, the outcome of the struggle was different. In America alone, democracy emerged victorious, not completely so, as we have seen, but victorious in principle. In Europe the religious revival expressed the ideals of triumphant reaction—the Holy Alliance, re-emphasis on the Anglican Church in England with tired liberals like Wordsworth, Coleridge, and Southey retreating into its shelter, the re-establishment of Catholicism in France welcomed by such erstwhile followers of Rousseau as Chateaubriand, the strengthening of illiberal Lutheranism in Germany with a renewed persecution of the radical Pietist sects. But in America the revival on the contrary expressed, at least emotionally, the ideals of democracy asserted through a liberalizing of the older churches or the setting up of new and more independent ones.

THE CONSERVATIVE CHURCHES

THE new spirit of democratic tolerance appeared immediately after the Revolution in the kindlier treatment accorded the Roman Catholics. The civil disabilities under which they had suffered were removed, and no objection was voiced when John Carroll, a cousin of Charles Carroll of Carrollton, was appointed as the first Roman Catholic bishop. At the time of his induction his diocese numbered only thirty thousand, and he recognized the ineluctable fact that his church was a minority group which would have to look to immigration, not proselytizing, for any increase in numbers and ultimate strength. But to this source it did not look in vain. Recruited from the vast numbers of Irish immigrants, it already in 1836 ranked fifth in size among American churches, being surpassed only by the Methodists, Baptists, Presbyterians, and Congregationalists; by 1850 it had left the Congregationalists behind; and during the decade from 1850 to 1860 its gain was more rapid than that of any other church body except the Disciples. Nevertheless, its membership was so largely illiterate and so new to the country that prior to the Civil War its chief function was to serve as an occasional scapegoat for Protestant discontent, as in the sacking of the Ursuline convent at Charlestown by a Boston mob in 1831, or in the political vituperations of the

Know-Nothing Party organized in the fifties under the slogan "America for the Americans" in the desperate hope of finding some other issue than that of the impending Civil War.

When it was sought to revive the Anglican Church in America after the Revolution, fundamental changes were, of course, necessary. Whereas the Anglicans had never accepted the designation "Protestant," or admitted that their church originated in the Reformation, the name of the American Church was changed to "Protestant Episcopal," thus emphasizing its kinship with other Protestant groups. Instead of the King as its head a governing body was formed on the analogy of Parliament: a General Convention, meeting every three years and consisting of a House of Bishops, and a lower house of ministers and clergy elected in equal proportions from every diocese. The prayer book was altered, the Athanasian Creed being dropped—an advance in liberalism unachieved by the Church of England—and a prayer for the President being substituted for the prayer for the King. Thus, at the outset, the Episcopal Church was made into a definitely American institution. Its membership, however, remained small, being practically restricted to the wealthiest classes.

The much more important Presbyterian Church was undeniably an American institution, but its Calvinistic doctrines of predestination, original sin, and election were utterly out of keeping with the optimism and voluntarism of the new democracy. To strengthen their defenses, the conservative Presbyterians formed a Plan of Union with the Trinitarian Congregationalists in 1801, and until 1837 their missionary expansion in western New York and Ohio was carried on ostensibly in the common interest. Of the forty colleges and universities established in the United States between 1780 and 1829, nearly half came into being under Presbyterian leadership. Realizing, however, that the frontier churches usually became in actual fact independent and Congregationalist in their form of organization, the Presbyterians in 1837 abrogated the Plan of Union. The conservative Presbyterians could never reconcile themselves to the two necessities of frontier missionary success, the subordination of dogma, and the employment of ministers not formally educated. Rather than yield on the former point, they cut off their most promising western community, that of the Cumberland Presbyterians in Kentucky. Yet while heresy trials continued frequent, it was noticeable that they resulted in an increasing number of acquittals, as in the celebrated trials of Albert Barnes, Asa Mahan, Edward Beecher, and Lyman Beecher in the early thirties. Finally, in 1838, the sect divided formally into the conservative "Old School Presbyterians" and the progressive "New School Presbyterians," about equal in number. Having enjoyed at the outset the most favorable opportunity of any sect for colonizing the frontier, the Presbyterians—aside from the single field of educational institutions—wasted in doctrinal quarrels the energy that might have gone into expansion. It remained for the Methodists, Baptists, and Disciples to do what they left undone.

THE METHODISM OF JOHN WESLEY

EMERSON's statement that an institution is "the lengthened shadow of one man" is particularly true of religious institutions. Methodism, the last of the great religious movements to be imported from Europe by Americans, was essentially the creation of John and Charles Wesley. They came of an eminently respectable and conservative family: through their mother, Susanna Annesley, they were distantly connected with the first Earl of Anglesea, while their father, the Reverend Samuel Wesley, was descended from a long line of clergymen. But what the phrenologists would have called the Reverend Samuel's "philoprogenitiveness" was his undoing. Nineteen children were too many for the income of an ordinary English rector. Without sinking into absolute poverty, the family was always on the edge of it. Educated at the charity school of the Charterhouse, John Wesley could later write, "From ten to fourteen I had little but bread to eat, and not great plenty of that." The two brothers were henceforward subject to a perpetual inner conflict; by birth and tradition they belonged to one social class, by personal experience to another.

So far as the mere name is concerned, Charles Wesley was the first Methodist. As with so many other group titles of popular origin—Lollards, Quakers, Shakers, Whigs, Tories—the word was originally a term of ridicule, applied by Charles Wesley's disrespectful fellow-students at Oxford to a group of earnest young men under his leadership who were particularly regular and "methodical" in taking the Holy Sacrament every week. When John Wesley came up to Oxford as tutor in 1729, he organized this group as the "Holy Club," which met every evening for Biblical reading and mutual criticism, and added Wednesday and Friday fasts to the ceremony of weekly Communion. From this, they advanced to the point of aiding the ministers of neighboring parishes in their duties of visiting the jails and consoling the sick. It was undoubtedly his memory of the fervor and devotion of this little band which later gave John Wesley the great idea of revitalizing the Anglican Church through the organization of small local societies throughout the realm. But the youthful enthusiasm of the Holy Club was almost entirely undirected; it might just as well have issued in an earlier High Church "Oxford Movement," emphasizing tradition and ritual and leading to Rome, as to the actual Methodism which resulted. Methodism owed to the Oxford group its name and the germinal form of its ecclesiastical organization, but its moving spirit and principles came from the Moravians.

On a tempestuous missionary voyage to Georgia in 1735, John Wesley was much impressed by the calmness of certain Moravian emigrants; he recognized that they possessed a faith surpassing anything that Anglicanism had given him. The impression was deepened by the contrast between their success as settlers in a foreign land and his own wretched failure in his Georgia parish. After his return to London in the agonized conviction that he was obviously among those predestined to eternal damnation, he met Peter Bohler, who was about to set out as a Moravian missionary to the Carolinas, and once more he perceived that the Moravians possessed that inner assurance in which he was lacking. Illumination at last came to him at a meeting in Aldersgate Street, the traditional center of religious radicalism, where, after listening to a reading of Luther's *Preface to the Epistle to the Romans*, his spirit was suddenly flooded by the conviction that God "had taken away *my* sins, even *mine*, and saved *me* from the law of sin and death." Even after this experience, Wesley's new sense of grace might have taken a Calvinistic direction but for a long visit to the Moravian settlement at Herrnhut, which completed his conversion to their essential principles with the exception of their communistic economics. With his conservative background, Wesley was not prepared to give up the principle of private property, nor did he feel any call to abandon the Church of England or openly attack the sacraments, but he had obtained from the Moravians a new conception of intrinsic human worth which was henceforth to be his guiding star.

From this time, in Wesley's theology, original virtue replaced original sin. Being a timid thinker, he never dared to deny the Fall or eternal punishment, but he held that man had the power, with God's loving assistance, to escape the consequences of the former and to avoid the latter. Instead of closing the gates of Heaven to all but the elect, he once more, like George Fox, threw them open to all who willed, truly willed, to enter. Indeed, he held that even in this life one might obtain absolute certitude of salvation. There were two steps or stages in the attainment of this inner conviction: the stage of "justification," wherein one knew that his former sins were forgiven, and the higher stage of "sanctification," when he knew that his present spirit was sinless. Since, under the pressure of objective evidence, Wesley was forced to admit that even a sanctified person might possibly fall into further sin, the distinction might seem to be practically valueless, but it has always been dear to Wesley's followers. To be absolutely perfect, if but for a moment, was a new goal of aspiration. In these ideas of Wesley lay the germ of the later Perfectionist movements.

Even after Wesley had equipped himself with a democratic theology, he was for some time inhibited from carrying his message to the multitude by his early regard for ecclesiastical ceremonies. As he was later to confess, "the saving of souls" still seemed to him "almost a sin if it had not been done in a church." From this ecclesiastical narrowness he was saved by the revivalist movement started by Whitefield in Bristol, Harris in Wales, and Robe in Scotland. Entering the movement later than these men, once he was in it Wesley proved himself the greatest of all revivalists. His courage was magnificent, his energy inexhaustible. Not allowed to speak in Anglican churches, denied the use of town halls, rotten-egged, stoned, and threatened with lynching, he held indomitably to his course. Up every morning at four, traveling annually an average of four thousand miles on horseback, preaching usually three sermons a day, establishing societies and Sunday schools wherever he went, he still found time to contribute to the Methodist hymnbook, to edit fifty volumes for the church library, and to take charge of the preparation of a series of foreign language grammars for the use of Methodist missionaries. Although he persisted in regarding himself as an Anglican clergyman, the adherence was only nominal. He took it upon himself to ordain ministers, appoint lay preachers, and establish circuits; he formulated codes of duties, diversions, and dress—plain dress, few diversions, and many duties. All in all, John Wesley was probably the greatest of Protestant missionaries.

Wesley could scarcely have done all that he did without developing a certain hardness of character. He was accused of being domineering and arbitrary, and was called "Pope John." In the rules formulated by him for the Kingswood School, which he founded for the children of his lay preachers, one reads: ". . . We have no play days . . . neither do we allow any time for play on any day; for he that plays as a child will play as a man." Fully accepting the revivalist standards of success, Wesley triumphantly reported in 1743 that in the four previous years his preaching had caused two hundred and thirty-four cases of hysteria, fourteen of temporary insanity, and nine of permanent insanity. Convinced that he was under the special protection of the deity, he was as superstitious as any Mather in his belief in illustrious providences. Like the early medievalists, he used the Bible in the manner of the *sortes vergilianae*, turning for guidance when in a quandary to the first chance text that met his eye. There was no slightest relation between Wesley's Methodism and contemporary science except the relation of complete opposition. Nor was Wesley able or willing to develop the democratic implications of his liberal theology. As he grew older, he became more and more of a Tory, denouncing John Wilkes and heartily disapproving of Burke and Pitt. He condemned every concession to the colonies, and went so far as to wish that George the Third would act as his own minister.

And yet, through all, Wesley's theology and even his ethics remained intelligent and humanitarian. The Apostolic Succession, he declared, "was a fable, which no man ever did or can prove." As to Trinitarianism, "I dare not insist," he wrote, "on any man using the word Trinity or Person." His ideal Methodism was to be a creedless religion of the heart! "Methodists alone do not insist on your holding this or that opinion, but they think or let think. Neither do they impose any particular mode of worship. . . . I do not know any other religious society wherein such liberty of conscience is now allowed, or has been allowed since the days of the Apostles. Herein is our glorying and a glorying peculiar to us."

Wesley was not a slave to the notion of Biblical infallibility. The Psalms of hate, he said, were "unfit for the mouths of Christian congregations." The hymns which he and his less strenuous, sweeter natured brother contributed to the Methodist hymnbook always stressed God's love and saving grace, the beauty and goodness of His world. The hymnbook was the most important feature of the Methodist ritual. It has been said that "As the whole German nation sang itself into Lutheran doctrine, so the English nation sang itself into Methodist doctrine." The literary quality of the hymns, those of the Wesleys excepted, was not as good as the Anglican, and the singing was not as good as the German, but the spirit of the words and tunes was much more humane and hopeful. With all its rigors, Methodism was at bottom a religion of joy and liberation.

AMERICAN METHODISM

As WERE the contradictions of Wesley, so were the contradictions of the religion he founded. Methodism was adapted to appeal both to the most generous impulses and to the most benighted prejudices of the American frontiersmen. But the spread of the Wesleyan gospel had merely begun in America when it was halted by Wesley's opposition to the Revolution. Every Methodist clergyman except Francis Asbury returned to England. That, with the stigma of Loyalism attached to its name, American Methodism was able to develop so quickly after the Revolution was primarily owing to the ability of the one man who had remained faithful to the American cause. Wesley sent over Thomas Coke, a Church of England clergyman, to be joint superintendent with Asbury, but the Conference which they called in Baltimore in 1784 wisely organized itself into an independent body under the name of the Methodist Episcopal Church, and elected Asbury as the first bishop. In mapping out his plans of campaign, Asbury devoted his attention chiefly to the frontier. The Baptists, Congregationalists, and Unitarians could fight over New England; the Presbyterians could have Pennsylvania; if the Methodists could win the expanding frontier, they would have gained more than the rest. For this crusading task, it was better fitted than any other sect. The system of itinerant preachers, going far back to the Waldenses, utilized by Wiclif, revived by Wesley, was precisely suited to the needs of the American wilderness. For the next thirty years the circuit riders would carry the glad news of salvation to isolated villages and lonely farms everywhere in the interior. Nor did they come only once and pass on; they had a regular itinerary, they created classes and societies in a cellular organization bound together in larger units under a centralized direction. Methodism conquered the wilderness in a methodical manner.

Francis Asbury was endowed with almost as much energy as Wesley himself, and he took his mission with the same abiding seriousness. Methodism was a deep fount of inward joy, but it was far from a merry religion. To be in a state of justification or sanctification entailed terrifying responsibilities toward God and man. A contemporary of Asbury thus described him: "I never saw him indulge in even innocent pleasantry. His was the solemnity of an apostle; it was so interwoven with his conduct that he could not put off the gravity of the bishop either in the parlor or the dining-room. He was a rigid enemy to ease; hence the pleasures of the study and the charm of recreation he alike sacrificed to the more sublime work of saving souls."

Asbury, living in the time of the Revolution, still possessed that starched and cleanly Puritan dignity which had set the pattern of colonial manners. But as the Methodist preachers rode westward with the pioneers, leaving civilization further and further behind, their speech and manners, like those of the laity, became rougher and simpler. A new type of muscular, fighting parson developed, such as Peter Cartwright, a preacher at eighteen, famous as "the Kentucky Boy," equally ready with tongue and fist, and at seventy-five, still hale and hearty, famous as "Uncle Pete," the progenitor of children, grandchildren, and great-grandchildren to the number of over a hundred. American humor, when it did not begin with the Negroes, had its origin in the religious rows of the frontier among Methodists, Baptists, Shakers, and others, in which a form of broad repartee, similar to the medieval "flytings," was more esteemed than logic or learning.

The religion of the frontier, whether Methodist, Baptist, Presbyterian, or Disciple, and no matter what its doctrinal basis, necessarily took on much of the coloration of its environment. And that coloration was still puritanic. The virtues of the pioneer were the virtues of the Puritan, and the vices of the Puritan were the vices of the pioneer. Like his ancestors, the pioneer was fighting for existence; his problem was not how to live beautifully, but how to live at all. The similarity of outward circumstance bred a similarity of inward character. The warlike virtues of energy and courage were once more emphasized at the expense of human sympathy. Work, whether of saving souls, killing Indians, or leveling forests, was regarded as a thing admirable in itself. A saved soul might be less amiable than it was before, a dead Indian and a dead tree might be less beautiful than living ones, but it was held to be none the less certain that these labors of salvation and destruction were approved by God. The clergymen of the frontier, like their Puritan predecessors, leveled their attacks against carnality. The terror of Hell was considered the chief incentive to righteousness; the torments of the damned still formed the staple theme of sermons.

But the westward-facing pioneer was not involved, as was the original Puritan, in a double struggle with Nature and with his fellow-men, but solely in a struggle with Nature. There was now no theocracy, no subtle theology, that needed defense. In the simple conflict with Nature, book learning was of little service. The circuit riding Methodists, and the Baptist missionaries who accompanied and moralized the westward migration, were innocent of classical scholarship. The requirements for the clergy were steadily lowered until they could be met by anyone with a native talent for exhortation. Prestige came to those handy with ax and gun as it had formerly gone to those expert in Greek and Hebrew. The last vestiges of the European intellectual tradition vanished in the American forest. And in its place developed steadily the great American tradition of the common man.

VARIETIES OF BAPTIST EXPERIENCE

AFTER the Methodists, the sect which expanded most rapidly at the beginning of the American religious revival was that of the Baptists. Unfortunately, they had never been able to agree for long as to their theology, being divided into "Soft Shell" and "Hard Shell," "General" and "Particular" Baptists, according to their denial or acceptance of the dogma of predestination. Logically, of course, they should have taken the same position as the Anabaptists from whom they stemmed; their protest against the idea of infant damnation and the supposed necessity of infant baptism was implicitly based on the conceptions of free will and the voluntary nature of ethical conduct; if sin could be involuntary and inheritable, as the Calvinists held, the Baptist restriction of baptism to adults was senseless. Nevertheless, environment and human association could do what logic could not, and gradually during the late seventeenth century most of the American Baptists had come to accept the views of their neighbors, and like all converts were more insistent upon them than those to the manner born. The liberalizing influence of the Great Awakening and the American Revolution had, however, as we have seen, been particularly powerful upon the Baptists, and, at least in intellectual New England, had brought a revival of the original Baptist spirit.

John Randall, the Revolutionary pastor of a "Hard Shell" Baptist church at New Durham, New Hampshire, being disfellowshipped for Arminianism in 1779, had immediately organized a group of "Free Will" Baptists whose influence spread throughout New Hampshire and into the adjoining states of Maine and Vermont. John Colby, Randall's missionary successor, succeeded during 1809–17 in reconquering the original Baptist centers of religious radicalism in Rhode Island, from which the movement spread into Massachusetts and Connecticut, and was gradually carried in the westward march of New England along the northern frontier into New York, Ohio, Indiana, Michigan, and Minnesota. A chain of liberal Baptist colleges was established from Colby and Bates colleges in Maine, through Keuka College, New York, to the far West of Hillsdale College in Michigan, and Parker College in Minnesota —true outposts of civilization in the frontier wilderness, genuine carriers of older cultural values, more adequately united than elsewhere with the new democratic equalitarian spirit.

Outside of the New England belt, the Baptists lacked intellectual leaders and relapsed into formalism. Having forgotten the original significance of their doctrine of adult baptism, they laid an ever-increasing emphasis on the mere rite of immersion as their main article of belief. Second only to the Methodists in their love of revivals and camp meetings, they soon had the woods of the West buzzing with angry disputes over the relative merits of immersion versus sprinkling as a means of salvation.

On the frontier, the Calvinistic art of casuistry degenerated from a lofty discussion of subtle metaphysical problems to concern about equally subtle but considerably more trivial questions of conduct, amusingly illustrated by the division between "Truthful" and "Lying" Baptists at Long Run, Kentucky, in 1804. The bone of contention was tossed up at a logrolling when someone propounded the following problem: Suppose a man has had four children killed by the Indians but still has a fifth one hidden near-by—if the Indians asked him whether he had another child, would he be justified in lying? The problem, unsolved at the logrolling, was taken up by the Long Run Baptist Church, where the dispute became so hot that the proponents of lying, being outvoted, withdrew from the church to form their own congregation. The incident was a perfect example of the kind of issues that were perpetually splitting the Protestant sects. It is also interesting, and quite typical, that the majority upheld a line of conduct that not a single member of the church would conceivably have followed in the given circumstances.

A much broader ground of dissension separated the northern and southern Baptists. The former, under the leadership of Adoniram Judson, a converted Congregationalist, became very active in the cause of foreign and domestic missions and in the circulation of Baptist translations of the Bible. In bitter opposition to such novelties, a group known as the "No Effort Baptists" arose in the South. Their chief representative was Daniel Parker, of whom the following unflattering description was transmitted to posterity by the Reverend J. M. Peck: "Raised on the frontiers of Georgia, without education, uncouth in manners, slovenly in dress, diminutive in person, unprepossessing in appearance, with shrivelled features and a small, piercing eye, few men, for a series of years, have exerted wider influence on the lower and less educated class of frontier people. With a zeal and enthusiasm bordering on insanity, firmness that amounted to obstinacy, and perseverance that would have done honor to a good cause, Daniel Parker exerted himself to the utmost to induce the churches within his range to declare non-fellowship with all Baptists who united with any missionary or other benevolent [or, as he called them, newfangled] societies." Another Georgia Baptist clergyman of the same sort is said to have exclaimed, "If an angel was to come from Heaven and declare the missionary cause was of God, he would not believe it"—the profanity of which utterance caused the official Baptist historian, J. H. Newman of Baylor College, to write in the eighteen-nineties, "If it be true that 'he immediately lost his speech, and remained in that deplorable situation until he died,' as is related on credible authority, it was no more than such blasphemy deserved." [1]

It was in the South that the Calvinistic Baptists made their greatest gains, among the poor whites and the Negroes. It was the *reductio ad absurdum* of Calvinism that its last stronghold should be found among such groups. Actually, of course, the Calvinism was largely nominal, as neither doctrinal subtlety nor moral rigidity was congenial to the lower class in the South, whether Negro or white. There was little but the name to distinguish the southern Baptists from the Methodists who shared with them the allegiance of the same groups. The real ground of appeal was the religious emotionalism which was present in equal amount in the faith of both sects.

It is easy to see that the Christianity of the Negro was essentially an escape. This did not prevent it from being profoundly meaningful. With the Negro, debarred as he was from all opportunities of earthly advancement, religion was the one source of hope. In his case, the Methodist and Baptist emotionalism rose into ecstasy. The Bacchic orgies of the camp meeting did not lead, as had the similar worship of Dionysus among the Greeks, to any high Apollonian drama—for the sun-bright Apollo had never been known in America—but they did produce in the Negro spirituals the only genuine folk literature which the country has ever had,

[1] J. H. Newman, American Church History Series (New York: American Society of Church Historians, 1893-97), II, 435-436.

infinitely superior to the crude exaggeration of the Paul Bunyan legend, or the cheap sentimentalism of the sea chanteys and the cowboy lyrics of which so much has been made. The eternal human dream of a land of bliss somewhere beyond the bounds of mortality, where injustice and misery should be no more—the dream which, so far as we have any reason to believe, no other animal but man ever has dreamt—this profoundest of human yearnings is expressed with peculiar poignancy in nearly every one of the spirituals.

THE ALL-TOLERANT DISCIPLES

THE third of the great frontier sects, that of the Disciples, or Christians, grew out of the American experiences of two Scotch-Irish Presbyterians, both graduates of the University of Glasgow, Thomas Campbell and his son Alexander. The reputation of Thomas Campbell has been submerged beneath that of his better known, more combative son; but he, not Alexander Campbell as is usually said, was the real founder of the movement. Already in the prime of life when he emigrated to America in 1807, leaving behind him an influential position as a Presbyterian minister in Ireland, Thomas Campbell brought with him a well-developed religious philosophy. The motivating principle of his life was the great, if at that time Utopian, conception that the various Protestant sects could be reunited in one single church if they would but abandon their elaborate theological creeds and return to the simple Biblical teachings. Assigned to the Presbytery of Chartiers in western Pennsylvania, he attempted to expound this novel idea and thereby aroused the wrath of his fellow-ministers. A committee was appointed to investigate his beliefs. Acting on its unfavorable report, the Synod passed a vote of censure on the too pacific Scotch-Irishman.

No longer permitted to preach as a Presbyterian in churches, Thomas Campbell could still preach as Thomas Campbell in the houses of friends. At one such meeting, which was to become historical, he proposed as a permanent rule of faith the principle: "Where the Scriptures speak, we speak; and where the Scriptures are silent, we are silent." Thereupon, Andrew Munro, the local postmaster, rose solemnly and said, "Mr. Campbell, if we adopt that as a rule of faith, then there is an end of infant baptism." Campbell answered, "Of course, if infant baptism be not found in Scripture, we can have nothing to do with it." At this, one of those present, Thomas Acheson, burst into tears, exclaiming, "I hope I may never see the day when my heart will renounce that blessed saying of the Scriptures, 'Suffer the little children to come unto me for of such is the kingdom of heaven' "; to whom the tougher minded James Foster replied, "Mr. Acheson, I would remark that in the portion of Scripture you have quoted there is no reference whatsoever to infant Baptism." The weeping Acheson left the meeting, and the rule was unanimously adopted by the others.

This was the real beginning of what the followers of Campbell termed "the Reformation," fondly hoping that their movement would prove as important in the history of religion as had those of Luther and Calvin. Unconsciously, they went back to the earliest principles of the pre-Reformation groups in seeking to base Christianity solely upon the Bible. Like Fox and Wesley, Thomas Campbell had no desire to found a separate sect. The Christian Association, organized under his leadership in 1809, was not a church; it had no paid ministry but trusted its cause to lay preachers who labored as farmers during the week and expounded the Scriptures to the best of their ability on the Sabbath. The Declaration of Principles written for the Association by Campbell made their position perfectly clear: "We have no nostrum, no peculiar discovery of our own, to propose to fellow-Christians, for the fancied importance of which they should become followers of us. We propose to patronize nothing but the inculcation of the express Word of God, either as to matter of faith or practise; but everyone who has a Bible and can read it, can read this for himself. Therefore, we have nothing new." They sought no converts, and they admitted the members of every Protestant church to their communion.

The fallacy in Thomas Campbell's position was, of course, the old fallacy of assuming that the Bible is self-interpreting, conveying the same meaning to all who read it. Alexander Campbell, who became associated in his father's work in 1810, was a much more vigorous thinker and better Biblical scholar than the irenic Thomas. Through a close study of all the relevant passages, he was able to prove that the only Scriptural form of baptism was adult immersion, as clearly shown in the cases of Jesus and the Ethiopian eunuch and implied by the various texts that refer to the subject.[2] Once this position was publicly taken by the Campbellites, it virtually forced them to affiliate with the Baptists, as they proceeded to do. From 1813 to 1832 they simply represented the most radical of the various groups in the Baptist Church.

But nothing could restrain Alexander Campbell within the bounds of real orthodoxy. Developing much further a mild suggestion made by his father, he casually tossed a thunderbolt into the meeting of the Christian Association in 1816 by delivering his celebrated "Sermon on the Law" which virtually discarded the Old Testament: ". . . There is an essential difference between law and gospel—the Old Testament and the New. No two words are more distinct in their signification than *law* and *gospel*. They are contradistinguished under various names in the New Testament. The law is denominated 'the letter,' 'the ministration of condemnation,' 'the ministration of death,' 'the Old Testament or Covenant,' and 'Moses.' The Gospel is denominated 'the Spirit,' 'the ministration of righteousness,' 'the New Testament or Covenant,' 'the law of liberty and Christ.' In respect of existence or duration, the former is denominated 'that which is done away'—the latter, 'that which remaineth'—the former was faulty, the latter faultless—the former demanded, this bestows righteousness—that gendered bondage, this liberty—that begat bond-slaves, this freemen. . . . The former waxed old, is abolished, and vanished away—the latter remains, lives and is everlasting."

Alexander Campbell's position was practically that of Anne Hutchinson and Roger Williams, but it was still not acceptable to orthodox Baptists in 1816. And there were other differences between them and the Campbellites. The Baptists required a public confession of Christian experience before baptism, the Campbellites did not; on the other hand, the Baptists did not claim that baptism brought remission of sins, whereas Alexander Campbell, keeping close to his New Testament sources, was forced to contend that it did bring absolution to those who came to the ceremony as "believing penitents." Walter Scott, a fiery Campbellite convert of

---

[2] Matthew 3:16; Mark 16:16; John 3:5, 23; Acts 2:38; 8:38, 39; 22:16; I Corinthians 6:11; Romans 6:4; Ephesians 4:5; I Peter 3:21.

1819, was a great evangelist, less scrupulous than the Campbells in winning adherents from other faiths. Under the influence of frontier optimism, Scott came to cherish a belief in the immediate Second Coming of Christ, and Alexander Campbell was sufficiently affected by the delusion to change the name of the important religious paper which he edited, so that the *Christian Baptist* became the *Millennial Harbinger*. Under all these circumstances it is not surprising that more and more Baptist churches closed their doors to the Campbellites, or that the Methodists began to launch bitter attacks against their new evangelical rivals. So at last in self-defense the Campbellites were forced to abandon the dream of a unified Protestant church and form themselves into a separate denomination. The name chosen was suggested by Alexander Campbell, the "Disciples of Christ." Their strength was soon augmented by an informal union with another heretical group known as the "Christians," composed of seceders from the three great sects—the Republican Methodists, organized as early as 1793 by James O'Kelly; a contingent of Vermont and New Hampshire Baptists led by Abner Jones; and an ex-Presbyterian group formed around Barton W. Stone—all of whom agreed with the Disciples in desiring a creedless church. As a result of this union, the terms "Disciples" and "Christians" both came to be applied to the Campbellites, the former being preferred by Alexander Campbell as more distinctive, the latter preferred by his father as the name of the original Christian Association formed by him on leaving the Presbyterian Church.

All the attacks on Alexander Campbell failed to affect his liberalism in the least. He continued to admit to communion the members of any other sect who wished to come. "I circumscribe not the Divine philanthropy," he exclaimed. "I dare not say there is no salvation in the church of Rome, or that of Constantinople." He was even willing to debate the value of religion itself with the "infidel" Robert Owen in a mighty series of arguments which ran on for fifteen meetings. Fanny Trollope, attending, was scandalized by the mutual courtesy of the debaters, who frequently dined together before their contests. ". . . This I think could only have happened in America," she said. "I am not quite sure that it was very desirable it should have happened anywhere."

Alexander Campbell continued all his life to live in the spirit of the early Reformation, attacking the greed and formality of the clergy, and preaching a simple equalitarian religion very close to that of Jesus of Nazareth. That it was welcomed by the frontier is shown by the extraordinary growth of his movement. The Disciples, beginning with two hundred members in their Brush Run congregation of 1811, numbered over ten thousand by 1830, over two hundred and fifty thousand by 1850, and half a million by 1865.

THE ORGIASTIC CAMP MEETINGS

THE most picturesque feature of nineteenth century American religion, the open-air camp meetings, was not identified with any one sect. They were simply an extension of the indoor revivals which had by now come to be accepted as part of the technique of all but the Catholic and Episcopal churches. The first camp meetings were held in 1794 on the North Carolina frontier under Presbyterian auspices. But the later ones were usually interdenominational popular gatherings where hundreds, and even thousands,[3] of people from widely separated settlements came together in a great religious fiesta, in white-tented towns set up for a week in some favorable meadow or valley, with exhortation and singing going on day and night—here, there, everywhere that a preacher could pick up an audience. The camp meeting was one place where no class distinctions held: every social group was represented, men and women, the very old and the very young and all ages between, the virtuous and the vicious, all moving to the common rhythm of sin and salvation, for a brief season forgetful of political and economic rivalries, glad to be simply human. The camp meeting was the perfect symbol of the motley, mongrel, praying, and laughing American democracy.

There were, of course, skeptics and scoffers in the crowd, pickpockets who plied their trade to advantage in the massed congregations, roués who well knew how favorable to the art of seduction was the emotional atmosphere of these open-air gatherings. Many a couple stole away from the singing and shouting in the flickering light of the torches into the darkness of the surrounding forest to

---

[3] It was estimated that in 1801 between ten and twenty thousand people attended the Cane Ridge meeting in Kentucky.

taste other joys than those of religion; not infrequently a stout farmer would return home from the camp meeting minus his wallet, and occasionally there would be unsettling arguments with some disputatious follower of the late Thomas Paine. But all this merely lent an added spice of danger to the attractiveness of the camp meetings. Sufficient danger even for those in grace, but danger truly terrible for the wicked whom God might smite down at any moment for profaning His assembly. Yet there was hope for them too if their hard hearts could be opened by some minister's preaching, or caught in the contagion of the multitude's groans and sighings.

A new religious phenomenon known as "the jerks" which became prevalent during the prolonged camp meetings is thus vividly described by Peter Cartwright:

"Just in the midst of our controversies on the subject of the powerful exercises among the people under preaching, a new exercise broke out among us, called 'the Jerks,' which was overwhelming in its effects upon the bodies and minds of the people. No matter whether they were saints or sinners, they would be taken under a warm song or sermon, and seized with a convulsive jerking all over, which they could not by any possibility avoid, and the more they resisted the more they jerked. If they would not strive against it and pray in good earnest, the jerking would usually abate. I have seen more than 500 persons jerking at one time in my large congregations. Most usually persons taken with the jerks, to obtain relief, as they said, would rise up and dance. Some would run, but could not get away. Some would resist; on such, the jerks were generally very severe.

"To see those proud young gentlemen and young ladies, dressed in their silks, jewelry and prunella, from top to toe, take the *jerks* would often excite my risibilities. The first jerk or so, you would see their fine bonnets, caps and combs fly; and so sudden would be the jerking of the head that their long loose hair would crack almost as loud as a waggoner's whip." [4]

The sexual basis of the revivalist and camp meeting orgies is too obvious to be overlooked. With all the physical exuberance of fron-

[4] *Autobiography of Peter Cartwright,* edited by W. P. Strickland (New York, 1857), p. 50.

tier life there was no frank recognition of natural impulses. The body was still denounced as the source of sin, sex was still insulted, and men still tried to convince themselves that they married and had children solely through a sense of duty. The neuroticism implanted by Puritanism in the American character at the beginning was reawakened and became even more intense because the restraints were now purely internal, unsupported by the outward authority of police and magistrates. When the repressed natural impulses could be dammed up no longer, they found expression in the excitement of the camp meeting, where, with howlings and rollings and sexual convulsions, souls were converted to God. The camp meetings afforded in more violent form the same emotional katharsis achieved in more settled societies through music, the drama, and the dance.

Fanny Trollope, attending a revival in Cincinnati in the early thirties, was shocked almost equally by the indecorum of the proceedings and by the open display of sexuality: "Two priests . . ." —one can imagine what would have been the indignation of the frontier preachers could they have known that the opprobrious term "priests" would ever be applied to them—"repeatedly mounted on the benches, and trumpet-mouthed proclaimed to the whole congregation 'the tidings of salvation,' and then from every corner of the building arose in reply, short sharp cries of 'Amen! Glory! Amen!' while the prostrate penitents continued to receive whispered comfortings, and from time to time a mystic caress. . . . More than once I saw a young neck encircled by a reverend arm. . . . One young girl, apparently not more than fourteen, was supported in the arms of another, some years older; her face was pale as death; her eyes wide open, and perfectly devoid of meaning; her chin and bosom wet with slaver; she had every appearance of idiotism. I saw a priest approach her, he took her delicate hand. 'Jesus is with her! Bless the Lord!' he said, and passed on.

"Did the men of America value their women as men ought to value their wives and daughters, would such scenes be permitted among them?" [5]

A more philosophical observer than Mrs. Trollope might have

[5] Frances Trollope, *Domestic Manners of the Americans* (London: Printed for Whittaker, Treacher & Co., 1832).

been less scandalized. He would have noted that the law of supply and demand affects domestic manners as well as prices and wages; that women were at a premium on the frontier through their scarcity, so that American men were no longer able to control the conduct of their wives and daughters as the British traveler thought they should; and that, if the attention of the clergy was mainly devoted to women, that in itself represented a clerical retreat from colonial days when they had dictated the laws of government. He would have recognized the medical value of the katharsis supplied by the revivalist movement, and he might have perceived another side of the movement which is more likely to be forgotten today. Not all of the revivals and camp meetings were as crude as those described by Cartwright and Fanny Trollope. The best of them met the need of isolated farms and straggling villages for some kind of contact with a larger life and higher interests than were afforded by a rather meager and narrowly practical daily existence. There can be no doubt that many did derive from them a mystical sense of communion with God and their fellow-men that gave renewed meaning and dignity to their lives. For a day or a week human equality and solidarity were made real in the camp meetings; the experience was not wholly forgotten when men returned to the more sordid necessities of competitive living. Essentially, more than all else, the camp meetings were an expression of community good will.

CHAPTER 23 . *The Rowdy Church of the Latter-Day Saints*

THE BOOK OF MORMON

WITH the exception of Jemima Wilkinson's abortive and unimportant Jerusalem movement,[1] Mormonism was the first truly American religion. Its founders and early followers were all born on American soil, and many of them had ancestry which in other circumstances would have been called "good New England stock." The two chief leaders, Joseph Smith and Brigham Young, both came out of Vermont, that fertile mother of early American radicals. But in spite of its respectable distant New England background, Mormonism was unquestionably a product of the frontier, the strangest, most ambiguous, adventurous, and colorful of all the movements emanating from that turbulent region.

It began in the year 1830 when there was published, in the little town of Palmyra in western New York, the most extraordinary work that had ever appeared up to that time in these United States of America. Everything about the book was remarkable, beginning with the exhilarating title page:

[1] For Jemima Wilkinson, see the sketch in the *Dictionary of American Biography*.

341

"The
BOOK OF MORMON
An Account Written by
THE HAND OF MORMON
Upon Plates
Taken From The Plates of Nephi

. . . sealed by the hand of Moroni, and hid up unto the Lord, to come forth in due time by way of the Gentile— The interpretation thereof by the Gift of God. . . .

By Joseph Smith, Junior, Author and Proprietor."

(The concluding assertion of authorship, conflicting with the earlier statements, was discreetly removed in later editions.)

The new Bible, written in an unsuccessful imitation of the style of the King James version, was, like the original, divided into books, fifteen in all. It purported to be a collection of records of prehistoric America, tracing the original inhabitants to various Jewish settlements and covering several thousand years from the time of the Tower of Babel to about 400 A. D. As a body of supposedly sacred scriptures supplementing the Biblical narratives, the volume was truly magnificent in its claims, and, if genuine, it would have well deserved the reverence which the Mormons accorded it.

It tells first how Christ came to a certain Lehi in the time of King Zedekiah; how Lehi's four sons, Laman, Lemuel, Nephi, and Sam, in order to escape persecution built a ship and came to America; how Laman and Lemuel sinned and their skin was turned dark in consequence; how their Indian descendants warred with the Nephites; how the latter penetrated into Zarahemla, where they found the descendants of another Jewish tribe, also emigrants in the time of Zedekiah, who preserved the records, written on gold plates, of still a third tribe, the mysterious Jaredites who had crossed the Atlantic after the fall of the Tower of Babel but had recently been totally destroyed in a civil war; and how the Nephites and Zarahemlaites were united in a single nation under the good King Benjamin.

Next it tells in more detail of King Mosiah, son of the good King Benjamin, who, becoming convinced that representative government was preferable to monarchy, voluntarily resigned his office to inaugurate an era of democratic equality in church and state, which resulted in great prosperity. But democratic prosperity brought luxury in its train. The Nephites commenced "to wax proud, because of their exceeding riches . . . for they began to wear very costly apparel . . . and they began to be scornful, one towards another, and they began to persecute those that did not believe according to their own will and pleasure." A series of prophets attempted to stem the tide of deterioration, but to no avail. The Nephites sank even lower than the Lamanites and became divided into social classes in which "some were ignorant because of their poverty, and others did receive great learning because of their riches." This period of widespread injustice was ready for the coming of the Messiah.

The Third Book of Nephi tells of the awful destruction that occurred in America at the time of Christ's crucifixion in Jerusalem. The cities of Moroni, Onihah, Mocum, sank into the depths of the sea; the cities of Moronihah, Gilgal, Gadiandi, Gadiomnah, Jacob, and Gimgimno were swallowed up by the earth; the great city, Zarahemla, was destroyed by fire from Heaven, as were the cities of Jacobugarth, Laman, Josh, Gad, and Kishkumen. For three days total darkness encircled the earth. Then the resurrected Christ appeared and established his church among the Nephites.

In subsequent years the power of the Christianized Nephites declined before that of the heathen Lamanites. By the middle of the third century A. D. the Nephite situation was desperate. Their great military leader, Mormon, managed to stave off defeat for a time, but when he made his compilation of the records at about 385 A. D. he knew that the end was inevitable. In a final tremendous battle near the Hill Cumorah the Nephites were decimated, all of them being slain save Mormon's son Moroni, who lived to complete the records and bury the plates in the neighboring hillside.

Mingled intermittently with the narrative in the Book of Mormon are moral and doctrinal teachings: simplicity of ritual is prescribed, infant baptism is denounced, and in one passage which is especially interesting in view of the Mormon future, polygamy is strongly condemned:

". . . Hearken unto the word of the Lord: For there shall not any man among you have save it be one wife; and concubines he shall have none;

"For I, the Lord God, delight in the chastity of women. And whoredoms are an abomination before me; thus saith the Lord of Hosts." [2]

The Book of Mormon contains a number of chapters lifted bodily from the Old and New Testaments and is full of unacknowledged quotations from them. Shakespeare was apparently known to Nephi, as he mentions "the undiscovered country from whose bourne no traveler returns." [3] It is foretold that in due time a mighty prophet shall arise, "by the name of Joseph," who shall make known the contents of the records to future generations, and mention is made of "three witnesses" who shall be permitted to see the plates themselves.

The account of the origin of the Book of Mormon was even more amazing than the book itself. The promoters of the work asserted that seven years earlier the spirit of the "angel Moroni" had appeared to an uneducated farm lad of eighteen in western New York; had told him where the plates were buried, together with a pair of magical glasses called the Urim and Thummim whereby they might be translated from the reformed Egyptian language in which they were written; and had appointed a yearly tryst with the youth at this spot on the Hill Cumorah not far from his dwelling. After four years the youth was instructed to dig up the plates and to begin the work of translation. The latter was dictated from behind a curtain to a country schoolteacher engaged as an amanuensis. When the task was finished, the plates and glasses were taken up into Heaven by Moroni, but three witnesses were allowed to see them: Oliver Cowdery, the amanuensis; David Whitmer, a friend at whose house the translation was made; and Martin Harris, a neighboring farmer who put up the money to publish the work. Such is the preposterous story which is still officially accepted by the Mormon Church and defended by its reputable and scholarly historians, such as John Henry Evans.

[2] Book of Jacob, 2:27–28. The curious inclusion of this passage in the Book of Mormon needs explanation. Possibly Joseph Smith's wife, Emma, had already developed the jealousy that she showed later, and the passage was put in to appease her.

[3] The Second Book of Nephi, 1:14.

JOE SMITH THE CHARLATAN

THE hero of this amusing tale, Joseph Smith, Jr., came of New England stock on both sides. His grandfather, Asael Smith, had been a fairly successful farmer of powerful physique and independent mind who belonged to no church but was inclined toward Universalism. Asael's son, Joseph Smith, Sr., was a shiftless individual, completely illiterate, who lost his inherited capital in a ginseng commercial venture and was thereafter a "frontier-drifter," moving nineteen times in ten years from one unsuccessful farm to another, ending as a squatter two miles from Manchester, in western New York. He was much addicted to the popular frontier sport of digging for buried treasure and was also given to religious visions—a habit encouraged by his wife, Lucy Mack, a tubercular woman with a woebegone countenance and large, staring, fanatical eyes, who outlived her famous son and wrote a life of him,[4] replete with marvelous happenings. Her father, Solomon Mack, was an epileptic, who after being converted to religion at the advanced age of seventy-six had immediately written and published an autobiography to celebrate the event.[5] Her brother, Jason Mack, belonged to the still existing sect of Seekers, who, as in the days of Roger Williams, were looking for further religious revelations to complete the Scriptures. Such a family, ignorant, superstitious, visionary, and eager, cherishing literary ambitions beyond their ability, was the perfect background for the Book of Mormon.

Joseph Smith, Jr., did not possess a particularly good character among the more respectable citizens in the New York villages of Palmyra and Manchester, between which his father's log cabin was located. Although large, strong, and of a particularly winning countenance with kindly, dreamy blue eyes, he was not popular or trusted, being considered lazy, fond of lying and hoaxing, and, like his father, the victim of a habit of hunting for buried treasure by the aid of "peep-stones."[6] We possess a vivid description of him at this time, written by David Hendrix, a resident of Palmyra

---

[4] Lucy Mack Smith, *History of the Prophet Joseph* (1853).
[5] Solomon Mack, *A Narrative of the Life of Solomon Mack* (c. 1810).
[6] That Smith's Urim and Thummim spectacles were evolved from the popular notion of "peep-stones" is a plausible theory, though it cannot be regarded as proven.

who assisted in the typesetting and proofreading of the Book of Mormon:

"Joe was the most ragged, lazy fellow in the place, and that is saying a good deal. . . . I can see him now in my mind's eye, with his torn and patched trousers held to his form by a pair of suspenders made out of sheeting, with his calico shirt as dirty and black as the earth, and his uncombed hair sticking through the holes in his old battered hat. In winter I used to pity him, for his shoes were so old and worn out that he must have suffered in the snow and slush; yet Joe had a jovial, easy, don't-care way about him that made him a lot of warm friends. . . . He was known among the young men I associated with as a romancer of the first water. I never knew so ignorant a man as Joe was to have such a fertile imagination. He never could tell a common occurrence in his daily life without embellishing the story with his imagination; yet I remember that he was grieved one day when old Parson Reed told Joe that he was going to hell for his lying habits."

If there is one fact in American history that can be regarded as definitely established it is that the engaging Joe Smith was a deliberate charlatan. Aside from the intrinsic improbability (to put it mildly) of his story regarding the plates, there is no slightest evidence of their existence other than the testimony of "the Three Witnesses," Oliver Cowdery, David Whitmer, and Martin Harris, who signed the statement published in the Book of Mormon: "We declare with words of soberness that an angel of God came down from heaven, and he brought and laid before our eyes, that we beheld and saw the plates, and the engravings thereon," [7] plus another statement of "Eight Witnesses," members of the Smith and Whitmer families, that they had "seen and hefted" the plates. Of the Three Witnesses, Martin Harris later testified in court that he had seen the plates not "as I do that pencil case" but "with the eye of faith . . . though at the time they were covered over with a cloth." Presumably, "the plates" were also covered with a cloth when the other witnesses did their seeing and hefting. Harris,[8]

---

[7] The phrase "engravings thereon" is in Smith's own telltale style.

[8] Martin Harris, on his expulsion by Smith, first joined the Shakers; then, after Smith's death, joined Strang's heretical Mormon sect in Wisconsin; and finally in 1870 was rebaptized in the true faith, went to Utah, and died there in his ninety-third year.

Whitmer, and Cowdery [9] were all later expelled from the Mormon Church, Whitmer and Cowdery being chased out of Missouri by a crowd of Mormons, eighty of whom signed a statement that they were thieves and counterfeiters.

Harris had, in fact, very early become suspicious of the Prophet and had insisted on taking a specimen of the "reformed Egyptian" characters to Professor Charles Anthon of New York for examination. According to Harris' alleged account of the interview, published in Smith's autobiography and probably written by Smith himself, "Professor Anthon stated that the translation was correct, more so than any he had before seen translated from the Egyptian." Professor Anthon's own account, written in answer to a letter from E. D. Howe, declared that the sample specimen was "a singular scrawl," consisting of "all kinds of crooked characters, disposed in columns, . . . evidently prepared by some person who had before him at the time a book containing various alphabets." [10] Professor Anthon does not mention any alleged translation of the scrawl, and it is most unlikely that any was ever submitted to him.

Further evidence of Joe Smith's knavery may be found: (1) in his and Rigdon's pretended translation of the Bible, simply plagiarized from the King James version with additions to the fiftieth chapter of Genesis and the twenty-ninth of Isaiah, prophesying the coming of a later Joseph and the future revelation in a sealed book; [11] (2) in Smith's fanciful "translation" of certain papyri purchased from a traveling showman at Kirtland, which Joe pretended were the writings "of Abraham and Joseph," whereas they were later shown to be simply a part of the well-known Egyptian "Book of the Dead"; [12] (3) in his solemn examination of six strangely marked plates of brass dug up in Kinderhook, Illinois, after which he

[9] Whitmer founded an ephemeral sect of his own called "The Church of Christ." Cowdery became a Methodist Sunday school superintendent, then joined Strang, and at the end was back with Whitmer in Missouri.

[10] E. D. Howe, *Mormonism Unveiled* (Painesville, Ohio, printed and published by the author, 1834), pp. 270–272.

[11] Even Smith did not quite have the audacity to publish this translation, the manuscript of which remained in the hands of his wife, Emma, until 1866, when it was given to the heretical Reorganized Mormon Church, which published it as *The Holy Scriptures Translated and Corrected by the Spirit of Revelation, by Joseph Smith, Jr., the Seer* (1867). It has never been accepted by the Church of Latter-day Saints.

[12] The hieroglyphics and Smith's translations of the Kirtland papyri were published in the two Mormon papers, the *Times and Seasons* and the *Millennial Star*.

announced that they recorded "the history of one of the descendants of Ham," when actually they had been marked and buried by several young men as a hoax.[13]

Finally, we have Smith's charming derivation of the name Mormon: "Before I give a definition to the word, let me say that the Bible, in its widest sense, means good. . . . We say from the Saxon, *good;* the Dane, *god;* the Gothic, *goda;* the German, *gut;* the Dutch, *goed;* the Latin, *bonus;* the Greek, *kalos;* the Hebrew, *tob;* the Egyptian, *mo.* Hence, with the addition of more, or the contraction *mor,* we have the word Mormon, which means literally *more good.*" [14]

The effrontery of the fellow was really superb. Knowing the credulity of his followers, he was ready to fool them to the top of their bent. Two of the sacred volumes of the Latter-day Saints, *The Book of Commandments for the Government of the Church of Christ* (1833) and *The Doctrines and Covenants of the Church of the Latter-day Saints* (1835), contain no less than one hundred and twenty-four special revelations from the Prophet Joseph. Most of them are exceedingly concrete and realistic. Thus, for example, the Lord announced to His Prophet that the Book of Mormon must not be sold for less than $1.25 "on pain of death," except that Joseph Smith, Sr., might sell it at a lower price; [15] He commanded the Prophet and Rigdon to make a new translation of the Bible; [16] He forbade Cowdery to be entrusted "with the monies which he shall carry into the land of Zion"; [17] He declared that "It is meet that my servant Joseph Smith, Jr. should have a house built in which to live." [18]

JOSEPH THE PROPHET

IT IS not surprising that Joe Smith's non-Mormon contemporaries, unversed in psychology, should have regarded him and his followers as merely a gang of liars and crooks. But very few of them

[13] The promoter of the hoax, W. Fulgate of Mound Station, Brown County, Illinois, testified to it before a justice of the peace on June 30, 1879.
[14] *Times and Seasons.*
[15] *Doctrines and Covenants,* Section 5.
[16] *Ibid.,* Section 25.
[17] *Ibid.,* Section 69.
[18] *Ibid.,* Section 41.

were merely that, and certainly not Joe Smith himself. Joe Smith was an extraordinary liar, but he was also a religious enthusiast. How far he believed in his own revelations it is impossible to tell, just as it is in the similar case of Mahomet, who used equally devious means. Probably his well-grounded contempt for his early followers caused him to justify his methods to himself as the only ones capable of bringing results with such a people. His end was noble— a new revelation—so what mattered the means? Joe Smith was not the first or the last to think in that fashion. His contemporaries could not believe that so uneducated a person could actually have written the Book of Mormon, and they concocted fantastic theories that it was the work of the Reverend Solomon Spaulding, or the Reverend Sidney Rigdon.[19] But, in the first place, nothing more was needed in the way of education than a familiarity with the Bible—which Joe undoubtedly had—and a school-teaching Cowdery at hand to furnish at need a quotation from Shakespeare; and in the second place, he possessed abundantly the sweeping vision, boundless ambition, and inner faith that were necessary for such a work.

For Smith to have converted his own family and such early followers as the Whitmers needed no great ability. But the further rapid spread of Mormonism, and Smith's continued dominance over really forceful disciples indicate quite extraordinary powers of leadership. The hardheaded Brigham Young, five years older than Smith, was not a man either to give devotion easily or to take orders easily, yet he never wavered in his loyalty to the Prophet. Orson Pratt was a scientist and expert mathematician, whose *Quadratic Equations* was used as a textbook in the University of Paris; yet he succumbed like others to the influence of the un-

---

[19] The Spaulding theory was invented by Philaster Hurlburt, who had been expelled from the Mormon Church, charged with adultery and an attempt on Smith's life. Hearing of an unpublished romance on the origin of the Indians written by the Pennsylvania clergyman, Solomon Spaulding, he leaped to the conclusion that Smith must have had access to it. He thereupon wrote to Spaulding's widow for the manuscript, intending to publish it, but discovered that it was different from what was expected. This did not prevent his continuing to circulate the story, nor did the actual publication of the rediscovered manuscript in 1885, showing that it was entirely dissimilar to the Book of Mormon, have any effect in discrediting the tale among anti-Mormon writers. The suggestion that Sidney Rigdon was the author is decisively negatived by the fact that Smith and Rigdon did not meet until after the Book of Mormon was published.

schooled Smith. Sidney Rigdon, ex-Baptist, ex-Disciple clergyman, known as "the great orator of the Mahoning Association," the friend of Alexander Campbell and Walter Scott, might venture to resist Smith momentarily, yet in the end he always submitted.

Smith was a genius in organization, as in other matters. The church which he now succeeded in setting up, with its center at Kirtland, was established on the strictest hierarchical basis, with six ascending orders of rank: deacon, teacher, priest, elder, member of the seventy, and high priest. Above these was the inner council of the Twelve Apostles, appointed by Smith as supreme dictator. The church was divided into an indeterminate number of dioceses or "stakes," each with its high priest and also with a practically more powerful lay official, called a bishop, in charge of its temporal affairs.

In his choice of the Twelve Apostles, Smith showed excellent judgment. Rigdon, whose loyalty he distrusted, was not included, although he was placated by the appointment of Orson Hyde, an ex-Disciple minister who had studied under him. Cowdery and Whitmer were not put on this highest council. In the organization of his church, Smith may be said to have effectively junked his earliest disciples in favor of the much abler members who came in a little later. Brigham Young, by far the most capable, was made "President" of the Twelve Apostles; the others were Heber C. Kimball, Orson and Parley Pratt, Luke and Lyman Johnson, Thomas B. Marsh, David W. Patten, William E. McLellin, John F. Boynton, Orson Hyde, and William Smith, the best of the Prophet's brothers, put on to safeguard his special interests. A number of these men continued to be prominent in Mormon history for thirty years after Smith's death. John Taylor, destined to succeed Brigham Young as head of the church, was a Canadian who was converted by Parley Pratt in 1836, while Taylor's future successor, Wilford Woodruff of New York, was converted in 1833. The men whom Smith gathered about him in Ohio, most of them zealous propagandists and good organizers, formed a fighting phalanx which soon made Mormonism a movement to be dreaded, if not respected.

During the whole decade of the thirties, Smith managed to inspire a most extraordinary missionary activity among his followers.

A constant stream of itinerant preachers went out from Kirtland. By the end of 1831 there were already Mormon churches in twenty states, the largest of them in Missouri, a state which Smith, visiting it in that year, declared to be "a century behind the times . . . without the benefit of civilization, refinement, or religion." Brigham Young and Orson Pratt struggled to plant the gospel on the stony soil of New England, Parley Pratt labored in Canada, while Kimball, Hyde, and others succeeded in winning two thousand converts in England within a single year. By 1836, when the little Mormon Temple at Kirtland was dedicated, the new religion is estimated to have had two thousand members in Ohio alone.

In the slaveholders' state of Missouri matters had not been going so well. By the middle of 1833 there were fifteen hundred Mormons peaceably settled there in Jackson County, with a thriving town in Zion City which supported a vigorous Mormon newspaper, the *Morning and Evening Star*. Unfortunately, the Mormons made no concealment of their antislavery sentiments and even invited free Negroes to settle among them. This was too much for the slaveowners. They held a mass meeting and then, with the unerring instinct of mob organizations, they struck at once at the Mormon press. The printing shop of the *Star* was destroyed and the editor's house was burned after his wife and a sick child had been thrown out of it. Edward Partridge, bishop of the Jackson County stake, was tarred and feathered. Mormon men were horsewhipped and Mormon women raped. Over two hundred houses were burned, with the standing timber surrounding them. The Mormon crops and cattle were seized. Finally, to cap an ironic climax, after the Mormons had been driven out of the county their lands were allowed to go to waste by their shiftless successors.

Permitted to settle in Clay and Calhoun counties, the Mormons after several years of diligent labor had succeeded in re-establishing their communities and were again on the road to prosperity when a new misfortune befell them. Joseph Smith got into trouble back in Ohio, owing to the failure of a wildcat banking scheme which he had promoted. To escape the wrath of the populace, he and Rigdon made a midnight ride out of Kirtland and by morning were well on the way to Missouri. Their arrival was the signal for a fresh outburst of persecution. Warned by their experience in Jackson

County, the Mormons had armed themselves, and Governor Boggs made this an excuse for calling out the militia against them. The massacre of Haun's Mill resulted, in which seventeen Mormons were ruthlessly slaughtered, among them two small boys and a Revolutionary veteran seventy-eight years old. The outrages of Jackson County were then repeated with the state soldiers playing the part of the mob. Smith, Rigdon, and Parley Pratt were seized and condemned, without the formality of a real trial, to be shot for treason. Their lives were saved by a hairsbreadth through the refusal of a subordinate officer to carry out the inhuman order. Smith lay in prison for four and a half months. By the time he was released, the Mormons had fled for safety across the Mississippi to the nonslaveholding state of Illinois, where he found them living in scattered shacks along the river in a demoralized condition.

In this dark hour, Smith's unbroken courage and organizational genius were invaluable to the Mormon cause. Within a few months, he established his followers in their own city of Nauvoo, for which, by skillfully playing the Whigs and Democrats in the state legislature against each other, he obtained a charter which erected Nauvoo into a practically independent community in which he held the combined offices of mayor, chief justice, and commander in chief of the Nauvoo Legion. There followed four golden years under his benevolent dictatorship, during which the Mormon population rose to twenty-five thousand, and the city became one of the most prosperous in the West.

In 1844 Smith announced himself as a candidate for the United States presidency on a more progressive platform than that offered by either the Whigs or the Democrats, containing three main planks: the abolition of slavery with compensation for the owners, to be obtained from the sale of public lands; government ownership of the banks; a national system of prison reform under which convicts should be employed on useful public works "where the culprit can be taught wisdom and virtue," as a substitute for the expensive penitentiary system which merely converted momentary criminals into habitual ones. The three planks were evidently derived from Smith's reflections upon his personal experience of the evils of slavery, private banking, and prison conditions. Needless to say, his proposals were not discussed on their merits but were simply regarded, outside of Nauvoo, as an example of Mormon crackpot philosophy. The number of votes he might have received was never brought to the test, since by the time of election Smith was dead, the victim of a particularly foul murder committed with the virtual connivance of Governor Ford of Illinois.

An article criticizing Smith's dictatorship had appeared in the anti-Mormon *Nauvoo Expositor*, edited by one William Law, who had been excommunicated from the church for adultery. Smith possibly feared that if this act of insubordination were allowed to go unpunished it might be followed by some disclosure of the practice of polygamy, which in 1841 he had been led by a special "revelation" to promulgate secretly among the elders. While the latter had quickly availed themselves of the privilege, they did so with such discretion that very few of the members of the church knew of the practice. Whatever his motives, Smith had the press of the *Nauvoo Expositor* destroyed. Considering the denial of constitutional rights to which the Mormons themselves had been subjected over a long course of years, Smith's action, however indefensible, was quite understandable. But a wave of high moral indignation swept over the state. Rightly accused of having exceeded even his broad chartered powers, Smith was summoned to Carthage for trial. Fully conscious that he was probably going to his death, he gave himself up, hoping that the storm might not fall on Nauvoo. After promising him full protection, Governor Ford deliberately failed to guard the flimsy jail; a mob was allowed to assemble in front of it; Smith and his brother Hyrum, arrested with him, were killed by shots through its wooden door. So perished Joseph the Prophet, one of the most remarkable, most misunderstood, and most puzzling characters in American history.

BRIGHAM THE OLD BOSS

For a few weeks after Smith's murder it looked as if the Church of the Latter-day Saints might disintegrate through the quarrels of rival leaders. Sidney Rigdon came forward with insane boasts of what he would do if the Mormons would follow him back to the East: "I will cross the Atlantic, encounter the Queen's forces, and overcome them—plant the American standard on English ground, and then march to the palace of Her Majesty and demand a portion of her riches and dominions, which if she refuse, I will take the little madam by the nose, and lead her out, and she shall have no power to help herself. If I do not do this, the Lord never spake by mortal." The Prophet's mother, Lucy Mack, demanded the leadership for her son, William Smith. James Jesse Strang, a half-crazed Mormon lawyer, demanded it for himself, producing a forged letter from the Prophet in support of his claims. There were still other pretenders to the Crown. It seemed as if the only prominent person who didn't desire it was the Prophet's first wife, Emma Hale, who apostatized from the faith, denied that she had ever credited her husband's visions or revelations, and, two years after his death, married L. C. Bidamon, a Nauvoo tavernkeeper.

With the return of Brigham Young, absent in New England at the time of the murder, the other contestants vanished like puffs of smoke. It was not merely that as President of the Twelve Apostles he had the best claim; the Mormons recognized in him the one man capable of dealing with the crisis in their affairs. Rigdon set up an obscure Mormon church in Pittsburg. Strang led his followers to deserted Beaver Island on Lake Michigan, where he discovered a new collection of buried gold plates, established his own order of Twelve Apostles, and had himself crowned as "King Strang"; Lucy Mack and William Smith founded a more permanent secessionist branch, "The Reorganized Church of Latter-day Saints," which, reverting to Smith's earlier teachings, refused to accept polygamy. But the vast majority of the Mormons remained in Nauvoo under Brigham Young.

When it became evident that the church was not going to disintegrate of itself, the Gentile persecutions were once more renewed in the usual form of mob actions tacitly endorsed by the state government. Realizing that the Mormons would never be safe until they had put the Rocky Mountains between them and their fellow-Americans, Brigham Young made a careful study of locations and routes before selecting the uninhabited region of the Great Salt Lake as the most suitable for his people. He then announced his one and only revelation, typical of the practical character of the man, directing some of the Saints to go in advance to Nebraska and prepare a temporary town, to be called "Winter

Quarters," as a resting place for the others on their long journey toward the Pacific.

The exodus from Nauvoo began on February 12, 1846, when Brigham Young and other Apostles crossed the frozen Mississippi to begin their hazardous undertaking; it was July 21, 1847, before the advance scouts, Orson Pratt and Erastus Snow, climbed out of a canyon and looked down into the valley of the Salt Lake. The first contingent of forty-six men started in to plow on the day of their arrival; five acres were ready when Brigham Young appeared with the main body of immigrants two days later. Though ill and shaking with mountain fever, the President of the Apostles stood up in his wagon and addressed his followers on the principles of the community they were to establish: "No man can buy land here, for no one has any land to sell. But every man shall have his land measured out to him, which he must cultivate in order to keep it. Besides, there shall be no private ownership of the streams that come out of the canyons nor of the timber that grows on the hills. These belong to the people—all the people."

The State of Deseret, so named from a word in the Book of Mormon meaning working bee, was economically a co-operative commonwealth. Each family was allotted a homestead in proportion to its size, and in every village and town there was a "Big Field" held in common. Roads were built, canals dug, timber felled, houses raised, all by community effort. Stores were usually started as co-operative undertakings. Toward the end of his life Brigham Young attempted to put into practice Joseph Smith's communistic ideal of the United Order of Enoch, and at least one communistic settlement was established at Orderville in southern Utah. Probably Young would have made such attempts much earlier but for his reluctance to do anything that might diminish the incentive toward individual labor. The moral value of work was the first and the last article of his creed.

The Mormons were far ahead of other groups in their day in the matter of recognizing a degree of social obligation for the maintenance of the destitute, but in the method of treatment Brigham Young was still true to his fundamental philosophy of labor. Seventy years ago he faced today's problem of direct relief versus work relief and decided in favor of the latter: "Some have wished me to explain why we build an adobe wall around this city. Are there any Saints who stumble at such things? Oh, slow of heart to understand and believe. I build walls, dig ditches, make bridges, and do a great amount and variety of labor that is of little consequence only to provide ways and means for sustaining and preserving the destitute. I annually expend hundreds and thousands of dollars almost solely to furnish employment to those in want of labor. Why? I have potatoes, flour, beef, and other articles of food, which I wish my brethren to have; and it is better for them to labor for those articles, so far as they are able and have opportunity, than to have them given to them." [20]

It was unquestionably the Mormon spirit of social solidarity that enabled them, like the Shakers, to surpass their more individualistic Gentile neighbors in worldly prosperity. This result had been evident even in Missouri and at Nauvoo; in Utah, undisturbed by neighborly interference, the Mormons advanced about twice as rapidly as other western communities.

The institution of polygamy, assuring an abundance of much needed labor, was undoubtedly an important factor in their success. Polygamy may have been first introduced by Joseph Smith merely in order to gratify his inordinate sexuality, but when publicly proclaimed by Brigham Young in 1852, it had an economic justification.

On the moral side, it was easy for Orson Pratt, the best of the Mormon polemicists, to defend polygamy not only on the ground of Biblical example but also by the sound argument that it did away with the adultery, concubinage, and prostitution that were prevalent among the Gentiles. It also, for good or ill, did away with romance. Brigham Young with twenty-seven wives and fifty-six children, John Doyle Lee with nineteen wives and sixty-four children, Heber Kimball with forty-five wives and sixty-five children—these exemplars found it impossible to concentrate much marital or parental affection on individuals. Shelley wrote in "Epipsychidion" that in the realm of love "To divide is not to take away," but he never had in mind such atomic division of love as the Mormons practiced. Brigham Young, to be sure, at the age of sixty-two conceived a be-

---

[20] *Journal of Discourses* (Liverpool: Bevvian Collection, 1854–85), VIII, 11. Quoted in Werner, *op. cit.*, p. 420.

lated romantic passion for his next-to-the-last wife, Amelia Folsom, an ambitious young lady of twenty-six, but this was highly exceptional. In general, polygamy with the Mormons and celibacy among the Shakers worked to the same end of turning attention away from individual to social well-being.

There is abundant evidence that the women as a rule did not object to the system. Ann Eliza, Brigham's last wife, jealous of his continued devotion to Amelia Folsom, did run away from him and publish her sensational and mendacious *Wife Number Nineteen,* but such scandals were very unusual. Every year hundreds of women took the perilous journey across the plains, eager to get to Deseret, and very few of them ever evinced any desire to leave. After Deseret had become a territory, with its name idiotically changed by Congress to Utah, naïve congressmen, thinking that Mormon women, if they had the chance, would abolish polygamy, introduced a bill to give them the vote. They were amazed when the Mormon Church immediately supported the measure; whereupon they themselves quickly abandoned it. Then Utah defiantly passed the measure itself, so sure were the Mormons of the loyalty of their women, who of course greatly outnumbered the men. They were right. The Mormon women never attempted to utilize the suffrage against the peculiar institution of Utah.

It must be admitted, however, that voting, always conducted by a show of hands, had little more meaning in Utah than it has today in Nazi Germany or Soviet Russia. The Mormons, both men and women, were quite content to leave the government in the hands of the priesthood. Brigham Young was an autocrat who appointed all the important local officers, whether civil or ecclesiastical; known as the "Old Boss," he expected to be consulted on a man's choice of wives, choice of business, and even his choice of guests for a ball. And in nine cases out of ten, his authority was willingly recognized. Heber Kimball expressed the common sentiment when he said in a sermon, "If Brother Brigham tells me to do a thing, it is the same as though the Lord told me to do it."

There was a further reason for the contentment of the Mormons under their supposedly inspired dictatorship. Their leaders always remained men of the people, close to the mass in their interests, their way of life, their manner of speech. Their addresses, collected in the *Journal of Discourses,* the last of the Mormon scriptures, were slangy, vulgar, humorous, realistic, and forceful, foreshadowing the popular style of Billy Sunday and Huey Long.

From the beginning, the Mormon movement had been characterized by a kind of earthy joviality. Smith and Young were essentially plebeian autocrats, who laid little emphasis on minutiae of conduct. Both, and especially Young, were fond of swearing. Though the use of tobacco was proscribed by the rules of the church, Brigham chewed and smoked it and recommended that it be planted in Utah. All the Mormons were excessively fond of dancing. Their formal balls, at which Brigham always led the first cotillion, began with prayer at four in the afternoon, and ended, again with prayer, at five in the morning. At Nauvoo, Smith had encouraged home dramatics, and the same interest was maintained in Salt Lake City so that after the opening of the railroad it became the most popular theatrical town west of Chicago. The choir of the Mormon Tabernacle was one of the best in the country. The untutored Mormons became devoted to their own schools and very early established a state university.

Everything, of course, had to yield to Brigham Young's personal crotchets. His moral disapproval of the polka, of fiction, and of tragedy sufficed to ban them. He hated lawyers and doctors, and so far as possible made their life unbearable. A thorough agrarian in his economic philosophy, he prevented the development of Utah's mines during his lifetime. The will of the Old Boss determined the course and limits of Mormon culture.

This was what America after two centuries had made of the Puritan. The theocratic dreams of Massachusetts Bay had come to fruition in a strange form. Deseret was a theocracy, but what a theocracy! Creedless, uninterested in theology, rowdy, plebeian, polygamous—all that the aristocratic Puritan would have most disapproved!

CHAPTER 24. *God's Peculiar People —*
the Shakers

"No sin can ever enter here—
Nor sinners rear a steeple;
'Tis kept by God's peculiar care,
For his peculiar people."

THERE were over a hundred communistic communities established in the United States during the nineteenth century, the overwhelming majority of them flourishing for
only brief periods in the two golden decades of social experiment
between 1825 and 1845, but a few of them beginning much earlier
and lasting much longer. None, of course, bore much relation to
the state-controlled Marxist communism of the twentieth century;
all were distinctly voluntary associations; and yet, undertaken, as
many of them were, under not unfavorable conditions, they shed
considerable light on the difficult question as to how far men will
ever be able to make a success of the attempt to build a society
which is not based on private property. But their answer to this
question is not as simple and unilateral as it is often considered.
The religious societies, such as the Shakers, Rappites, Zoarites, True
Inspirationists, and others, enjoyed one type of communistic experience; the nonreligious organizations of the Owenites and the
Fourierists met with quite another; while the Oneida Community
introduced special features which separated it from all the rest. By
and large, the religious communistic societies were relatively successful. The Zoarites in the village of Zoar, Ohio, named by them
after the "little city" to which Lot fled from Sodom, survived for

359

two generations; the Rappites lasted for three generations, with their prosperous towns of Harmony, Indiana (sold to Robert Owen), and Economy, Pennsylvania; the True Inspirationists in Ebenezer, New York, and later in Amana, Iowa, continued to flourish under their communistic organization until less than ten years ago. But since the characteristics of these German sects were virtually the same as those of the American Shakers, who have not yet entirely disappeared, we may confine our attention here to the Shakers.

Of all the nineteenth century communistic or semicommunistic communities, the Shakers were the first, the most successful, and the longest lived. Their importance has only once been recognized adequately: that was by John Humphrey Noyes, the founder of the Oneida Community. "It is no more than bare justice," he wrote, "to say that we are indebted to the Shakers more than to any or all other social architects of modern times. Their success has been the 'specie basis' that has upheld all the paper theories, and counteracted the failures, of the French and English schools. It is very doubtful whether Owenism or Fourierism would ever have existed, or if they had, whether they would have moved the practical American nation, if the facts of Shakerism had not existed before them, and gone along with them. But to do complete justice we must go a step further. While we say that the Rappites, the Zoarites, the Ebenezers, the Owenites and even the Fourierists are all echoes of the Shakers, we must also say that the Shakers are the far-off echoes of the Primitive Christian Church."

Noyes may have slightly overemphasized the influence of the Shakers, but he was completely right as to their origin. The Primitive Church, that ideal of all the most vigorous Protestant sects, was taken as a model much more closely and literally by the Shakers than it was by the individualistic Methodists and Disciples, who avoided its economic example.[1] They represented one more pure revival of the Left Reformation, being composed of the same lower-class social elements and deriving ultimately from the same medi-

---

[1] Even Alexander Campbell, debating with Rigdon the Mormon, resorted to sophistry in trying to show that Acts 2:44-45 need not be interpreted communistically.

eval sources as the German Pietists, and like them seeking an escape from the world to establish a community of the Lowly Elect where the will of God might rule among the few.

In 1685 the revocation of the Edict of Nantes had roused special protest in Languedoc, the old land of the Cathars. The Protestant peasants at first offered passive resistance to the re-establishment of the Catholic Church; then the rack and the thumbscrew, the galleys and dungeons, wrought their usual result, and disobedience flamed into violence. Prophets arose announcing Armageddon at hand when the Catholic Church would be overthrown and a millenarian reign of equality introduced, when men should be free in conscience and should enjoy all things in common. Under the pressure of this rhapsodic dream, men and women thought they conversed with the spirits of the dead who urged them to rise in the last war that would end all wars. It took Louis the Fourteenth three years and a hundred thousand troops to suppress the eight thousand Camisards [2] under Jean Cavalier, an ex-baker. Many fled to England, where some of their leaders, known as the "French Prophets," continued to preach their communistic-millenarian doctrines. A few members of the upper class were attracted by the novelty of the Prophets, among them one John Lacy who is said to have "entered into all their absurdities, except that of a community of goods, to which he strongly objected, having an income of two thousand pounds." The Prophets, reverting to pacifism after their military defeats, found more permanent adherents among the poorer English Quakers. A group of these, known as "Shaking Quakers" from their ecstatic ritual, began to meet in 1747 at the house of James Wardley, a tailor of Bolton, near Manchester. They were joined in 1758 by a young girl in her early twenties, named Ann Lee.

She was short and thickset, with blue eyes and a mild and grave countenance which was often thought beautiful. She was totally illiterate. The daughter of a blacksmith, she worked at various times in a cotton factory, as a cook, and in a hatter's establishment; all her associations were with the poor. In 1762, when she was twenty-six, she married Abraham Standerin, a rather brutal blacksmith whom she soon ceased to love but to whom she bore four children,

[2] Their name came from *camise*, a jacket worn in fighting.

all of whom died in infancy. This bitter personal experience left her with an enduring hatred of marriage which later occasioned the adoption of celibacy among her followers.

In 1770 occurred an event that was to become one of the most cherished of Shaker traditions: "She was thrown into a stone prison, and kept there for fourteen days with the purpose of starving her to death. A little boy, whom she had brought up, inserted a pipe-stem through the key-hole, and poured wine and milk into the bowl, and kept her alive while in prison, with the help of the good Spirit, so that she came out in very good condition, when they expected to find her dead." [3] She had been consoled in her affliction by a vision of Christ in his glory, and emerged from prison with renewed faith and zeal. From this time she assumed a position of leadership in the little Wardley group.

The proverbial Shaker cleanness and neatness came directly from the injunctions of "Mother Ann." "You ought to be neat and clean," she would say, "for there are no slovens or sluts in Heaven." So she said to Lucy Bishop, "Clean your room well; for good spirits will not live where there is dirt." And to Zeruah Clark she said at more length: "Be faithful to keep the gospel; be neat and industrious; keep your family's clothes clean and decent; see that your house is kept clean and your victuals are prepared in good order, that when the Brethren come in from their hard work they can bless you, and eat their food with thankfulness, without murmuring, and be able to worship in the beauty of holiness. Watch, and be careful, don't speak harsh, nor cast reflections upon them; but let your words be few, and seasoned with grace." To John Robinson, she said, "Never put on silver spoons nor tablecloths for me, but let your tables be clean enough to eat from without cloths." And she said to all: "Put your hands to work and your hearts to God; pay all your just debts, and right all your wrongs. Remember the poor; if you have but little to spare, give to them that need. Be neat and clean, and keep the fear of God in all your goings-forth." [4]

In 1774 Ann Lee, Abraham Standerin, and seven others came to

[3] Frederick W. Evans, *Religious Communism* (pamphlet), London, 1871, p. 19.
[4] Quotations given in Clara Endicott Sears, *Gleanings from Old Shaker Journals* (Boston: Houghton Mifflin Co., 1916), pp. 46–47.

America. The seven others proceeded to establish a Shaker settlement at Watervliet, seven miles northwest of Albany, but Ann lingered for two years in New York with her husband. Was she still uncertain of her true mission, or did she feel it her duty to give her worthless husband a further chance? Whatever her motives, it was not until Standerin deserted her for another woman that she rejoined the rest of her group at Watervliet. In 1780 they were strengthened by the conversion of a small Baptist community at New Lebanon (now Mount Lebanon), twenty-five miles southeast of Albany on the New York–Massachusetts border. "Mother Ann" then went on a missionary journey through New England which resulted, after much hardship and persecution, in the establishment of half a dozen additional settlements. Returning to Watervliet, she died there in 1784.

In the absence of definite early records, it is impossible to tell how far Ann Lee herself was responsible for the peculiar Shaker theology. She seems always to have remained simple and sincere, with no desire to receive particular honors; dictatorship and autocracy were foreign to all the Shaker ideals; much of their theology, like many of their customs, probably grew up unconsciously in a kind of folklore which would have been impossible in a more learned or self-conscious group. Still, it seems evident that Ann Lee fairly early came to be regarded, and presumably regarded herself, as the realization of Christ's prophesied Second Coming and as one who symbolized a radically new conception of deity: that of "the Father-Mother God," declared by later Shaker theologians to be "one in essence, nature, and union, but two in their office and manner of operation." The Shakers, like the Quakers from whom they sprang, considered the Bible to be a much corrupted record of the Word of God, but on the central point of their theology they claimed direct Scriptural sanction. Elder Frederick Evans of New Lebanon put their argument very plausibly in an address which he delivered in London in 1871:

"Your Scriptures say, 'In the beginning God created man in his own image, in the image of God created he him, male and female created he them.' . . . How could man and woman, I ask, be in the image of God if God himself has no element of the feminine in him? There is, you may depend, so far as my testimony can go, and that of my people, as truly in existence a Heavenly Divine Mother as there is a Heavenly Divine Father unto whom you pray. And indeed, my friends, how could there be a father when there is no mother? Is it not a little out of order to use the term father? Why do you not use the term 'it'?" [5]

The feminist element in the Shaker theology naturally appealed especially to women, so that they nearly always outnumbered the men in the Shaker communities two to one and sometimes by a much larger proportion. At Shirley, Massachusetts, for example, in 1874 there were six men and thirty women; and at Enfield, New Hampshire, there were one hundred and three women to thirty-seven men. In the remnant of the community at Hancock, Massachusetts, today there are eight women and a single man. This feminine preponderance makes the economic success of the Shakers the more surprising, especially since their women never worked in the fields as did those of the German communistic groups.

The Shakers originated the idea of the Fourieristic "phalanstery" before Fourier ever dreamed of it. Their settlements were divided into "families," often several miles apart, each family occupying what was really a large double house, usually three stories high, with separate entrances and staircases for men and women, who rarely met except at mealtime and at the religious services. Even at the latter they sat on opposite sides of the room and, although the ritualistic dances were often ecstatic in character, sex decorum was never violated, the men and women going through the movements of the dance in separate lines which did not intermingle. The equality and mutual respect of the sexes were preserved by keeping them apart, and apparently both men and women were quite willing to have it so.

Every family had its elder and eldresses, who were known as "the Leads." They exercised a mild paternalistic authority, censoring mail and seeing to it that no sinful novels or dramas were smuggled into the settlements. But as this was done with the full approval of the community, it was hardly an exercise of dictatorial power. The elders worked in the fields like the others, ate the same meals, shared the same simple rooms, and were in all ways one with their people. The Shakers always asserted that the greatest charm

[5] *Ibid.*, p. 8.

in their manner of life was the sentiment of equality that prevailed.

The first great success of the Shakers was in New England, where by 1800 they had nine thriving villages, in addition to the original two in New York. Then expanding into Ohio and Kentucky, by 1830 they had in all eighteen villages with fifty-eight families.

The Shakers made a practice of locating their villages far enough away from cities to be uncontaminated by urban depravity, yet near enough to enjoy the advantages of trade. They early became great dairy farmers with the best cattle in the countryside. Their stone barns rose four and five stories high, substantial buildings designed for eternity, in notable contrast to the hasty wooden structures too often put up by the Gentiles. Their flower and vegetable gardens were famous when the nursery art was still in its infancy in America. Their seeds were reputed to be the best on the market. They were the first to do a large business in canned vegetables. They claimed to have originated straw brooms. The Shaker sisters made "the Dorothy cloak," "the Shaker sweater," the "Shaker-knit underwear." The Shakers prospered exactly as the early Quakers had prospered because their workmanship was good and they kept their word.

And they did much better than the Quakers in resisting the lure of wealth. Successful as they were in their business dealings, their trade was always kept subservient to a subsistence economy. No money circulated within the community. And although the advantages of the division of labor were fully understood so that each member was assigned his allotted task, there were no fixed hours of labor. The usual number was not more than six hours a day. The Shakers, unlike the Puritans and the Quakers, did not make a fetish of work. With half the labor, they lived more comfortably than the Gentiles. Their houses were simpler, but they were also warmer and better lighted. The communist Utopia was actually realized in the Shaker communities for over a century.

Their villages were everywhere noted for their extraordinary cleanliness, their harmonious spirit, and their hospitality. Shaker communism was an expression of Shaker solidarity and sense of human brotherhood. Their statement of principles reads: "The bond of union which unites all Shakers is spiritual and religious, hence unselfish. All are equal before God and one another; and, as in the institutions of the primitive Christian church, all share one interest in spiritual and temporal blessings, according to individual needs; no rich, no poor. The strong bear the infirmities of the weak and all are sustained, promoting each other in Christian fellowship, as one family of brethren and sisters in Christ." These were not simply ideals; they were put into daily practice. In the raucous competitive America of the thirties, the Shaker villages were little oases of peace. All visitors noticed the soft, gentle voices of the Shakers, their invariable courtesy, their hospitality. They were always on good terms with the Indians, and they were the only white communities to receive Negroes simply and naturally on a basis of human equality. Every village had a hobo house on its outskirts for the use of tramps. During the winters many temporary converts would flock to the warmth of the Shaker settlements, departing like birds in the spring. The Shakers were well aware of their character, calling them "Winter Shakers" derisively, but they nevertheless continued to take them in. In the peaceful surroundings which they made for themselves, the lives of the Shakers passed slowly. All of the religious communists were noted for their longevity, but the Shakers above all the rest. Even today when no converts come to their doors, and no voices of children are heard in the still communities that are lingering out their long twilight, one still meets there hale and hearty octogenarians and nonagenarians just as men did a century ago.

CHAPTER 25. *Philanthropic Communism:*
the Owenists

THE decades of the twenties, thirties, and forties constituted a Utopian era in American history. The whole nation was infected with the optimism of the frontier. It was in a fine mood for social experiments, though it did not very well know just how to go about them. Accustomed to thinking in religious and political terms, not only the average American but also his intellectual leaders found it very difficult to conceive of economic and social realities as they were. Political liberty and equality had been won, but obviously this was not enough. They, however, at least left the field open. If Americans wanted to try out new ways of living, they were free to do so without interference from government. But what ways should be tried? It is not surprising that the first answers came from Europe, where people had been thinking about the problem much longer. Robert Owen and Charles Fourier had behind them a more mature social experience at the same time that they were as Utopian-minded as any American.

Even the simplest of people are rarely consistent. Robert Owen was one of the simplest of men; yet his life was full of contradictions. As an industrialist, he was shrewd and careful, as a philanthropist, he was reckless and wasteful; he acquired his wealth through twenty years of unremitting attention to business, and he lost most of it in four years of improvident spending for others; he was intensely emotional, but his writings were, with a few ex-

367

ceptions, amazingly dull; uncommonly ugly, with a nose of Cyrano size, he loved to appear on the platform. The best characterization of him is that of Lillian Symes in *Rebel America:* "He was probably one of the world's worst bores and poorest listeners, a visionary, and at times, no doubt, pretty much of a fool. But he was also one of the most disinterested, benevolent and farsighted men modern England has produced." [1]

Owen was one poor boy who never forgot his beginnings. The son of a saddler in Wales, he was sent away to London at the age of ten to make his own living, clerked in various shops, won the confidence of his employers, was appointed manager of a cotton factory in Manchester, purchased, with several partners, the New Lanark Mills from the millionaire David Dale, and finally married the millionaire's daughter. The usual effect of such a Horatio Alger career—as shown in the cases of the first Astor, the first Gould, the first Vanderbilt, and scores of others—is to give the hero of the success story an overweening sense of the importance of individual ability and achievement. Few have been so modest as Mary Baker Eddy and John D. Rockefeller, who said that their money "came from God." But Owen, more modest still, believed neither in the self-made man nor in the divine right to riches. A slender reader, but something of an original thinker, he early concluded from the strife of religious sects that their arguments canceled out, leaving nothing but the general Deistic conception of a benevolent ruler of the universe who worked out his purposes through natural causes. Human beings, he professed to believe, were wholly created by their environment; but behind this profession lay a passionate faith in the natural goodness of men who, if given decent living conditions and a rational education, would live moral, industrious, and rational lives quite as easily as the bees make their honey.

If Owen learned little from books, he learned much from the liberal acquaintances whom he sought out. Among his friends were William Godwin, Arthur Young, James Mill, John Dalton the Quaker, Erasmus Darwin, Thomas Percival, and Francis Place, "the radical tailor of Charing Cross," who lent his highly critical assistance to Owen's most important book, *A New View of Society*

---

[1] Lillian Symes and Travers Clement, *Rebel America* (New York and London: Harper & Brothers, 1934), p. 21.

(1813). In 1816 the millowner visited the schools of Frederick Oberlin, Pestalozzi, and Fellenberg, being so much impressed by the work of the last-named that he sent his sons, William and Robert Dale Owen, to him to be educated.

He was confirmed in all his convictions by his experience at New Lanark. The working conditions there were considered to be among the best in Great Britain, yet the mills were largely maintained by the labor of children between five and seven who worked at pitiful wages thirteen hours a day. The villages were unsanitary and filthy, there were no schools, and the only joy to be found was in drunkenness. Forced to make profits for his partners, Owen could only cut the hours a little; but he organized a company store with low prices which raised the real wages, compelled the workers to keep the yards and streets clean, instituted special rewards for sobriety, and built two model schools, including a kindergarten, which emphasized nature study and the use of pictures and maps, included singing and dancing in their curriculum, and forbade the use of corporal punishment. When obliged to close the mills for four months because of the American embargo, he paid full wages during that time. Under Owen's benevolent paternalism the villages were transformed, and the New Lanark experiments were soon the talk of the kingdom.

Unfortunately, Owen's partners were Quakers, sympathetic with his reforms on their material side, but distrustful of an educational scheme which made no place for religious instruction. They interfered more and more with his plans, abolished the singing and dancing, dismissed the teachers of natural science, and finally supplanted Owen's whole system by adopting the formalized methods of the British and Foreign Schools Society. So ended the first attempt at experimental education in England.

Owen might have put up a fight for his schools but by that time he was involved in larger issues. A parliamentary investigation revealed shocking labor conditions throughout the kingdom; called on to testify, Owen pleaded earnestly for a ten and a half hour law and the appointment of government inspectors for mills and factories; the law that was actually passed was a twelve hour law with no inspectors. During his testimony, Owen was bitterly assailed by the cotton manufacturers, well represented in Parliament, those devoutly Christian gentlemen striving desperately to undermine his evidence as that of an "infidel" who could not be trusted.

But meanwhile Owen had come under the influence of a new type of thinking. He happened upon a forgotten Elizabethan work by John Bellers, entitled *Proposals for raising A Colledge of Industry of all useful Trades and Husbandry* (1696), in which the author suggested the establishment of co-operative communities, with common houses and meals, the profits to be divided only after the comfort of the workers and the education of their children had been taken care of. With his interest thoroughly aroused, Owen went on to make a study of the Shakers, who seemed to be successfully exemplifying these very ideas, the result being that he republished Bellers' treatise, together with an enthusiastic sketch of the Shakers written by himself. He now only awaited a suitable time and place to inaugurate a communistic enterprise of his own, so when the Rappite offer came in 1824 he embraced it eagerly.

No other communistic experiment was ever begun under such favorable auspices. There was plenty of capital behind it, and the initial difficulties of taming the wilderness had already been overcome by the Rappites. Owen inherited a well laid out town with successful industries and prosperous farms. With a modicum of intelligence, the experiment might possibly have been successful. But at this crucial moment, Owen suddenly went mildly mad, letting his imagination run away with his common sense. Putting his inexperienced twenty-four year old son William in charge of "New Harmony," as the town was renamed, Owen himself set out on an extensive lecture tour. The tone of his speeches is illustrated by the one which he delivered in the Hall of Representatives at Washington, D.C., before a select audience of congressmen, senators, and judges, with the President and his full cabinet in attendance. He began: "The Power which governs and directs the Universe and every action of man . . . permits me to announce a new empire of peace and goodwill to men"; and he concluded by issuing a general invitation to "the industrious and well-disposed of all nations" to join in the enterprise. After three months of this nonsense, he abruptly returned to England, leaving poor William Owen to struggle as best he could with the crowd of penniless cranks whom his father's indiscreet utterances sent to New Harmony.

Embarrassed at the outset by some eight hundred enthusiasts who came to the community before he had had time to make any suitable preparation for their employment, William Owen did his best to maintain discipline and get the industries going. As he wrote to his father: "We have been much puzzled to know what to do with those who profess to do anything and everything; they are perfect drones and can never be satisfied here. We have got rid of a good many such although we still have a few left." Robert Dale Owen, who came over to join his brother in the following spring, was still less optimistic. The community, he wrote, consisted of "a heterogeneous collection of radicals, enthusiastic devotees to principle, honest latitudinarians and lazy theorists, with a sprinkling of unprincipled sharpers thrown in." With such a personnel to work with, it speaks volumes for the ability and energy of the two youthful brothers in charge of the enterprise that they were able to maintain some sort of order until the return of their father in 1826.

This time, on his return, Owen brought with him, down the Ohio River from Pittsburgh, what the press termed "the Boatload of Knowledge." As a university faculty in the departments of science and education the group could hardly have been rivaled anywhere. It included William Maclure, a founder of the Philadelphia Academy of Natural Sciences and probably the ablest geologist of his day; Thomas Say the zoologist; Charles Alexander Lesueur, a French naturalist; Dr. Gerard Troost, a Dutch chemist; and three competent disciples of Pestalozzi, William Phiquepal d'Arusmont, Joseph Neef, and Madame Maria Fretageot.

New Harmony, for a brief period, now made a very genuine cultural contribution to American life. The *New Harmony Gazette*, launched the previous year by William Owen and Robert L. Jennings, later edited by William Pelham and finally by Robert Dale Owen and Frances Wright, began as a mere community chronicle but eventually became the most fearless and inspiring magazine in the country. The schools were the most progressive yet seen on this side of the Atlantic. The kindergarten of Madame

Fretageot was a marvel. William Phiquepal proved himself an astounding master of vocational training, teaching his students to make their own clothes, hats, and shoes, giving them a knowledge of blacksmithing, tanning, and grazing, so that they learned from this extraordinary Parisian Frenchman how to adapt themselves to the conditions of the American frontier. The scientific instruction in the schools was, of course, excellent. The Rappite meetinghouse was thrown open to any visiting clergymen who might care to use it, with the provision that after the sermon the audience should be free to ask questions—an ordeal that few cared to meet. With an abundance of musical talent in the community, it was easy to form a good band which gave a concert every Friday. Once a week there was also a public forum. There were innumerable picnics; and there were dances every night, including Sunday. New Harmony, termed by Lyman Beecher "the infidel trumpet call to all the envious and vicious poor," was certainly for two years a spirited and joyous community.

Full communism was not adopted until Owen's final arrival in 1826. At that time it was decided that all should participate in manual labor, should be paid equal wages, and should receive food, clothing, and shelter free of charge. But since practically every social class was represented in the community the principle of equality was difficult to enforce. A straw showed the trend of the wind. To prevent class distinctions in the dances, lots were drawn for partners. Charles Bernard, Grand Duke of Saxe-Weimar-Eisenach, a sharp-eyed visitor at New Harmony, observed that "the young ladies turned up their noses at the democratic dancers who often in this way fell to their lot." No doubt, the Grand Duke of Saxe-Weimar-Eisenach was somewhat unsympathetic, but there was only too much ground for the charge that social cliques continued to exist in the equalitarian Utopia. The intellectual workers also felt that they should be paid higher wages than those accorded to manual labor. Maclure with his Scottish Presbyterian ancestry was not ready to accept Owen's Deism. To add to these several sources of dissension, Owen was uncertain as to the proper form of government for the community. During a year and a half, seven successive constitutions were adopted, ranging from a dictatorship of Owen by common consent to a decentralized organization under ten committees. The social snobbishness of the English immigrants caused them to withdraw and form the separate community of "Feiba Peveli." The religious conservatives withdrew to try to build up a new town, "Macluria." Soon eight other subdivisions occurred. This critical moment was chosen by Owen for one of his frequent visits to England, but before going he made matters worse by giving out a number of individual leases. On his final return a year later, he learned that a number of his tenants had used their land for individual profit, one rascal named Taylor having gone so far as to set up a distillery. Owen thereupon disgustedly closed his undertaking in April, 1828.

He remained undisillusioned, however, as to the merits of communism. After a vain trip to Mexico in an attempt to secure lands in Coahuila and Texas for a second venture, he still dreamed that sometime, somewhere, under more favorable stars, he would be able to carry out his vast plans. Meanwhile, he did yeoman service in England on behalf of factory legislation, co-operative stores, and trade unions. He organized a group of Equitable Banks of Labor Exchange which offered easy terms to workingmen. His rather grandiloquent "Association of All Classes and Nations" was the first official socialist organization. But to the end his projected solution remained philanthropic, his hope being that if enough capitalists like himself would join with the working classes, private property could be done to death painlessly. He saw the specter of class warfare clearly enough on the horizon, but hoped that it might be exorcised in time. He was never able to recognize, more than momentarily, the actual amount of greed and shortsightedness in the world. Shortly before his death in 1858, he found such escape as was possible for him by becoming a believer in spiritualism.

CHAPTER 26. *The Fourierist Folly*

IT TOOK a little over ten years for the Owenist failures to be so far forgotten that renewed experiments in community living could be undertaken with any chance of a popular following. But in the forties a new and much more widespread interest was aroused in them. Noyes denominated the era "the Fourier period," which was correct enough since the teachings of the erratic Frenchman dominated the aims and methods of the community experiments after 1843; but their basic impulse was older and much more religious. The Oneida Community, to be discussed later, was in a class by itself, and of course owed nothing to Fourier. But neither did Hopedale, the most successful of the later undertakings; Brook Farm, in its inception, was uninfluenced by Fourierism; Fruitlands was the dream child of Charles Lane and Bronson Alcott. Had Fourier never existed, some such movement as that in the forties would still have occurred and might have been much more significant if it had not been deflected from its true course by the foreign influence. The inciting cause behind it was a deep dissatisfaction with the increasingly capitalistic and industrial character of American society: hence the fact that the first communities sprang up in New England, where the evils were most in evidence.

THE HIGH HOPES OF HOPEDALE

THE earliest of them, and in many ways the most interesting, stemmed from the reformist zeal of Adin Ballou, the American founder of Christian Socialism. As a poor farmboy, he had been perforce self-educated—but the education that he achieved, while more limited, was more dynamic and vital than that of the schools. At the age of eighteen, he began to preach as a member of the Rhode Island "Christian Connection," soon being expelled, however, for holding Universalist views. From 1823 to 1831 he was, next to his kinsman, Hosea Ballou, the leading figure in the Universalist Society. Gradually he came to realize that there had developed a Universalist orthodoxy, similar to the Unitarian orthodoxy against which Channing rebelled: a respectable, complacent staticism which used the once liberating doctrine of universal salvation as a cloak to cover existing evils. In 1831 he withdrew from his church and organized the "Massachusetts Association of Universal Redemptionists," which was, in spite of its theological name, inspired by an activist idea of redemption as something to be worked out on this earth through the struggle for social justice. No less than thirty-one heretical ministers joined the group. Out of this movement there developed, ten years later, the Hopedale Community.

In January, 1841, some months before Brook Farm was started, Ballou organized a joint stock company with a capital of four thousand dollars, which purchased about six hundred acres near Milford, Massachusetts, where they erected a village of some thirty houses, three mechanic shops, and a chapel. By 1851 there were nearly two hundred people engaged in the movement with every prospect of enduring success. John Humphrey Noyes, that best of authorities on early American socialisms, wrote of Hopedale: "As it came nearest to being a religious community, so it commenced earlier, lasted longer, and was really more scientific and sensible than any of the other experiments of the Fourier epoch." [1]

As usual, Noyes picked out the essential features in the object of his study. Scientific and sensible though Hopedale was in some measure, its inspiration was primarily religious and moral. Fundamentally, it represented a revival of the Cathar ideal, an attempt to carry on the Left Reformation in nineteenth century America through the addition of a kind of Quakerism brought up to date.

---

[1] J. H. Noyes, *History of American Socialisms* (Philadelphia: J. B. Lippincott & Co., 1870), p. 120.

This appears clearly in Ballou's account of the enterprise, published in 1851:

"It is a church of Christ . . . based on a simple declaration of faith in the religion of Jesus Christ, as he taught and exemplified it. . . . No precise theological dogmas, ordinances, or ceremonies are prescribed or prohibited. In such matters all the members are free, with mutual love and toleration, to follow their own highest convictions of truth and religious duty. . . . But in practical Christianity this church is precise and strict. . . . It insists on supreme love to God and man—that love which 'worketh no ill' to friend or foe. It enjoins total abstinence from all God-contemning words and deeds; all unchastity; all intoxicating beverages; all oath-taking; all slave-holding and pro-slavery compromises; all war and preparations for war; all capital and other vindictive punishments; all insurrectionary, seditious, mobocratic and personal violence against any government, society, family, or individual; all voluntary participation in any anti-Christian government, under promise of unqualified support—whether by doing military service, commencing actions at law, holding office, voting, petitioning for penal laws, aiding a legal posse by injurious force, or asking public interference for protection which can be given only by such force; all resistance of evil with evil; in fine, from all things known to be sinful against God or human Nature."

Here we have the familiar withdrawal from government, the familiar opposition to oaths, capital punishment, and all forms of violence. Peter Waldo or George Fox would have felt at home in Hopedale. But besides its negative, medieval aspect of withdrawal, Hopedale had also a very positive centemporary program which Ballou went on to emphasize:

"It is a universal religious, moral, philanthropic, and social reform Association. It is a Missionary Society, for the promulgation of New Testament Christianity, the reformation of the nominal church, and the conversion of the world. It is a moral suasion Temperance Society on the teetotal basis. It is a moral power Anti-Slavery Society, radical and without compromise. It is a Peace Society on the only impregnable foundation of Christian non-resistance. It is a sound theoretical and practical Women's Rights Association. It is a Charitable Society for the relief of suffering humanity, to the extent of its humble ability. It is an Educational Society, preparing to act an important part in the training of the young. It is a socialistic Community, successfully actualizing, as well as promulgating, practical Christian Socialism—the only kind of Socialism likely to establish a true social state on earth."

The program of Hopedale, in other words, embodied virtually all of the most enlightened humanitarian aims of the period. It was a far more militant program than that of Brook Farm, openly espousing, as it did, the dangerous causes of antislavery and women's rights. Finally, Hopedale was, in the eyes of Ballou, the very apotheosis of the principle of local self-government: "It is," he wrote, "a Civil State, a miniature Christian Republic, existing within, peaceably subject to, and tolerated by the governments of Massachusetts and the United States, but otherwise a commonwealth complete within itself. . . . It asks of them no corporate powers, no military or penal protection. It has its own Constitution, laws, regulations and municipal police; its own Legislative, Judiciary and Executive authorities; its own moral and religious safeguards, its own fire insurance and savings institutions; its own internal arrangements for the holding of property, the management of industry, and the raising of revenue; in fact, all the elements and organic constituents of a Christian Republic, on a miniature scale."

All this was admirable, but Ballou neglected one fundamental consideration. The question of the location of government, whether local or national, was of less importance than that of the nature of its control. The weakness of the joint stock form of association was that control was vested in a limited number of stockholders. The high ambitions of Hopedale collapsed through this basic defect. As long as the social-minded Ballou remained at the helm the community prospered, but in 1852 he resigned the presidency to devote himself to writing his prophetic *Practical Christian Socialism* (1854). Ballou's successor, Ebenezer D. Draper, together with his brother, George Draper, owned three fourths of the stock; they were shrewd businessmen whose idealism waned as they became alarmed over the expenditures for the improvement of the community. Seeing more chance for personal profit in private industry, they withdrew their stock in 1856 and invested it in their own Hopedale Manufacturing Company. This, of course, killed the co-operative community and, although its ghost survived as a kind of moral uplift society until 1868, the living Hopedale was transformed into a company-owned town maintained by the Draper industries. As such, it still was vastly cleaner and better kept up than most New England factory towns, but otherwise it did not differ greatly from all the rest.

THE ESSENCE OF BROOK FARM

BROOK FARM, much better known than Hopedale, has been called both a Unitarian and a Transcendentalist community; but, strictly speaking, it was neither. Its founder, George Ripley, a Harvard graduate and classical scholar, influential in bringing contemporary European culture to New England through his fourteen-volume edition of *Specimens of Standard Foreign Literature*, was indeed a prominent member of the Transcendental Club and had long been the Unitarian pastor of the wealthy Purchase Street Church in Boston. But in the latter capacity he had met with discouragement similar to that of Ballou. In 1841 he resigned his pastorate, because, as he said, "the liberal churches had begun to fear liberality" and failed to realize that the aim of Christianity was "to redeem society as well as the individual." With those last words, he also escaped from the charmed circle of Transcendentalism. His Transcendentalist friends, Emerson, Thoreau, Bronson Alcott, and Margaret Fuller, were mildly sympathetic with his Brook Farm experiment and came often to visit the Farm, but none of them actively participated in the undertaking. Hawthorne was the only one of the Concord group really to take part in the movement.

The modest little community organized by Ripley, consisting at first of not more than twenty members, took over a dairy farm of a hundred and sixty acres near West Roxbury, nine miles from Boston. The land was beautiful rolling country, there was a brook, there were pine woods and meadows. The Charles River was close by for swimming and boating. It was an idyllic spot, the perfect site for that union of labor and leisure, that combination of the work of the head and the hand, which the founders envisaged. The spirit of the place was expressed in the pleasant poetic names given to the buildings as they arose one after another the Hive, the Eyrie, the Nest, the Cottage, the Pilgrim House.

The distinctive feature of Brook Farm, which made it unique among the co-operative movements, was its preservation of individual cultural values in the midst of its socialized aims. It had no bold reformist program like Hopedale: the atmosphere was one of intellectual tolerance enlivened by curiosity, inquiry, and free discussion. Catholics would not have felt happy at Hopedale, but at Brook Farm the founder's wife, Sophia Ripley, was already on the way to Rome, as were Charles King Newcomb and Isaac Hecker, the future organizer of the Paulist Fathers, the most liberal of Catholic orders. The classics were never better taught than in the Brook Farm school: philosophy by Ripley, Dante by Mrs. Ripley, Greek and German by Charles A. Dana, whose youthful idealism was later to degenerate, after a transitional Fourierist phase, into the crass opportunism of the editor of the New York *Sun*. There were classes in music under the many-sided John Sullivan Dwight, Unitarian minister, musical critic, translator of Goethe. There were classes in botany and geology. The personnel of the students was almost as distinguished as that of the faculty: George and James Burrill Curtis were there, along with two sons of Orestes Brownson, two sons of George Bancroft, and a younger brother of Margaret Fuller. All subjects were elective, rules and regulations were minimized, and, instead of the traditional reliance on memorizing and discipline, attention was centered on the development of individual creative ability. It was such a school as every real educator has dreamed of and but few have encountered.

The Farm, though near enough to Boston for frequent visits, was not dependent on outside sources for excitement and entertainment. As Van Wyck Brooks writes in *The Flowering of New England*, "There were merry dances every night, picnics on Cow Island or in the grove, boating parties on the Charles, close by, Shakespeare readings, Elizabethan pageants, tableaux, charades, plays, scenes from Byron's *Corsair* and Sheridan's *Pizarro*." [2]

[2] Van Wyck Brooks, *The Flowering of New England* (New York: E. P. Dutton and Company, 1936), p. 245.

When Emerson, however, referred to Brook Farm as a "perpetual picnic," he was guilty of slander. Everyone, teacher and student alike, had an arduous amount of physical labor. In fact, Hawthorne found this too taxing to allow him to continue his writing, as he had hoped. Ripley never forgot the social aims of the Farm. In his report to the New York Convention of Associationists in April, 1844, he did not stress the excellence of the school but the point that it was free. And he laid his chief emphasis on two entirely different aspects of the movement: the refusal to employ domestic servants, and the equal wages paid for all forms of labor.

"This institution of domestic servitude," he said, "was one of the first considerations; it gave one of the first impulses to the movement at Brook Farm. . . . It was a deadly sin—a thing to be escaped from. Accordingly, it was escaped from, and we have now for three years lived at Brook Farm and have carried on all the business of life without it. At Brook Farm they are all servants of each other; no man is master. We do freely, from the love of it, those duties which are usually discharged by domestics." There can be no doubt of the practice of equality at Brook Farm. Among its members were the son of an English baronet and an English baronet's valet. The social snobbishness which Owen had been unable to conquer at New Harmony was successfully overcome at Brook Farm. This seemed to Ripley its first and greatest achievement.

And the second was like unto it: "In the best society that has ever been in this world, with very small exceptions, labor has never had its just reward. Everywhere the gain is to the pocket of the employer. He makes the money. The laborer toils for him and is his servant. The interest of the laborer is not consulted in the arrangements of industry; but the whole tendency of industry is perpetually to disgrace the laborer, to grind him down and reduce his wages, and to render deceit and fraud almost necessary for him. And all for the benefit of whom? For the benefit of our excellent companies, our excellent employers. The stream all runs into their pockets, and not one little rill is suffered to run into the pockets of those who do the work. Now in Association already we have changed all this; we have established a true relation between labor and the people. . . ." [3]

So Ripley spoke, with justifiable pride, in 1844, just as he and Brook Farm were coming under the influence of the deceitful Fourierism which was destined to dissolve the Brook Farm synthesis of the individual and society and wholly alter the community's spirit. As the Fourierist Brook Farm was another Brook Farm, consideration of it may be conveniently postponed for a moment.

TRANSCENDENTALIST FRUITLANDS

BRONSON ALCOTT's Fruitlands, much more than Brook Farm, was a truly Transcendentalist enterprise. Co-operative in theory, it was anarchistic in practice; supposed to afford a union of leisure and labor, it turned out to be nearly all leisure; and it ended in a serio-comic debacle—serious enough to Alcott, but comic to all observers.

Alcott was in truth a divided soul. The most transcendental of the Transcendentalists, spontaneity was the very spring of his being. Logic, rules, routine, mechanisms of any sort were abhorrent to him. He perceived that they could easily stifle the spirit, as they finally did at Brook Farm; he failed to see that, properly used, they were also necessary means for almost any enduring achievement. And yet, inconsistently, he was, unlike Thoreau and Emerson, an essentially socialized person, a constant attendant at all reform meetings, loving above all things to be with people and to talk to them. He stoutly maintained that the individual only becomes a person through social relationships. At one of the meetings of the Transcendental Club he condemned the tendency "to confirm the student or inquirer in what was peculiar to himself, more than to lead himself forth into what belongs to all mankind." These two opposed drives, Alcott was never able to reconcile; his life was passed in alternately listening to the inner and the outer voice. His was, in exacerbated form, the problem of the New

[3] Quoted by J. H. Noyes, *History of American Socialisms* (Philadelphia: J. B. Lippincott & Co., 1870), pp. 222–224.

England conscience itself, once it was complicated by the new sense of social responsibility.

Hopedale and Brook Farm had vainly invited him to join their communities; neither enterprise, he thought, was sufficiently "idealistic." But in 1842 during a six months' visit to England, generously financed by Emerson, he came into intimate relationship with a group of former correspondents who had founded in London a school conducted on his principles and named in his honor "Alcott House." Charles Lane, a leader in that undertaking, offered to assist, personally and financially, in another American community venture which should be as idealistic as Alcott could wish. Lane was a fanatical weathercock who blew with every wind, but always saw one point of the compass as the whole horizon. He was the last man under whose influence the gentle Alcott should have come, but at the moment their ideas seemed to coincide so nearly that the American was persuaded to take advantage of the opportunity offered by Lane's assistance.

Lane and his young son accompanied Alcott on his return, and the Englishman made good his promise by purchasing a ninety-acre farm at Harvard, fourteen miles west of Concord. Everyone is familiar with the amusing story of their seven months' enterprise; how, disbelieving in human slavery, they refused also to "enslave" any other animals, thus depriving themselves of the aid of horses and cows, and restricting their diet to a meager vegetarianism, deprived of eggs, milk, cheese, or butter; how they shivered in linen because they could not wear cotton, as a product of slavery, or wool as a robbery of the sheep; how they planted at the wrong time, and when harvesting came were away on a walking trip to consult other social reformers—a trip that carried them as far as New York. The oft-repeated story that Alcott drew a distinction between the "aspiring vegetables" that grew above ground and those that burrowed beneath has been recently proven a myth,[4] but in other respects the traditional tale is true enough. Yet, ridiculous as it was the Fruitlands adventure had its aspect of misguided heroism. It was an idealistic, Promethean defiance of Nature, a vain attempt to assert the supremacy of the pure spirit,

[4] Odell Shepard, *Pedlar's Progress* (Boston: Little, Brown and Company, 1937), p. 367.

a refusal to admit the all-constraining power of nonmoral natural laws. If the universe had been, as the Transcendentalists believed, an expression of Spirit, it should have responded more generously to Alcott's endeavors. From this point of view, Fruitlands may be regarded as a scientific test of the Transcendentalist hypothesis—a test from which all the other Transcendentalists shrank.

Nature being what it is, Fruitlands, the smallest of the American co-operative communities, never including more than eleven persons, was the most ineffective of them all. Emerson had written of the Fruitlanders in the early summer: "They look well in July; we shall see them in December." But by December, Fruitlands was no more.

Only two miles away the Shaker village of Harvard was still prospering after fifty years through continued observance of Mother Ann's wise counsel: "Every faithful man will go forth to put up his fences in season, and will plow his ground in season, and put his crops into the ground in season; and such a man may with confidence look for a blessing. But the slothful and indolent will say: 'Tomorrow will do as well,—and tomorrow will do as well.' Such a man never finds a blessing,—if he has anything it is afterwards, and there seems no blessing in it. Just so he is in spiritual things;—he will be slothful in the work of God, and he will reap his reward. He that is unfaithful in the unrighteous Mammon, how can he be trusted with the true riches?" [5] Alcott and Lane visited the Shaker village, but they had no ears for its teachings, no eyes for its lesson.

Lane, to be sure, did join the Shakers temporarily, after the failure of Fruitlands, but it was not their rational methods of labor which attracted him, but their irrational asceticism. He had earlier made an unhappy marriage and in his reaction against that experience was all for the celibate life, writing envenomed articles depicting the evils of matrimony; but he proved to be only a "Winter Shaker": in the spring when the sap began once more to flow, he was off for England, there to contract a second marriage.

As for Alcott, who had conducted his scientific experiment in a most unscientific spirit, he did not give up Transcendentalism, but

---

[5] Clara Endicott Sears, *Gleanings from Old Shaker Journals* (Boston: Houghton Mifflin Company, 1916), p. 47.

Associationism. And the co-operative movement, forgetting him as a mere leaf fallen by the wayside, marched on joyously into the pitfalls of Fourierism.

FOURIERISM

PERHAPS no other historical figure quite so self-contradictory as Charles Fourier ever exercised so great an influence over the mind of a whole generation. A timid bourgeois and a high-souled idealist, a pedantic mathematician, a shrewd economist, and a lunatic poet —Fourier was all of these. Born in 1772, the son of a linen draper, he received a small inheritance which, like many a larger one, was swept away by the French Revolution. The experience left him with a deadly fear of class struggles and a meritorious determination to formulate some scheme of society which would prevent their future recurrence. He wished to right the wrongs of labor and at the same time to preserve the status of the petty bourgeois class to which he belonged. As frugal-minded as most Frenchmen, he was shocked by the extravagance and wastefulness of big business. Caught between the upper and nether millstones of expanding capitalist enterprise and growing labor organization, he sought an escape by reversal. But it seemed to him not enough, as the physiocrats had taught, merely to return to agriculture. His proposal was also to divide up society into small self-sufficient units or "phalanxes," each to contain exactly sixteen hundred people, to be three miles square, and to have a huge "phalanstery" at its center where the inhabitants would live in common. Eventually, as he carefully figured out, there would be precisely two million phalanxes in the world.

In a long succession of volumes, Fourier worked out his system in minutest detail. Each phalanx was to be ruled by a general council, divided into four branches to oversee the separate "groups" of industry, agriculture, science, and finance, their decisions in case of conflict to be referred to a council of arbiters, seven in number, a majority of whom must be women. Each "group" was to be subdivided into "series"—agriculture, for example, having a "farming series," a "planting series," and a "cattle series." Great attention must be paid to these "groups" and "series," or the system would not be successful. Work was to be divided into three classes, necessary, useful, and attractive, the last-named to be the least paid. Much seemingly unattractive work, however, could be made attractive through adaptation to age and disposition. Having observed that children were fond of playing in dirt and making mud pies, Fourier proposed to organize them in "Little Hordes" for spreading manure, cleaning sewers, etc. Where even the Little Hordes failed, a "Sacred Legion" would step in, composed of those whose high sense of duty would impel them to perform the unpleasant tasks that all others refused.

In order to insure the peaceful co-operation of his two million phalanxes, Fourier gave them the cosmic setting of an optimistic universe ruled by an internal spirit of progress. Under its beneficent operation, the most remarkable changes were due to occur. The earth would come to have five satellites instead of one, a second aurora borealis would warm the North Pole, the ocean would lose its salt and acquire the pleasant taste of mineral water, lions and sharks would be replaced by amiable domesticated "anti-lions" and "anti-sharks," and man himself would grow a tail equipped with eyes. Dead bodies would become sweet aromas, floating from planet to planet, sun to sun.

Fourier's best of all possible worlds and societies was strictly respectable in manners and morals. "That man," he wrote, "has no claim to confidence who advocates such absurdities as community of property or absence of divine worship or rash abolition of marriage." Nevertheless, as a tolerant person, Fourier held that exceptional individuals, who were by nature inconstant, should be permitted to supplement marriage by concubinage—a provision that caused some of his pious American disciples considerable embarrassment until they decided conveniently to forget it.

In these small units, economic business methods could be obtained through a division of labor based upon individual talents. Since men do best that for which they are best fitted by Nature, the phalanxes could not be otherwise than successful; and since men are happiest when most successful, the phalanxes would be filled with joyous people. Any individual reluctances would be overcome through the spirit of solidarity engendered by the community life in the phalanstery.

Fourier, being a most obscure writer, badly needed disciples to popularize his ideas. It was his good fortune to inspire two young men admirably adapted for just that work: Prosper Victor Considérant, of whom more hereafter, to spread Fourierism in France; and Albert Brisbane to give it a suitable American garb. Brisbane (1809–90), the son of a wealthy landowner of Batavia, New York, was early impressed with the evils of modern society by his tutor, the liberal John Monesca. At the age of eighteen, idealistic and ardent, he went to Europe to study social philosophy. After working under Cousin, Guizot, and Hegel, he was still dissatisfied, as they all seemed to accept current European civilization at its face value. He took a trip to Constantinople to familiarize himself with Mohammedan culture, but found nothing there that could solve his problems. Returning to Paris, he was intrigued at first by the teachings of Saint-Simon, but was soon led to reject them. Then one day he happened by chance to pick up a copy of Fourier's *L'Association Domestique-Agricole:*

"I came to the following phrase printed in large type: 'ATTRACTIVE INDUSTRY.' Those two words made on me an indescribable impression. In the few lines of explanation that followed, I saw that the author conceived the idea of so organizing human labor as to dignify it and render it attractive. I sprang to my feet, threw down the book and commenced pacing the floor in a tumult of emotion. I was carried away into a world of new conceptions. . . ."

By good luck, Brisbane had come at the outset upon the most inspiring idea in Fourier. With the enthusiasm of youth he hurried through the book, bought and read all the other works of Fourier which he could find, and made the personal acquaintance of his new god. As soon as he felt that he had thoroughly mastered the doctrine, he returned to America to spread the glad tidings. His presentation of Fourierism in *The Social Destiny of Man* (1840) had few literary merits but was sensible and judicious. It consisted in large part of well-selected quotations which showed the French writer at his infrequent best; it left out the most bizarre elements in his teachings; and it stressed those most likely to appeal to Americans: the making labor attractive, the efficiency program, the virtue of association, and the religiosity of spirit. Horace Greeley, quickly converted, allowed Brisbane to run a daily column in the New York *Tribune* during 1842–43—seventy years before his son, Arthur Brisbane, would succeed his father as a New York columnist with the rather notable difference that whereas Albert Brisbane was interested in social welfare, Arthur Brisbane would be interested only in the welfare of Arthur Brisbane. Besides his column in the *Tribune*, Albert Brisbane started a Fourierist paper, *The Phalanx*, edited by himself and Osborne Macdaniel. Soon a second appeared, *The Prospect*, edited by W. H. Channing. Then Parke Godwin, son-in-law of William Liggett, the most liberal of the editorial writers on the *Evening Post*, became a convert, bringing out his *Popular View of the Doctrines of Charles Fourier* (1844). During the winter of 1843–44 a two-weeks' Fourierist convention was held in Boston, and the enthusiasm reached its height. Brook Farm came over to Fourierism; the North American Phalanx, launched a little earlier with a great fanfare of trumpets, started joyously on its course; and no less than thirty other phalanxes sprang up like mushrooms all the way from New York to Wisconsin.

The effect of Fourierism on Brook Farm was wholly disastrous. The happy spontaneity, the atmosphere of free discussion and inquiry disappeared. Emerson, Thoreau, Orestes Brownson ceased to visit the Farm. Instead, Albert Brisbane, grown pontifical with success, came often to deliver long monologues to submissive hearers. He was fond of lecturing on "the origin of evil," which he traced to three causes, "matter, transition, and individuality"—and George Ripley, that erstwhile Transcendentalist, meekly stood by and listened! The whole place became mechanized, standardized, staticized. The school deteriorated. The Brook Farm magazine, *The Harbinger*—or "The Porringer, food for babes," as Theodore Parker derisively called it—was little more than a chronicle of Fourierist undertakings. The talk at the Farm was all of "groups" and "series." Parker insisted that one day he met a wild-eyed member running about the Farm shouting, "The pigs have got into the cornfield, and I'm looking for one of the Miscellaneous Group to drive them out." Everyone became concerned with outward success and increase in numbers. That end was gained; the increased numbers came, and with them came factions. The spirit of unity was lost. The old delightful costume parties and private theatricals were replaced by separate meetings to play whist and to gossip. And then, having sold its soul to gain the world, Brook Farm lost even the little part of the world which it had possessed. The money which should have been spent on the school or the farm was diverted into erecting a great, ugly phalanstery. The day after it was virtually completed, the building burned down. The Brook Farmers had no spirit left to go on with their enterprise, and the community soon dissolved.

Brisbane, the involuntary cause of Brook Farm's decline, had never wholly approved of that enterprise, which was on too small a scale to satisfy his desires. He demanded an initial membership of at least four hundred and an initial capital of four hundred thousand dollars, which was quite in line with Fourier's own lordly ideals. But Brisbane's financial requirements proved much too high for his American followers. The best endowed of the American communities, his own special venture, the North American Phalanx, had an initial capital of only eight thousand dollars, and was begun with less than eighty members.

The North American Phalanx, outwardly the most nearly successful of the Fourierist experiments, was located near Red Bank in Monmouth County, New Jersey. Besides Brisbane, the other Fourierist leaders—W. H. Channing, Parke Godwin, and Greeley —all took part in the enterprise. A three-story phalanstery and a large grist mill were erected, other mills and shops followed, extensive orchards were planted, and excellent crops of corn, potatoes, tomatoes, and melons were raised. Without developing many intellectual or cultural interests, the phalanx was economically prosperous, the value of the property rising to eighty thousand dollars within nine years. According to Charles Sears, the capable manager of the enterprise, wages and profits were regulated by the following principle: "For labors that are necessary, but repulsive or exhausting, we award the highest rates; for such as are useful, but less repugnant or taxing, a relatively smaller award is made; and for the more agreeable pursuits, a still smaller rate is allowed."

In 1852 the phalanx had a hundred and twelve members, but, a controversy arising over some obscure religious issue, a considerable number seceded to form the short-lived Raritan Bay Association. This so weakened the original colony that when a disastrous fire swept away the mills and shops in 1854, it could not recover. After struggling gallantly for another year, the North American Phalanx went the way of Brook Farm.

Most of the other Fourierist enterprises were hasty, ill-advised adventures, led by impatient enthusiasts. With little capital and no knowledge of farming, they were usually forced into buying the cheapest land, normally barren and rocky and far from the industrial centers. Within a few months, or at most a year or two, these phalanxes vanished almost as suddenly as they had appeared. The only one which was not an economic failure was the Wisconsin Phalanx founded by Warren Chase, a spiritualist, in Fond du Lac County, Wisconsin; its members were experienced farmers who, aided by a rise in land values, were able to sell out at a small profit when the community dissolved in 1850. None of the phalanxes succeeded in making either labor or life particularly attractive. The intimacy upon which Fourier had counted to breed the necessary spirit of social solidarity worked in the opposite direction as a cause of personal jealousy and strife. However successful community living might be, as the Shakers and other religious sects proved, among groups inspired beforehand by a common ideal, it could not be trusted, in the mechanical manner of Fourierism, to produce such results of itself. On the contrary, community living vitiated the co-operation it was supposed to sustain. The net result of the movement was self-defeating, discrediting the idealism that had given it birth.

CHAPTER 27. *Perfectionism and Sex:*
the Oneida Community

DURING the thirties the first of the ever-recurrent movements in America for sex liberation reached its height. It was, with good reason, inextricably tied up with the revolt against private property and against the subjection of women. The question of the origin of the family institution is not particularly relevant. Westermarck may be right in insisting that the institution goes back to the very beginning of human society, and Briffault may also be right in pointing to many examples of complete promiscuity among the higher apes and primitive peoples; it would not be the only instance in which the earliest men apparently followed quite opposite behavior patterns in different places, since as far back as we can go we find examples of both competitive and communistic organization, of both extremely warlike and extremely peaceful tribes. What is relevant, however, is that the institution of marriage, as we know it historically, bears indisputable evidence of its connection with private property and masculine superiority. Confining the question to our own historical past, we need only remind ourselves of the facts that the family until recent times has been almost invariably patriarchal, with the father possessing what amounted practically to rights of ownership over wife and children (as in the Tenth Commandment one was forbidden to covet his neighbor's wife or daughter or oxen or asses or anything that was his); that the symbols of marriage, such as the ring, originally were tokens of feminine bondage; that marriage ceremonies have included the wife's promise to "obey" her husband; and that infractions of the sex code have been visited upon women with far greater severity than upon men.

It was wholly natural that Calvinism, on its economic side a glorification of private property, should on its sex side have been the most rigoristic of disciplines. Fallen human nature had fallen, Calvinism believed, precisely through sex and disobedience. It was also natural that the recovery of faith in human nature, which was the work of the eighteenth century, should eventually carry over into the field of sex. Women, the greatest sufferers under the existent code, furnished the most radical rebels, the Mary Wollstonecrafts and Fanny Wrights. But there were hundreds of men ready to second their efforts as a part of their own belief in liberty and equality. Marriage was attacked from two sides: by anarchists like Josiah Warren who saw in it an interference with individual freedom, and by communists who believed that it diverted attention from social welfare. In this respect, the situation was not different in the twenties and thirties from that of recent times; but whereas modern protests have sought a basis in science, those of the earlier period were inevitably more often couched in terms of religion. And because these earlier rebels had behind them an era of much stronger sex inhibition than any modern can know, their revolt was correspondingly the more violent.

We have noted the unadmitted eroticism of the camp meetings. In Swedenborgianism, as we shall see later, the sexual motive was openly proclaimed and justified. Mormonism included it in its economics, twisting it back once more into a masculine privilege. Perfectionism, now to be considered, gave it romantic glorification and in the Oneida Community attempted to work out a rational social experiment in its honor.

Because of the enduring fame of John Humphrey Noyes and the Oneida Community, Perfectionism is sometimes identified with that particular movement. In reality, however, it appeared in the thirties in three distinct types or stages, of which the Oneida Community represented only the last, being preceded by the Ohio and New York schools. It was really of western origin, a kind of frontier analogue of Transcendentalism, cruder, more Biblical, in which philosophic communion with the oversoul was replaced by a more emotional union with the traditional Holy Spirit, the refined inner freedom of the Transcendentalists efflorescing into an outward antinomianism. Historically, Perfectionism went back to John Wesley's idea of momentary sanctification already discussed. Like a thief in the night, this Methodist doctrine crept into Presbyterianism as the latter's Calvinistic basis began to collapse under the impact of the postrevolutionary American optimism. Once the logical Presbyterian mind got to work upon it, the notion of momentary sanctification was expanded into that of a permanent state of sinlessness. This idea obtained its first full self-conscious development in what was known as the "Oberlin Perfectionism" centered in the new coeducational college of that name in Ohio. Rules of discipline and taboo were written on every wall of that college. The very sign and symbol of Oberlin Perfectionism was its supposed ability to withstand every temptation of sex. But this emphasis only lent added interest to the dangerous instinct. If the strength of one's virtue was shown by ability to overcome temptation, how could one be sure of absolute perfection unless tried in the uttermost fires? In fact, a single supreme temptation was not enough; perhaps yesterday one was strong enough to resist, but how could he be certain that he was still strong enough today unless subjected to equal trial? A dual technique for arousing and then resisting passion was needed. No better place for testing these ideas could have been found than in what was called "the Burnt Over Region" of western New York recently set ablaze by the revivals of Charles Grandison Finney, later president of Oberlin College. For, as John Humphrey Noyes was to put it bluntly: "Revivals lead to religious love; religious love excites passions." At Delphi, New York, Lucinia Umphreville, a convert of Finney, proclaimed a doctrine of "Spiritual Marriage" which spread far and wide. According to Lucinia, the state of perfection was only attained when men and women passionately in love with each other lived together without carnal union. If, in spite of their efforts, they fell from grace, that was a sign that their spiritual marriage was imperfect and that they should seek other soulmates. In this badly disguised form, erotic Perfectionism invaded New York State as a sequel to the purely spiritual Perfectionism of Oberlin.

From disguised to open eroticism was only a step, and the New York Perfectionists themselves hardly knew which was which. In either case religious justification was proffered. During the early thirties more than twenty Perfectionist congregations sprang up in New York State, the largest under John B. Foot at Albany, with subcolonies in Oneida and Madison counties. James Latourette headed a group of New York City Perfectionists, and there was another in Newark, New Jersey. Theophilus Gates put out a paper, *The Battle-Axe*, in support of the movement.

The New York Perfectionists as good proselytizers extended their sphere of influence into Massachusetts, finding congenial groups in Westfield, Southampton, and Brimfield. Here they ran into a Perfectionist of a somewhat different type, the virginal John Humphrey Noyes, twenty-four years old, recently deprived of his ministerial license because of his heretical views.

The career of John Humphrey Noyes and his Putney-Oneida community has recently been so fully told [1] that there is no necessity here to do more than recall the main incidents, stressing those that seem of greatest importance. Born in 1811, he came of a cultured and fairly well-to-do family; his father, known as "Squire Noyes" in the little town of Brattleboro, Vermont, where he conducted a general store, was a Dartmouth graduate, an erstwhile lawyer, and for a short time representative from Vermont in the United States Congress; his mother, Polly Hayes, a great-aunt of President Rutherford B. Hayes, was a woman of strong character, deeply religious. John Humphrey combined the rationality of his father with his mother's mysticism, but both were slow to awaken. When he entered Dartmouth, as he wrote, "Fishing and hunting and ease were the *summa bona* of my existence"; college aroused his intellectual interests, but religion left him untouched until, while studying law, he was suddenly converted at a revival in 1831. His course then lay through Andover and Yale Divinity School into the ministry, but it was marked by a constant unavailing struggle to obtain a due conviction of sin. His diary of the period is full

---

[1] Robert Allerton Parker, *A Yankee Saint* (New York: G. P. Putnam's Sons, 1935); George Wallingford Noyes, *Religious Experience of John Humphrey Noyes* (New York: The Macmillan Co., 1923); *John Humphrey Noyes, the Putney Community* (edited by George Wallingford Noyes, 1931); Pierrepont B. Noyes, *My Father's House* (New York: Farrar and Rinehart, Inc., 1937).

of such reflections as these—"I could not produce that feeling of despair which I had felt before"—"I have not that sense of my own sinfulness which the Bible commands"—and he was never to have it, except momentarily. The truth was that John Humphrey Noyes did not really believe that he was a desperate sinner, thereby indicating that he was living in the historical present. The efforts of all the revivalists to turn back the clock to the seventeenth century were almost over.

In vain Noyes applied to himself the supreme Calvinistic test: "I asked myself, Can I consign a certain impenitent friend, for whom I have long prayed, to eternal burnings without murmuring, if it be the will of God? Alas! How quickly was the whole aspect of my spirit changed! The peace and blessedness which I had hoped would be perpetual were gone, and rebellion usurped their place." Here was concrete proof of his sinfulness, yet instead of bringing him to repentance it merely left him rebellious.

At last he decided to accept himself as he was. Not that he put it that way. Being a New Englander, he of course had to find a theological sanction for his position, and being an ingenious thinker, he was able to discover it. The Gospel texts showed clearly that Jesus promised his followers that he would return to set up his kingdom during their lifetime; therefore he must have done so, even though no record was left of the fact. If the Second Coming had already occurred and the kingdom was already established, it must be possible for men now to be in the sinless state that was to follow upon those events.

With Noyes to have a conviction was to act upon it. He at once preached a sermon on the text, "He that committeth sin is of the devil," and when afterwards challenged by the question, "Don't you yourself commit sin?" he boldly answered, "No." The news of his heresy ran like wildfire through New Haven, and the Association of the Western District of New Haven County rescinded his license to preach. Noyes merely commented, "I have taken away their license to sin, and they keep on sinning. So, though they have taken away my license to preach, I shall keep on preaching." Bold words, not so easy to practice. To be outlawed by his church was for Noyes worse than to be outlawed by the state. He at first sought companionship among the other Perfectionists; visited Latourette and Gates and was disappointed in both of them; started a paper, *The Perfectionist*, in collaboration with one James Boyle, a Canadian who had already passed through Catholicism, Methodism, and Presbyterianism; and was forced to abandon it when Boyle became convinced that it was a violation of personal liberty for them to attempt to force their personal opinions on others in that way through the press. He had nothing but contempt for the self-deception and irresponsibility of the New York group. His own views on the sexual relation were set forth in the famous "Battle-Axe Letter" of 1837, written to a friend who allowed it to be published by Theophilus Gates. Its most significant portion read: "When the will of God is done on earth, as it is in heaven, *there will be no marriage.* The marriage supper of the Lamb is a feast at which *every dish is free to every guest.* Exclusiveness, jealousy, quarreling, have no place there, for the same reason as that which forbids the guests at a thanksgiving dinner to claim each his separate dish, and quarrel with the rest for his rights. In a holy community, there is no more reason why sexual intercourse should be restrained by law, than why eating and drinking should be— and there is as little occasion for shame in the one case as in the other."

It will be noticed that Noyes' gospel of sexual freedom, like Wiclif's communism, did not apply outside of a "holy community." But where was such a holy community to be found? If it was to come into being at all, he must establish it himself. As a first step he believed that he needed a suitable helpmate, whom he discovered in Harriet Holton, the well-educated and idealistic granddaughter of Mark Richards, lieutenant governor of Vermont.

Noyes' proposal to Harriet Holton was probably unlike any other hitherto mailed in America. It suggested a partnership, "which I will not call marriage until I have defined it. . . . We can enter into no engagements with each other which shall limit the range of our affections as they are limited in matrimonial engagements by the fashion of this world. I desire and expect my yoke-fellow will love all who love God, whether man or woman, with a warmth and strength of affection which is unknown to earthly lovers, and as freely as if she stood in no particular connection with me."

Harriet Holton, who was already familiar with Noyes' ideas and who shared them completely, replied in the same key: "In gladly accepting this proposal for an external union, I agree with you that it will not 'limit the range of our affections.' The grace of God will exclude jealousy and everything with which the marriage state is defiled as we see it in the world."

The first act of the newly married couple was to purchase a secondhand press on which to print in their home in Putney, Vermont, Noyes' paper, *The Witness*, which he had begun to publish in the previous summer. Like Joseph Smith, Noyes gained his first converts among the members of his own family—his wife, two sisters, and a younger brother. (It is interesting to note that these two great foes of the family, Smith and Noyes, could neither of them have got started without it.) Polly Hayes was slower in yielding to the influence of her son. In 1838 she wrote to a friend: "His wife thinks he is a prophet. . . . Harriet and Charlotte say that he is Christ's representative upon earth, the savior mentioned in Obadiah; that he is infallible in spirit but not in the letter. . . . Is there anything more in him than in other great reformers, such as Luther, Calvin and Erasmus?" But there were few in his immediate circle who could stand out for long against the will and self-confidence of John Humphrey Noyes. After a bitter struggle, Polly Hayes capitulated, and *The Witness* of March, 1839, carried the following item over her signature: "I am not governed by parental partiality and self-exaltation in the testimony which I now give to John H. Noyes as being to me a teacher and father in spiritual things." Poor Polly Hayes! There was indeed no self-exaltation in thus giving up her position as the head of her family and abandoning her cherished orthodoxy in favor of the new untried heresy. It was simply the surrender of a strong but defeated will to one still stronger.

Gradually, a few other members joined the group, and in 1840 the Putney Association was formally organized. A community store and community mansion were built. In 1844 full communism was introduced, Noyes, like Robert Owen, having become interested in the subject through a reading of Shaker books, followed by a visit in 1838 to the Shaker village of Harvard, Massachusetts. The most distinctive features of his social scheme, however, the ideas of Male Continence and Complex Marriage, were not arrived at by him until 1846, the crucial year of his life.

They were reached as the result of reflection upon the unhappy lot of his wife, who in six years had given birth to five children, four of them stillborn. Noyes saw no justification for the continued suffering of women under the curse of Eve in this fashion. He objected to the use of contraceptives advocated by Robert Dale Owen, which seemed to him a disgracefully easy solution—he was still enough of a Puritan to cherish discipline for its own sake—but he came to believe that the same end could be accomplished through the practice of self-control in male continence (coitus interruptus). Furthermore, since the woman with whom one happened to be in love, or to whom one was legally married, manifestly might be, as in the case of his own Harriet, unfit to bear children, one should be permitted to become a father by other women. Eugenic results, in which Noyes was greatly interested, could be obtained through what he called "Stirpiculture"—the deliberate selection by the heads of the community of those members who should be allowed to have offspring.

The motivation of the Oneida system was dual: it was a revolt against the slavery of women to childbirth, and it was a revolt against the creation of the unfit. Noyes made this perfectly clear in his *Bible Communism:* "We are opposed to excessive, and of course oppressive procreation, which is almost universal. We are opposed to random procreation, which is unavoidable in the marriage system. But we are in favor of intelligent, well-ordered procreation. The physiologists say that the race cannot be raised from ruin till propagation is made a matter of science; but they point out no way of making it so. Procreation is controlled and reduced to a science in the case of valuable domestic brutes; but marriage and fashion forbid any such system among human beings. We believe the time will come when involuntary and random propagation will cease, and when scientific combination will be applied to human generation as freely and successfully as it is to that of other animals. The way will be open for this when amativeness can have its proper gratification without drawing after it procreation as a necessary sequence. And at all events, we believe that good sense and benevolence will very soon sanction and enforce the rule that women shall bear children only when they choose. They have the principal burdens of breeding to bear, and they rather than men should have their choice of time and circumstances, at least till science takes charge of the business."

Noyes, using the popular phrenological terms of his day, considered the separation of "amativeness" from "procreation" to be fundamental to human happiness. The former, he always believed, was essentially pluralistic: "Men and women find universally that their susceptibility to love is not burnt out by one honeymoon, or satisfied by one lover. On the contrary, the secret history of the human heart will bear out the assertion that it is capable of loving any number of times and any number of persons, and that the more it loves the more it can love." The shocking feature of this argument was that it applied to both sexes. That men, the vile creatures, were naturally polygamous had often been granted, but Noyes maintained that women were equally versatile in their affections—and was prepared to prove it in his community. So far as romantic love was concerned, he held that perfect freedom of individual choice could be permitted, if male continence were observed, without the slightest loss to society, whereas the interest of society demanded that the propagation of children should be strictly regulated. Here, as in most things, the state had got matters exactly topsy-turvy, placing no bar to the creation of children, however unfit, but attempting to coerce errant love which cannot be controlled.

After prolonged discussion, the Putney Association adopted the principle of complex marriage in 1846. Evil rumors soon began to circulate through the village, and busybodies began to collect evidence. Within a year, a grand jury was persuaded to indict Noyes for adultery. Sensibly shunning a meaningless martyrdom, he fled from the state. But not for a moment did he intend to abandon the struggle. After careful investigation, he discovered a suitable location for his community at Oneida, New York, where he purchased twenty-three acres, including a log house, barn, and shoemaker's shop. Twenty-six of his followers—thirteen men, thirteen women, accompanied by twenty-five children—arrived in March, 1848, and the Putney Association entered upon its heroic days as the Oneida Community.

The first thought of Noyes, once the members were settled in their new surroundings, was for the continuance of the community paper. During the years, *The Witness* had become *The Perfectionist and Theocratic Watchman* and the latter had become *The Spiritual Magazine*, but the society had never lacked an organ, under one or another name, and never should, if Noyes could prevail. "Let the private fortune of the Oneida Community be what it may," he said, "its first business is to see that God has a press." Desiring a more central office for the paper, Noyes and Harriet Holton accordingly betook themselves to Brooklyn, New York, where they lived for the next five years, always in close correspondence with the community but with their chief efforts concentrated on a desperate struggle to keep the paper alive.

Meanwhile at Oneida the members of the community were struggling desperately to keep themselves alive. They had invested heavily in a sloop, the *Rebecca Ford*, to carry their produce down the Hudson, but it was wrecked on its maiden trip, leaving the colony in hard straits. John Miller, a brother-in-law of Noyes, who had been left at the head of the community during its leader's absence in Brooklyn, fairly worked himself to death on its behalf. Noyes, called back to Oneida by this sad event in 1854, took personal charge of affairs but he could do little to improve economic conditions. The members of the community were driven to sell their personal belongings, while many of them went on the road as peddlers to sell the few trinkets that their Yankee ingenuity enabled them to produce. Then in 1857, when the community seemed at its last gasp, it was joined by Sewall Newhouse, the inventor of steel traps, and with this new industry matters began to improve. Through the manufacture of traps and the development of a second industry in fruit preserving, Oneida not only recovered but became exceedingly prosperous. More land was added, up to seven hundred acres, new buildings were erected, the school was improved, and an excellent community orchestra came into being, this orchestra alone being as large as the whole adult membership of the original colony. From 1860 to 1870 Oneida enjoyed a golden age. Like the other religious communes, it was a place of health, happiness, and longevity.

CHAPTER 28. *The Complex Faith of New England*

UNITARIANISM AND UNIVERSALISM

IN THE second quarter of the nineteenth century, New England, and in New England, Massachusetts, almost monopolized the literary production of the nation. As it was the proud boast of Massachusetts that she furnished more soldiers during the Revolution than all the other colonies north of the Potomac, so it was equally true that in this later period she gave birth to more thinkers of note than all the other states put together.

Why this sudden emergence of New England? Back of it lay the facts that this section was the only part of the United States with a real tradition of intellectual culture—one beneficial heritage from Calvinism—and that this tradition had managed to incorporate in the Unitarian movement all that was left in America of the influence of the French Enlightenment. All but two of the authors of the New England renaissance were direct products of the Unitarian movement, and those two—Whittier, the born Quaker, and Bronson Alcott, the half-Quaker—would not have developed as they did without the Unitarian environment in which they moved.

The question of Trinitarianism versus Unitarianism has long since become a rather idle topic of purely theological speculation. But until well into the nineteenth century it carried with it intellectual and social considerations of the utmost importance. The practical significance of the Trinitarian dogma was double. By subordinating

400

the human personality of Jesus, it minimized the equalitarianism of his teachings and transformed his revolutionary conception that all men were sons of God into the socially harmless one of his own unique divinity; and by placing an insoluble mystery at the heart of the Christian religion, it discredited in advance the authority of reason. On the first count, the dogma was openly denied by the Anabaptists and was disregarded by the half-Unitarian Quakers; on the second, it had been attacked by the seventeenth century rationalists, Michael Servetus in Switzerland, Faustus Socinus in Poland, and Franz David in Transylvania. Originating in those "backward countries," the specific Unitarian movement at last reached America toward the end of the eighteenth century and proved a welcome substitute for the similar but more radical Deism.

The redoubtable Jonathan Mayhew had been a Unitarian in all but name; in 1782 the name itself was adopted by King's Chapel in Boston; from 1783 to 1819 the pulpit of the East Church in Salem was occupied by William Bentley, the greatest linguistic scholar in the United States. In 1803, William Ellery Channing became pastor of the important Federal Street Church in Boston, and in 1805, the Reverend Henry Ware was appointed to the Hollis Professorship of Divinity at Harvard. Professor Eliphalet Pearson, who had vainly fought the appointment on the ground that the appointee must be a Calvinist, resigned in wrath and established Andover Theological Seminary as a home for the orthodox. Yet in reality Ware represented only the right wing of Unitarianism, between which and the left wing led by Channing there was a profound intellectual cleavage. Ware maintained that, in case of a conflict between revelation and reason, revelation must always be trusted because "You can never be so certain of the correctness of what takes place in your own mind as of what is written in the Bible." Channing, on the other hand, declared: "If after a deliberate and impartial use of our best faculties a professed revelation seems to us plainly to disagree with itself or clash with great principles which we cannot question, we ought not to hesitate in withholding from it our belief. I am surer that my rational nature is from God than that any book is."

United, however, in their opposition to Calvinism and Trinitarianism, the two wings moved on together to the conquest of Massachusetts. From there the movement spread to the other New England states and extended into New York, New Jersey, and Pennsylvania, reaching the point of national organization in 1825 when the American Unitarian Association was established. What was ultimately to prove the greatest contribution of Unitarianism —its influence in liberalizing more orthodox sects—appeared as early as 1827, when Elias Hicks, a New York Quaker, led about half of the Friends to adopt Unitarian principles. Beyond the Alleghenies, the movement met with much less response, though James Freeman Clarke was able to establish an influential nucleus of Unitarian liberal thought in Louisville, Kentucky, and Thomas Starr King later achieved the same result in far-off San Francisco.

Outwardly, the Unitarian creed consisted mainly of negations. It rejected the dogma of the Trinity, the dogma of the divinity of Christ, the dogma of a material Hell; it rejected the belief in miracles; it rejected, in spite of Henry Ware, the literal authority of the Scriptures; the whole traditional mythology and methodology of orthodox Christianity was abandoned by it. But beneath this negativism lay a very positive urge. A sanction for morality was sought, where Rousseau had sought it, in human nature. "All virtue," Channing declared, "has its foundation in the moral nature of man." In line with the dynamic principles of the Enlightenment, Channing criticized the imitativeness of American authors, pled for adult education—fifty years in advance of his time—and, foreseeing the coming of the Civil War, made a desperate attempt to forestall it by an eloquent appeal to the conscience of the South to end slavery while there was still opportunity for a peaceful solution. He proved even more prophetic on the lesser issue of prohibition, a newly born reform with which he sympathized but in connection with which he warned against coercion. "Men cannot be driven into temperance," he declared.

Unfortunately, the "Channing Unitarians," as they were called, failed to carry their church actively with them. The majority of its members were comfortable bourgeois who found in the negations of their creed a pleasant relief from the disturbing excesses of emotional religion, but who were quite unwilling to sacrifice altogether the traditional belief in supernatural assistance: "A majority of our brethren," wrote Channing, "believe that Jesus Christ is more than man, that he existed before the world, that he literally came from heaven to save our race, that he sustains other offices than those of a teacher and witness to the truth, and that he still acts for our benefit and is our intercessor with the Father." Ralph Waldo Emerson's Boston church accepted his resignation rather than accept his purely symbolic interpretation of the Lord's Supper; and when in his Divinity School Address he set forth Jesus' own teaching that all men are the sons of God, he so shocked the Harvard authorities that he was not invited to speak there again for more than forty years. Unitarianism had become wholly respectable. "And now," Channing wrote sadly in 1841, "we have a Unitarian orthodoxy."

But Unitarianism had a disreputable twin brother, Universalism. The movement was started in England by one of Whitefield's former associates, a Welshman named James Relly, who in his tract, *Union, or a Treatise of the Consanguinity and Affinity between Christ and his Church* (1759), advanced a highly mystical philosophy based on the spiritual identity of Christ with the whole human race. He took the dogma of the Atonement seriously: he believed with the Unitarians (and all orthodox sects) that Christ "came to save our race" but he differed from them in actually including everybody under that head, regardless of character, wealth, or social position. He preached universal redemption, a wholly joyous Second Coming, and the vanity of all ceremonies. We know by now the social class to which such doctrines were sure to appeal. Brought to America as early as 1770 by Relly's disciple, John Murray, who labored at first in New York and New Jersey but eventually found New England a more fertile field, Universalism spread gradually from Murray's church in Boston to the old radical groups in Rhode Island, Maine, New Hampshire, and Vermont. Without representation, such as the Unitarians enjoyed, on bench and bar and boards of trade, its growth was slow, while the strong Separatist tendency within it prevented adequate ecclesiastical organization. The upper-class religious groups looked down on the Universalists and were fond of calling them "atheists."

THE TRANSCENDENTALIST MOVEMENT

THE small group of about a dozen New England writers, mostly Unitarian clergymen, heirs of the Channing tradition, who in 1836 began to meet in Boston in what was nicknamed the "Transcendental Club," were interested generally in German philosophy —which was beginning to exercise its potent influence on New England thought—and were interested specifically in the problem of pouring new life and warmth into the veins of the chill and dying Unitarianism about them. Of its members, Orestes Brownson, as yet untouched by the Catholicism about to engulf him, was busily organizing his workingmen's "Church of the Future." George Ripley, J. S. Dwight, and W. H. Channing were soon to spend their idealistic energy in the Brook Farm and Fourierist movements. It was only the Concord group, headed by Emerson and Bronson Alcott, which was to make Transcendentalism in the coming years the foremost intellectual expression of the American faith.

Back of their movement was the whole emotional ferment of the thirties and forties, to which they were keenly responsive. Alcott and Emerson were widely traveled in the America of their day, and Thoreau was, as he boasted, widely traveled in Concord. Though they found their ideational inspiration in sources strange to the multitude, they reflected in the more subdued Massachusetts atmosphere the same eager frenzy of the unloosed spirit that drove the Methodist circuit riders over hill and dale to preach to their Maenadic followers in the Kentucky forests.

Transcendentalism was essentially the religion of romanticism. The name and ultimate intellectual foundation of the movement were derived, of course, from Immanuel Kant, though in impulse and outcome the movement itself was strictly American. Kant represented romanticism in its beginning when it still wore the heavy armor of eighteenth century rationalism; American Transcendentalism represented the same romanticism in a later nudist stage, dancing nakedly, though still decorously, on the mountaintops. Kant had repeated Bishop Berkeley's interesting discovery that one cannot think without thinking, and had extracted a remarkable amount of juice from that apparently barren twig of thought. He showed with infinite care and logical elaboration that all our ideas of the outer world are fashioned by the mind itself, and hence are entirely relative to the mind without possible proof of correspondence to any external reality. Having thus in *The Critique of Pure Reason* used the intellect to blast the authority of the intellect— and incidentally sent philosophy off on a century-long wild goose adventure in epistemology—he turned in *The Critique of Practical Reason* to examine the claims of conscience, and ended by justifying them, when properly chastened, as constituting a probable revelation of the moral nature of the universe. As he himself summed up the result, he had done away with knowledge in order to make room for faith. This faith was intuitive, the quintessence of Protestantism stripped of all authoritarian dogmas, enlightened by reason and invigorated by Deistic and democratic aspirations. It gave equal recognition to the fact that every individual is an end in himself and to the correlative fact that all are integrated in the common life of humanity. It was probably the most admirable philosophic presentation of universal laws of conduct ever achieved. But when Kant's Transcendental philosophy went beyond this and asserted, in its author's rather arrogant language, that the mind prescribed laws to Nature, it made possible the whole series of grandiose metaphysical mythologies worked out by Fichte, Schelling, Hegel, and Schopenhauer—with none of whom Kant himself would have had much sympathy.

All this immense imaginative effort, cast in the form of rigorous logic, enhanced the already great appeal of German romanticism and established the prestige of Germany as the home of profundity. American students began to go to German universities to complete their education—Edward Everett, George Ticknor, Frederick Henry Hedge, and countless others—and even those who, like Longfellow, were incapable of the slightest philosophical ideation, brought back, in addition to a pleasant sense of the picturesqueness of the Rhine and the beauty of German romances and lyrics, a definite knowledge of strict educational methodology. In fact, as the German universities in their later development turned more and more to science, the stream of American students continuing until the first World War tended to follow the same course, so that the final influence of Germany upon American education was almost entirely scientific and methodological—a result directly the opposite of that which the Transcendentalists had desired.

EMERSON

THEY, in truth, owed much less to German thought than their name would imply. Emerson, the greatest of them, did not even learn German until late in life; his acquaintance with Kant and the other German philosophers was at second hand through Coleridge and Carlyle, and in the development of his thought Plato and Berkeley counted for as much as the Germans. Picking and choosing in an eclectic manner, he was interested in the ideas of these thinkers mainly because they corroborated his own feeling of the innate value of man and Nature. Believing this conviction to be wholly a matter of intuitive insight, and that it was foolish to defend intuition by argument when it was, by hypothesis, superior to argument, he quite logically cared nothing for the logical apparatus of the German system makers. A poet and mystic, he was, like Spinoza, "God-intoxicated," though he saw divinity, not in the necessary working out of the law of sufficient reason which seemed divine to the tempered mind of Spinoza, but in the beauty of the moral order which he fancied he found exemplified in Nature. His creative intellect played swiftly over the world, detecting in lightning flashes new relationships, new instances of the universal harmony. The earth in his shaping hands lost every trace of mechanical causality and became a kind of winged spirit, urged on its course by its own inner impulses, which yet in some strange way were the very impulses of New England with all its Yankee shrewdness retained but sublimated.

Those critics who, seeking rather desperately through American literature for a still "usable past," have found it in Emerson are at least partially justified. To the degree that spontaneity, originality, self-trust, the acceptance of inward discipline rather than outward authority, and the achievement of a unified whole life instead of a compartmentalized one are goods more difficult to attain today than formerly, Emerson is still an abiding inspiration. He will always be, in Matthew Arnold's final phrase, "a friend to those who would live in the spirit," a liberalizing force. Owing to his splendid

Humanism, there is much in his work to outlast time; he belongs among the immortals like Epictetus and Marcus Aurelius; but the very part of his work that was more dear to him, its Transcendentalist creed, is as dead as the Stoicism of the Greek slave or the Roman emperor. Even in his own hands, as he all but realized, Transcendentalism went to pieces, wrecked on the "problem of evil."

To a materialist, there is, of course, no more a special problem of evil than there is a problem of good, creation and destruction being equally evident and inseparable parts of the natural order. But to one who, like Emerson, believes that the natural order is also the moral order, the presence of real evil offers not only a problem but an insoluble problem. Emerson was too honest to blink the unpleasant facts, and he tried desperately to account for them by a number of intellectual expedients, none of them entirely satisfactory even to himself. He advanced his celebrated law of compensation according to which every evil is accompanied and nullified by some correlative blessing; he dallied with the idea that evil is only the lesser good; and he found some consolation in the doctrine of Plotinus that evil is pure negation and nothing in itself.

Nature obstinately refused, as Emerson saw clearly enough, to give more than a partial sanction to any of these idealistic explanations: "What front can we make," he cried despairingly, "against these unavoidable, victorious, maleficent forces? What can I do against the influence of Race, in my history? What can I do against hereditary and constitutional habits, against scrofula, lymph, impotence? against climate, against barbarism, in my country? I can reason down or deny everything, except this perpetual Belly; feed he must and will, and I cannot make him respectable."

Among these evils that Emerson was forced to recognize, none weighed more heavily on his heart than the contemporary barbarism of his country: "In America," he wrote, "out of doors all seems a market; in doors an air-tight stove of conventionalism. Everybody who comes into our houses savors of these habits; the men of the market; the women of the custom. I find no expression in our state papers or legislative debate, in our lyceums or churches, specially in our newspapers, of a high national feeling, no lofty counsels that rightfully stir the blood. I speak of those organs that can be presumed to speak a popular sense. They recommend conventional virtues, whatever will earn and preserve property; always the capitalist, the college, the church, the hospital, the theatre, the hotel, the road, the ship, of the capitalist,—whatever goes to secure, adorn, enlarge these is good; what jeopardizes any of these is damnable. The 'opposition' papers, so-called, are on the same side. They attack the great capitalist, but with the aim to make a capitalist of the poor man. The opposition is against those who have money, from those who wish to have money."

It is evident that not only was Emerson aware of the evils of his day, and ours, but that he traced them correctly to their economic root. But what to do? Here he had no wisdom. His idealism in regard to human nature failed him completely in the crisis. Although he deplored the tendency of the law to protect property rather than persons, he put this among those natural evils against which there is no defense. "The law," he wrote, "may in a mad freak say that all shall have power except the owners of property; they shall have no vote. Nevertheless, by a higher law, the property will, year after year, write every statute that respects property." At times he spoke sympathetically of socialism, as of almost everything else, but his real convictions tended in the direction of philosophical anarchy. Believing that "the less government we have, the better," he was unable to take seriously the ideal of making the government or any other institution a concrete agent of justice and culture.

And in the long run Emerson surrendered to the enemy. In "Experience," the most sadly sincere of his later essays, he wrote: "The ardors of piety agree at last with the coldest skepticism,—that nothing is of us or our works,—that all is of God. Nature will not spare us the smallest leaf of laurel. All writing comes by the grace of God, and all doing and having. I would gladly be moral, and keep due metes and bounds, which I dearly love, and allow the most to the will of man, but I have set my heart on honesty in this chapter, and I can see nothing at last, in success or failure, than more or less of vital force supplied from the Eternal."

The same thought occurs frequently in his poems, as in these verses of "The World-Soul":

> "For destiny never swerves,
>   Nor yields to men the helm;
> He shoots his thought, by hidden nerves,

Throughout the solid realm.
He serveth the servant,
The brave he loves amain;
He kills the cripple and the sick,
And straight begins again,"

or in these lines of "Destiny":

"One thing is forever good;
That one thing is Success,"

or in the advice of "Alphonso of Castile":

"Earth, crowded, cries, 'Too many men!'
My counsel is, kill nine in ten,
And bestow the shares of all
On the remnant decimal . . .

So shall ye have a man of the sphere
Fit to grace the solar year."

This is clearly a going back to Calvinism, and even beyond Calvinism to the sheer naturalistic struggle for existence. It was this note in Emerson that made him dear to Nietzsche and congenial to Carlyle. And it explains why Emerson's lofty idealism did nothing to weaken the drive of capitalistic exploitation. For, in the end, Emerson's Transcendentalism, like nearly all philosophical idealisms, turned out to be an apology for the natural nonmoral order. The penalty for attempting to moralize the universe is that morality, once universalized, ceases to be morality at all, and man, through attempting to be divine, ceases even to be completely human.

THOREAU

EMERSON's disciple, Henry Thoreau, was much more than a mere disciple. Outwardly, he was not a heroic figure—long-legged, short-bodied, narrow-shouldered, phthisic, always carrying an umbrella in his explorations of the woods, and assuming mighty airs of hardihood because he dared to go three miles out of town and live alone at Walden Pond; and yet he had a kind of moral heroism, an inflexible inner rectitude which led him to attempt to harmonize thought and conduct with a directness unknown to Emerson. From the thesis, "The less government the better," he drew the logical conclusion, "That government is best which governs not at all." To be sure, he qualified this doctrine of philosophical anarchy by the statement that its general adoption must wait until "men are prepared for it"—but this did not relieve those who were prepared from the responsibility of acting in accord with their insight. Majority rule had come to be accepted, he thought, for no better reason than that the majority was "physically the strongest." When unjust laws were passed with the consent of the majority, as in the case of the Fugitive Slave Act, it became the duty of the civilized minority to nullify them.

Thoreau was not the first to proclaim the duty of civil disobedience whenever the government violated the moral law. Even in the celebrated instance of his refusal to pay his poll tax he had been preceded by Bronson Alcott, and on the larger issue he had been also preceded by John Humphrey Noyes, William Lloyd Garrison, and Adin Ballou. Indeed, the principle could be traced back through the practice of the Quakers and the German Baptists to the earliest left-wing sects of the Reformation. It was deeply imbedded in the American character, as was to be seen later in the southern nullification of the Reconstruction Acts, and, in our own time, in the nullification of Prohibition. But it was Thoreau's distinction that he produced in his essay on "Civil Disobedience" probably the ablest presentation of the principle that has ever been made, an essay that directly inspired Mahatma Gandhi's policy of passive resistance, so that in its few pages Thoreau may be said to have affected the destiny of several hundred million people.

Where the inspiration to be derived from Emerson is mainly intellectual, that of Thoreau is almost wholly moral. The one demanded freedom of thought, the other freedom of conscience. And Thoreau's conscience was both enlightened and also, in whatever concerned the pure individual, immensely practical. In his *Journal* he stated beautifully the central problem of life in its most personal form: "How to make the getting our living poetic; for if it is not poetic, it is not life but death that we get," which reappeared in his essay, "Life Without Principle," in the slightly expanded phrasing, "How to make getting a living not merely honest and honorable, but altogether inviting and glorious." He brought to this effort more zest than Emerson, a racier sense of humor, a more accurate study of books, and a more intense love of Nature which led him to a much closer observation of her ways. At the same time, his individualism, even more exaggerated than Emerson's, left him still further from any constructive social program.

In 1842, reviewing the second edition of a remarkably prophetic work by J. A. Etzler, flamboyantly entitled *The Paradise Within Reach of All Men, Without Labor, by Powers of Nature and Machinery*, in which the author advanced the now familiar argument that technological development could be made to reduce human labor to a minimum, Thoreau treated the whole idea jestingly, and then added, in his most moralistic vein: "The chief fault of this book is, that it aims to secure the greatest degree of gross comfort and pleasure merely. Nature is to be controlled, wealth is to be controlled, pleasure is to be distributed by a corporation, and not the slightest concern for the moral control of man and his wants." That the control of Nature and of wealth has a great deal to do with the moral control of man, Thoreau did not for a moment see.

His Transcendentalism was no more able to escape the power test than Emerson's. Of the struggle for existence in Nature, he wrote: "I love to see that Nature is so rife with life that myriads can be afforded to be sacrificed and suffered to prey upon one another; that tender organisms can be serenely squashed out of existence like pulp—tadpoles which herons gobble up, and tortoises and toads run over in the road; and that sometimes it has rained flesh and blood. With the liability to accident, we must see how little account is to be made of it. The impression made on a wise man is that of universal innocence. Poison is not poison after all, nor any wounds fatal." Considering that Thoreau's own organism was to be squashed out of existence by consumption at the age of forty-five, these were brave words, indicative of a large natural piety. But philosophically, they indicate a more complete confusion of values than anything to be found in Emerson. The innocent wastefulness which Thoreau admired in Nature was the very principle on which the pioneers slaughtered the American forests, on which southern plantation owners ground their slaves into cotton, on which northern capitalists exploited their workers —the natural principle of ruthless competition which every humane effort of Thoreau's wise men, including those of Thoreau himself, had striven to abrogate.

BRONSON ALCOTT

THOREAU's reputation has latterly risen so high that at the moment it threatens to overshadow that of his master, as is natural in an age impatient with Emersonian compromise and desperately in need of a gospel to strengthen its moral fiber. But the other members of Emerson's circle have not weathered the changing years so well.

The very name of Bronson Alcott, the third of the Transcendentalist leaders, had come to be accepted, prior to the recent sympathetic biography by Odell Shepard, as almost a synonym for the vaguest and most boring kind of mystical enthusiasm. He deserved a far different fate, for he had the sanest, broadest, and most practical ideas on education of any American of his generation with the exception of Horace Mann. Born and brought up in poverty on a Connecticut farm, he spent the crucial years from nineteen to twenty-four as a peddler in the South, where he came deeply under the influence of the Carolina Quakers, from whom he derived a trust in the inner nature of man which led him on to a Rousseauesque conception of education as the development of native capacity rather than as either mental discipline or the acquisition of learning; and this natural development he thought of as an organic thing, involving the body as well as the mind, the will and the imagination as well as the intellect. These ideas he worked out in actual practice during nearly a score of years as a schoolteacher in Connecticut, Pennsylvania, and Massachusetts, introducing in his schools gymnastics, organized play, the honor system, and juvenile libraries, reducing corporal punishment to a minimum, beautifying the schoolroom, and striving in every way to make the process of study seem a pleasant and desirable occupation.

As long as Alcott's heretical methods were not widely known, he had no insuperable difficulty in introducing them, but while conducting a school in the Masonic Temple in Boston he imprudently published two volumes which told of his work, *The Record of a School Exemplifying the General Principles of Spiritual Cul-*

ture and Conversations with Children on the Gospels (1836). These books revealed the fact that he was teaching his pupils to think for themselves, something that the ruling Unitarians regarded as most unbecoming. One particular passage gave great offense, in which, answering a pupil's question as to the nature of childbirth, he said: "The mother suffers when she has a child. When she is going to have a child, she gives up her body to God, and he works upon it in a mysterious way, and with her aid, brings forth the Child's Spirit in a little Body of its own." Even this cautious and distant approach toward physiologic fact was too daring for the Boston of 1836; the *Daily Advertiser* and the *Courier* denounced the passage as obscene and blasphemous, Professor Andrews Norton of the Harvard faculty joined in the attack, and though Emerson and James Freeman Clarke came to Alcott's defense, the outraged parents withdrew their children in such numbers that the school was reduced to a third of its former registration. When, a little later, Alcott, uncowed by the public hostility, ventured to admit a Negro girl to the school, he lost this small remnant of his pupils.

With the closing of his school, Alcott's constructive work was over. Until the failure of his Fruitlands experiment, he kept up some sort of contact with the outer world, but thereafter he withdrew into a mystical realm of his own, writing a few poems, contributing his "Orphic Sayings" to the *Dial*, and earning a meager support for his family by a highly original series of "conversation-lectures" which he delivered wherever he could—until the success of his daughter Louisa in producing the sentimental best seller, *Little Women*, at last redeemed the household from poverty. The philosophy which Alcott developed during these years of discouragement with practical action was a curious kind of Neoplatonic subjective idealism that considered the world to be a visionary creation of the fallen human soul imprisoned in the illusory flesh with which it had surrounded itself, but from which it could escape by reverting to its own source in the indwelling deity of which it was an emanation.

Yet all these years, secured by a kind of rift in his personality, Alcott's educational theories had remained intact, uncorrupted by his mysticism, and when at the age of sixty he was appointed superintendent of the Concord schools, he at once introduced into the curriculum singing, calisthenics, and the study of physiology quite as if the body were substantially real, organized an informal parent-teachers' society, and advocated the introduction of dancing, hours of directed conversation, and a course of readings aloud.

But when this work was over, and the momentary link with actuality was again severed, Alcott once more withdrew into the mists. In his seventies, he fell a ready victim to the kindred subjective idealism of Mrs. Eddy, reading with great enthusiasm the copy of *Science and Health* which she sent him, and cultivating the acquaintance of the author for a few months until disillusioned by her inveterate habit of using everyone as a means to her own ends. Meanwhile, he was instrumental in establishing the Concord School of Philosophy, where, under the influence of William Torrey Harris, a form of Hegelian idealism was taught, with which he would have had no sympathy had he not been too old and tired to make the effort to understand it. Outliving nearly all of his Transcendentalist friends, he died in the midst of an alien world which had almost forgotten his very existence.

HAWTHORNE

IN THE work of Nathaniel Hawthorne, we have the self-criticism of Transcendentalism. Not that Hawthorne, who cared little for abstruse speculation, was ever deeply affected by idealistic philosophy. While esteeming Emerson as a man, he had only contempt for his writing, an attitude that Emerson precisely reciprocated; to Hawthorne the great Transcendentalist was "that everlasting rejector of all that is and seeker for he knows not what," while Emerson wrote of Hawthorne's work, "His reputation as a writer is a very pleasing fact, because his writing is not good for anything, and this is a tribute to the man." But for all that, Hawthorne was organically, if not intellectually, a Transcendentalist. The concern with the inner self which the Transcendentalists deliberately cultivated was with Hawthorne an obsession; they proclaimed the world to be visionary and then tried to deal with it realistically; Hawthorne, without believing it to be such, could not help but see it as a vision. In spite of his utmost effort, the characters he created remained unreal and wraithlike, not so much through his inability to give them fleshly garments as through their positive possession of ghostly quality, enhanced by the twilight atmosphere in which he loved to place them. Something stronger than his will forced him to write in a manner of which he by no means approved. He was the supreme solipsist in American literature, but an unconsenting solipsist. Valiant and unceasing were his endeavors to come into warm human contact with his fellows, at Brook Farm, in the custom house, in the consulate; he performed his duties efficiently, he was the kindest and most generous of friends, but at heart he still remained aloof from all but Sophia Peabody, whose unswerving devotion brought him the sense of reality which he could find nowhere else. Critics in his own day demanded that he be something other than he was. "Let him mend his pen," wrote Poe, the most sympathetic of them, "use visible ink, cut Mr. Alcott, and hang (if it be possible) the editor of the *Dial.*" Hawthorne agreed; he tried to mend, not only his pen but his ways; he declined to visit the Alcotts; even the hanging of Margaret Fuller he attempted, metaphorically, in *The Blithedale Romance;* but it was of no avail.

He was, essentially, a Transcendentalist without faith. The flight to the inner soul which was Alcott's final way of escaping the evils of the world was no escape for Hawthorne, because he dwelt there constantly and found in the solitude of the individual, prescribed irrefragably by Nature, the deepest of tragedies. Every man, shut up with his own consciousness, can communicate with his fellows only indirectly through misleading symbols; it is doubtful whether human beings ever understand one another, and impossible to verify it if they do. This ancient wisdom, first announced by Gorgias of Leontini, was reaffirmed by Hawthorne in story after story in which the inherent isolation of the individual is enhanced by secret sins that lead to the putting on of mask after mask over the inevitable one already lent by Nature. The very need for human sympathy necessitates concealment, for if all one's real thoughts were known even the appearance of such sympathy would be withdrawn. This mingling of solitude, sin, and hypocrisy constituted the moral atmosphere of Hawthorne's world.

Concerned as he was with sin, Hawthorne was naturally attracted to the Puritan past—but again only as a distant spectator. His reveries on the subject of sin, for they were reveries rather than definite thoughts, brought to him gradually a realization of how intimately good and evil were intertwined in his visionary world, which for all the prominence accorded in it to moral issues, was curiously nonmoral at heart. The opening of *The Scarlet Letter*, with its unforgettable picture of Hesther Prynne's emergence from prison, seemed to some of Hawthorne's contemporaries positively blasphemous in its juxtaposition of the sacred and the profane: "Had there been a Papist among the crowd of Puritans, he might have seen in this beautiful woman, so picturesque in her attire and mien, and with the infant at her bosom, an object to remind him of Divine Maternity, which so many illustrious painters have vied with one another to present; something which should remind him, indeed, but only by contrast, of that sacred image of sinless motherhood, whose infant was to redeem the world. Here, there was the taint of deepest sin in the most sacred quality of human life, working such effect, that the world was only the darker for this woman's beauty, and the more lost for the infant that she had borne."

In the working out of *The Scarlet Letter*, this juxtaposition of good and evil enters into the characters so completely as to make utter shipwreck of conventional morality. It is the really unrepentant Hesther who dominates life, while the more "spiritual" Dimmesdale, immersed in his egoistic conviction of sin, deteriorates until it is hardly clear whether his final confession is a dying reassertion of strength or simply an expression of the exhaustion of his will to live. In *The Marble Faun*, inferior though it is as a novel, Hawthorne carried his analysis of the problem a step further in showing how the purely pagan Donatello is transformed by his crime into a moral, responsible human being. Whether the wages of sin is death, or on the contrary, a more abundant, though sadder, life, seems to depend in Hawthorne upon the spirit of the sinner, who may be led merely to a fruitless subjective repentance or to an active social atonement. Once again, the realm of the subjective in which Hawthorne loved to dwell is regarded by him as the realm of defeat.

Yet there was much confusion in Hawthorne's reflections. The man who could mistake Emerson's great affirmation for a rejection was evidently not in the habit of thinking things through. Hawthorne's unconventionality was all in the subconscious; it evaporated when brought to the surface. So completely did he in his actions and conscious thought accept the mores of his period that he regarded nude pictures as vaguely immoral and refused, when in England, to meet George Eliot because of her violation of the social code in living with George Henry Lewes.

Herman Melville was badly deceived in the picture he draws in his celebrated letter to Hawthorne: "There is the grand truth about Nathaniel Hawthorne, he says No! in thunder; but the Devil himself cannot make him say *yes*. For all men who say *yes*, lie; and all men who say *no*,—why, they are in the happy condition of judicious, unencumbered travellers in Europe; they cross the frontiers into Eternity with nothing but a carpet-bag,—that is to say, the Ego. Whereas those *yes* gentry, they travel with heaps of baggage, and, damn them! they will never get through the Custom House." It was the bold adventurer, much richer in experience though ten years younger, who spoke thus to a shy, hesitating provincial, full of doubts which he never dared to carry to the point of open denial. Hawthorne did not say "No" in thunder; he whispered it softly, more than half believing that he ought to say "Yes." Therein he was a true Transcendentalist.

AMERICAN SWEDENBORGIANISM AND SPIRITUALISM

GENUINE mysticism of the Transcendentalist type is too austere, too unworldly, ever to win a wide popular following; its goods are all of the spirit; it promises no material gains of wealth, or comfort, or power. But the lean Don Quixote always has his attendant in a paunchy Sancho Panza. Pseudomysticisms, dabbling in the occult, and attempting to conquer both worlds at once, acquiring an intimacy with Heaven while remaining on familiar terms with the earth—these are well-fitted to bring many recruits. Nineteenth century America, even twentieth century America, has been fertile in "mystical" movements on this lower plane: Swedenborgianism, Spiritualism, Theosophy, Christian Science, Russellism, Dowieism, the Prince of the House of David, the Four-square Gospel of Aimee Semple McPherson, the Moral Rearmament of Buchmanism. Swedenborgianism, the first of these movements and the parent of all the others, had the most distinguished founder of any of them and came the nearest to possessing a coherent philosophy.

Emanuel Swedenborg (1688–1772) was, if judged in terms of his knowledge rather than of his influence, the greatest scientist of the great eighteenth century. His writings, uncollected in systematic form until a hundred years after his death, reveal him to have been, in the words of A. J. Grieve of Victorian University, Manchester, "ahead of his time . . . in almost every department of scientific activity." In physics, he forecast the nebular hypothesis of Kant and Laplace, advanced a prophetic theory of molecular magnetism, and made an important study of phosphorescence; in chemistry, he was the first to recognize the subscience of crystallography; in geology, he made original discoveries in paleontology; in physiology, he anticipated later research in emphasizing the cellular structure of the brain, the importance of the cerebrum, and even that most recent of discoveries, the functioning of the ductless glands.

This universal creative genius was also of a practical turn, making all sorts of inventions that ranged from ear trumpets and stoves to flying machines, steam engines, submarines, and machine guns. When his native country of Sweden, engaged in a war, needed to transport some boats for fourteen miles overland, Swedenborg discovered the means to do it. As assayer-extraordinary of the Swedish Board of Mines, he published valuable works on mineralogy and the processes of smelting and assaying. As a member of the Swedish House of Nobles, he took a prominent part in formulating policies on currency, trade, and liquor control. Nor were his political interests confined to Sweden. He traveled widely in England, Holland, Germany, and France, and was in his outlook what Nietzsche would have called a "good European."

But this belated man of the Renaissance whom Alberti and Leonardo would have delighted to meet was also an heir of the Reformation. His father, Dr. Joseph Swedberg (the "en," equivalent to the German "von" or French "de," being an aristocratic addition when Swedenborg was ennobled in 1719), had been professor of theology at the University of Upsala and bishop of Aksara, well known for his liberal religious views. Religion ran in Swedenborg's veins, and as Swedenborg grew older he devoted his energies to working out a cosmology that would be both religious and scientific. At the age of fifty-seven he began to have a series of visions in which, as he believed, Heaven and Hell were opened to him, or rather, the heavens and the hells, since he discovered them to be many; he was permitted to have long conversations with departed spirits, now living as angels or demons; and he was instructed as to the meaning of all that he saw by the Lord and given by Him an understanding of the "spiritual sense of the Bible." From these experiences he emerged with alleged telepathic and clairvoyant powers which he and his followers believed that he exercised in a number of remarkable instances.

The central principles of Swedenborg's system were those of continuity and correspondence. The universe, in his view, was one seamless garment, or better, one living body sustained by the breath of indwelling deity, from whom all things emanated; there was a minute correspondence between all its parts, the physical sun being paralleled by a heavenly sun, physical dwellings by heavenly mansions, the activities of men by those of angels and demons; and there was continuity everywhere, passing by infinite gradations from the lowest physical order to the highest spiritual realm, the fundamental distinction between spirit and matter being that between activity and passivity—wherein passivity itself was a lower form of activity—so that the whole universe was a dynamic process drawn upward, or inward, toward God, its source.

With his organic viewpoint, Swedenborg looked upon men less as individuals than as members of groups, finding that the heavens were organized as separate societies of angels, according to the type of activity in which they engaged. Thus, though well aware of the deadening formalism of the churches, he ventured to dream of a universal Church of the New Jerusalem, creedless and free, with members bound together only by their common worship of God as the source of all love and by activities of kindness and charity. Even before his death, the beginnings of such a church were attempted in London, and in 1784 James Glenn, one of its members, brought Swedenborgianism to America in a series of lectures delivered in Boston and Philadelphia. But at that time little interest was aroused, and the gift to Harvard College of the Latin edition of Swedenborg's *Arcana Coelestia* was allowed to rest in the rubbishroom until it was accidentally discovered by a student, Thomas Worcester, in 1816. Greatly excited by the character of his find, Worcester gathered a group of students about him for Swedenborgian study, and in 1818 they organized the Boston Society of the New Jerusalem. A knowledge of Swedenborg soon became a necessary part of the liberal culture fostered by the Channing Unitarians and Transcendentalists.

There was enough intellectual pith and marrow in Swedenborg's system, with its inclusion of Platonic and Aristotelian elements, to give it philosophical interest. Emerson was much influenced by the Swedish writer and deemed him worthy of one of the most brilliant chapters in his *Representative Men*. The boldest and most incisive of contemporary literary and religious critics, Henry James, Sr., falling into a strange spiritual despondency—a state termed by Swedenborg a "vastation" and by the Catholics, more poetically, "the dark night of the soul"—was rescued by a reading of Swedenborg's *Divine Love and Wisdom* and later produced a number of volumes on Swedenborgianism.

Owing to the social emphasis in Swedenborg's writings, a considerable number of Swedenborgians, such as Henry James, Sr., took an active part in the Owenist or Fourierist movement. Swedenborg also exercised a potent influence in the revolt against marriage which characterized the America of the twenties, thirties, and forties. Since Swedenborg himself was a stout upholder of the matrimonial institution, finding it in existence even among the angels, a word of explanation is needed at this point.

When the religious revival in America flowered into romantic freedom it brought with it in many quarters, as we have seen, a demand for a loosening of sex bonds as well as others. And here Swedenborg, as always, was on the side of spiritual liberation. He was interested in upholding matrimony, not for its own sake, but for what he called "Conjugial Love" centered on the welfare of the children; it was thus not a creation of romantic love but a social obligation; romantic love being, however, a fact, and one obviously not confinable within matrimonial limits, he made a kind of safety valve place for it in his system.

"For those," he wrote, "who on account of salacity cannot control their lusts, it is possible that this conjugial love may be preserved if the wandering love of the sex be confined to one mistress. Pellicacy is to be preferred to wandering lust if only it be not entered into with more than one; and not with a virgin . . . ; nor with a married woman; and if it be kept apart from conjugial loves. . . . In this way one may avoid the lust of defloration, the lust of varieties, the lust of violation, and the lust of seducing innocence." Concubinage was thus sanctioned by Swedenborg only as a lesser evil, but it was none the less sanctioned. Hence in America he gave aid and comfort both to those moderates who sought more liberal divorce laws and to the radicals who were satisfied with nothing less than free love.

Finally, Swedenborg was the immediate father of American spiritualism. The latter was in fact simply a democratization of Swedenborg's own experience. The ease and familiarity of his communications with the dead, the barely supramundane character of his angelic visitants engaged in heavenly activities differing only slightly from those on earth, and the traditional nature of his clairvoyant-telepathic faculties all encouraged an easy hope that his experiences could be shared by the multitude. Swedenborg's account of the future life as a mere continuation of the present under slightly altered conditions supplied the peculiar coloration of spiritualism which brought the distant Christian Heaven close to earth, satisfied the tenderest human feelings by the intimacy of communication which it claimed to establish between the two realms, permitted its votaries to enlarge their own stature by converse with the mighty dead, and brought a new excitement, greater than that of the camp meetings, into lives dulled by routine and devoid of cultural interests.

The first victims of the spiritualist craze were the New England Shakers, the somewhat boring decorum of their peaceful communal life making them peculiarly susceptible to this call of the wild. The Shakers, of course, had always been spiritualists in theory, but they were not deeply affected until between 1838 and 1845 a wave of visionary enthusiasm swept over their communities to such an extent that during those seven years their villages were closed to outsiders. Their religious meetings were turned into séances where spirits of the dead, angels, and demons vied with each other in clamoring for attention. Among the most frequent heavenly visitants were spirits of Indians from the Blue City, and Negroes from the City of Delight who told how in that abode of poetic justice former slaveowners were obliged to act as servants to their erstwhile slaves. Characters from the Bible came very often: St. Peter, St. John, Elisha, Ezekiel, Noah, Isaiah, and Malachi. But the most valued of all these celestial intruders were the four mysterious angels: Holy Assan De La Jah, the Angel of the East; Michael Van Ce Va Ne, the Angel of the West; Ga Bry Ven Do Vester Run, the Angel of the North; Ven Den De Pa Rol Jew Le Jah, the Angel of the South.

Some of the wondrous revelations that were vouchsafed to the Shakers during this mystical period were written down by Hervey Elkins in his *Fifteen Years in the Senior Order of Shakers, a Holy, Sacred and Divine Roll and Book, from the Lord God of Heaven to the Inhabitants of Earth, Revealed in the United Society at New Lebanon* (1843). A similar work was *The Divine Book of Holy and Eternal Wisdom* (1849) by Paulina Bates. Both works, at first accepted in the Shaker Canon but later looked on askance, show that during this period of prolonged extravagance the Shakers for once completely lost their sense of decorum, shouting and rolling and speaking with tongues like a Methodist camp meeting. Many of their best and worst hymns were supposed to have been given them by the spirits. One of these preserves a modified sample of the speaking with tongues:

> "Lo all vo, hark ye, dear children, and listen to me,
> For I am that holy Se loné se kára an vé;
> My work upon earth is holy, holy and pure,
> That work which will ever forever endure.
>
> "Yea, my heavenly Father hath se-vé-ned to you
> That power which is holy and that faith which is true;
> O then, my beloved, why will ye delay?
> O la hó le en sé ren, now while it is day."

The excitement soon spread beyond the Shakers to other sects. The Universalists, with their special interest in the future life, furnished a great many converts to the new faith. Next, the extraordinary performances of Andrew Jackson Davis, the mesmeric shoemaker and psychic healer, who in his trances could speak, not precisely with tongues, but in languages unknown to his waking self and with an amount of philosophical knowledge far beyond anything that his meager education could apparently have supplied, aroused the interest of the learned in the phenomena of spiritualism, while at the same time the movement was given a pseudo-metaphysical basis in Davis' interesting work, *The Principles of Nature* (1847). Finally, in 1848, a definite technique for communication with the spirits seemed to be discovered in the famous "Rochester rappings" of the Fox sisters in Hydesville, New York. Margaret and Kate Fox, aged eight and a half and six years respectively, were farmers' daughters living in a traditionally haunted house, who suddenly became attended by unaccountable rappings until one day Kate held up several fingers and uttered the mysterious words, "Here, Mr. Splitfoot, do as I do"—and the spirit responded with the right number of knocks. This remark of the little six year old girl became the rock on which the Spiritualist Church was founded. Within four years its members were publishing three widely circulated papers, *The Spirit Messenger, The Star of Truth*, and the *Northwestern Orient*.

Meanwhile, the two rapping Fox girls had been taken in charge by their older sister Leah, aged twenty-nine, who learned the technique and then put on public exhibitions at which, by the advice of Horace Greeley, an admission fee of five dollars was charged. The sisters were a nine days' wonder, but after a time the fickle public turned its interest elsewhere. Many years later Margaret Fox confessed that the rappings had been caused by a skillful manipulation of the joints of the big toe—explaining little Kate's ingenuous utterance—and demonstrated the fact in further public exhibitions; but much less interest was aroused by her belated honesty than that which had greeted her original trickery. Mediumship was established as a minor industry of an industrial period, and a long succession of noted mediums followed: Daniel Douglas Home, Ann O'Delia Diss Debar alias the Baroness Rosenthal, Eusapia Palladino, William James' Mrs. Piper, and the Harvard faculty's Margery. Always the same story of apparently inexplicable phenomena and eventual exposés, with an endless succession of victimizers and victims. If the Spiritualists did not solve the problem of communication with Heaven, they at least solved that of perpetual motion.

THE MILLERITES

ONE more notable attempt to take Heaven by storm came out of New England. The enduring fascination exercised by the idea of the End of the World and the Second Coming of Christ would be an interesting subject of study. It satisfied that yearning for the dramatic which has played a larger part in human history than historians have admitted; in calling upon abstruse mathematical calculations to determine, on the basis of Biblical prophecies, the exact date of the coming event, it gratified the pseudoscientific delight in the solution of oracular puzzles which still finds expression today in the reading of horoscopes; and in times of doubt and depression, it bore out the observations of pessimism and at the same time sustained an underlying, ultimate optimism. As long as the conception of original sin was widely prevalent, the thought of expediting the Last Judgment could only be welcome to exclusive sects who regarded themselves as exceptions to the condemnation awaiting the mass of mankind; but once the masses themselves no longer really feared damnation, thousands were ready to embrace a doctrine which promised them an immediate salvation within their own lifetime. These considerations may help to explain the enormous vogue of the Adventist teachings of William Miller in the eighteen-forties. The Millerite movement, as David M. Ludlum remarks, "represented the summation of all the reforms of the age." [1] Mormonism, Perfectionism, Owenism, and Fourierism had all been Messianic movements that looked forward to some Utopia. Millerism promised a cosmic social revolution to be followed by a cosmic Utopia. It took a shorter cut to a more magnificent conclusion.

William Miller (1782–1849) had been born in Pittsfield, Massachusetts, but was brought up in the frontier town of Poultney, Vermont, in an environment that had proved a hothouse for the development of wild and radical sects. Out of Vermont had come, in addition to Joseph Smith, Brigham Young, and John Hum-

[1] David M. Ludlum, *Social Ferment in Vermont, 1791–1850* (New York: 1939), p. 251.

phrey Noyes, such ambiguous groups as the Dorrilites, whose leader boasted that his body could not be injured—until driven to retract under the beating administered by an irate soldier—and the "Pilgrims," who specialized in rolling in the dust of the highways and never bathed, because bathing was not enjoined by the Bible. It was in such an atmosphere that William Miller, on the basis of the prophecies of the Second Coming contained in the Book of Revelation, worked out to his own satisfaction a mathematical proof that the date would be some time between March 21, 1843, and March 21, 1844. For fourteen years he kept this knowledge to himself, but then, deciding that the public needed time to prepare for the great event, he published his first article on it in the Brandon *Vermont Telegraph* in May, 1832.

But though Millerism was thus a product of the Vermont frontier, on the fringe of New England, its influence reached to Boston itself. In the famous Chardon Street Convention of 1840, arranged by Bronson Alcott, Parker, and Ripley, in which representatives from all the radical religious sects met in tumultuous conclave, the Millerites were the noisiest, if not the most numerous. Joshua Himes, pastor of the Chardon Street Baptist Church, became a convert, and spread the news of the Second Coming far and wide through his articles in the Boston *Signs of the Times* and the New York *Midnight Cry*. Thousands of Baptists and Methodists became adherents. When March 21, 1844, passed quite as usual, Miller perceived that he should have used the Jewish Calendar as the basis of his calculations, and this time confidently announced the approaching October twentieth as the exact date. As the fatal day drew nigh, groups of men and women throughout New England, New York, and Ohio prepared their white ascension robes; the harvesting was neglected; and at dawn of the appointed day many climbed trees and perched on housetops in order to gain a special advantage in the coming heavenward race. Even a second disappointment did not dampen Miller's own ardor, and with renewed calculations he was able to organize the first formal Adventist Church at Albany, New York, in 1845. But the mass of his followers put away their white garments and returned to sobriety. There ensued what the Baptist *Vermont Observer* called a "time of spiritual death and famine." Sadly the same paper went on:

"There is an almost total dearth of revivals throughout the country. A moral chill has pervaded the churches . . . the like of which has not often been witnessed." [2] In the Millerite movement, the mysticism of New England had reached its highest point of extravagant faith; after that flaming episode it fell back exhausted. But there remained the solid New England conscience, content henceforward to take the path of piecemeal reforms, moving toward Utopia only by inches, but moving toward it in the actual world.

THE NEW ENGLAND CONSCIENCE IN ACTION

ONE is likely today to smile at the spirit of universal reform which seemed to animate the New England leaders in the period just before the Civil War. Theirs appeared to be the attitude of Anthony Trollope's John Bold,[3] whose passion was "the reform of all abuses; state abuses, church abuses, corporation abuses, . . . abuses in medical practise, and general abuses in the world at large." Everything came within their purview, from vegetarianism to international peace. When their attention eventually became focused on the evil of slavery, it was easy for Southerners to regard this as an instance of the old human habit of being more concerned about the mote in one's neighbor's eye than the beam in one's own. Yet the charge was unjust. The New Englanders began by attempting to put their own house in order, and it was only when they perceived that nearly every major reform movement sooner or later led up to the slavery issue that they concentrated their efforts on abolition. Nor were any of these major reforms either trivial or without enduring result. On the contrary, they in large part set the pattern of the post-Civil War period through the practical results achieved, the ideals enunciated, or the problems raised. The widely ramifying program of educational reform was carried out so energetically that it created the general framework of modern American education; the feminist program had before it a slowly expanding future of immeasurable import; the more ambiguous temperance program brought out a problem that happens to be in abeyance today but has in no way been solved; and the program

[2] *Ibid.*, p. 259.
[3] A character in *The Warden*, by Anthony Trollope.

for world peace prefigured what is likely to be the chief concern of the twentieth century.

The earliest of these reform movements was that connected with temperance. The issue was, of course, an old one. All of the colonies had laws against excessive drunkenness, but toward the end of the eighteenth century attempts began to be made to remove the external cause instead of merely penalizing the effect. Anthony Benezet the Quaker, John Wesley, and Benjamin Rush all wrote against the use of distilled liquors, and one of the first acts of the newly formed Methodist Church in America was to issue a declaration against it. Lyman Beecher in Litchfield, Connecticut, began a notable temperance crusade in 1810, which was to occupy much of his time for the next twenty years and was to bring the majority of Presbyterians to its support. During the twenties the growth of temperance societies was so rapid that by 1833 they enjoyed an estimated total membership of over a million. In the following year, the chairman of the New York State Temperance Society was able to issue a manifesto signed by three United States Presidents, James Madison, Andrew Jackson, and John Quincy Adams. It read: "Being satisfied from observation and experience, as well as from Medical Testimony, that ardent spirit, as a drink, is not only needless but hurtful; and that the entire disuse of it would tend to promote the health, the virtue, and happiness of the community, we hereby express our conviction, that would the Citizens of the United States, and especially all Young Men, discontinue the use of it, they would not only promote their personal benefit, but the good of their country and of the world."

Not infrequently the expression of the temperance ideal was less felicitous, as in the song of the Philadelphia Mechanics' and Workingmen's Temperance Society at their Fourth of July meeting in 1835:

> "No, let us rise united
> And the great monster crush,
> By water draughts excited,
> We to the rescue rush."

But in spite of the occasional absurdity and exaggeration of the movement, and its overreliance on the effectiveness of personal pledges, it still, during these years when it sought only voluntary co-operation, undoubtedly exercised a beneficial influence in checking the habitual drunkenness which was one of the ugliest features of the American scene. In 1846, however, Colonel Neil Dow, a Maine businessman who had calculated the number of days of labor lost to the employers every year through the drunkenness of their employees, proposed the fatal policy of calling for legislation to prohibit the sale of liquor, thereby changing the movement from one for temperance into one for prohibition. During the next decade, Maine and ten other states were induced to give the new policy a trial, but the violation of personal liberties which it entailed caused all of these laws, outside of Maine itself, to be either repealed or declared unconstitutional. The problem was handed on unsolved to the post-Civil War period.

The much more important reform movement in education also had behind it a long history. Washington, Jefferson, and Madison again and again pointed out that popular education was essential if democracy were to succeed. Jefferson considered his own work in founding the University of Virginia, with its bold experiment of the honor system, as one of his greatest achievements. Madison, and later John Quincy Adams, tried to establish an "American University" under government auspices in the national capital. But the wholly negative theory of government held by most congressmen prevented federal entrance into the educational field. To this day there is no national department of education, and it was more than fifty years before the inadequate Bureau of Education was established. The fostering of common schools was left to the individual states; these in turn left it to the counties; and the counties left it to individual citizens. As a result, there arose the situation described in the Book of Mormon: "some were ignorant because of their poverty, and others did receive great learning because of their riches."

The first insistent demand for public education came from the short-lived Workingmen's Party in 1829–30 in New York City. Its organ, *The Working Man's Advocate*, edited by George Henry Evans, carried as its leading motto "All children are entitled to equal education." The English feminist, Frances Wright, successor of Mary Wollstonecraft, was then ending a five years' American campaign for social reform as editor of *The Free Enquirer,* and in it she advanced a radical program for the state to set up boarding schools for all children, who were to be taken from their parents at the age of two and given an absolutely equal education, regardless of wealth or social position. Needless to say, this ran too counter to American habits of domesticity to have any chance of success, but after this time the demand for equal education formed part of every labor program. Unfortunately, in the absence of an organized labor movement, the demand carried little weight.

When James Carter, as a member of the Massachusetts Legislature, chose to look into the matter of public education during the twenties, he found that the schools had been utterly neglected for forty years. By his active propaganda, Carter paved the way for the work of Horace Mann, who, as secretary of the State Board of Education from 1838 to 1848, really established the Massachusetts public school system, and, through its example, the public school system throughout the United States. Mann, who had himself risen from poverty, was aware of the danger that capitalism might capture the system, and he denounced the industrialism of his day as unsparingly as did Ripley, or Emerson, or Orestes Brownson. "The power of money," he wrote, "is as imperial as the power of the sword; and I may as well depend upon another for my head, as for my bread. The day is sure to come, when men will look back upon the prerogatives of Capital, at the present time, with as severe and as just a condemnation as we now look back upon the predatory Chieftains of the Dark Ages." [4]

But Horace Mann's successor in educational influence, Henry Barnard of Connecticut, moderately wealthy, a devout Episcopalian, and married to a Roman Catholic wife, took a different view of the situation. As editor of the nationally circulated *American Journal of Education,* he excluded all references to slavery but was willing enough to publish a capitalist catechism which included such edifying questions and answers as these:

Q. Suppose a capitalist in employing his capital makes large profits, would that harm the working man?

A. No. There would be more capital to pay wages. . . .

---

[4] Quoted in Merle Curti, *Social Ideas of American Educators* (New York: Charles Scribner's Sons, 1935), p. 116.

Q. Are you sorry, then, that capitalists should have great profits?
A. Glad.

Thus, in spite of Horace Mann, public education, when it came into actual being in the United States, was not the equal education of which Frances Wright dreamed but was already heavily weighted on the side of the wealthier classes. Nevertheless, it was better, in the long run, to have even a biased education than no education, and to that extent Horace Mann was successful.

Much the same may be said of the movement for the education of women. The leaders in that field, Catherine Beecher, Emma Willard, and Mary Lyon, sought primarily to train women for their domestic duties as wives and mothers, discountenanced the suffrage movement, and believed wholeheartedly in the efficacy of religious revivals. Yet in opening to women in their seminaries the hitherto closed field of higher education, they unconsciously prepared the way for the entrance of women into the professions and for their active participation in public life.

The new enlargement of the privileges of education did not stop with women. The kindergarten, first introduced in America by Robert Owen, received Horace Mann's endorsement and henceforth became a part, though too often a neglected part, of the American system. Thomas Hopkins Gallaudet, a descendant of Connecticut's Thomas Hooker, was the first in three generations of Gallaudets who devoted themselves successfully to the education of the deaf and dumb. Samuel Gridley Howe, who as a youth had fought beside Byron for the freedom of Greece, founded the Massachusetts School for the Blind of which Horace Mann said, "I would rather have built up the Blind Asylum than have written Hamlet." These movements quite literally brought the possibility of intelligent life to the deaf-blind Laura Bridgman, trained by Howe, and to the more recent Helen Keller, while they rendered invaluable aid to many thousands of those less terribly handicapped. Dorothea Dix broadened the concept of education still further through her work first for convicts and then for the insane; out of the beginnings she made grew the modern methods of prison reform, the modern methods of treating insanity.

The essence of all these New England educational movements was that they broadened the concept of *man*. As Odell Shepard well says, "That innocent-sounding little phrase 'all men' in the Declaration of Independence was now to be interpreted." Hitherto, by tacit consent, the full rights of humanity had not been extended to women, to children, to deaf-mutes or the blind, to the insane or to convicts; no attempts had been made to lighten the handicaps of sex, age, or infirmity; on the basis of existent inequalities, all opportunity to decrease them had been neglected.

When, through the efforts of these New England reformers, women, children, convicts, and the insane at last came to be recognized as human beings, it was inevitable that Negroes should also be brought under that head. But here the reformers met with insuperable difficulties. When Bronson Alcott admitted Negro students into his Boston school, we have seen that he lost all his white pupils. When Prudence Crandall attempted to establish a school for Negro girls in Canterbury, Connecticut, she was put in jail and obtained her release only after a long and expensive lawsuit carried up to the state Supreme Court. When an academy for free Negroes was built in Canaan, New Hampshire, it was destroyed by a mob. Is it any wonder that Horace Mann, interested in every phase of education, should at last have resigned his position on the state board and have gone to Washington to take part in the fight against slavery in the halls of Congress?

Frances Wright, foremost in the early battle for popular education, had also been a harbinger of the suffragist movement. She was particularly concerned with the nonexistence of property rights in the case of married women. If a woman was really a human being and not merely a part of a husband, she asked, why should her property be transferred to the latter at marriage? But in the twenties such feminist arguments met with little response, and the movement for women's rights, when it came, had a different source. In 1837, the appearance on a public platform of "Carolina's high-souled daughters," Angelica and Sarah Grimke, speaking against slavery, was assailed as unwomanly in a "Pastoral Letter" issued by the General Association of Congregational Ministers of Massachusetts. In 1840, when Lucretia Mott and Elizabeth Cady Stanton went to London as delegates to an international antislavery conference they were refused the right to speak on the ground that their sex had no political standing. In 1852, Susan Anthony, rising to speak at a temperance meeting to which she went as an authorized delegate, was informed that "the sisters were not invited there to speak but to listen and learn." These and many similar experiences on the part of other women reformers brought them to see the necessity of securing political rights if they wished to take part effectively in the life of their own times.

Although the woman's suffrage movement belongs in the main to a later period than that covered in this volume, it should be remembered that it was organized as early as 1848, and was widely publicized in the fifties by the defiant wearing of "bloomers," a short skirt over full trousers, similar to the costume of the feminine Perfectionists at Oneida but named for the originator, Mrs. Amelia Bloomer. As nearly all the suffragists were also abolitionists, however, the feminist issue was perforce to be subordinated to the more immediate aim. "First free the Negro, then women," was the cry. Few imagined that in this "land of liberty" the first could not be accomplished without a civil war, or the second attained until fifty years later.

Finally, there was the peace movement initiated by Elihu Burritt, "the Learned Blacksmith" of New Britain, Connecticut. That extraordinary genius, while working at his forge, carried out a program of self-education sufficiently illustrated by a typical excerpt from his journal: "June 19, Sixty lines of Hebrew; thirty pages of French; ten pages of Cuvier's Theory of the Earth; eight lines of Syriac; ten lines of Danish; ten ditto Bohemian; nine ditto of Polish; fifteen names of stars; ten hours' forging." His studies gave Burritt a conception of the interdependence of all aspects of culture, and looking upon international politics from this viewpoint he was so profoundly shocked by the irrationality of nationalist policies that he decided to devote his life to the cause of world peace. Through the circulation of his weekly pacifist paper, *The Christian Citizen*, he gained enough followers in America and England to be able to organize in 1846 a League of Universal Brotherhood with twenty thousand members, which led on to the Brussels Peace Congress of 1848, and no less than eighteen peace conventions in the United States—all aiming to establish a Court of Nations not unsimilar to the later World Court at The Hague.

Burritt's movement was halted, as were the educational and

feminist reforms, by the problem of slavery. How that single issue came to overtop and absorb all others will be the theme of the remainder of this book. Before tracing the steps whereby the North ultimately arrived at the point where it saw in the struggle over slavery a conflict between irreconcilable ideologies, it will be necessary to turn our attention to the southern attitude which gave rise to that conflict.

Those writers of the eighteenth century who believed that all men are guided merely by self-interest were superficial thinkers. One of the most striking examples of the fallacy of their supposition is furnished by the history of the southern states between 1790 and 1860. At the former date, the population and wealth of the North and the South were approximately equal. But by 1860 the white population of the North had risen to over nineteen millions, and that of the South was only eight millions, while three fourths of the wealth of the nation was in northern hands. The North had manufactures and mines, canals and railroads; the South was deficient in all of them. As to the cause of this change in the relative prosperity of the two regions, no economist of today, whether northern or southern, would disagree with the statement of Ernest L. Bogart, "The reason for the industrial backwardness [of the South] was the existence there of slavery." [5] That is, purely from an economic standpoint, regardless of its moral aspects, the expensive, wasteful, and unproductive system of slavery was a curse to the South. And yet for half a century, southern energy was chiefly expended in endeavoring to preserve and perpetuate an institution which all the laws of self-interest should have led that section itself to abolish.

[5] Ernest L. Bogart, *Economic History of the United States* (New York: Longmans Green & Co., 1937), p. 442.

CHAPTER 29 . *Southern Romanticizing of Slavery*

WHAT remains true, however, is, not that all men but that some men are guided merely by self-interest, and that, if they are in positions of power, they can impose their own ideology, by romanticizing it, upon the mass of the people, who will then fight and die for a cause in every way disadvantageous to them. This was the case in the South, where the profits of slavery, such as they were, were limited to the slave-owning class, which constituted less than five per cent of the population. Indeed, strictly speaking, the profits inured only to that one fourth of the slaveholders, or one twentieth of the population, who owned more than ten slaves and worked the larger plantations. In this one twentieth nearly all the political power was vested. Such a condition was clearly a travesty of democracy.

The impact of slavery on southern culture was still more deadly than was its effect on economics. Where the North gave birth to scores of notable writers during the period, one could sum up those of the South on the fingers of his two hands. The intellectual ferment of Transcendentalism, the idealistic efforts toward social justice, the extension of democratic concepts on the frontier, the attempts at community living—all this mental and spiritual excitement fell on deaf ears in the South, which set itself doggedly to develop a very different antidemocratic philosophy of its own. Thus it came about that by the fifties the South was so different

434

from the North that northern visitors like Frederick Olmsted felt as if they were traveling in a foreign land.

That at some time between the American Revolution and the Civil War the South changed its political faith is sufficiently obvious. A popular myth, promulgated by southern writers, would have it that the change came in the thirties as a reaction to the Nat Turner slave revolt and to the northern abolitionist movement. In actuality, the change was much less marked than is often supposed, and it began long before Turner or Garrison.

We have seen how the planters of the deep South, in an unholy alliance with New England merchants, kept Jefferson's denunciation of the slave trade out of the Declaration of Independence, how they were able to defeat his proposed ordinance of 1784, and how they threatened to wreck the Constitutional Convention rather than yield their inequitable voting power derived from the possession of slaves. It is true that under the generous impulse of the Revolutionary movement they temporarily abolished the slave trade, but they very soon re-established it. At no time was there any widespread antislavery sentiment in the South outside of Virginia, Kentucky, and the hill country of North Carolina and Tennessee.

In other words, those sections of the South which were most open to northern influence, which were most democratic in spirit, and which specialized in tobacco and other crops easily raised by white workers, were in 1790 eager to be rid of slavery; while those farthest removed from northern influence, most aristocratic in temper, and most dependent upon slave labor because their crops of rice and cotton involved a type of labor too disagreeable for white men to render, were even more eager to maintain the slave system. The change that now gradually came about was simply that the deep South was able to convert the border states to its views, and that those views themselves shifted from an apology for slavery as a necessary evil to a eulogy of it as a providential good.

THE EFFECTS OF THE COTTON GIN

IT WAS indeed a New Englander who was unintentionally responsible for the change, but it was not William Lloyd Garrison the abolitionist, but that inventive Connecticut Yankee, Eli Whitney, forty years earlier. Prior to Whitney's epochal invention of the cotton gin in 1793, the best worker could clean only ten pounds of cotton a day; the gin made it possible for a man to clean three hundred pounds in the same time. That one little mechanical fact changed the fate of the South.

The cotton boom that resulted, foreshadowing the mining and oil booms after the Civil War, was more important than those ever became. It shattered the emergent Jeffersonian pattern of small farm agrarianism, so far as the South was concerned, re-establishing on a much larger and cruder scale the older plantation system and thereby separating the South from the rest of the nation in way of life and way of thought.

Hitherto, the only get-rich-quick opportunities offered by America had been in the hazards of land speculation, but now an apparently sure gamble was seen in cotton production. The tale of pounds produced per year is sufficiently revealing: a million and a half in 1790, over eighteen million in 1800, over eighty million in 1810, over one hundred and forty million in 1820. After that, production continued to increase, but prices fell.

Cotton lent itself ideally to the demands of slavery. Its production required but little skill and for many years the profits increased with the size of the crop. The quickest rewards came through exploiting the soil and then moving on to fresh land, so that cotton became a symbol for expansion as its cultivation spread in triumphal progress from Georgia and South Carolina westward through Alabama, Mississippi, and Louisiana, on to Texas. To the older Tidewater aristocracy was now added a *nouveau riche* frontier aristocracy, devoid of humane traditions, devoted wholly to getting rich, and calling constantly for more land and more slaves. The Mexican War, the invasion of Kansas, the desperate attempt to introduce slavery into the northwest territories, were distant but absolutely natural results of Eli Whitney's invention of the cotton gin.

THE AMERICAN COLONIZATION SOCIETY

ONCE slavery was accepted as a permanent instead of a temporary feature of southern society, the changing attitude brought with it certain very definite consequences: (1) The southern clergy devoted themselves to producing a religious justification of slavery based on the example of the patriarchs in the Old Testament, and on the oft-quoted commandment to do one's duty in that state of life into which God had called one; since God (with the help of the slavetraders) had called the Negroes into a state of slavery, there must be no interference with that divinely ordained institution. (2) The practice of manumission must be discouraged. (3) The Negro must be prevented from cherishing false hopes that he or his descendants would ever be liberated. (4) The large number of free Negroes already in the country, constituting by their very existence a stimulus to such false hopes, must be kept from all contact with the slaves, and, if possible, removed to foreign shores.

The ambiguous American Colonization Society, organized under a cloak of philanthropy in 1817 and largely financed by southern capital, contained in its statement of policy all four of these items of the new program. Its foremost aim—to colonize the free Negroes in Liberia on the west coast of Africa, where they could set up a Negro republic—looked on the surface like a highly idealistic one, and the Society boasted a number of distinguished names on its list of officers—Lafayette, Madison, John Marshall, Henry Clay, Daniel Webster, Gerrit Smith, James Gillespie Birney, John Tyler. Many of these members joined the Society from humanitarian motives. Fundamentally, however, the purpose of the organization was simply the preservation of slavery through the removal of the dangerous free Negro group. This motive appears again and again in the utterances of the Society's organ, the *Colonization Journal:*

"You cannot abolish slavery, for God is pledged to sustain it.

"Policy, and even the voice of humanity, forbid the progress of manumission. It would be as humane to throw them from the decks in the Middle Passage as to set them free in this country. Free blacks are a greater nuisance than slaves. This class of persons is a curse and a contagion where they reside . . . an anomalous race of beings, the most depraved on earth.

"Christianity cannot do for them here what it will do for them in Africa. This is no fault of the colored man, nor the white man, but an ordinance of Providence, and no more to be changed than the laws of motion.

"If the free people of color were generally taught to read, it might be an inducement for them to remain in this country. We should offer them no such inducement."

In spite of great efforts, the colonization scheme was a failure, owing to inadequate capital, the unwillingness of the free Negroes to emigrate, and the inability of those of them who did go to Liberia to develop any kind of prosperous community in that equatorial region—their failure, of course, being taken as conclusive evidence of the Negro's incapacity for self-government. The chief result of the Colonization Society's crusade was the passage of laws in the southern states prohibiting the education of Negroes, whether slave or free, under penalty of fine and imprisonment. This drew from Joseph Doddridge, an unusually enlightened Episcopal minister in northern Virginia, the following withering comment:

"It is a curious circumstance that while our missionaries are generously traversing the most inhospitable regions, and endeavoring with incessant toil to give the science of Europe and America, together with the Christian revelation, to the benighted pagans, most of the legislatures of the slave-holding States have made it a highly penal offense to teach a slave a single letter. While, at great expense and waste of valuable lives, we are endeavoring to teach the natives of Africa the use of letters, no one durst attempt to do the same thing for the wretched descendants of that ill-fated people, bound in the fetters of slavery in America. . . . We debase them to the condition of brutes, and then use that debasement as an argument for perpetuating their slavery." [1]

THE DYING PROTEST OF VIRGINIA

In the early thirties, the Jeffersonian Virginians made their last stand against slavery. How little the insignificant Nat Turner slave rebellion had to do with sharpening the proslavery sentiment of the South may be seen from the fact that immediately afterward in the very state where it occurred a resurgent demand for emancipation appeared. Slavery was never denounced more bitterly, on both economic and moral grounds, than in the Virginia Legislature

[1] Quoted in Walter Wilson Jennings, *Origin and Early History of the Disciples of Christ* (Cincinnati: The Standard Publishing Co., 1919), pp. 315–316.

of 1831–32; not a single speaker had the hardihood to defend it; one listening to the debate might have thought abolition close at hand. But after all the fine words had been uttered, nothing whatever was done. The Virginia legislators had intelligence, they had a sense of justice, but they no longer possessed the will to act.

The reason for Virginia's inaction was that her planters were discovering a new source of revenue in the sale of surplus slaves to the deep South. Thomas R. Dew, a teacher in the formerly liberal William and Mary College but trained in the authoritarian atmosphere of German universities, was the first to point out that Virginia derived almost as much profit from the sale of slaves as from tobacco, and to urge the raising of Negroes as an industry like cattle breeding. Dew's *Review of the Debates in the Virginia Legislature of 1832*, in which he set forth the supposed moral and economic advantages of slavery, was esteemed so highly that he received the presidency of William and Mary as a reward.

The new industry involved a change of attitude toward the sexual morality of the Negroes. Chancellor William Harper of the Supreme Court of South Carolina wrote in *A Memoir on Slavery* (1838): "In northern communities the unmarried woman who becomes a mother is an outcast from society. She has given birth to a human being who is commonly educated to a course of vice, depravity, and crime. It is not so with the female slave. She is not a less useful member of society than before. . . . Her offspring is not a burden but an acquisition to her owner. The want of chastity among slaves hardly deserves a harsher name than weakness." [2]

The actual practice on the Border was frankly admitted by the Reverend Moncure Conway of Virginia, who wrote, "As a general thing, the chief pecuniary resource in the Border States is the breeding of slaves; and I grieve to say that there is too much ground for the charges that general licentiousness among the slaves, for the purpose of a large increase, is compelled by some masters and encouraged by many." [3] An authoritative southern utterance quoted by Frederick Olmsted was to the same effect: "In the states of Maryland, Virginia, North Carolina, Kentucky, Tennessee, and Missouri,

---

[2] Quoted in William E. Dodd, *The Cotton Kingdom* (New Haven: Yale University Press, 1919), pp. 55–56.

[3] Quoted in W. E. B. Du Bois, *Black Reconstruction* (New York: Harcourt, Brace and Co., 1935), p. 44.

as much attention is paid to the breeding and growth of Negroes as to that of horses and mules. . . . Planters command their girls and women (married or unmarried) to have children; and I have known a great many Negro girls to be sold off because they did not have children."

It is estimated that from fifty to eighty thousand slaves were sent south from the Border States every year. Between 1840 and 1850, one hundred thousand were exported from Virginia alone. Thus, the slave trade, the guilt of which Jefferson had tried to throw on George the Third—the trade supposedly abolished by Congress in 1808— had now definitely become an American institution. There was a slave market in Washington itself not many blocks from the Capitol in whose marble halls congressmen, senators, and Presidents continued to prate about human rights.

The innate brutality of the slave system was revealed in all its nakedness in the slave marts, where husbands were separated from wives, mothers from children, never to see each other again. The Negroes were stripped and examined like animals, the buyers feeling their muscles, looking at their teeth, searching for signs of disease or weakness exactly as if dealing with dogs or horses. The slave-traders, usually men of the lowest type, were of course not received in southern society, but the planters dealt with them, encouraged them, and depended upon them.

Less outwardly brutal, but even more devastating, was the increased miscegenation which naturally accompanied the breaking up of Negro families in the slave market and the changing attitude toward the sex morality of female slaves. By 1860 the official census was to record the presence of 518,360 mulattoes, constituting twelve per cent of all Negroes. This meant that many thousands of white fathers had suffered the moral tragedy of watching their own children grow up as slaves, that many thousands of Negro mothers had suffered the greater tragedy of seeing them doubly deprived of their birthright as human beings and as sons and daughters.

THE CAROLINA PHILOSOPHY

To EVOLVE a system of philosophy idealizing so inherently barbarous an institution as slavery required no little intellectual ability, but the South was equal to the task. Ironically, the first in the field was one whom Jefferson had called the profoundest thinker in America, his old friend the materialistic philosopher, Thomas Cooper, who as professor of chemistry and political economy in South Carolina College launched the first attack on Jeffersonian equalitarianism in his *Lectures on the Elements of Political Economy* in 1828. Thirty years before Darwin, Cooper pictured life in grim terms as a struggle for survival wherein victory inevitably went to the strongest and cleverest. But although his nonmoral materialism supplied a much better logical basis for proslavery argument than did the transmogrified Biblical Christianity that was forced into service for the same end, it lacked the emotional afflatus of the latter and was, of course, condemned by the southern clergy. Psychologically, Calhoun, the South Carolina Calvinist who studied at Yale under Timothy Dwight, was much more closely in touch with southern sentiment. Calhoun himself was not an original thinker even in the limited field of political science; he simply took over theories worked out in the first instance by others. But he gave the whole movement a centralized political leadership, transforming its ideology into a practical power philosophy. That ideology was a curious amalgam of elements from many sources: the Calvinistic doctrine of the elect, an inverted theory of natural rights, liberal criticism of industrial capitalism, laissez-faire economics, states' rights, the romanticism of Sir Walter Scott, arguments from ancient history and from biology. All this varied material was now given a semblance of organic unity by the predetermined purpose to defend slavery.

The Carolina philosophy was one the conclusions of which were given in advance, but it was none the less cogent, claiming to be founded upon a view of Nature more realistic than that of Jefferson, since it recognized the fact of natural inequality as basic and drew the conclusion that liberty is a privilege conferred upon recognized merit, not a right belonging to all. Chancellor Harper stated the observed fact very baldly: "Is it not palpably nearer the truth to say that no man was ever born free and that no two men were ever born equal, than to say that all men are born free and equal? . . . Man is born to subjection. . . . The proclivity of the natural man is to domineer or to be subservient." [4] Calhoun in his *Disquisition on Gov-*

[4] Quoted in William E. Dodd, *The Cotton Kingdom* (New Haven: Yale University Press, 1919), pp. 56–57.

ernment (1851) voiced the hasty conclusion: "It is a great and dangerous error to suppose that all people are equally entitled to liberty. It is a reward to be earned, not a blessing to be gratuitously lavished on all alike."

From this there followed a hierarchical conception of society with a division of labor according to native talents and a gradation of rights as dependent upon social service: at the bottom, the majority of men fit only for manual labor; above them the professional classes capable of intellectual labor; at the summit the elite of political and economic rulers who in a well-governed community must form a single class in charge of the material and spiritual development of society. Such was the more realistic version of Platonic sociology elaborated most fully by George Fitzhugh in his *Sociology for the South* (1854), reprinted in an enlarged form as his popular *Cannibals All; or Slaves Without Masters* (1856). Fitzhugh was so certain of the correctness of his social analysis that he confidently predicted the return of northern white laborers to a condition of serfdom within a few years. "Slavery," he wrote, "will everywhere be abolished or everywhere be reinstated," and he had no doubt that the latter alternative was the one which would be adopted.

While Fitzhugh was bolder than most of his colleagues, a host of lesser southern writers advanced very similar views during the decade of the fifties: J. Campbell, *Negro-Mania: being an Examination of the Falsely Assumed Equality of the Various Races of Men* (1851); J. Fletcher, *Studies in Slavery* (1852); A. W. Smith, *Lectures on the Philosophy and Practice of Slavery* (1856); G. S. Sawyer, *Southern Institutes* (1859); and finally in the year of the beginning of the Civil War, S. Seabury, *American Slavery Distinguished from the Slavery of English Theorists and Justified by the Law of Nature* (1861).

It is hardly necessary today to point out the fallacies in this philosophy. Granting, as one must, that men have always been born in a condition of inequality and varying states of subjection, and that the struggle for survival is dominant throughout the rest of the animal kingdom, it still is true that the southern writers sinned against Nature more than did Jefferson. Their attempt to carry the biological argument into sociology neglected the vital difference between men and other animals in that human beings have a capacity of individual thinking and individual choice; and their acceptance of natural inequality was formulated in static terms which attempted to immobilize in a caste system what actually is a matter of individual variation and dynamic change. The southern philosophy strove to erect a new feudalism which inevitably suffered from the same limitations as those of the old medieval feudalism. The strength of the original natural rights philosophy lay, in spite of its inadequate formulation, in its outlook toward the future; its significance was not in its false assertions of existent equality but in its demand for equal opportunity for all as the necessary basis for whatever subsequent inequality of talent might appear. The Negroes and even the poor whites of the South had no chance whatever to show whether they were by nature intellectually or morally equal to the ruling caste. The latter merely took advantage of their temporary possession of power and attempted, to their cost, to eternalize the passing moment.

The Carolina argument from ancient history, with its constant appeal to Hebrew, Greek, and Roman example, was plausible rather than convincing. The ideal of Greek democracy, which was the one most often cited, was particularly appealing to the southern mind: all manual labor performed by an inferior class, with the rest left free to devote themselves to matters of government, art, and philosophy. But the comparison of Charleston, the cultural capital of the South after the decline of Virginia, with Athens, was rather pathetic—Charleston being an Athens devoid of sculpture, painting, poetry, or drama, a city in which so little attention was paid to literature that William Gilmore Simms, the one southern novelist of distinction, lived and died there without the slightest recognition from the upper class which he idolized. It was a beautiful city with its jeweled bay, esplanades, and magnolia gardens; it was a rich city, Josiah Quincy of Massachusetts confessing in 1773 that "In grandeur, splendor of buildings, decorations, equipages, number, commerce, shipping, and indeed everything it far surpasses all I ever saw, or expect to see in America"; it was a city delighting in entertainment, cultivating the arts of the drawing room, unproductive of drama but devoted to the theater, so charming the Duke de la Rochefoucauld-Liancourt that he wrote of its inhabitants in 1796, "From the hour of four in the afternoon, they rarely think of aught but pleasure and amusement." But it was moored in still water, still trying in 1850 to lead the life of half a century earlier; its pleasant culture was superficial; its aristocracy of rice, indigo, and cotton barons had no serious intellectual interests outside of history, law, and politics, cherished primarily as economic defenses.

There can be no doubt that the South gradually convinced itself that slavery was in the best interest of the Negroes themselves. Race superiority was taken for granted—a more pardonable attitude then, in the absence of ethnological science, than it is today. The Negroes, it was argued, were accustomed to slavery in their native Africa, and they were better off in a Christian community than they would have been if enslaved to the barbarous chiefs of the Congo. In fact, the argument proceeded, they were much better off than the laborers of the North since they were assured of food, shelter, and maintenance. Here the southern writers were able to take the offensive and made the most of their advantage in devastating studies of the New England factory system. The contrast between the evils of wage slavery and the benefits of chattel slavery inspired the notable southern poem of "The Hireling and the Slave," written, in the style of Goldsmith, by William J. Grayson, whose intense controlled satire was fully equal in literary merit to the impassioned odes of Whittier on the other side. In prose, John Pendleton Kennedy and William Gilmore Simms depicted the happiness of the slaves in such glowing colors that they created a myth which has endured in the South down to the present era, as seen in the recent *Gone With the Wind* of Margaret Mitchell. The myth was, of course, not wholly myth. In the case of the house slaves, a kindly paternalism was certainly the general rule; on the tobacco plantations, working conditions were mild enough; but in the mass labor of the rice swamps, cane brakes, and cotton plantations where the Negroes worked in gangs under hired overseers paid to get the last erg of energy out of them, the myth bore almost no relation to the facts. And, unfortunately, the most pleasant relations between slave and master were always liable to interruption if the latter was obliged to economize, so that the dread of being "sold down the river" was almost as terrible to the slaves of Kentucky and Missouri as the reality was to those of Mississippi and Louisiana.

The southern comparison between chattel slavery and wage slavery suffered like the rest of the argument from oversimplification. In the first place, it confined its attention to purely economic factors, neglecting the northern laborer's opportunities for education and his enjoyment of civil rights; and in the second place, even in its own terms it falsified the situation by neglecting the distinction between static and dynamic conditions. Granting, for the sake of the argument, that the southern slave was on the average materially better off than the northern laborer, the status of the latter was still preferable because it was capable of improvement through individual effort. The slave's lot was hopeless; neither he nor his children could ever anticipate any substantial amelioration of it this side of Heaven.

The absence of all incentive to effort in slavery made the system terribly costly. It was currently estimated that it took at least two slaves to perform the work of one free laborer. Instead of recognizing that this inefficiency was an inevitable outgrowth of the slave system, made worse by the dense ignorance in which the Southerners, less wise than the Greeks and the Romans, insisted on keeping their slaves, an explanation was sought in the alleged inherent laziness and incompetence of the Negro.

THE DEFEAT OF FREE SPEECH

LIKE all ruling minority elites, the southern slave-owning oligarchy was fearful of public discussion and criticism. When in the early thirties the abolitionists began to mail their magazines into the South, the local postmasters illegally refused to deliver them. Amos Kendall of Kentucky, the postmaster general, took the position that the federal mails were in this one instance subject to state laws, and President Andrew Jackson of Tennessee sought to have Congress legalize the suppression—which Congress, for once remembering the First Amendment, refused to do. The abolitionist literature continued to be confiscated, however, by the southern postmasters on the ground that the very sending of it was a gross interference with southern rights. Governor McDuffie of South

Carolina declared that "The laws of every community should punish this species of interference with death without benefit of clergy." The South Carolina Legislature adopted a resolution calling upon the nonslaveholding states to suppress all abolition societies—a resolution actually endorsed by Governor Edward Everett of Massachusetts and Governor Marcy of New York. When in 1836 the Charleston Quakeress, Angelica Grimke, published in the North her *Appeal to Southern Women*, in which she begged them to use their persuasive influence to secure gradual emancipation, the answer of Charleston was to burn all the copies of her book on their arrival and to threaten the authoress with imprisonment should she ever return to her birthplace. For thirty years the South was kept insulated against every criticism of slavery. The old truth was strikingly illustrated, that he who enslaves others enslaves himself.

Southern politicians did their best to impose the same enforced silence on the rest of the nation. Their influence in the national House of Representatives was sufficient to secure the passage of the celebrated "Gag Rule" under which that body for nine years refused to consider any petitions concerning slavery—nine years during which Congressman John Quincy Adams of Massachusetts, no abolitionist but a friend of free speech, fought a singlehanded battle against the whole House until the oppressive rule was at last withdrawn.

From censorship to vigilanteism is psychologically only a step, both being based fundamentally on the same fear of free speech. The social system of the South rested in the last analysis on force, not consent, and the logic of the situation was quite inevitable. Lynchings began to appear in the South in the thirties, and although prior to the Civil War poor whites were more often the victims than Negroes, owing to the greater economic value of the latter, during the decade of the fifties thirteen Negroes were burned at the stake. It was no accident that the outrages upon the Mormons were much greater in slaveholding Missouri than elsewhere, or that the Missourians entered Kansas with pistol and bowie knife to control the ballot, precipitating a civil war that was a rehearsal of the greater war soon to come. Nor was it an accident that in 1856, after Congressman Preston Brooks of South Carolina had made his nearly murderous assault with a heavy cane upon Senator Sumner, unarmed and seated at his desk in the Senate chamber, only one congressman south of the Mason and Dixon line voted for the cowardly bully's expulsion. When Brooks resigned and returned to South Carolina, his admiring fellow-citizens gave a great banquet in his honor, presented him with a new cane bearing the inscription, "Use Knockdown arguments," and triumphantly re-elected him to Congress. Such was the level to which planter chivalry had sunk under the operation of lynch psychology.

Yet the Civil War was not to arrive without one last southern protest against slavery, based now not upon its injustice to the Negroes but upon its evil economic consequences to the once proud yeomanry degraded by slavery to the state of "poor whites." A few Southerners had awakened too late to a realization that in sacrificing the development of their mines, manufactures, and most of their agriculture to the single cause of cotton, they had been worshiping a hungry idol rather than a beneficent deity. George M. Weston and Daniel R. Goodlow both ventured a little timidly in 1857 to raise the question of the economic value of slavery. But there was nothing timid in the third work of that year, *The Impending Crisis* by Hinton Rowan Helper of North Carolina—the most violent attack upon slavery ever penned. The author cared nothing for the Negroes; his was the voice of the southern poor white, raised this once in all the years. Denied the vote, denied education, denied even an equal place in the churches, the southern poor white had at last in Hinton Helper an adequate spokesman whose words came from his pen scorching and flaming with the sense of injustice:

". . . Chevaliers of the lash, and worshippers of slavery, . . . your villainous institution has retarded the development of our commercial and manufacturing interest, . . . it has stifled the aspirations of inventive genius. . . . Fully advised, however, of your indigent circumstances, . . . we shall . . . in your behalf, make another draft on the fund of non-slaveholding generosity. . . . Though we have given you all the offices, and you have given us none of the benefits of legislation; though we have fought the battles of the South, while you were either lolling in your piazzas, or playing the tory, and endeavoring to filch from us the birthright of freedom; though you have absorbed the wealth of our communities in sending your own children to Northern seminaries and colleges, or in employing Yankee teachers to officiate exclusively in your own families, and have refused to us the limited privileges of common schools; though you have scorned to patronize our mechanics and industrial enterprises, and have passed to the North for every article of apparel, utility, and adornment; and though you have maltreated, outraged and defrauded us in every relation of life, civil, social, and political, yet we are willing to forgive and *forget you*, if you will but do us justice on a single count. . . .

"It is for you to decide whether we are to have justice peaceably or by violence, for whatever consequences may follow, we are determined to have it one way or the other. Do you aspire to become the victims of white non-slaveholding vengeance by day, and of barbarous massacres by the negroes at night? . . .

"Sirs, we would not wantonly pluck a single hair from your heads; but we have endured long, we have endured much; slaves only of the most despicable class would endure more. . . . Out of our effects you have long since overpaid yourselves for your negroes; and now, Sirs, you *must* emancipate them, or we will emancipate them for you. Every non-slaveholder in the South is, or ought to be, and will be, against you."

There was bitter truth in nearly every line of this diatribe. Its one weakness lay in its final identification of what ought to be with what will be. The class of nonslaveholding whites to whom Helper's book was addressed never even saw it, as its circulation was strictly forbidden in the South. Had they been permitted to read it, one may doubt whether it would have had the effect that its author intended. For the poor whites of the South, though they hated the planters, hated the Negroes still more as a rival class of protected labor. At the first hint of the Negro insurrection that Helper prophesied, racial ties would have reasserted themselves, and the poor whites and the planters would have made common cause as they did later under Reconstruction—aided and abetted by none other than Hinton Helper himself, who composed his later works, *Nojoque* and *Negroes in Negroland*, in order to "write the negro out of America . . . and out of existence."

The warnings of Goodlow, Weston, and Helper went unheeded.

The South remained solidly united in defense of slavery, with a few unimportant exceptions such as West Virginia, East Tennessee, and individual outlaws like Newt Kight of Ellisville, who said, "I jist aint mad at no Yanks," and set up in the heart of Mississippi "The Free State of Jones," suppressed almost as soon as it was born. By and large there was less deviation from the correct political line in the southern states than there is today in Nazi Germany or Soviet Russia. In the authoritative words of William E. Dodd, "No newspaper of any importance, no college or university professor, no prominent preacher, and no politician of any party offered effective resistance. . . . There was the most perfect agreement ever known in Anglo-Saxon history. Men thought the ideal social organization had been found." [5]

"THE GREAT PHYSICAL AND MORAL TRUTH OF SLAVERY"

MEN also thought that this ideal social organization, oligarchic, authoritarian, and standardized, was essentially democratic. All the external forms of American democracy were preserved: the triple division of powers among executive, legislative, and judiciary; a representative government, even though the representation was limited by property interests; rule by majority decision among those who possessed the suffrage; the principle of revocable contract. On the last point, the South was nearer than the North to the intent of such early radicals as Paine and Jefferson. That the original states had formed their union by a compact among them was a historical fact: the very name, "United States," implied a federated system; the Constitution had been adopted by the states, which in accepting it had never intended to give up their local sovereignty except to a limited degree. How far the limitation extended or just where the ultimate sovereignty resided was not made entirely clear in the Constitution, but voluntary entrance seemed to imply voluntary withdrawal, and the right of secession was asserted in Massachusetts during the War of 1812 and again during the Mexican War almost as violently as it was asserted, on other issues, in South Carolina. Webster's principle of indissoluble union, first urged by him in 1830, lacked conclusive historical sup-

[5] William E. Dodd, *The Cotton Kingdom* (1919), p. 79.

port, and in resisting it the South stood on its own traditional interpretation of the Constitution. Thus, the South could feel that it was fighting on behalf of the cherished democratic ideal of local self-government (or, in recent terminology, "self-determination"). No more ardent defender of "liberty," in this sense, ever existed than Alexander Stephens of Georgia, the ablest of the southern constitutional writers, and no word was more often on southern lips.

And yet the whole constitutional discussion of seventy years, during which the leading congressional debaters, Hamilton, Madison, Clay, Calhoun, and Webster, all changed back and forth in accordance with the economic interests involved, was, if not essentially barren, at least conducted in a barren manner on a legalistic and unreal plane. No conclusive answer was possible in terms of the argument: first, because the Founding Fathers had themselves been divided, and often uncertain of their own views, on the questions of indeterminable contract and the location of ultimate sovereignty; and second, because the Constitution, a result of compromise, permitted of opposite interpretations that were equally plausible.

The doctrine of states' rights unquestionably had a strong emotional appeal as a defense of one's homeland, the soil on which one had grown up, the ways of life with which one was familiar, but its equivalence to liberty was more than doubtful in states ruled politically and economically by small minority groups. The theory was not upheld in the South because of its constitutional merits or its democratic implications but because it afforded an adequate defense of the institution of slavery.

Alexander Stephens, as vice-president of the newly formed Confederacy, stated in unequivocal language that the immediate cause of the southern secession was simply and solely the slavery issue:

"The new Constitution has put at rest forever all the agitating questions relating to our peculiar institutions—African slavery as it exists among us—the proper status of the Negro in our form of civilization. This was the immediate cause of the late rupture and present evolution. Jefferson in his forecast, had anticipated this as the 'rock upon which the old union would split.' He was right. What was conjecture with him is now a realized fact. But whether he comprehended the great truth upon which that rock stood and stands may be doubted. The prevailing ideas entertained by him and most of the leading statesmen at the time of the formation of the old Constitution, were that the enslavement of the African was in violation of the laws of nature; that it was wrong in principle, socially, morally and politically. It was an evil they knew not well how to deal with, but the general opinion of the men of that day was that, somehow or other, in the order of Providence, the institution would be evanescent and pass away. . . . Those ideas, however, were fundamentally wrong. They rested upon the assumption of the equality of races. This was an error. It was a sandy foundation, and the idea of a government built upon it; when the 'storm came and the winds blew, it fell.'

"Our new government is founded upon exactly the opposite idea, its foundations are laid, its corner-stone rests upon the great truth that the Negro is not equal to the white man. That slavery—subordination to the superior race—is his natural and normal condition. This, our new government, is the first in the history of the world, based upon this great physical and moral truth."

Southern statesmen like Stephens considered the struggle between the South and the North to be that between a superior and an inferior civilization; but the southern clergy went much further and gave the conflict a cosmic, religious setting. In the division of the churches that developed between 1840 and 1860, the Roman Catholic and Episcopal churches, true to their authoritarian bias, generally tended at first in both the North and the South to support the institution of slavery on religious and moral grounds, while the truly Protestant churches early split in accordance with the economic beliefs of their sections. As the war approached, official Christianity on both sides took up the sword, as it has always done in similar crises.

The southern clergy, traditionally hostile to Jefferson, seized every opportunity to denounce the Declaration of Independence. After scornfully quoting its language, the Reverend Frederick A. Ross went on to declare in his *Slavery Ordained of God* (1857): "All this, every word of it, every jot and tittle, is the liberty and equality claimed by infidelity. God has cursed it seven times in France since 1793." Albert Taylor Bledsoe of the University of

Virginia in his influential *Essay on Liberty and Slavery* (1856) asserted, parroting Martin Luther, that the true equality was purely spiritual: "The poorest slave on earth possesses the inherent and inalienable right to serve God according to his own conscience; and he possesses it as completely as the proudest monarch on his throne." "It is not simply a contest between different forms of civil polity or of civilizations," declared a southern Baptist minister, quoted in the Charleston *Mercury*, November 17, 1860. "It is a conflict between divine revelation and human reason—between the Providence of God and the devices of man." The very phrasing, as well as the ideas, of autocratic John Cotton were thus echoed, after two hundred years, in autocratic South Carolina.

Because through the united efforts of the leaders of southern thought slavery had been successfully romanticized, moralized, and made an article of religion, the eight million white population of the South fought for four years to defend the property interests of three hundred and fifty thousand.

CHAPTER 30 . *The Northern Faith Militant*

THE nineteenth century abolitionist movement was in the beginning only a continuation of the old Quaker protest. The Friends were never long silent on the subject of slavery. Petition after petition was sent to the early Congresses begging for such indirect control of the slave trade as was possible under the Constitution. After the nominal abolition of the trade in 1808, the church as an organized body was somewhat less active, but its members, as individuals or groups, continued for many years to furnish the nucleus of the slowly growing opposition to the whole institution of slavery.

The first to organize antislavery societies and the first to publish an abolitionist paper was the young New Jersey Quaker, Benjamin Lundy. Apprenticed in his youth to a saddler at Wheeling in western Virginia, a center of the slave trade, in his four years there he saw enough of the evils of slavery to determine him to devote his life to its overthrow. Settling temporarily in St. Clairsville, Ohio, at the age of twenty-six he organized there in 1815 "The Union Humane Society," the precursor of hundreds of similar groups to be established by him during the next twenty years. As a believer in gradual emancipation to be effected by persuasion, he labored at first among the Quakers in Virginia, North Carolina, Tennessee, and Kentucky, the Border States which furnished the overwhelming majority of the antislavery societies established during the

453

twenties. Meanwhile, in 1821, he began to edit at Mount Pleasant, Ohio, *The Genius of Universal Emancipation*, issued first as a monthly but after 1824 as a weekly. In 1828, being attracted by the vigorous editorials in a small paper published in the village of Bennington, Vermont, by a young temperance advocate named William Lloyd Garrison, Lundy walked three hundred and some miles from Baltimore to Bennington to secure Garrison's aid in his own cause. There was a notable meeting of minds, except that Garrison had no faith in the colonization efforts which Lundy mildly supported. When they could reach no agreement on that particular point, Lundy said, "Well, thee may put thy initials to thy articles, and I will put my witness to mine, and each will bear his own burden," and on those terms the two came together.

The gentle Quaker quickly learned that he had brought a fiery Hebraic prophet into his camp. Garrison, no respecter of persons, was soon in jail for seven months for the crime of printing the name of a highly respected merchant of Newburyport who was secretly engaged in the coast slave traffic. Next, as a result of Garrison's more outspoken policies, Lundy himself was attacked and nearly killed by a slavedealer named Austin Woolfolk. The office of the paper moved peripatetically through Baltimore, Washington, and Philadelphia, and its name was changed to *The National Inquirer* and then to *The Pennsylvania Freeman*, but neither the perfect title nor the perfect location was found. Garrison's language continuing too violent for Lundy's taste, their collaboration ceased after three years, although their mutual regard never lapsed. To Lundy's influence Garrison was permanently indebted for his policy of passive resistance and political nonco-operation. The question of slavery, as they saw it, was purely a moral one, and theirs was the task of rousing the conscience of the nation against it. They would not degrade their mission by associating it with the intrigues of political parties. But Lundy's temperament was pacific, Garrison's militant; the one used persuasion, the other denunciation; and so their ways parted.

In 1831 Garrison started his own paper, *The Liberator*, which was to exercise far more influence than *The Genius of Universal Emancipation* ever had. This was partly because Garrison was to confine himself to the single issue, exercising the concentrated power of a magnet, whereas the tolerant Lundy had thrown the pages of his paper open to all sorts of causes, thereby dissipating his strength; and partly because Garrison succeeded much better than Lundy in tying up antislavery with the tradition of American liberty. In a prospectus issued before the first appearance of *The Liberator*, he made a ringing declaration of principles:

"I shall assume, as self-evident truths, that the liberty of a people is a gift of God and nature:—That liberty consists in an independency upon the will of another:—That by the name of slave we understand a man who can neither dispose of his person or goods, but enjoys all at the will of his master:—That no man can have a right over others, unless it be by them granted to him. . . . That that which is not just is not law; and that that which is not law, ought not to be in force. . . . That the right to be free is a truth planted in the hearts of men, and acknowledged so to be by all that have hearkened to the voice of nature."

This was in both manner and matter a reassertion of the Jeffersonian theory of natural rights, coupled with the Quaker appeal from law to justice, from man to God. The original spirit of the Reformation was once more reborn, and the old struggle between freedom and power was renewed almost in its original terms. Where the proslavery writers pointed to the authority of the Bible and the churches and the laws of the state, the abolitionists went behind these outward forms to appeal to the individual conscience and the higher law of morality supposed to be written in the nature of God and man. In combining the moral force of the Reformation with the equalitarianism of the Enlightenment, Garrison drew together the strongest dynamic traditions of the seventeenth and eighteenth centuries and stood forth as the successor of Jefferson.

A fundamental change came over the spirit of the antislavery movement during the thirties. Theretofore slavery had been regarded as a misfortune which the South had inherited but for which it was not morally responsible; thereafter, slavery was considered a crime wickedly defended by southern self-interest. Although the new attitude was much influenced by Garrison, who expressed it perfectly, it developed mainly in response to changing outward conditions. In 1829 slavery was abolished in Mexico, and a strong movement for emancipation in Cuba was only checked by a notification to Spain from the United States government under Andrew Jackson that the abolition of Cuban slavery would not be permitted by the United States government. The revelation that there was less regard for human liberty in the States than in despised Latin America brought a natural feeling of shame to northern liberals. Then in 1833 the long efforts of Wilberforce in England were crowned with success, and slavery was abolished in the British West Indies. This left the United States as the only nation in North America in which the institution was still preserved. Americans, at least in the North, suddenly realized that after leading the world in political progressivism at the time of the Revolution, the nation had now fallen behind even the rest of its own continent. The utter incompatibility between democracy and slavery stood out more starkly than ever before. At the same time, the newly militant attitude of the South in defense of its peculiar institution made the former spirit of tolerance much more difficult, if not impossible. The South assumed full responsibility for slavery by endorsing the evil thing and striving to perpetuate and extend it. When thus deliberately upheld, the institution ceased to be a mere misfortune and became a crime.

The most powerful class in the community was arrayed against the abolitionists because the representatives of commerce and industry considered that the antislavery movement was likely to interfere with their southern trade. One of many similar editorials in James Gordon Bennett's New York *Herald* may be taken as an example of the fascist creed proclaimed by the commercial organs:

"What business have all the religious lunatics of the free states to gather in this commercial city for purposes which, if carried into effect, would ruin and destroy its prosperity? . . . Public opinion should be regulated. . . . When free discussion does not promote the public good, it has no more right to exist than a bad government that is dangerous and oppressive to the common weal. It should be overthrown. On the question of the usefulness to the public of the packed, organized meetings of these abolitionists, socialists, Sabbath-breakers, and anarchists, there can be but one result arrived at by prudence and patriotism. They are dangerous assemblies—calculated for mischief, and treasonable in their character and purposes."

At the other end of the social scale were the mobs, easily amenable to such incitements to violence as those in the *Herald*, and particularly resentful of the abolitionist attempt to set up the Negroes as their equals. Double victims of mob-minded businessmen and business-minded mobs, the abolitionists received little protection from the police or the courts, who were disposed as usual to favor the cause of property.

It is unnecessary to mention more than a few of the outrages that for a decade played havoc with the constitutional right of free speech. Dr. Reuben Crandall, brother of Prudence Crandall, was held for eight months without trial in a prison in Georgetown, District of Columbia, simply for possessing abolitionist literature; the hardships he endured during this period so broke his health that he died soon after release. The printing office and press of James G. Birney in Cincinnati were thrice demolished by mobs. Antislavery meetings were broken up in New York, in New Haven —where Yale students headed the mob—and in Boston, where Garrison was dragged through the streets with a rope round his neck. Pennsylvania Hall, erected in Philadelphia as a forum for free discussion, was burned by a mob the day after it was completed; a Negro church and hall in the same city were destroyed, and many Negro homes were burned or looted in a two days' race riot. The escaped slave, Frederick Douglass, one of the ablest of abolitionist writers,[1] was nearly killed while attempting to speak in Pendleton, Illinois. The Reverend Elijah P. Lovejoy, a fearless abolitionist editor in Alton, Illinois, who refused to be driven out of the community by threats against his life, was murdered during a mob attack on his press.

During this dangerous period, the antislavery movement was essentially a New England movement. This appears clearly from a roll call of its leaders. The New England contingent included Garrison, Whittier, Lowell, Bronson Alcott, Theodore Parker, Horace Mann, Charles Sumner, Wendell Phillips, Thomas Wentworth Higginson, Samuel May, C. C. Burleigh, the Crandalls, Henry Ward Beecher, Edmund Quincy, Jonathan Sewall, Maria White,

---

[1] Douglass was a much better thinker and writer than Booker T. Washington. See *The Narrative of Frederick Douglass* (Boston: Published at the Anti-Slavery Office, 1845) and *My Bondage and My Freedom* (Syracuse, N.Y.: J. G. K. Truair, 1855).

Lydia Maria Child, without counting such fellow-travelers as Emerson, Thoreau, Longfellow, and others. In comparison with this solid phalanx, the membership in other states was scattering: from New York, Gerrit Smith, and Arthur and Lewis Tappan, New England born; Lundy from New Jersey; Lucretia Mott from Pennsylvania; the Grimke sisters from South Carolina; James G. Birney from Kentucky; Charles G. Finney, another New Englander by birth, and Asa Mahan in Ohio.

Harriet Martineau, who knew whereof she was speaking, wrote in 1838 that "A just survey of the whole world can leave little doubt that the abolitionists of the United States are the greatest people now living and moving in it." They were poor economists, they were bad political strategists, they were often fanatical, but they represented the old heroic strain in the American character. With utter unselfishness and undeviating courage, they gave their time, energy, money, and risked even their lives solely for the sake of social justice. In them, American idealism reached the highest point it ever attained.

On the other hand, the American labor movement, such as it was, remained more than cool toward the antislavery cause. For this unfortunate result, the abolitionists were themselves partly responsible. Garrison, in the first number of *The Liberator*, attacked the New England Association of Farmers, Mechanics, and Other Workingmen because of its efforts to "inflame the minds of our working classes against the more opulent and to persuade them that they are contemned and oppressed by a wealthy aristocracy." Utterly ignorant of economics, Garrison and most of his followers saw in slavery merely a form of race discrimination, whereas it was in reality even more a form of labor exploitation. But even had the abolitionists understood the true nature of slavery they could hardly have gained the support of northern labor without a long and intensive campaign. For the northern worker, like the southern poor white, looked upon the slave simply as a labor competitor. The Irish laborers tended to follow the lead of the Roman Catholic Church, which, through the mouth of such spokesmen as Orestes Brownson, sanctioned the institution of slavery. The German laborers, coming from an authoritarian background, were equally hostile or indifferent toward the abolitionist movement.

Both groups concentrated their efforts on securing a homestead law which, they fancied, would prove the salvation of labor by giving it an outlet in the West that would, at the same time, raise eastern wages. Concerned with the immediate problem of their own wages, they had no interest in broader humanitarian issues. Hermann Kriege, the German immigrant who is said to have gained the support of six hundred newspapers for his land reform program, was bitterly opposed to the abolitionists, while the Congress of Trade Unions, with one hundred and ten members, called by Wilhelm Weitling in Philadelphia in 1850, never even mentioned the subject of slavery in its long list of resolutions. Not until the formation of the class-conscious *Arbeiterbund* in 1853 by Joseph Weydemeyer, the friend of Karl Marx, did any part of organized northern labor protest against Negro slavery. In this respect, as in most others, the American labor movement lagged far behind that in England, where Marx's influence was very much stronger.

On an unlucky day in 1837 William Lloyd Garrison received a visit from that Putney firebrand, John Humphrey Noyes. Inspired by their talk, Noyes subsequently sent him a letter which Garrison promptly published, without the author's name, in *The Liberator* of October 20, 1837. This extraordinary communication read as follows:

"I am writing that all men should know that I have subscribed my name to an instrument similar to the Declaration of '76, renouncing allegiance to the government of the United States, and asserting the title of Jesus Christ to the throne of the world.

"I will give you the reasons for this 'wild' deed. When I wish to form a conception of the government of the United States (using a personified representation), I picture to myself a bloated, swaggering libertine, trampling on the Bible—its own Constitution—its treaties with the Indians—the petitions of its citizens; with one hand whipping a Negro tied to a liberty-pole, and with the other dashing an emaciated Indian to the ground. On one side stand the despots of Europe, laughing and mocking at the boasted liberty of their neighbor; on the other stands the Devil saying 'Esto perpetua.' . . ."

Having thus relieved his mind, John Humphrey Noyes went his own way with far other fish to fry; but Garrison, brooding over his strange visitor's declaration and watching year by year the federal government sink into southern control, at last decided that he, too, must reject the Constitution. In 1843 *The Liberator* began to carry on its masthead these words: "The compact which exists between the North and the South is a covenant with death and an agreement with Hell—involving both parties in atrocious criminality and should be immediately annulled."

Garrison's rash action alienated many of his closest followers, including Whittier, and split the abolitionist movement. The leadership of the majority passed to the less violent James Birney of Kentucky, ex-slaveholder, ex-member of the Kentucky and Alabama legislatures, a onetime officer of the Colonization Society who had long since outgrown such compromises and now looked to political action to secure general emancipation. Having lived for many years in the South, where he had labored vainly for restriction of the slave trade, Birney understood the aggressiveness of the southern temper and the meaning of the southern expansionist program. Long before Lincoln, he saw that the nation could not endure, half-slave and half-free. "There will be no cessation of conflict," he maintained, "until slavery shall be exterminated or liberty destroyed. Liberty and slavery cannot live in juxtaposition." [2] Thus, in spite of his moderate beginnings, Birney was in the end quite as radical as Garrison and much more of a statesman. Moral suasion, certainly, he said, but unless moral suasion led to some form of political or economic action it remained merely verbal. Hence he demanded the organization of a political party to attack slavery by all the legal means at hand.

To Garrison's uncompromising individualism this seemed another covenant with death, which was certain to infect the moral issue with the corruption of politics and was likely to result only in further futile gestures of the type which the Whigs and Democrats had already made too familiar. The political skepticism of the Garrisonians, which they shared with the Perfectionists and Transcendentalists, constituted a tremendous indictment of American democracy, but it was also an unconscious indictment of themselves, virtually admitting that they had no immediate program. The union

---

[2] Quoted in Jesse Macy, *The Anti-Slavery Crusade* (New Haven: Yale University Press, 1919), p. 38.

of Quakerism and Jeffersonianism broke down at this point. In the last analysis, Garrison was a Primitive Christian while Birney was a nineteenth century democrat. The strife between the two leaders became exceedingly bitter—so bitter indeed that long after their death it was continued retrospectively by their children.[3] On the immediate issue, Birney was victorious. The Liberty party was organized, nominated him for the presidency, and, although it polled only seven thousand votes in 1840, obtained sixty-five thousand four years later—still an insignificant number but indicating a remarkable growth.

In their second platform, the Liberty party stole a little of Garrison's thunder by boldly announcing their determination, as individuals or as officeholders, to regard the fugitive slave clause of the Constitution as being "utterly null and void." That the party should have grown sevenfold in four years, and that sixty-five thousand voters should thus publicly pledge themselves to disregard a part of the Constitution, seemed portentous enough.

Yet when Birney was incapacitated by a serious accident which tragically ended his political career, his party wandered in 1848 into the fold of the Free Soil Democrats, pledged only to resist the further extension of slavery, and led by that wily old politician, Martin Van Buren. Garrison's political skepticism seemed justified after all.

Next came the Compromise of 1850, formulated by Clay and supported by Webster, in which six out of the eight provisions favored the South, including the retention of slavery in the District of Columbia, the abnegation by the federal government of the right to interfere with the interstate slave trade, and the passage of a more effective fugitive slave law under which alleged slaves could be arrested without warrant and tried without jury before special commissioners who received a larger fee for extradition than for discharge. The most that could be said for the so-called "Compromise" from the northern viewpoint was that it secured the admission of California as a free state and gave the North a further breathing spell in which to increase its industrial lead. The Com-

[3] See W. P. and F. J. Garrison's *William Lloyd Garrison* (Boston: Houghton Mifflin and Company, 1894), and William Birney's *James G. Birney* (New York: D. Appleton and Company, 1890).

promise of 1850 was ridiculous as a final solution of the questions at issue, yet it was hailed throughout the nation as being exactly that; and it was followed by a two years' conspiracy of silence in Congress during which Whigs and Democrats refused even to mention the subject of slavery. The abolitionist cause had never seemed so hopeless as it did at this moment after thirty long years of agitation.

Suddenly the wintry silence was broken by the appearance of *Uncle Tom's Cabin,* first run as a serial in the Washington *National Era,* then immediately published in book form with a sale running into the millions, and soon translated into every civilized language. Almost the only part of the world where the book was not widely read was the southern section of the United States, a section which the author had particularly hoped to influence.

Harriet Beecher Stowe was the one great northern writer equipped by personal experience to understand slavery as it was. In her years in Cincinnati on one of the routes of the Underground Railway, she had opportunity to meet many an escaped slave and hear his story; she visited in Kentucky; she was in constant touch with direct reports of conditions in the deep South. In the writing of *Uncle Tom's Cabin* she showed her awareness not only of the plight of the slave but of that of the slaveholder, and she put into the mouths of the best of her southern characters all that could be said in defense of the institution. Her delineation of slavery was, of course, hostile, but not her delineation of the South. On the contrary, her contrast between the typical intolerance of Miss Olivia from New England and the typical generosity of St. Clair of New Orleans was decidedly unfavorable to her own section. Mrs. Stowe's obvious attempt throughout to be fair-minded was appreciated everywhere except in the South, and it had a vast deal to do with the success of her book. Modern writers of propaganda might learn much in this respect from *Uncle Tom's Cabin,* the most influential propaganda novel ever published.

Now that propagandist literature has once more come into favor, the time may be ripe for a revision of the derogatory estimate of *Uncle Tom's Cabin* with which the later nineteenth century critics more than counterbalanced the exaggerated praise accorded the work on its appearance. For there were unacknowledged reasons behind that derogatory estimate. The Civil War over and done with, once the bitterness of the Reconstruction Period was past, the sentiment of the nation set strongly toward a reconciliation of the sections, and anything that tended to reopen the old wounds was frowned upon. Furthermore, the smugness of the Gilded Age liked to believe not only that this is the best of all possible worlds, but that it always was the best, at least in that part of it contained between the Atlantic and Pacific oceans. Hence, out of deference to southern prejudice and northern optimism it became the fashion in the schools to deny all literary value to *Uncle Tom's Cabin* as a hopelessly untrue and sentimental story which had owed its extraordinary contemporary vogue solely to its timeliness. But the fact that this charge of sentimentalism originated in a period itself much more sentimental than that of Mrs. Stowe makes it suspect: for the true sentimentalist always regards as unseemly any attempt to translate generous emotion into action, preferring to cherish lofty emotions as a private source of pride and satisfaction, such as the ostensibly noble but quite fatuous sentiments abounding in Aldrich, Stedman, Stoddard, Cale Young Rice, and their sort.

The timeliness explanation of Mrs. Stowe's contemporary popularity will not hold water. Adequate possibly for America, where, conceivably, any fervent novel on the slavery issue might have sold a million copies within a year of publication, it certainly does not account for the vogue of *Uncle Tom's Cabin* in England and on the Continent. The English critics of that day, particularly, were not given to tossing light compliments across the Atlantic, nor were they at all excited about slavery; they were no subtler than the reviewers of our own day, but when they welcomed *Uncle Tom's Cabin* as the first great American novel they did so because of the genuine literary merits that they perceived, or at least thought they perceived, in the work. And such genuine merits it in truth possesses abundantly.

Uncle Tom's Cabin, as anyone will discover on rereading it, is, in the first place, an absorbingly interesting narrative. Mrs. Stowe knew how to tell a story—an art that many modern novelists of much greater intellect have forgotten, or never have learned. Events move rapidly in her writing, there is constant variety of scene and situation, the descriptions are vivid. After all, who can forget the escape of Eliza on the ice, the sale of Uncle Tom down the river, the charm of the St. Clair household, or the horrors of the Legree plantation? Melodramatic, yes—as Scott and Dumas, Dickens and the Brontës were melodramatic. Melodrama is a form of literature, not a denial of literature. It is the essential form of all pure narrative where the interest is primarily in action rather than in characterization.

Yet the drawing of character in *Uncle Tom's Cabin* is done with firm, broad strokes, without subtlety, indeed, but defining the author's types as she wished them to be defined. In literature types are quite as legitimate as individual sketches—witness Molière or Ben Jonson, or for that matter Homer—provided they realize the author's intention and are not simply caused by the failure to achieve an attempted individualization. In the case of *Uncle Tom's Cabin* the types were carefully selected to reveal slavery at its best and worst according to the locality and the kind of slave labor involved. The three sorts of slaveowner: the efficient and coldly kind Kentuckian, Shelby; the languorous, warmer hearted St. Clair of Louisiana; the villainous, transplanted New Englander of the cane swamp, Legree; and the correspondent types of Negro, George the rebel, Uncle Tom the pious Christian, Topsy the incarnation of Negro whim and irresponsibility, Sam the informer, and Sambo the brutal agent of Legree: all these are clearly marked and distinguished. Intended to be unchanging representative types, they are, of course, too consistent ever to have been encountered in the flesh; but they live in the book, and at least three of them, Legree, Topsy, and Uncle Tom, live on in the American memory as part of its traditional furnishing. Of how many other characters in American fiction can the same be said?

Uncle Tom's Cabin was the first American social novel of great importance, holding in germ all our later literature, the first to depict the many-sided life of an entire section of the country, the first to take advantage of the objective opportunities of fiction in drawing characters from observation instead of by imaginative projection from within, the first to attempt realistic dialogue taken from speech rather than from books, the first to develop the scattered sketches of Kennedy, Caruthers, and Longstreet into a unified whole.

The essential truth of its picture was long denied by southern writers, but latterly has been unconsciously affirmed by a newer group of southern novelists whose own report of the later treatment of the Negro in the South is far more bitter than anything to be found in the writing of Mrs. Stowe. In fact, her prudence, or perhaps her prudery, caused her to leave untouched the most abhorrent feature of slavery—the fairly constant miscegenation that brought with it the unacknowledged parenthood of mulatto children. The evils which she did deal with—the activities of the slave-traders, the separation of families, the dreaded "sale down the river," the floggings, and the use of bloodhounds—were all matters of common knowledge. That the book contains many exaggerated and mawkish passages, especially in the interpolated moralizings, must, of course, be admitted. Little Eva may be dismissed to join the company of Little Nell and Elsie Dinsmore in the limbo of impossible children. But as a whole, *Uncle Tom's Cabin* remains, what it was meant to be, a convincing indictment of the evils prevalent, though by no means universal, under the slave system.

Harriet Beecher Stowe's personal solution of the slavery problem, advanced in her less successful second novel, *Dred, A Tale of the Great Dismal Swamp* (1857), was akin to an idea of Frances Wright's, consisting in a scheme of gradual emancipation for which the slaves were to be educated by their masters. Whatever the merits of the conception, the time for it was past by at least thirty years. While the author of *Uncle Tom's Cabin* was developing her hopelessly moderate program, her first work was having an effect the very opposite of that which she had desired. It embittered the South, and it made innumerable northern converts to the cause of immediate emancipation. Harriet Stowe had portrayed the evils of slavery only too powerfully. The moral injustice of the system had burned itself indelibly into her pages. After the appearance of *Uncle Tom's Cabin* silence on the subject of slavery was no longer possible. Mrs. Stowe, who was not an abolitionist in either the Garrison or Birney sense of the word, had done more for their cause than all of them put together. It was an unanswerable reply to the fugitive slave law in the Compromise of 1850. And as soon as the North had recovered from its momentary relief at the passage of that measure, and southern agents hot on the trail of their slaves began to appear and demand northern co-operation in hunting down their unfortunate victims, the moral indignation of the North, kindled anew by *Uncle Tom's Cabin*, flamed forth in the almost open activity of the Underground Railway.

That boldest of all the measures adopted for the relief of the slaves dated from the early twenties. It originated in the successful efforts of certain North Carolina Quakers to transport to the free states a few individual Negroes who were the victims of especially flagrant injustice. The first of these was a free Negro kidnaped into slavery, who was rescued by the Quakers at considerable danger to themselves; the second was a freedman who fled to them for refuge, because he was about to be returned into bondage by court order owing to the breaking of the will under which he was manumitted; a third was a slave who had been treated with exceptional inhumanity by a cruel master. The Quakers who saved them were of course violating the statutes, but this mattered little to the more zealous members of a sect which had always placed the unwritten law of conscience above state enactments. Levi Coffin, a North Carolina Quaker settled in Newport, Indiana, became the receiving agent upon whom devolved the duty of helping the fugitives on toward Canada along a chain of friendly houses and farms. He kept a special horse and wagon for these journeys, always made at night along unfrequented roads, and hardly a week went by when he was not thus engaged for a part of his time. Coffin was often called "the president of the Underground Railroad," but there was no formal organization of this strictly illegal and highly dangerous traffic. Rather, there were many men in various parts of the North who gradually took up the work, and there were many underground railroads. Of the other leaders besides Coffin, the most important were William Still and William Whipple of Philadelphia, Thomas Downing and James McCune Smith of New York, William Rich of Troy, Stephen J. Myers of Albany, and J. W. Loguen of Syracuse. The invisible tracks of one railroad ran through Philadelphia to New York and thence up the Hudson and along Lake Champlain; another deviated at New York to run up the Connecticut River and along the Green Mountains; another went through the mountains of Pennsylvania and the western lake region of New York to Niagara Falls; others through Ohio, Indiana, or

Illinois to the Great Lakes; still another from St. Louis to Lawrence, Kansas, and thence to Keokuk, Iowa, where the fugitive was in comparative safety. For thirty years the number of slaves thus rescued increased slowly but steadily until in the fifties it went up by leaps and bounds so that many hundreds and possibly thousands of Negroes were escaping from bondage each year.

And yet it proved impossible to obtain legal evidence to convict any of the leaders in this lawless humanitarian enterprise, well-known though their activities were. The general sentiment of the North was behind them. If a slave had enough courage and energy to escape, it was felt that he richly deserved his freedom. Emerson, for example, was not a violent person, but the day that he read the Fugitive Slave Act he wrote in his journal, "By God, I will not obey it!" There were thousands who made the same vow as Emerson.

Although the slavecatchers in the North were not treated as the abolitionists were in the South, the attitude toward them was not unsimilar. The fugitive slave law proved a boomerang, coming to be regarded in the North as an establishment of the slave system within free territory. So strong was this feeling that in 1851 a recaptured fugitive slave named Shadrach was openly rescued in Boston—the city where, fifteen years before, Garrison had been nearly lynched, and in 1854 Thomas Wentworth Higginson led an attack on the jail in an unsuccessful attempt to rescue the fugitive slave, Anthony Burns. Thus the North, like the South, moved toward direct action.

This meant only that the North was at last united in its determination to resist any further extension of slavery. Not a single northern leader of any importance—with the single exception of the religious fanatic, John Brown of Osawatomie—ever countenanced the idea of imposing the system of free labor on the South. When Brown formed his mad scheme of inciting a slave insurrection at Harpers Ferry, he deemed it necessary to conceal his design even from his antislavery friends by the plea that he was simply raising arms and money to continue the struggle for the freedom of Kansas. But since, as pointed out earlier, the economics of slavery made its preservation dependent upon its expansion, the purely defensive attitude of the North amounted, practically, to an offensive.

Once the southern planters had lost their struggles for California and Kansas, no alternatives remained open to them except either to resign themselves to a position of political and economic inferiority, or to carry their states into a secession which, if successful, would open the way to exploitation of the Caribbean. With their psychology already geared to a program of militarism and their class interest vitally at stake, it is not surprising that the southern political leaders made the second choice, even though it involved a war of less than eight million people against twenty-two million.

It is easy to argue today that the war was foolish on both sides. Slavery was doomed in any case owing to its economic waste and inefficiency. Sooner or later, the South would have been forced to abandon it on its own initiative, and such voluntary emancipation would have had far better consequences for both whites and blacks, avoiding the devastation of war and the tragedy of the Reconstruction Period. Financially, it would have been cheaper for the North to have bought all the slaves at the highest price asked for them, cheaper for the South to have paid the North to take them. The centralized power of the federal government that resulted from the war was immediately seized by industrial capitalism, producing new class divisions and inequalities. During the actual conflict, war profiteering flourished on a hitherto unheard of scale. Civil liberties were in abeyance, and were never afterwards fully recovered. The war was in no sense a people's war: on both sides, after the initial enthusiasm had waned, conscription was adopted, thus introducing into American democracy that most undemocratic of customs, derived from Napoleon, which makes it legal to send good citizens to their death without their consent— and introducing it with the most flagrant concessions to wealth by permitting the payment of substitutes in the North and by exempting in the South the large planters in whose interest the conflict was fought. Finally the war in itself involved a rejection of the principle of peaceful discussion and compromise which was so essential a part of the democratic faith.

And yet the contemporary rhetoric of the struggle was not merely rhetoric. The war was more than a power war, more even than an economic war. Those who look upon it as the latter—which happens to be the fashionable attitude at the moment—are guilty of the same fallacy of abstraction as were those who at the time looked upon it as solely a moral struggle. Even so excellent a historian as Charles Beard has given countenance to the fallacy in such statements as, "It took more than a finite eye to discern where slavery as an ethical question left off and economics—the struggle over the distribution of wealth—began"—as if the distribution of wealth were not also an ethical question. The isolation of economics from morals and politics had been the central weakness in American democracy which made the Civil War inevitable: not inevitable, of course, had men been wholly rational, but inevitable, men being as they were. But although the war was a devastating revelation of democratic weakness, it was also a belated reassertion of democratic strength: political and moral principles *were* involved; and the triumph of the North insured the survival of the basic American tradition in however mutilated a form.

It is quite true that the war was nominally fought on the issue of union versus secession, not the slavery issue; and that on the constitutional point of the "right of secession," the arguments of the South were at least as good as those of the North; but beyond the legalistic contentions was the stubborn fact that to continue to allow the interests (or the supposed interests) of three hundred thousand planters to control the destiny of thirty millions would have been a *reductio ad absurdum* of the democratic principle of majority rule. It is also true that the North was much more divided in attacking slavery than was the South in defending it; and that Lincoln, desirous of the support, or at least the neutrality, of the Border States, made no move against slavery for two whole years. But again, behind all this, was the unquestionable fact that slavery was the real cause of the war. If the songs of a people are more significant than its laws, it cannot be overlooked that the popular northern war songs were "John Brown's Body," "The Battle Hymn of the Republic" with its climactic line—"As He [Christ] died to make men holy, let us die to make men free"—and "We Are Coming, Father Abraham . . . To lay us down, for Freedom's sake. . . ." That the North believed it was fighting for freedom will not be denied; that it actually was fighting for freedom, though often doubted today, was equally true. Indeed, the North could with reason have claimed that it was fighting not only for the liberty of the Negro, but for that of every white man in the South deprived, with or without his own consent, of the basic human right of individual opinion. Once again, as so often before in American history, the cause of the individual was tied up with the cause of the many. Liberalism and democracy, the two ideal values for which America had stood, were genuinely at stake in the Civil War, and the outcome of the war determined that they should be preserved, maimed indeed but still living, to be transmitted to the future as the main articles of American faith.

Index

Abolitionists, 445, 453-462, 467
Adams, Henry, 12
Adams, John, 217, 226, 249, 263, 264, 266, 269, 273, 279, 284, 293, 302
Adams, John Quincy, 312, 427, 428, 446
Adams, Samuel, 226, 260, 261, 263, 275, 284, 289
Adventurers, see Merchant Adventurers
Ainsworth, see Separatists
Alabama, 436
Albigensian, see Cathars
Alcott, Bronson, 183, 378, 381, 382, 383, 400, 404, 412, 413, 414, 415, 425, 431
Alden, John, 104, 114, 118
Alden, Priscilla, 136
Alien and Sedition Acts, 301
Allen, Ethan, 226, 231, 232
Allerton, Isaac, 108, 114, 118
Althusius, Johannes, 238
Ambrose, Saint, 29, 30
Ambrosiaster, 29
American Alien Law, 141
American Capitalism, 85, 86, 89, 299, 374, 429, 468
American Church History Series, 10, 17, 332
American Civil Liberties Union, 106
Ames, William, 125
Amish, 199
Anabaptism, Anabaptists, 52-55, 75, 129, 401; origin of, 52; transformation into Baptists, 55-57
Andrews, Charles M., 84, 109, 124, 132
Andros, Sir Edmund, 161, 162
Angell, Thomas, 134
Anglican Church and Anglicanism,

American, 123, 219; in Virginia, 94, 95, 96; Church of England, 47, 57, 60, 61, 62, 72, 75, 78, 95, 128, 219, 220; Ecclesiastical Commission, 72, 73
Anthony, Susan, 431
Anti-Federalist Party, 299, 300, 301
Aquinas, Thomas, 18, 19, 23, 164
Archdale, John, 183
Argall, Sir Samuel, 92, 94
Aristotle, 219, 230, 240
Arnold, Benedict, 268
Articles of Confederation, 289, 290
Arundell, Sir Thomas, 171
Asbury, Francis, 327, 328
Ashton, Robert, 105
Athanasian Creed, 31, 32
Augustine, Saint, 18, 30, 31, 32, 44, 64
Auricular Confession, 23, 40, 47, 61

Backus, Isaac, 217
Bacon, Leonard Woolsey, 17, 136
Bacon, Nathaniel, 97
Bacon, Roger, 39
Ballou, Adin, 374-377, 410
Baltimore, Lord, see Calverts
Baptism, 27, 29, 30, 36, 38, 46, 53, 95, 158; adult, 10, 36, 52, 57; infant, 27, 31, 52, 56, 57, 156, 158, 330, 334
Baptists, 9, 52, 56, 106, 176; affiliation of Campbellites, 335; colleges, 330; in America, 96, 130, 149, 170, 216, 217, 329, 330, 425; in England, 57, 58, 78, 179; persecution of, 156, 157
Barclay, Robert, 226
Barlow, Joel, 226
Barnard, Henry, 429

Barrowe, Henry, 77
Bates, Paulina, 422
Bax, Belfort, 21, 54
Baxter, Rev. Richard, 69, 70, 125, 165, 181
Beard, Charles, 9, 116, 123, 243, 251, 289, 469
Becker, Carl Lotus, 240
Beecher, Edward, 323
Beecher, Lyman, 323, 372, 427
Bellamy, Joseph, 214
Bellarmine, Robert, 238
Bellers, John, 370
Bellomont (Richard Coote, Earl of), Governor, 254
Benezet, Anthony, 204, 429
Bennett, James Gordon, 456
Berengar of Tours, 31
Berkeley, Sir William, 97
Beston, Henry, 95
Biddle, Nicholas, 314
Birney, James, 460, 461
Birney, William, 460
Bledsoe, Albert Taylor, 451
Blue Laws, 95, 154
Bodin, Jean, 238
Bogart, Ernest L., 433
Bohler, Peter, 324
Book of Common Prayer (English Prayer Book), 61, 72, 107, 109
Bora, Katherine, 47
Boston, 83, 115, 117, 119, 120, 123, 126, 128, 133, 168, 425; Port Bill, 262; tea dumpings, 261
Boyle, James, 395
Braddock, Gen. Edward, 265
Bradford, William, 104-118, 130, 131, 132, 134, 195
Brattle, Thomas, 166, 168
Brattle, William, 168
Brend, William, 158
Brewster, William, 104, 106-110, 114, 116, 118, 130
Brisbane, Albert, 386, 387, 388
Brisbane, Arthur, 387
Brook Farm, 374, 375, 378-380, 387, 388, 389
Brooks, Van Wyck, 379
Browne, Robert, 74-77, 105, 124
Brownism, *see* Robert Browne
Brownson, Orestes, 387, 404, 429, 458
Bulkeley, Peter, 144
Burke, Edmund, 305
Burling, William, 204
Burrage, Champlin, 77

Burritt, Elihu, 432
Burroughs, Rev. George, 163, 166
Busher, Leonard, 130
Butzer, Martin, 25
Byllinge, Edward, 186, 187
Byrd, William, 97

Caine, Hall, 21
Calderwood, David, 109
Calef, Robert, 167, 168
Calhoun, Arthur W., 90
Calhoun, John C., 441, 450
Callender, James, 301
Calverton, V. F., 51, 195
Calverts, The, 172-175, 190
Calvin, John, 28, 34, 54, 63-70, 74; theology, 64, 65, 66
Calvinism, 51, 62, 64-71, 75, 78, 116, 117, 167, 219, 220, 332, 409; ideal of government, 125-126
Calvinists, *see* Calvinism
Cambridge Platform of 1648, 70, 159
Campbell, Alexander, 333-336, 360
Campbell, J., 442
Campbell, Thomas, 333, 334, 335, 336
Campbellites, *see* Disciples
Camp Meetings, 337-340, 391
Carlstadt, Andreas, 48, 49
Carmer, Carl, 256
Carolinas (North and South), 83, 86, 87, 100, 183, 251, 252, 253, 273, 282, 283, 436, 440-444, 452, 453
Carroll, John, 321
Carter, James, 429
Carteret, Sir George, 187
Cartwright, Peter, 328, 338, 340
Cartwright, Thomas, 74
Carver, Gov. John, 104, 111
Cathars, 34-38, 46, 129, 176
Catholicism, Roman, and Catholic Church, 17-20, 25, 26, 29, 31-34, 38, 43, 47, 48, 52, 53, 61, 63, 66, 74, 78, 86, 125, 156, 173, 174, 175, 181, 223, 237, 267, 268, 321, 361, 451
Cavalier, Jean, 361
Cavaliers, 90
Celibacy of Clergy, 22, 31, 40, 47, 61
Ceremonies of Church, 19, 27, 31, 36, 56, 138, 325; attacks on, 31; the Lord's Supper, 31, 36, 38, 61
Chalkley, Capt. Thomas, 202
Channing, Edward, 163
Channing, W. H., 387, 388, 404
Channing, William Ellery, 401-404
Chaucer, Geoffrey, 41

Chauncy, Charles, 159, 211, 222
Christians, *see* Disciples
Church of Latter Day Saints, *see* Mormonism
Civil War, 11, 86, 90, 267, 447, 470
Clapp, Thomas, 225
Clark, John, 156, 157
Clark, Joseph, 232
Clarke, James Freeman, 402, 413
Clay, Henry, 312-315, 450
Clement, Travers, 368
Cluny Reform, 18
Clyfton, Richard, 105, 106
Coddington, Judge William, 139, 141, 144, 146, 149
Coffin, Levi, 466
Cohen, Morris R., 239
Coke, Thomas, 327
Colby, John, 330
Colden, Lt. Gov. Cadwallader, 254
Coleman, Elihu, 204
Communism, 54, 86; at Plymouth, 113, 114; medieval, 113; Moravian, 55
Communistic Communities in U.S., *see* Shakers, Owenites, Fourierists, Oneida Community
Congregationalism, Congregational Church, 52, 74, 75, 77, 95, 105, 119, 123, 124, 152, 169, 217
Connecticut, 83, 119, 128, 151-154, 161, 214; founding of New Haven, 154; "Fundamental Orders" of Constitution, 152, 153; liberalism and reaction in, 151-154; settlements, 152
Considérant, Victor Prosper, 386
Constitutional Convention, 289-293, 296, 435
Constitution of U.S., 85, 188, 248, 283, 292, 296, 297, 449, 450, 451
Continental Congress, 263, 264, 265, 267, 278, 284, 288, 293
Coode, John, 175
Cooper, Thomas, 301, 441
Corey, Giles, 166
Corey, Martha, 166
Cotton, John, 10, 11, 121, 124, 125, 126, 128, 132, 134, 137, 140, 142-145, 154, 155, 157, 452
Council for New England, *see* Virginia Company
Covenant of Grace, 140, 142
Covenant of Works, 140, 142
Coverdale, Miles, 61
Cowdery, Oliver, 344, 346-350
Crandall, John, 156, 157

Cranmer, Thomas, 62
Creighton, Mandell, 57
Curti, Merle, 429

Dabney, Virginius, 280
Dale, Sir Thomas, 92
Dana, Charles A., 379
Dante Alighieri, 18, 24, 25
Dare, Virginia, 87, 88
Davenport, John, 124, 154, 159
da Vertazano, Giovanni, 133
Davis, Andrew Jackson, 422, 423
Dawson, Henry B., 287
de Cassolis, Jacobus, 24
Declaration of Faith (1611), 57
Declaration of Independence, 9, 170, 265, 273-280, 435, 451
Declaration of Religious Tolerance, 102
Defoe, Daniel, 70
Deism, Deists, 11, 193, 218, 223-226, 233, 304, 305, 307; Benjamin Franklin a Deist, 226-230; danger of, 225; Ethan Allen's Deism, 231, 232; Jefferson's, 304; leaders of Revolution, 226; Paine a Deist, 307; rise of, 218, 219
Delaware, 161, 283
Democracy, 9, 12, 75, 85, 102, 103, 121, 125, 449, 450, 456, 460, 469, 470
Denck, Hans, 55, 56
Dennie, John, 306
Dew, Thomas R., 439
Dewey, John, 193
Dewsbury, William, 180
Dexter, H. M., 157
Dickinson, John, 263
Diet of Spires, 53
"Directory of Church Government," 74
Disciples (Christians), 321, 323, 333, 336, 337, 360
"Divine Right of the King," 125
"Divine Right of the Pope," 125
Dix, Dorothea, 430
Doctrine of Natural Rights, 238, 239, 244, 245, 246
Dodd, William E., 439, 441, 449
Doddridge, Joseph, 438
"Dominion of New England," 161
Douglas, Frederick, 457
Dow, Col. Neil, 428
Draper, Ebenezer R. and George, 377
Dred Scott Decision, 277, 278
Du Bois, W. E. B., 439
Dudley, Joseph, 141, 142, 143, 162
Dunbar, William, 24
Dunster, Pres. Henry, 157, 158

Dürer, Albrecht, 26
Dwight, J. S., 404
Dwight, Sereno Edwards, 212, 213
Dwight, Timothy, 214, 231, 278, 304
Dyer, Mrs. Mary, 145, 146

Eaton, Nathaniel, 158
Eaton, Theophilus, 154
Eck, John, 45
Eddy, Mary Baker, 368, 414
Edwards, Jonathan, 207-214, 247; philosophy, 207-210; sermons, 210, 211; "The Great Awakening," 211, 212
Edwards, Jonathan, Jr., 214
Edwards, Morgan, 217
Eliot, George, 417
Eliot, John, 128, 132
Elkins, Hervey, 422
Ellsworth, Oliver, 294
Emerson, Ralph Waldo, 144, 264, 378, 380, 381, 383, 406-409, 411, 414, 416, 420, 429
Emmons, Nathaniel, 214
Emmott, Elizabeth Braithwaite, 181, 198
Encyclopedists, 243, 245
Endicott, John, 120
Episcopacy, *see* Anglican Church
Episcopius, Simon, 107
Erasmus, Desiderius, 45, 48, 65
Established Church, *see* Anglican Church
Etzler, J. A., 411
Evans, Frederick W., 362, 363
Evans, George Henry, 428
Evans, John Henry, 344
Everett, Gov. Edward, 446

Farel, William, 65
Fascism, 11, 86
Fay, Bernard, 231
Federalists, 298, 299, 301, 302
Fell, Judge Thomas, 179
Feudalism, 20, 21, 22, 25, 59, 78
Finney, Charles Grandison, 392
Fiske, John, 152
Fitzhugh, George, 442
Fletcher, J., 442
Flower, Enoch, 190
Fourier, Charles and Fourierism, 360, 364, 367, 374, 381, 384-389, 424
Fox, George, 177-183, 376
Fox, Margaret and Kate, 423
Franciscans, 18
Franklin, Benjamin, 220, 226-230, 263, 269, 282, 284, 289, 320

Franklin, James, 227
Freedom of Conscience, 9, 78, 142, 155, 174, 185, 186, 187, 225, 327, 410
Freedom of Speech, 9, 237, 301, 310, 445, 446, 457
French Political Theory, 242-247
Freneau, Philip, 226
Fretageot, Mme. Maria, 371
Fruitlands, 374, 381, 382, 383
Fuggers of Augsburg, 26
Fuller, Samuel, 119, 123

Gadsden, Christopher, 278
Gage, Gen. Thomas, 255
Gallaudet, Thomas Hopkins, 430
Galloway, Joseph, 263
Garrison, W. P. and F. J., 461
Garrison, William Lloyd, 410, 454-460
Gavin, Rev. Anthony, 95
Gay, Rev. Ebenezer, 221, 222
General Court, 115, 133, 140, 141, 143, 147, 151, 152, 158, 161, 168
Geneva Bible, 73
George the Third, 13, 241, 248, 271, 272, 275, 279
Georgia, 83, 84, 85, 253, 436
Godwin, Parke, 388
Goodlow, Daniel R., 447, 448
Goodwin children, 165
Gorges, Sir Fernando, 100-103, 121
Gorges, Robert, 100
Gorges, Thomas, 101, 102
Gorton, Samuel, 116, 146-149
Gratian, 25, 33
Grayson, William J., 444
"Great Awakening," 211, 212, 215, 216, 217, 219, 330
Greeley, Horace, 386, 388, 423
Greenwood, John, 77
Grimke, Angelica, 431, 446
Grimke, Sarah, 431
Grotius, Hugo, 238, 239
Guilds, 20, 22, 107
Guyer, Florian, 49

Halfway Covenant, 159, 213
Hall, Joseph, 105, 107
Hamilton, Alexander, 226, 289, 290, 291, 298, 300, 309, 450
Hamilton, Edith, 35
Hansard Knolly Society, 130
Harper, Chancellor William, 439, 441
Harris, Martin, 346, 347
Harrison, Gen. William Henry, 315
Harvard Corporation, 168

Hawthorne, Nathaniel, 378, 380, 414-417
Hayne, Robert, 238
Hell, 27, 58, 167, 402
Helper, Hinton Rowan, 447, 448
Helwys, Thomas, 57, 58, 107
Hendrix, David, 345
Henry, Patrick, 204, 261, 263, 273, 275, 278, 281, 289
Henry the Eighth, 60, 61, 62, 74
Hicks, Elias, 402
Higginson, Francis, 123, 128
Higginson, Thomas Wentworth, 467
Himes, Joshua, 425
Hobbes, Thomas, 238, 243
Hofmann, Melchior, 53
Holton, Harriet, 395, 396, 397
Holland, 54, 62, 75-78, 88, 106-109, 113, 115
Holmes, Obadiah, 156, 157
Hooker, Richard, 238
Hooker, Thomas, 128, 151-154
Hopedale Community, 374-378, 382
Hopkins, Samuel, 214
Howe, E. D., 347
Howe, Samuel Gridley, 430
Hubmaier, Balthasar, 55
Humanists, 45, 48, 221, 225
Hunter, Jacob, 55
Hus, John, 42, 47
Hussites, 34, 43, 46
Hutchinson, Anne, 135-146, 149, 154, 169
Hutchinson, Thomas, 149, 277
Hutchinson, William, 137, 138, 139, 145

Independents, *see* Separatists
Indians, 88, 101, 112, 114, 117, 128, 131, 132, 134, 150, 172, 183, 190, 195, 200, 267; massacre of 1622, 94; Mohegan, 148, 149; Narragansett, 134, 148
Indulgences, 23, 31, 38, 45, 47
"Inhabitants, The," 115
Innocent the Third, 18, 31, 37
Inquisition, 37

Jackson, Andrew, 312-316, 427, 445, 456
Jacobs, H. E., 61
James, William, 10, 176, 230
Jameson, J. Franklin, 259
James the First, 74, 93, 96, 109
Jay, John, 226, 262, 263, 267, 268, 278, 284
Jefferson, Thomas, 12, 170, 204, 226, 230, 273, 275, 278, 279, 280, 284, 289, 291, 293, 296, 299, 301, 302, 303, 307, 428, 442, 451; President of U.S., 304, 305,

306; theory of natural rights, 236, 276
Jennings, Walter Wilson, 438
Jerome of Prague, 42
Jesuits, 18, 171, 174, 238
John of Leyden (Johann Bockholdt), 54
Johnson, Francis, *see* Separatists
Johnson, Samuel, 220-223
Jonson, Ben, 73
Judson, Adoniram, 331
"Justification by Faith," 44, 45
"Justification by Works," 45
Justin Martyr, 18, 28, 31

Kant, Immanuel, 319, 404, 405, 418
Kennedy, John Pendleton, 444
Kentucky, 249, 435, 444, 453
King James Bible, 73
Knox, Gen. Henry, 288
Knox, John, 74

Lane, Charles, 382, 383
Langland, William, 41
Latimer, Hugh, 62
Laud, Archbishop, 123
Law, Andrew, 264
Lay, Benjamin, 204
Lechford, Thomas, 126
Lee, "Mother" Ann, 361-363, 383
Lee, Richard Henry, 263
Leisler, Capt. Jacob, 254
Leland, John, 232, 233
Leo the Great, 18
Lerner, Max, 33
Leverett, John, 140, 142, 168
Lincoln, Abraham, 283, 314, 469
Lloyd, David, 194, 195
Lobb, Stephen, 192
Locke, John, 237-244, 247, 248, 251, 296
Loe, Thomas, 184, 185
Lollards, 35, 39-42, 46, 55, 59, 129, 176
London Company, *see* Virginia Company
Lord, Arthur, 115
Lothrop, John, 138
Louisiana, 308, 436, 445
Loyalists, 266
Ludlum, David M., 424
Lundy, Benjamin, 453, 454, 455
Luther, Martin, 32, 34, 43-51, 53, 56, 61, 63, 245, 334
Lutheranism, Lutherans, 28, 52, 53, 66, 78, 266
Lyon, Matthew, 301

Macaulay, Thomas Babington, 191
Mack, Solomon, 345

Macy, Jesse, 460
Madison, James, 226, 273, 278, 290, 293, 299, 427, 428
Magna Charta, 236
Magnus, Albertus, 18
Maine, 99-103, 117, 172, 174
Mann, Horace, 412, 429, 430, 431
Manning, James, 217
Marcy, Gov. William Learned, 446
Mariana, Juan, 238
Maryland, 100, 171-175, 283
Mason, George, 273, 275, 276, 278
Mason, Capt. John, 103
Mass, 19, 38, 46, 47, 171
Massachusetts, 83, 85, 95, 102, 103, 117-146, 148, 155-162, 168, 172
Massachusetts Bay Company, *see* Massachusetts
Massasoit, Chief, 112, 134
Mather, Cotton, 157, 159, 160, 162, 164, 165, 166
Mather, Increase, 160, 164, 167
Matthiesen, Johann, 53, 56
Mayflower, The, 104, 110, 119, 120; Compact, 110, 111, 115, 119, 152
Mayhew, Jonathan, 222, 401
Melville, Alexander, 74
Melville, Herman, 202, 417
Melville, James, 74
Mennonites, Menno Simons, 56, 57, 75, 106, 199
"Mercantile Theory," 257
Merchant Adventurers, 109, 110, 113, 114, 118
Methodism, Methodists, 43, 215, 323-329, 332, 360, 425, 427
Miantonomo, Chief, 148, 149
Millerite Movement, William Miller, 424, 425, 426
Milton, John, 38, 148
Missouri, 446
Molasses Act, 259, 260; Sugar Act (revision of Molasses Act), 261
Monaghan, Frank, 262
Morais, Herbert, 232
Moravian Brethren, 43, 176, 199, 324
Morgan, Rev. Joseph, 71
Morison, Samuel, 163
Mormonism, Mormon Church, 341-358; polygamy, 85, 353, 356, 357; sexual motive, 391
Morris, Gouverneur, 262
Morris, Roger, 284
Morton, Thomas, 116, 117, 132
Motley, John L., 115

Muggleton, Lodowicke, 185, 186
Mumford, Lewis, 19, 21, 22
Münster, 53, 54
Münzer, Thomas, 49, 50, 53, 55, 56
Murdock, Kenneth, 163

Natural Religion, *see* Deism
Navigation Acts, 260
Negro Spirituals, 332, 333
New England Courant, see Franklin, James
New Hampshire, 83, 103, 146, 147, 249, 283
Newhouse, Sewall, 399
New Jersey, 83, 186, 187, 283
Newman, J. H., 332
New Testament, 20, 27, 35, 39, 335; Tyndale's translation of, 60, 61
New York, 83, 85, 100, 221, 253-256, 428
Nicholas of Hereford, 39
Niles, Nathaniel, 264
North American Phalanx, 388, 389
Norton, Prof. Andrews, 413
Norton, Rev. John, 158, 159
Norton, William Warder, 203
Norton Memorials, 158
Noyes, George Wallingford, 393
Noyes, John Humphrey, 360, 374, 375, 391-399, 410, 424, 425, 459
Noyes, Pierrepont B., 393
Nurse, Samuel, 166

Ockham, William of, 39, 44; theory of "consubstantiation," 48
Oecolampadius, 45, 48
Oglethorpe, Sir James, 253, 270
Oglethorpe, Owen, 62
Oligarchy, at Plymouth, 114; Hitlerian, 52; in New York, 254; in Pennsylvania, 201; of Massachusetts Bay Colony, 124, 129, 130, 133, 134; Pilgrim, 118, 130; Puritan, 121, 130
Oneida Community, 359, 391, 398, 399
Origen, 29
Orrery, Lord, 185
Otis, James, 260, 261, 266, 275, 296
Owen, Robert, and Owenism, 336, 359, 360, 367-373, 424, 430
Owen, Robert Dale and William, 371

Pacelli, Cardinal, 19
Paine, Thomas, 269-273, 305-307
Palfrey, J. G., 130, 157
Palmer, Elihu, 305
Parker, Daniel, 331, 332

Parker, Robert Allerton, 393
Parker, Theodore, 387
Paul, Saint, 21, 28, 44, 45, 48
Peasants' Revolt of 1525, 49, 53, 55
Peck, J. M., 331
Penn, Adm. Sir William, 184, 185, 187
Penn, William, 9, 136, 164, 180, 181, 184-197, 203, 262, 270, 296
Pennsylvania, 43, 56, 83, 187-190, 192, 194-201, 204, 266, 285
Penry, John, 77
Pepys, Samuel, 184
Perfectionism, 391-399; attitude on sex, 391, 392, 398
Peter, Saint, 20, 21, 38
Peters, Hugh, 124, 139, 154
Philip of Hesse, 48, 53
Phipps, Sir William, 162
Phiquepal, William, 372
Pilgrims, 9, 77, 93, 99, 101, 104, 105, 106, 109; in America, 110-119, 132; in Holland, 106-110; Pilgrim Fathers, 104
Pinckney, C. C., 295
Pitt, William, 259
Plymouth, 83, 101, 114, 115, 116, 118, 119, 129, 130, 147; Company, *see* Virginia Company
Polygamy, 54, 85, 343, 353, 356, 357
Popham, Lord Chief-Justice, 99
Porter, Ebenezer, 214
Pratt, Orson, 349, 350, 351, 355, 356
Pratt, Parley, 351, 352
Prence, Thomas, 114, 115, 118
Prendergast, William, 255
Presbyterianism, Presbyterians, 71, 72, 76, 78, 124, 169, 215, 321, 322, 427
Presbyters, Presbyteries, *see* Presbyterianism
Preston, John, 125
Priestley, Joseph, 243
Procter, John, 166
Protestant Episcopal Church, *see* Anglican Church
Protestantism and Protestants, 17, 26, 31, 56, 62-67, 84, 125, 156, 171, 173, 174, 175, 176
Pufendorf, Samuel, 169, 238, 239
Puritans, Puritanism, 62, 67, 68, 73, 77, 99, 117, 119, 120-125, 129, 130, 143, 148, 159; apologists, 163; autocracy, 158; of Virginia, 94, 97, 175; oligarchy, 121, 130

Quakers, Quakerism, 9, 26, 41, 52, 56, 97, 115, 129, 149, 159, 170, 176, 177, 180-204, 254, 255, 256; hangings, 83, 146; laws against, 158; persecution of, 155, 159, 163
Quebec Act of 1774, 267
Quincy, Josiah, 443

Raleigh, Sir Walter, 87-89
Randall, John, 330
Rappites, 359, 360, 370
Reeve, John, 185
Reformation, 9, 11, 17, 34, 38, 39, 43, 47, 56, 79, 127, 176, 237, 360, 375, 410, 455; in England and Scotland, 59-63, 73-79; religious issues, 26-33; social causes of, 21-26
Reform Movements, 426-433; education, 428-431; peace movement, 432; suffrage, 431, 432; temperance, 427, 428
Religion of the Frontier, 329, 331
Relly, James, 403
Restoration, 90, 161, 176
Revivalist Movement, 325, 326
Revolution, American, 83, 85, 90, 247, 248, 257-265, 282-285
Revolution of 1688, 175, 241, 282
Rhode Island, 83, 102, 119, 128, 146-149, 161, 174, 278, 283
Ridley, Nicholas, 62
Rigdon, Sidney, 349-354
Riley, Isaac Woodbridge, 223, 307
Ripley, George, 378-381, 387, 404, 425, 429
Roanoke Island, *see* Carolinas
Robinson, John, 105, 107, 109, 110, 116, 119, 124
Rockefeller, John D., 368
Rolfe, John, 96
Ross, Frederick A., 451
Roswell, Sir Henry, 121
Rothmann, Bernard, 53
Rousseau, Jean Jacques, 238, 239, 244-247
Rush, Benjamin, 427
Rutledge, John and Henry, 263

Salem (Mass.), 70, 119, 120, 123, 131, 134; agitation in 1692, 165, 166
Saltonstall, Nathaniel, 166
Saltonstall, Sir Richard, 121
Sandiford, Ralph, 204
Sandys, Sir Edwin, 93, 94, 96, 97, 109, 152, 188
Sawyer, G. S., 442
Schwenkfelders, Caspar Schwenkfeld, 56, 199
Scott, Reginald, 164

Scott, Walter, 335
Scotus, Duns, 39, 44
Seabury, S., 442
Sears, Clara Endicott, 362, 383
Ségur, Philippe Paul, Comte de, 250
Separation of Church and State, 9, 36, 56, 57, 58, 75, 79, 125, 130, 131, 146, 156, 283
Separatists, Separatism, 57, 58, 74, 106-110, 123, 124, 128, 129; Ainsworth-Johnson group, 77, 106; Gainsborough, 57, 106; in England and Holland, 77, 78, 106-110
Servetus, Michael, 66
Sevier, "Noluchucky Jack," 253
Sewall, Justice Samuel, 167
Shakers, 85, 180, 360-366, 370, 421, 422; communism, 365; feminism, 364; idea of "phalanstery," 364; settlement at Watervliet, 363; spiritualism, 421, 422; theology, 363
Shay, Daniel, 287
Shepard, Odell, 214, 382, 412, 430
Shepard, Rev. Thomas, 122
Sherman, Roger, 226
Sherman, Stuart, 163
Simms, William Gilmore, 443, 444
Sin, 26, 27; doctrine of original, 27-31, 52, 424
Slavery, 95, 97, 195, 203, 204, 215, 267, 276-281, 293, 294, 295, 352, 433-450, 467, 469; Underground Railway, 466, 467
Smalley, John, 214
Smith, Hezekiah, 217
Smith, J. Allen, 287
Smith, Capt. John, 90, 91, 99
Smith, Joseph, Jr., 341, 342, 345-353, 356, 358
Smith, Logan Pearsall, 201, 202
Smith, Lucy Mack, 345, 354
Smith, William, 249
Smyth, John, 57, 58, 105, 106
Snow, Erastus, 355
Social Contract, Theory of, 237-240
Sons of Liberty, 261, 262
Spaulding, Rev. Solomon, 349
Spiritualism, 417, 421, 422, 423
Spottswood, Gov. Alexander, 97
Standish, Miles, 104, 114, 116, 118
Steele, Rev. Richard, 70
Stephens, Alexander, 450
Stiles, Ezra, 225, 232, 288
Storch, Nicholas, 48, 49
Stowe, Harriet Beecher, 462, 463, 465
Strachey, John, 12

Strang, James Jesse, 354
Stuart, Mary, 74
Supernaturalistic Religion, 319, 320
Swedenborgianism, Emanuel Swedenborg, 319, 417-421; father of Spiritualism, 421; sex liberation, 391, 420, 421
Symes, Lillian, 368
Symmes, Zechariah, 138, 140
Synods, *see* Presbyterianism

Taborites, 55
Talleyrand, 300, 301, 302
Taney, Chief Justice Roger B., 277, 279
Tarbell, John, 166
Taxes, *see* Tithes and Taxes
Taylor, John, 314
Tea Act of 1773, 261
Tennant, Gilbert, 215
Tennessee, 249, 253, 435, 453
Tertullian, 27, 28
Texas, 436
Theocracy, 64, 78, 95, 121, 125, 126, 139, 156, 160, 168
Thirty Years' War, 55
Thoreau, Henry, 378, 387, 404, 409-412; "Civil Disobedience," 410
Tithes and Taxes, 23, 49, 76, 115, 126, 161, 173, 200, 217
Tobacco-raising, *see* Virginia
Trading Companies, *see* Virginia Company
Transcendentalism, Transcendentalists, 11, 183, 378, 381, 392, 404-407, 420, 434; Emerson's, 409; Hawthorne's, 414-416; Thoreau's, 411
Transubstantiation, 31, 40, 41, 42, 61, 62
Trollope, Anthony, 426
Trollope, Fanny, 336, 339, 340
Tudor, Mary, 61; Marian persecutions, 62
Twelve Articles of the Peasants, *see* Peasants' Revolt
Tyler, Wat, 40
Tyndall, William, 47, 60, 61

Umphreville, Lucinia, 392
Uncas, Chief, 148, 149
Uncle Tom's Cabin, 462-466
"Undertakers," 114, 118
Unitarians, Unitarianism, 52, 221, 222, 400-403, 413, 420
Universalism, Universalists, 29, 221, 222, 232, 375, 403, 422
Upham, Charles W., 167

Usher, Roland, 114
Utah, *see* Mormons

Van Buren, Martin, 461
Vane, Harry, 139, 141, 142
van Loon, Hendrik, 156
Van Tyne, Claude H., 248
Vermont, 103, 281, 285; Declaration of Independence in 1777, 249, 281
Virginia, 83, 84, 85, 87-98, 108, 117, 172, 175, 435; attitude against slavery, 438, 453; Bill of Rights, 274, 275; Clergy, 95; founding of University, 428; Statute of Religious Liberty, 283; tobacco-raising, 95-97; "Tuckahoes" and "Cohees," 98
Virginia Company, 87, 96, 108, 109, 121, 172, 188; Plymouth branch, 99, 100
von Berlichingen, Goetz, 49

Waldenses, Peter Waldo, 34, 37, 38, 46, 52, 55, 56, 176, 328, 376
Walpole, Horace, 243
Ward, Nathaniel, 140
Warder, John, 203
Ware, Rev. Henry, 401, 402
War of the Roses, 59
Warwick, Earl of, 120, 148
Washington, George, 12, 204, 226, 263, 265, 268, 280, 286, 290, 313, 428
Waymouth, George, 172
Weber, Max, 230
Webster, Daniel, 238, 314, 449, 450
Webster, Noah, 288, 289
Wells, H. G., 230
Wentworth, Gov. Sir John, 284
Wertenbaker, Thomas J., 84, 90
Wesley, Charles, 323
Wesley, John, 70, 71, 207, 323-327, 392, 427; as revivalist, 325, 326; his theology, 325; hymns, 327
Weston, George M., 447, 448
Wheelwright, John, 139-142

White, John, 87
Whitefield, George, 207
Whitmer, David, 344, 346, 347, 349, 350
Whitney, Eli, 435; cotton gin, 435, 436
Whittier, John Greenleaf, 400, 444, 460
Wiclif, John, 39-42, 60, 62; Bible, 39, 41
Wiedemann, Jacob, 55
Wigglesworth, Michael, 30
Wilkins, Thomas, 166
Wilkinson, Jemima, 341
Willard and Moody, 166
William of Orange, 162, 192
Williams, Roger, 9, 10, 57, 119, 127-135, 145, 146, 148, 149, 150, 152, 155, 168, 169, 270, 296; attitude to Indians, 132, 133; founding of Providence, 134, 135; views of, 129
Wilson, James, 263, 294
Wilson, John, 124, 128, 140, 142, 145, 157, 159
Wilson, M. L., 295
Winslow, Gov. Edward, 101, 104, 108, 115, 118, 134
Winter, William, 156
Winthrop, John, 115, 120, 121, 122, 129, 132, 139-144, 147, 151, 153, 155, 156, 169
Wise, John, of Ipswich, 161, 166, 169, 170
Witchcraft, 83, 162-167
Wollaston, Captain, 117
Wollaston, William, 228, 230
Woolman, John, 204
Wright, Frances, 371, 428, 430, 431, 465
"Writs of Assistance," 260, 261
Wyncop, John (Wyncop Patent), 109

Yeardley, Sir George, 93
Young, Brigham, 341, 349, 350, 354-358, 424
Young, Sir John, 121

Zenger, Peter, 195
Zwingli, Huldereich, 47, 48, 52, 61